# CASE STUDIES
## IN US TRADE
## NEGOTIATION

### VOL. 1: MAKING THE RULES

INSTITUTE FOR INTERNATIONAL ECONOMICS

# CASE STUDIES IN **US TRADE** NEGOTIATION

## VOL. 1: MAKING THE RULES

CHARAN DEVEREAUX   ROBERT Z. LAWRENCE   MICHAEL D. WATKINS

Washington, DC
September 2006

**Charan Devereaux** is a senior researcher at the John F. Kennedy School of Government's Trade and Negotiations Program and the Harvard Law School Program on Negotiation, where she writes on international trade issues.

**Robert Z. Lawrence**, senior fellow at the Institute for International Economics since 2001, is the Albert L. Williams Professor of Trade and Investment at the John F. Kennedy School of Government at Harvard University. He was appointed by President Clinton to serve as a member of his Council of Economic Advisers in 1999. He held the New Century Chair as a nonresident senior fellow at the Brookings Institution and founded and edited the *Brookings Trade Forum*. He has been a senior fellow in the Economic Studies Program at Brookings, a professorial lecturer at the Johns Hopkins School of Advanced International Studies, and an instructor at Yale University. He is the author or coauthor of several books, including *Has Globalization Gone Far Enough? The Costs of Fragmented Markets* (2004) and *Crimes and Punishments? Retaliation under the WTO* (2003).

**Michael D. Watkins** is a professor of practice in organizational behavior at INSEAD, Fontainebleau, and was a professor at Harvard's Kennedy School of Government and the Business School. He also taught negotiation in the Senior Executive Program at the Program on Negotiation at Harvard Law School. He is founding partner of Genesis Advisers, a leadership strategy consultancy. He is the author of *The First 90 Days: Critical Success Strategies for New Leaders at all Levels* (Harvard Business School Press, 2003) and *Breakthrough Business Negotiation: A Toolbox for Managers* (Jossey-Bass, winner of the CPR Institute prize for best negotiation book in 2002).

**INSTITUTE FOR INTERNATIONAL ECONOMICS**
1750 Massachusetts Avenue, NW
Washington, DC 20036-1903
(202) 328-9000   FAX: (202) 659-3225
www.iie.com

C. Fred Bergsten, *Director*
Valerie Norville, *Director of Publications and Web Development*
Edward Tureen, *Director of Marketing*

*Typesetting by BMWW*
*Printing by Automated Graphic Systems, Inc.*

Printed in the United States of America
08 07 06   5 4 3 2 1

**Library of Congress Cataloging-in-Publication Data**

Devereaux, Charan.
  Case studies in US trade negotiation / Charan Devereaux, Robert Z. Lawrence, Michael D. Watkins.
      p.  cm.
  Includes bibliographical references and index.
      ISBN-10: 0-88132-362-4 (v. 1 : alk. paper)
      ISBN-10: 0-88132-363-2 (v. 2 : alk. paper)
      ISBN-13: 978-0-88132-362-7 (v. 1 : alk. paper)
      ISBN-13: 978-0-88132-363-4 (v. 2 : alk. paper)
      1. United States—Commercial policy—History.   2. International trade.
  3. Foreign trade regulation—Cases.
  4. Agreement on Trade-Related Aspects of Intellectual Property Rights (1994)
  I. Lawrence, Robert Z., 1949–
  II. Watkins, Michael, 1956–    III. Title.

  HF1455.D49 2006
  382'.973—dc22                    2006022687

# Contents

## Tables

## Figures

# Preface

Trade policy is central to the Institute's research program. A number of our studies have analyzed the functioning of the World Trade Organization (WTO), and the General Agreement on Tariffs and Trade (GATT) before it, and proposed reform of the international trading rules; others have assessed bilateral and regional trade agreements; still others have measured the costs of protection and delved into the American trade policymaking process.

This new volume presents case studies on five important trade negotiations. Authors Charan Devereaux, Robert Z. Lawrence, and Michael Watkins focus on "making the rules"—the process of establishing how the trade system operates. They pay particular attention to how decision making on trade occurs within the context of the American political system. Some of the cases take place in the United States without direct participation of other nations; others involve bilateral, regional, or multilateral negotiations. But all the cases concentrate on exploring the policies, politics, and processes that are used to make rules about trade.

The five major rulemaking events presented here are the introduction of intellectual property rules into the WTO, the negotiations between the United States and the European Union to establish mutual recognition agreements, the negotiations at the Organization for Economic Cooperation and Development for a Multilateral Agreement on Investment, the negotiations over granting the US president trade promotion (fast-track) authority, and the negotiations between the United States and China over China's accession to the WTO. A companion volume, *Resolving Disputes*, offers case studies on major trade disputes and the efforts to resolve them through the WTO dispute settlement mechanism. The two volumes thus provide an important complement to the Institute's earlier studies on the substance of these topics.

The Institute for International Economics is a private, nonprofit institution for the study and discussion of international economic policy. Its purpose is to analyze important issues in that area and to develop and communicate practical new approaches for dealing with them. The Institute is completely nonpartisan.

The Institute is funded by a highly diversified group of philanthropic foundations, private corporations, and interested individuals. Major institutional grants are now being received from the William M. Keck, Jr. Foundation and the Starr Foundation. About 33 percent of the Institute's resources in our latest fiscal year were provided by contributors outside the United States, including about 16 percent from Japan.

The Institute's Board of Directors bears overall responsibilities for the Institute and gives general guidance and approval to its research program, including the identification of topics that are likely to become important over the medium run (one to three years) and that should be addressed by the Institute. The director, working closely with the staff and outside Advisory Committee, is responsible for the development of particular projects and makes the final decision to publish an individual study.

The Institute hopes that its studies and other activities will contribute to building a stronger foundation for international economic policy around the world. We invite readers of these publications to let us know how they think we can best accomplish this objective.

C. FRED BERGSTEN
Director
August 2006

# Acknowledgments

In compiling this volume, we received help from a number of generous people who agreed to be interviewed for the case studies. Some of these individuals are quoted in the text, while others preferred to remain anonymous. We thank them for their time and assistance. We would also like to thank all those who read drafts and made suggestions, including Ellen Frost, I. M. Destler, Edward M. Graham, and Nicholas Lardy.

We are grateful to the participants of the John F. Kennedy School of Government (KSG) Executive Program, "The Practice of Trade Policy: Economics, Negotiations, and Rules," and to the participants of the Institute for International Economics work sessions on "Case Studies on International Trade Rules Negotiation and Enforcement," who commented and offered their ideas on much of this work. The case studies in this volume were developed as KSG cases, and we thank the staff of Harvard's KSG Case Program for their help.

Finally, we would like to thank Madona Devasahayam, Marla Banov, Helen Hillebrand, and Valerie Norville at the Institute for International Economics for their assistance with the editing and publishing process. Though there are many to thank, the views expressed here are the authors' and should not be attributed to anyone else.

# Introduction

International trade negotiations once focused on reducing border barriers such as tariffs and quotas that protected markets for manufactured goods. Such discussions took place in a rules-based, multilateral global system centered on the General Agreement on Tariffs and Trade—the GATT. The GATT was spectacularly successful in reducing border barriers. On average, tariffs on industrial goods fell from around 40 percent in 1947 to below 5 percent in the late 1980s. But as tariffs fell and markets opened, the challenges presented by the different laws and practices of different trading nations became apparent. In response, the focus of trade policy-making shifted. Trade negotiations now often center on policies and rules once thought of as purely domestic in nature. Trading nations commonly seek not only to negotiate over tariffs but also to change practices by constraining, reconciling, or even harmonizing rules.

The cases presented in this volume describe negotiations to set trade rules in this new context. Our aim is to present the facts coherently and in a manner that will raise questions and inspire discussion. To that end, the cases both explore the substance of trade agreements and delve into the negotiation process. As well as the *what* of trade, they describe the *who*, *how*, and *why* of decision making. By examining some of the most important recent negotiations, the reader can come to understand not only the larger issues surrounding trade policy today but also how participants seek to exert influence and how the system evolves as a result of these pressures.

We have tried here, both in our introductions and in the cases themselves, to avoid policy advocacy. The idea is neither to undertake an analysis of trade policy from the perspective of a particular discipline (e.g., economics, politics, law, negotiation) nor to provide normative prescriptions. The cases in this volume cover five important trade negotiations, all focused on "making the rules"—the process of establishing how the trade system will operate. A companion volume will offer cases on settling—or attempting to settle—trade disputes. In both volumes we pay particular attention to how decision making on trade occurs within the context of the American political system. Some of the cases in this volume take place in the United States without the direct participation of other nations; others involve bilateral, regional, or multilateral negotiations. But all the cases concentrate on exploring the policies, politics, and processes that are used to make rules about trade.

The five major rule-making events treated here are the introduction of rules for intellectual property into the World Trade Organization (WTO), the negotiations at the Organization for Economic Cooperation and Development (OECD) for a Multilateral Agreement on Investment (MAI), the negotiations over granting the US president trade promotion (fast-track) authority, the negotiations between the United States and China over China's accession to the WTO, and the negotiations between the United States and the European Union to establish mutual recognition of conformity assessment procedures.[1] The cases are summarized below.

## The Agreement on Trade-Related Aspects of Intellectual Property Rights

To what extent should international trade agreements require participating nations to harmonize their policies? A two-part case on the 1994 Agreement on Trade-Related Aspects of Intellectual Property Rights (TRIPS) explores this critically important question. The case also provides insight into the distribution of power within the WTO and the importance of effective negotiation in determining outcomes. Negotiated during the Uruguay Round of trade talks, the TRIPS agreement significantly broadened the reach of the trading regime by establishing the most comprehensive set of global trade rules for intellectual property. It obligated WTO members to adopt policies protecting patents, trademarks, and copyrights. While countries remained free to provide even more protection than TRIPS required, the agreement set minimum standards. But the TRIPS negotiation might not have happened without a concerted effort by the pharmaceutical, software, and entertainment industries to get intellectual property on the Uruguay Round agenda and to press for completion of an agreement. How was this landmark agreement negotiated? What were the challenges?

---

1. We have chosen not to present a case on the North American Free Trade Agreement (NAFTA), arguably the most crucial US trade policy negotiation in the past decade, because a superb study of the agreement—Frederick Mayer's *Interpreting NAFTA: The Science and Art of Political Analysis* (1998)—already exists.

In the aftermath of the Uruguay Round, some argued that the TRIPS agreement would largely benefit richer countries while hurting poorer nations. Some representatives of developing countries and nongovernmental organizations (NGOs) were especially concerned that TRIPS would decrease access to medicines in developing countries. These groups organized to fight for their cause, both at the WTO and around the world. The second part of the case describes their efforts to secure the Declaration on TRIPS and Public Health at the 2001 WTO ministerial meeting in Doha.

## The Multilateral Agreement on Investment

Negotiations for the Multilateral Agreement on Investment began in 1993 at the OECD with great expectations. However, the talks failed to produce an agreement. A well-organized campaign against the MAI negotiations played a role in the treaty's demise: 600 organizations in 70 countries fought strenuously against it. But some observers say that difficulties that emerged in the talks themselves were just as important—if not more so. Negotiators had substantive disagreements about what the treaty should achieve. In addition, governments were often unready or unable to make the commitments necessary to reach agreement. How and why did this negotiation come to be held at the OECD? Who gains and who loses from foreign direct investment? Should international trade agreements cover foreign direct investment? Are investment agreements even necessary?

## Fast Track/Trade Promotion Authority

How well-suited is the US system for negotiating modern trade agreements? The Constitution gives the president the authority to negotiate international trade agreements. However, Congress must approve any such agreement and the legislation to implement consequent changes in US statutory law. To many trade policymakers, this arrangement blunts the negotiating power of the United States in trade talks because other countries know that any commitments made at the table can be altered or rejected by Congress. Therefore, from 1974 to 1993, Congress granted the president fast-track authority: In return for regular consultations and timely notification by the executive, the legislature committed to an expeditious yes-or-no vote to implement trade agreements with no amendments or changes. But beginning in the early 1990s, fast track became the subject of fierce political debate, largely centered on concerns about global trade liberalization. Can the United States pursue trade agreements without fast track? Why did fast track become so contentious? Should provisions on core labor standards and environmental standards be included in trade agreements? Why was President Clinton unsuccessful in obtaining fast-track authority in 1997 and President George W. Bush able to obtain it (renamed trade promotion authority) in July 2002?

## China's WTO Accession:
## The 1999 US-China Bilateral Agreement and
## the Battle for Permanent Normal Trade Relations

On December 11, 2001, China became a member of the World Trade Organization. Many say the 1999 US-China bilateral trade agreement and the vote in Congress to permanently establish normal trade relations with China paved the way for China's WTO accession. Even though China was not a WTO member, the United States had granted China most favored nation (MFN) trading status since 1979. Yet US law required annual renewal of China's trade status, a process that often became a focal point in Congress for protests over human rights issues, security concerns, and the growing US trade deficit with China. In order to support China's WTO accession, the United States had to commit itself to nondiscriminatory treatment by agreeing to make China's MFN status permanent—granting permanent normal trade relations, or PNTR—and thereby giving up the right to annual reviews. The vote in Congress generated a lobbying battle on Capitol Hill of historic proportions. Why did PNTR pass? What role should trade agreements play in promoting human rights, enhancing domestic reform, encouraging the rule of law, and promoting national security? How were the US-China bilateral agreement and the PNTR vote linked to other key negotiations? What is the role of trade in advancing America's economic interests?

## The US-EU Mutual Recognition Agreements

In 1998, the United States and the European Union recognized each other's inspection, testing, and certification requirements for a wide range of traded products in a set of agreements known as mutual recognition agreements. The MRAs applied to nearly $50 billion in transatlantic trade in six sectors: medical devices, pharmaceuticals, recreational craft, telecommunications, electromagnetic compatibility (EMC) services, and electrical equipment. The MRAs were intended to enhance the US-EU trade relationship by eliminating duplicative testing, streamlining procedures, lowering costs, and decreasing the amount of time needed to bring new products to market. According to the US Commerce Department, the agreement would save US industries more than $1 billion annually in testing and certification costs. According to Stuart Eizenstat, the MRAs would "cut red tape and save money for industry, consumers, and regulators and make the USA more competitive."[2]

An important player in the MRA negotiations was the Transatlantic Business Dialogue (TABD), a group of American and European business leaders that came together as part of a US government initiative. The MRA negotiations were also notable for involving regulatory agencies in trade talks. Indeed, that involvement created some tension domestically, for the US regulatory agencies, with a mission of safeguarding consumers, had run-ins with the agencies seeking to facilitate trade. Tension also arose between US and European agencies that had different standards and methods for certifying products. Though an agreement was concluded, there were problems with implementation. Should trade agencies take the lead in such areas? If not, how can nations deal with their differences in certification, inspection, and regulatory standards? What is the appropriate role for industry in these discussions? Is regulatory harmonization the goal?

---

2. Eizenstat, quoted in "US Industry Urged to Back MRAs with EU," *Marketletter*, October 13, 1997.

# Making Trade Policy

In each of the cases in this volume, we see a variety of participants work-ing to influence and design trade policy. Interested parties debate four basic questions as they negotiate international trade agreements and pol-icy changes: What issues and sectors should be included in the agree-ment? How deep should trade agreements be? How will any decisions be enforced? And should all signatories be treated equally—in particular, how should developing countries be treated?

The answers to these policy questions are not determined by quiet an-alytical reflection in an ivory tower. Rather, decisions are made in a polit-ical context through negotiations between governments, corporations, nongovernmental organizations, and interest groups. Therefore, address-ing two other questions that are fundamental to any political debate can help to clarify how trade policy is made. First, who wins and who loses? Any new policy will benefit some groups more than others. And second, how does the agreement affect governance? International agreements not only determine rules, they also determine who makes those rules and who enforces them. In short, international trade agreements are highly political endeavors because they affect the distribution of both income and power.

For each case, we provide an introduction that considers each of the above questions and its application to the decision at hand. Here, we briefly note some commonalities—themes that emerge repeatedly from these highlighted trade talks. In all the cases, we find changes that add to the comprehensive scope of trade agreements, deepen their requirements, make their enforcement stronger, and place more demanding require-ments on developing countries.

# Coverage

What issues and sectors should be included in any particular trade agreement? What is the appropriate scope for discussions? On the one hand, some believe that the scope of trade agreements should be narrow, limited only to policies that are directly related to trade (such as tariffs, quotas, and export subsidies) and to those aspects of domestic policy that explicitly discriminate against foreign goods. Proponents of this view, concerned about mission creep, argue that having too many targets may prevent any from being attained. An institution that takes on too much can blunt its effectiveness and even call its own legitimacy into question. The World Trade Organization (WTO), for example, may be well suited to deal with trade liberalization, but it lacks the expertise or legitimacy to tackle environmental policies, competition policies, or labor standards—not to mention human rights. In addition, some argue, any WTO rules in these areas threaten national sovereignty by compromising a nation's ability to determine its own domestic policies. They worry that by increasing efforts to create rules on issues such as labor and the environment, the WTO would increase the difficulties of its members (especially developing countries) in implementing them, and thus increase their likelihood of becoming subject to trade sanctions. Finally, some say, broadening the coverage of trade agreements could ultimately stymie liberalization by attracting political actors whose main interest is in promoting their policies, not in trade.

On the other hand, others believe that the trading system *requires* rules on a broad range of issues. Some emphasize the need to include under the trade umbrella additional economic concerns, such as investment and competition policy. Investment rules, proponents argue, further facilitate economic integration, especially since multinational corporations play such an important role in the services trade. Competition rules ensure that international markets are contestable, blocking anticompetitive behavior by private firms that can inhibit trade. Other advocates of a broader trade agenda emphasize the need to explicitly address social issues. In order to build broad support for free trade, they argue, policymakers must alleviate concerns that globalization will undermine standards in areas such as labor rights and environmental regulation. Since trade rules affect workers and the environment, some believe that these issues need to be considered when agreements are negotiated.

In the early postwar years, trade agreements were limited in scope, covering mainly border barriers such as tariffs and quotas that protected markets for manufactured goods. From its inception in 1947 until 1967, multilateral trade negations under the General Agreement on Tariffs and Trade (GATT) concentrated on reducing these tariffs. In the Tokyo Round, concluded in 1979, the GATT's purview was extended to nontariff barriers; six codes were negotiated on import licensing, technical barriers to trade, customs valuation, subsidies and countervailing duties, antidumping provisions, and government procurement. However, the focus remained on rules and barriers that were clearly related to trade in goods.

But in the 1980s, the scope of trade agreements was dramatically broadened in numerous bilateral, regional, and multilateral negotiations. The United States and Japan, for example, negotiated the Structural Impediments Initiative (SII), which covered such issues as Japan's laws regarding large retail stores, the behavior of corporate groups known as *keiretsu*, enforcement of antitrust laws, and spending on infrastructure. The United States and Canada negotiated a free trade agreement that covered not only goods but also services and investment. Europe launched its EC92 initiative to complete its internal market and facilitate the movement of goods, services, capital, and labor by removing barriers and reconciling regulatory differences. The Uruguay Round, negotiated between 1986 and 1993, also reflected this trend as it liberalized the flow of services, agricultural goods, and investment. Finally, the North American Free Trade Agreement (NAFTA) both pushed further into these areas and also included side agreements on labor and the environment.

The cases in this volume demonstrate the expanding scope of trade agreements. The introduction of intellectual property rules, as described in the case on the 1994 Agreement on Trade-Related Aspects of Intellectual Property Rights (TRIPS), exemplifies the broadening of multilateral trade rules to include new concerns. The case that treats the fight to grant China permanent normal trade relations (PNTR) reveals how trade agreements have grown to cover all goods (including the agricultural), as well as services, investment, intellectual property, and domestic regulatory regimes. In addition, the China case illustrates the role trade agreements are asked to play in establishing the rule of law and promoting domestic economic reform.

Nonetheless, as several cases bring out, the question of what issues should be included in trade agreements remains controversial. Efforts to negotiate more extensive rules on foreign direct investment through a Multilateral Agreement on Investment (MAI) ended in failure. Debate continues as to whether trade should be used as a mechanism for enforcing human rights, as seen in the China case. The case on fast-track authority (now called trade promotion authority, or TPA) demonstrates the deep divide in Congress over the use of trade agreements to enforce workers' rights and environmental standards. And finally, in the case on the US-EU mutual recognition agreements (MRAs), legislators and government officials wondered if a trade agreement was the appropriate venue for dealing with regulatory issues.

These controversies over the scope of trade agreements are unlikely to be resolved anytime soon. The WTO ministerial in Seattle failed to launch a new round in 1999, in part because of strong disagreements over the issue of labor standards. And although a round was launched at Doha in 2001, negotiations on the so-called Singapore issues (competition, investment, and transparency in government procurement and trade facilitation) were postponed. Later, because of the fundamental international conflicts on these issues, only trade facilitation remained on the Doha agenda.

## Depth

How deep should trade agreements be? What should they require of their signatories? The central issue here is how deeply trade agreements should reach into areas generally controlled by domestic governments. In their least invasive form, agreements can simply require that governments operate without discrimination and transparently. At the other extreme, agreements can seek full policy harmonization. An intermediate approach sets minimum standards that all signatories must adhere to.

The first approach facilitates diversity and allows nations to express their own preferences by minimizing constraints on domestic policies. Harmonization, though imposing a greater constraint on national sovereignty and autonomy, brings greater benefits: uniformity, similarity of treatment, and economy in information costs. For some, the use of trade agreements to constrain or change domestic rules presents an attractive opportunity. For others, it results in an unwarranted intrusion on domestic sovereignty.

The traditional approach of the GATT was to require only that nations (1) engage in reciprocal reductions of border barriers, (2) treat all GATT members equally—commonly referred to as most favored nation (MFN) treatment, and (3) treat foreign and domestic goods in the same way—known as national treatment. The GATT did not seek to harmonize standards or policies; it simply required the same treatment of domestic and imported products. Provided they respected this principle, countries remained free to implement any domestic policies or rules they desired. After the Tokyo Round, GATT parties were subject to more constraints under the Code on Technical Barriers to Trade. However, although members were encouraged to adopt international standards, they could set their own so long as those standards were applied transparently, were not discriminatory, and erected no unnecessary obstacles to trade.

By contrast, the agreements in the cases in this volume were all intended to move beyond the basic requirements of national treatment and nondiscrimination. The TRIPS agreement, for example, requires countries to implement policy regimes that achieve a minimum level of intellectual property protection. The draft MAI required signatories to grant foreign firms guarantees against expropriation (a government's seizure of an investor's property). This and other rights could actually have resulted in better than national treatment for some foreign investors—that is, foreign investors could be entitled to compensation under circumstances in which domestic firms would receive nothing. The case on the MRAs also illustrates the deepening of trade agreements. While the MRA allowed the United States and the European Union to maintain their own regulatory standards, it required them to mutually recognize certifiers. In addition, some representatives of business and industry saw the MRAs as a steppingstone toward harmonization of standards. And in the China case, China was required to implement a large number of domestic policy changes; these included abandoning its interventionist industrial policies and limiting agricultural subsidies in order to enter the WTO. Each of these examples shows how the new issues in trade are moving beyond national borders into the arena of domestic policy.

## Enforcement

How should trade agreements be enforced? For international agreements to be effective, they must be adhered to. Some agreements are nonbinding; countries proclaim their intention to comply but suffer no consequences if they fail to follow through. Other international agreements are binding but lack a formal enforcement mechanism; countries adhere to them out of self-interest, respect for international law, and concern about their reputation. In a third group, the primary enforcers of binding agreements are domestic, but international participants may respond to noncompliance by withdrawing benefits. In a fourth type, noncompliance can result in fines or penalties. Finally, in a fifth type, countries may actually turn over to an international body their ability to determine or regulate certain policies. Thus countries within Europe have ceded sovereignty to the European Union in trade and other matters.

The GATT is an example of the third type of system, though implemented without much force before the Uruguay Round. A country's failure to comply with the GATT agreement could be challenged by other parties, but full consensus was required before a dispute could be heard, panel findings accepted, and the withdrawal of concessions authorized. The requirement for unanimous agreement in essence gave each country veto power. Moreover, some of the codes negotiated under the Tokyo Round were separate instruments to which all GATT parties did not necessarily subscribe; several had their own dispute settlement systems. In addition to the challenges within the GATT system, sometimes member nations—particularly the United States—would take matters into their own hands and attempt to enforce trade agreements unilaterally by threatening trade sanctions. Though other international organizations outside of the GATT dealt with trade-related issues, including intellectual property (the World Intellectual Property Organization, or WIPO), health standards (the Codex Alimentarius Commission, or Codex), labor standards (the International Labor Organization, or ILO), investment (the Organization for Economic Cooperation and Development, or OECD), and the environment. However, aside from publicizing violations, these organizations generally had limited or no ability to enforce agreements.

The WTO dispute settlement system enhanced the power of the dispute settlement body (DSB) to enforce trade rules. Because the new system required unanimity not to undertake but to prevent proceedings, no one country could block the panel from hearing a dispute. The Uruguay Round was also a single undertaking in which all WTO members agreed to all rules, rules that were subject to a single dispute settlement mechanism. This change dramatically increased enforcement by giving WTO members the option of cross-sectoral retaliation. For example, if a country violated the TRIPS agreement's intellectual property rules, it might lose other trade benefits, such as low tariffs on manufactured goods. As a result, advocates of labor and environmental standards (as well as of other causes) strengthened their efforts to have their issues taken on by the WTO, which could use the trade dispute settlement mechanism to enforce its decisions. These efforts were controversial, however, and led among other things to difficulties in securing fast-track negotiating authority for the US president.

As the world economy becomes more deeply integrated, countries face the prospect of increasingly sharing their sovereignty. For example, enforcement measures outside the WTO have been considered. The MAI negotiations took place under the auspices of the OECD, so the agreement was not intended to be subject to the WTO's procedures. Nonetheless, the MAI would have required signatories to commit to a binding process of settling disputes between investors and states. Thus, in principle, an independent body could have had the authority to challenge a country's laws and policies that violated the agreement. That possibility gave rise to concerns that the agreement would eventually undermine national sovereignty.

## Developing Countries

Should developing countries be provided with special and differential treatment in the trading system? On one view, they should, as their experiences with global integration have not all been positive. In particular, colonialism is widely seen as having retarded development. After world commodity and debt markets collapsed during the 1930s, many developing countries in the 1950s sought to reduce their dependence on the world economy by pursuing import substitution and protection strategies. Their suffering also gave rise to the view that developing countries should not be obligated to extensively open their domestic markets as a precondition for GATT membership. In addition, countries with limited means—and with governance a scarce resource—are often seen as unable to enforce commitments undertaken in trade agreements. For example, poor countries may simply lack the resources needed to implement social policies to regulate labor standards. Another widely accepted argument in defense of favorable terms is that an increase in exports can contribute significantly to a country's economic development. All these considerations suggest that developing countries should be expected to meet relatively less stringent legal obligations and conditions for market access than more developed countries.

But others do not see the need for such favorable treatment. In particular, many developing countries themselves have decided that liberalization is in their interest, believing that a commitment to binding international agreements will encourage potential investors by heightening the visibility, credibility, and apparent permanence of their domestic reforms. Other critics of special treatment question the assumption that the value of economic policies differs in developed and developing countries. If particular rules are well crafted and promote growth, they argue, then shouldn't those rules be applied to all members? In addition, as several developing countries have become formidable international competitors, the developed world has pressed for the removal of their special market access. Finally, though providing special treatment is relatively easy in matters of tariffs and quotas, rules are more difficult to manage. Thus, while tariffs can be set at different levels for different members, most rules either are or are not enforced. Accordingly, as trade agreements increasingly focus on rules, special treatment has become more difficult to implement.

Developing countries were granted differential and special treatment in the GATT. For example, unlike developed countries, developing countries were allowed to promote infant industries and to raise trade barriers in the face of balance of payment problems. They also were given more freedom to form preferential trading arrangements among themselves. Finally, a special Enabling Clause adopted in the Tokyo Round made permanent a set of waivers originally adopted in 1971 that allowed, but did not require, developed countries to provide developing countries with better than MFN treatment through the Generalized System of Preferences (GSP). Practice and principle do not always jibe, however. Developing countries were subject to more restrictive arrangements in textile trade than developed countries, and trade barriers against their most competitive goods, especially agricultural and labor-intensive products, often remained high.

The cases in this volume reveal a noteworthy shift regarding developing countries. Though they continue to enjoy more lenient treatment in some areas, in many others they are expected to meet the same obligations as other members. For example, the TRIPS agreement enforces the same regime on both developed and developing countries, although the latter are given more time to adjust. Moreover, since the trading system has dramatically extended its coverage and depth, countries that hope to join the WTO find themselves saddled with many more commitments than the developing countries that entered years ago. In particular, the

United States insisted that China enter the WTO on "commercial terms"—
that is, complying with the rules—rather than on more lenient terms. The
expansion of the system has raised questions about whether developing
countries can undertake such far-reaching international obligations—and
indeed about whether enacting strict disciplines at early stages of development is desirable. At the same time, developing countries often have
had little input into the system. For example, most were excluded from
the MAI negotiations, and the attempt to design multilateral investment
rules that would have been presented to them on a take-it-or-leave-it basis
created great controversy. Participants in the 1999 Seattle WTO ministerial meeting had already raised concerns about the failure to incorporate
the particular needs and interests of developing countries.

## Winners and Losers

Who wins and who loses in trade agreements? Traditionally, trade agreements affected readily identifiable interests, of both producers and consumers. Altering border barriers, for example, has a fairly predictable effect on prices and thus on incomes. Economic theory suggests that under
competitive conditions, trade in general benefits a nation. But trade liberalization can also create winners and losers: specifically, import-competing
producers and consumers of exports can lose while export producers and
consumers of imports can gain. Theory also suggests some aggregate effects on the distribution of income, with gains in the relatively abundant
factors of production and losses in the relatively scarce factors of production. Thus, in a typical developed country, the beneficiaries of trade liberalization will be skilled workers and capitalists; in developing countries,
they will be unskilled workers and farmers (if the country is an agricultural exporter). Conversely, unskilled workers in developed countries will
lose, as will skilled workers in developing countries. China's entry into the
WTO may affect distribution significantly along these traditional lines—
benefiting producers associated with exports, hurting those involved in
imports. The impact of WTO membership could be even greater, as domestic reforms and the rule of law are imposed. For example, state-owned
enterprises and financial institutions could be required to downsize, hurting workers, and Chinese farmers could receive fewer subsidies.

As trade agreements have penetrated more deeply into formerly domestic matters, many potential winners and losers have emerged. Intellectual property protection, for example, obviously rewards the producers given that protection and, at least in the short run, could raise costs for
consumers. The hope is that over the long run, consumers will also gain
from enhanced intellectual property rights (IPRs) as productivity increases
and new products are developed. But for intellectual property, unlike
trade, there is no reason to believe that enhancements will benefit nations

as a whole. Indeed, countries that lack innovations could be losers, although they might gain more foreign investment and diffusion of technology if stronger protection of intellectual property rights removed the worry of theft.

Introducing workers' rights and environmental standards into trade agreements could similarly create new winners and losers. For example, guaranteeing workers the rights to freedom of association and to collective bargaining could lead to higher wages for unionized workers and lower profits for owners. Stronger environmental controls might improve a nation's environment but add to the costs of pollution-intensive industries. Because developed countries have already enacted many labor and environmental standards, the initial burden of adjusting to such agreements would fall heavily on developing countries. However, the impact would also be felt in developed countries, as the heated debate over labor and environmental issues that arose in connection with US fast-track authority illustrates.

The MAI was clearly intended to increase the rights of multinational corporations and to enhance their ability to operate abroad. Corporations and host countries believed that benefits such as increased exports would follow its implementation. But some workers in home countries objected to enhancing the international mobility of firms. The MRA was similarly an opportunity for firms to reduce their costs, but it also reduced the power of some government certifiers in the United States, who went from holding a monopoly to being forced to compete with private-sector certifiers in Europe.

## Governance

How do the new trade agreements affect governance? The arrangements detailed in trade agreements can change who makes decisions, what is decided, and who enforces the rules. For example, fast-track authority/TPA alters the balance of power between the president and Congress. While the Constitution empowers Congress to regulate international trade, fast track gives the president the ability to insist that trade agreements not be amended, thereby taking power from Congress. As trade agreements become more far-reaching, congressional committees that work on international trade gain some of the power formerly wielded by committees drafting domestic legislation. With the introduction of issues relating to labor and environment into the trade debate, new political alignments may arise that increase the partisanship in arguments over trade policy. For example, parties aligned with the workers and unions might be hard-pressed to support trade agreements that fail to enforce workers' rights. The same is true of issues relating to the environment. Rather than focusing, as is traditional, on purely economic concerns (e.g., free trade versus protection), trade policy becomes a forum where all social concerns are addressed.

Trade agreements' effects on governance extend beyond the executive and legislative branches of government. As noted above, the MRA raised concerns among US domestic regulators deprived of their monopolies to certify compliance (though they retained the right to set their own rules). By entering into the international negotiations on this issue, firms also gained a new opportunity to change their relationship with their regulating bodies.

Of course, the United States is not alone in feeling the consequences of trade agreements on power relationships in domestic government. In China, the impact of WTO membership on governance will be profound. WTO accession may enhance the power of reformers to implement market-oriented changes that promote the rule of law and reduce bureaucratic discretion. But it also may enhance the role of the central government and reduce provincial autonomy. By signing the MAI, most developed countries would have agreed to new constraints on their domestic policy autonomy. In particular, environmentalists and others raised concerns that the MAI could have constrained environmental initiatives: independent arbitration panels, reviewing government decisions on the environment, could have required compensation for adversely affected foreign firms.

Trade agreements affect not just domestic governance but also the relationships between governments of different countries. By granting China permanent MFN status, Congress reduced the United States' ability to threaten or impose trade sanctions in response to human rights violations. As this brief account makes clear, international trade negotiations can profoundly shift power relations among interest groups, corporations, and policymakers—an outcome that helps to explain why they have become increasingly controversial.

## Looking Forward

In sum, the cases in this volume illustrate how trade agreements are being transformed. Coverage has become broader, commitments have become deeper, enforcement has become stronger, and the requirements placed on developing countries have become more demanding. In addition, we find new losers and winners, and fundamental changes to governance. However, we must also take a closer look at how different parties work to influence the far-reaching effects of trade policy. The next chapter will detail some tactics these groups use and how their strategies are changing as they seek to control the important variables in reaching a final agreement—not just power and knowledge but also building coalitions, setting agendas, determining the location of the negotiation, and organizing grassroots support.

# 2

# Negotiating Trade Agreements

The literature on international trade tends to focus on policy analysis: What should trade agreements cover? How do trade rules affect national economies? What policy changes should be pursued? However, the process by which trade policy is negotiated has received far less attention (one notable exception is Mayer 1998). This neglect is somewhat surprising, because international trade rules emerge from, are clarified by, and are implemented through processes of negotiation. Trade rules result from the actions of a host of interested parties—domestic, national, and supranational—competing and cooperating to shape agreements by using such tactics as forum shopping, coalition building, agenda setting, and grassroots organizing. And signing an agreement is by no means the end of the story—many details and ambiguities often remain to be negotiated and sometimes renegotiated during implementation. The processes by which agreements are enforced involve further strategic efforts to influence outcomes.

This is not to say that trade policy is captive to those who are best able to advance their partisan interests in negotiations. Macropolitical and macroeconomic forces play a major role in policymaking and in shaping how the trading system evolves. But within the boundaries established by these macro forces, substantial scope for process entrepreneurship remains. In all the case studies in this volume, the actions of individuals or small groups had significant impacts.

The ability to understand and undertake complex "negotiation games" is therefore essential for those who aspire to shape international trade policy. By viewing international trade through the conceptual lens of negotiation analysis, we pose questions different from, but complementary to, those illuminated by policy analysis: How do negotiation processes shape trade rules? How are key decisions made, and who makes them? Which players are the most influential, and what strategies do they employ?

The cases in this volume therefore look beyond the changing substance of trade agreements, deeply exploring patterns of influence. They examine both the *what* of trade and the *who*, *how*, and *why* of decision making. By focusing attention on some of the most important recent trade negotiation processes, the reader can come to understand not just the larger issues surrounding trade but also how players seek to exert influence and how the system is evolving day to day.

## Foundations of Negotiation Analysis

The point of departure for negotiation analysis is the treatment of negotiations as games, or sets of interactions among a group of parties who formulate and enact strategies to exert influence so that they may reach a favorable agreement on some cluster of issues.[1] Outcomes in negotiation are bounded but not determined by the structure of the game. In other words, there are no preset outcomes or equilibrium solutions;[2] rather, outcomes emerge from the choices made by the participating parties and from the evolving environment in which negotiations take place.

Games have structure—in classic game theory, a set of players, a range of potential outcomes and associated payoffs for the players, and rules governing the timing of moves. The structure of negotiating games likewise can be analyzed along four dimensions: issues, parties, levels, and linkages.[3] The simplest negotiating games involve just two monolithic parties negotiating over a single issue. By definition, these negotiations occur at one level: because the parties are of one mind, internal negotiations within each side do not complicate the process. And because the two parties negotiate in a single episode or round, the precedents and relationships that shape negotiations that are linked in time are not important (though reputations may be).

On the other end of the spectrum, the most complex negotiations involve multiple issues, many parties and levels of negotiating activity, and linked rounds of ongoing interactions. Even relatively straightforward bilateral trade negotiations are in fact quite complicated. Multilat-

---

1. This discussion draws on Howard Raiffa's seminal work on negotiation analysis; see Raiffa (1982).

2. *Equilibrium* in game theory means having one or a few undominated outcomes. Game theorists have devised several powerful notions of dominance—static or dynamic logics through which certain outcomes can be determined to be dominated by others. See Myerson (1997).

3. For an early effort to define the structure of negotiations, see Raiffa (1982, chapter 1). For developed frameworks, see Sebenius (1992).

**Figure 2.1    The structure-strategy-process-outcomes model**

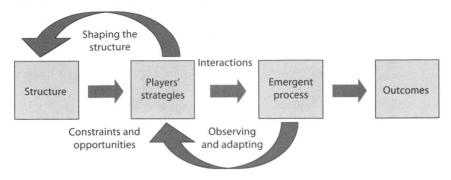

eral rounds of trade negotiations under the auspices of the General Agreement on Tariffs and Trade (GATT) or the World Trade Organization (WTO) are arguably the most complex negotiations ever undertaken: they involve complicated agendas; perhaps hundreds of parties, each engaged in internal negotiations and decision-making processes; and years of linked interactions.

The structure of a negotiation strongly influences each party's constraints and opportunities. As the structure-strategy-process-outcomes model in figure 2.1 illustrates, structure shapes the strategies the players employ, the process that emerges from their interactions, and the eventual outcomes.[4] At the same time, the players learn and adapt their strategies as the negotiations proceed. Also, as discussed later, they can take actions to alter the structure of the situation.

## The Structure of Simple Negotiations

Consider a negotiation over a used car between a buyer and seller who are meeting for the first and only time. From a structural point of view, this is as simple as negotiations get. The interaction involves just two parties, both of whom are monolithic, negotiating over a single issue—the price of the car—in a single round. If the buyer and seller reach agreement, they exchange the car for some amount of money; if not, they walk away.

---

4. This model bridges the structure-process gap in the study of negotiation, accounting for both the impact of structure on process and the impact of process on structure. An earlier version of it is presented in Watkins (2000). Walton, Cutcher-Gershenfeld, and McKersie (1994) develop a related framework, analyzing negotiation in terms of forces shaping negotiators' choices and the interactions of strategies, processes, and structures. Sebenius (1996) analyzes negotiation in terms of structure, people, and context, as well as barriers and opportunities for creating and claiming value.

## Figure 2.2 Bargaining range in a distributed negotiation

Here, the overriding goal of both sides is simply to *claim value*.[5] The buyer and seller of the car have bottom lines, defined by what Roger Fisher and William Ury (1981) called BATNAs (best alternatives to a negotiated agreement); real-life negotiators would call them fallback options. For the seller of the used car, the best alternative may be a take-it-or-leave-it offer from another interested party; for the buyer, it may be purchasing another car. These BATNAs are translated into bottom-line prices for the two sides. If they overlap, there exists a *bargaining range* within which the parties negotiate; if not, then no agreement is possible.

Suppose that a buyer is willing to pay up to $5,000 for the car and the seller will accept no less than $4,000. The result, illustrated in figure 2.2, is a bargaining range of $1,000. Given the size of the range, we would expect the parties to reach agreement somewhere within it.

This negotiation game does not have a predefined equilibrium outcome. Instead, each side seeks to claim the maximum amount of value. In this *distributive negotiation*, the negotiation process is purely competitive in nature. The outcome is determined by the strategies each side employs to shape the perceptions of the other. In particular, value is claimed through the dance of offers and concessions, threats and commitments as the parties progressively converge on an agreement or break off their talks (see Raiffa 1982, chapter 4).

## The Structure of Complex Negotiations

If trade negotiations were as simple as bargaining for a used car, the world would be a much less interesting place. However, the negotiations that

---

5. Walton and McKersie (1965, chapters 2–5) make the important distinction between distributive and integrative bargaining. They also note that negotiations might involve a mix of distributive and integrative bargaining (in their terms, "mixed-motive"; see their chapter 5). Lax and Sebenius (1986) reconceptualize the distinction between distributive and integrative bargaining, viewing value claiming and value creating as processes that go on in parallel in most negotiations rather than as discrete types of bargaining.

result in trade agreements have structures that are far more complex in the four key dimensions mentioned earlier: issues, parties, levels, and linkages. Increasing the complexity of each dimension significantly changes the nature of the emergent process, creating strategic opportunities and vulnerabilities for the negotiators.

## From Single-Issue to Multi-Issue Negotiations

The move from negotiating one issue to negotiating multiple issues changes the nature of the process dramatically, because it gives the parties opportunities to *create value* as well as *claim value*. As David Lax and Jim Sebenius (1986, 33) put it, "Value creating and value claiming are linked parts of negotiation. Both processes are present. No matter how much creative problem-solving enlarges the pie, it still must be divided; value that has been created must be claimed."

The positions taken by parties in negotiations represent their efforts to advance underlying *interests*.[6] To the extent that negotiators can identify complementary interests, they are able to make cross-issue trades and thereby enlarge the pie.[7] In fact, the agendas of trade negotiations are explicitly constructed to open up possibilities for trades across issues—for example, tariff concessions in different sectors. Trade negotiators also create value through mechanisms such as side payments to compensate losers or phase-in provisions to permit time for adjustment.

To explore how the move to multiple issues affects the players' strategies and the resulting process, we might add an issue to the used car negotiation: now, the buyer and seller are bargaining over the timing of transfer of the car as well as over price. Suppose that the seller hopes to keep the car for 10 more days, in order to have time to buy another. And suppose that the prospective buyer has some flexibility, but really wants to acquire a car within 5 days—immediately, if possible. If the buyer is willing to pay more in return for getting the car earlier than the seller's minimum price for giving it up, then they can make a mutually beneficial cross-issue trade of money for time.

The result is an *integrative negotiation* in which the parties seek simultaneously to create value and to claim value. The bargaining range in such a negotiation is not a line, as in the case of purely distributive negotiation (see figure 2.2), but a zone as shown in figure 2.3. Both sides may gain if they can identify and capitalize on the potential to make mutually ben-

---

6. Fisher and Ury (1981) make the crucial distinction between positions and interests. For a deeper treatment of approaches to evaluating trade-offs and making better decisions, see Hammond, Keeney, and Raiffa (1999).

7. For a detailed discussion of differences as a potential source of joint gains, see Sebenius (1984, chapter 5) and Lax and Sebenius (1986, chapter 5).

## Figure 2.3  Bargaining range in an interactive negotiation

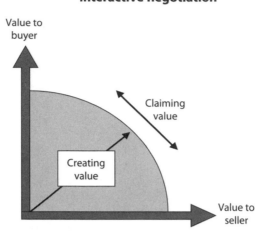

Note: "Value" means the total value to each of the parties of different (price, delivery time) combinations.

eficial trades (moving toward the frontier of feasible agreements). Of course, the value that is created has to be claimed or divided between the sides (moving along the frontier).

As in single-issue negotiations, parties engaged in multi-issue negotiations seek to influence each other's perceptions of their alternatives to a negotiated agreement. But they also seek to influence each other's perceptions of their interests and hence the possible trade-offs across issues. When they identify shared or complementary interests that are the basis for mutually beneficial trades, they create value and make possible greater joint gains. To create and claim more value, parties control what issues are up for negotiation by framing what is at stake, setting the agenda, and similar strategies.

The extent to which value can be created and claimed in trade negotiations is strongly influenced by how the *issue agenda* is constructed. If the agenda is too narrow, the parties may have difficulty creating enough value to make agreement possible. This was a key factor in the failed Organization for Economic Cooperation and Development (OECD) negotiations over a Multilateral Agreement on Investment (MAI). The talks focused so narrowly on investment issues between developed nations that they lacked the grist—the multiple issues across which trades could be made—for reaching an agreement. Conversely, if the agenda for a negotiation is very broad, the process may become unmanageable unless it is divided into smaller subnegotiations. For this reason, trade negotiations—and indeed all negotiations with broad agendas—usually get broken down or "unbundled"[8] into smaller clusters of issues. But the precise form of this breakdown is critical. Each cluster must contain a range of issues sufficiently broad to enable value to be created and claimed. At the same time, the results of the subnegotiations must ultimately be integrated; failure to reach agreement in one issue-cluster can poison the entire process.

Issues can be negotiated sequentially as well as in parallel subsets, making *issue sequencing* important. A common approach is first to negotiate a few easier issues, hoping to thereby build confidence and momentum. But overreliance on sequential negotiation eliminates cross-issue trades and thus the potential for value creation. The sequence in which issues are negotiated can also influence how coalitions form and eventually how gains and losses are distributed.[9] Parties therefore often compete to shape not just the agenda's contents but also the order in which those contents are addressed.

Finally, the need both to create and to claim value in multi-issue negotiations results in a fundamental tension. In order to create value, the parties have to share some information about their preferences. But information sharing leaves them vulnerable to being misled by the other side. The result is what Lax and Sebenius (1986) term "the negotiator's dilemma": negotiators must balance cooperative efforts to enlarge the pie and competitive efforts to get the biggest share.[10] This tension often leads to defensive behavior (e.g., not sharing sufficient information about true preferences) that can end in missed opportunities for value creation. By failing to share sufficient information or by engaging in strategic behavior, the parties may leave value on the table.

### From Two-Party to Multiparty Negotiations

As Howard Raiffa, one of the founders of the field of negotiation analysis, once noted, "significant conceptual complexities arise when even a single new party is added to two-party negotiations: coalitions . . . can now form"

---

8. This term is borrowed from Lax and Sebenius (1986, 94): "Where different interests are bundled into a negotiation, a good strategy can be to unbundle and seek creative ways to dovetail them."

9. For a fascinating discussion of the relationship between issue sequencing and coalition formation, see Riker (1986).

10. Walton and McKersie (1965, 183) had earlier observed that tensions often arise when negotiators engage in mixed-motive negotiations: "At virtually every turn the negotiator finds himself in a dilemma: Should he conceal information in order to make his tactical commitment more credible, or should he reveal information in order to pursue integrative bargaining; should he bring militant constituents into the session to affirm feeling, or should he use small subcommittees in which new ideas can be quietly explored." Lax and Sebenius (1986) place this strategic tension between value creating and value claiming at the heart of negotiation.

(Raiffa 1982, 257). In negotiations involving more than two parties, when none is able to unilaterally impose (or veto) the outcome, coalitions can profoundly alter parties' perceptions of their bargaining power. A group of parties that succeeds in building a *winning coalition* can improve their desired outcomes; but a *blocking coalition* may be able to frustrate the plans of even the most powerful individual player (see Lax and Sebenius 1991).

But building coalitions is one thing—sustaining them is quite another. Coalitions founded on strongly aligned interests and long-term relationships are inherently stable. However, alliances that are short-term and more opportunistic are often vulnerable. The breakup of a coalition can be triggered by changes in external conditions or by the active efforts of other parties, bargaining with or punishing members of an opposing coalition in order to induce them to defect.[11]

Like multiple issues, the sheer number of the parties in trade negotiations can powerfully complicate the process. By definition, multilateral trade negotiations involve many parties. National governments and, in the case of the European Union, a negotiation unit representing many national governments, sit at the table. But numerous other parties, including nongovernmental organizations (NGOs) and lobbying groups, exert influence on the process.

As the number of parties to a negotiation rises, so too does the challenge of reaching a mutually acceptable agreement—especially when consensus is required for a decision, making it possible for a single determined spoiler to halt the process. For example, India nearly blocked the launch of the Doha Round of trade talks over concerns about negotiations on foreign investment and other issues.

As noted above, dividing a negotiation into subnegotiations over subsets of issues can be helpful in reaching agreement. Often, the key to simplifying the process is reducing the number of parties participating in the core negotiation to a manageable level. Such a reduction occurs voluntarily when *patterns of deference* emerge over the course of a negotiation: some parties agree to subordinate themselves (i.e., be represented by others) in the process (Myerson 1997, chapters 8, 9). Such patterns of deference often arise; but as the case of the Agreement on Trade-Related Aspects of Intellectual Property Rights (TRIPS) will show, they come into play most strongly at the time of key deadlines or "action-forcing events" (Watkins 1998).

## From Unitary to Multilevel Negotiations

In the used car negotiation, the two parties are individuals and hence assumed to be monolithic or of one mind. But negotiations that take place

---

11. Much of the discussion of negotiation in this section is implicitly framed in terms of non-cooperative game theory, but the issue of coalition stability is also a central concern in the literature on cooperative game theory. See Myerson (1997, chapters 8, 9).

among groups, organizations, or nations simultaneously occur *within* the parties. Even if trade negotiations are bilateral, such as those in 1999 between China and the United States over market access, negotiations within the parties interact strongly with negotiations between the parties, resulting in what Robert Putnam termed "the two level game" (Putnam 1988; see also Lax and Sebenius 1986, chapter 17).

Along this dimension, too, the move from simplicity to complexity profoundly alters the character of the game and hence of effective strategies of influence. Any bargain between two sides really involves three separate agreements: one across the table and one within each side.[12] More precisely, reaching agreement between the parties requires that a critical mass of support—in other words, a sufficiently powerful coalition—be built within each side.

Negotiators must therefore synchronize talks held at the various internal and external tables so that the agreement is accepted at all of them. Each negotiator must both vigorously seek to advance the interests of his or her side and at the same time sell the agreement to internal decision makers. One tool for gaining internal approval is ambiguous language, which can enable the parties to sell differing interpretations to their respective constituencies. Of course, such reliance on ambiguity can create major problems when the resulting agreements are implemented and disputes must subsequently be resolved.

Synchronizing internal and external negotiations involves a delicate balancing act, because their interactions may restrict tactical flexibility. For example, exhibiting unyielding behavior in the external talks may make a leader appear to be a tough negotiator and thereby bolster internal political support; but it may also lock him or her into untenable positions with outside counterparts. Later retreat from these positions may prove impossible because the resulting internal loss of face would be unacceptable. Likewise, negotiators must pay close attention to how positions taken at the table will influence internal negotiation processes. A leader's willingness to make concessions in external negotiations can easily become grist for internal political struggles, as we will see clearly in the cases of the negotiation for permanent normal trade relations (PNTR) with China and the battle for fast track.

Finally, success in managing multilevel negotiation rests, in part, on the negotiator's ability to understand how the other side or sides make decisions. Negotiators must ask key questions, such as, Who has authority to negotiate and to ratify trade agreements? How will decisions be made within governments? Who influences these decisions? For example, the decision-making process in the United States contains multiple levels of

---

12. For an extensive discussion of bureaucratic politics and its impact on decision making, see Allison (1971); see also Iklé (1964).

authority—the administration can negotiate trade agreements, but Congress must ratify any associated changes in domestic law.

International trade negotiations are not just two-level games; they are multilevel or *network games*. In multilateral negotiations, each participating nation must both negotiate at the table and engage in some form of domestic decision-making process away from the table. Additional levels of negotiating may occur within or among the supranational agencies concerned about trade issues. The resulting need to synchronize these linked negotiations is perhaps the most difficult challenge confronting the facilitators of trade talks and is a principal reason why major rounds of multilateral trade negotiations tend to be so time-consuming.

### From Single-Round to Multiround Negotiations

The final dimension of structural complexity concerns linkages in time among sets of negotiations. In our used car example, the parties met, negotiated, reached agreement, and parted company for good. But trade policy is shaped through multiple rounds of negotiations involving the same parties, a change that alters the character of the negotiating process in several important ways.

First and most obviously, prior relationships—good and bad—strongly shape outcomes. Sometimes, prior relationships lead to a more challenging negotiation. The perception among developing countries that they were stiffed in the Uruguay Round powerfully influenced how they approached the negotiations to start a new round of multilateral trade talks at Doha. Such rules of thumb adopted by real-life negotiators as "build the relationship" and "safeguard your reputation" make a great deal of sense in this context. The ongoing relationships created by linkages in time can also project into the future. For example, concessions may be made in one round of negotiations with the expectation that future rounds will bring reciprocal concessions.

Another complication in multiround processes is that agreements are not *self-enforcing*. In the used car negotiation, the parties traded the car for some cash; the exchange immediately followed the agreement, and neither side could renege. But trade negotiations are rarely so happily foolproof. In fact, the agreements reached in trade negotiations may be quite insecure, in that powerful parties can and do abrogate provisions and insist on highly questionable interpretations of terms. Weaker parties therefore face a dual challenge: they must both advance their interests in the rule-making negotiations and also increase the security of agreements. The latter requires that they strengthen the mechanisms and institutions for resolving collective disputes and negotiate regimes to monitor and verify agreements.

A related change is that complex trade agreements are implemented, in part, through later clarifying rounds. In other words, the gains made in the main negotiation can easily be lost (and losses made up) in the subsequent negotiations concerning implementation. Disputes over implementation themselves may well be addressed in part through further negotiations. Therefore, in a fundamental sense, the game of negotiating trade rules never really ends.

The negotiations that shape international trade rules are clearly among the most complex possible. This complexity is both good news and bad news. Because the negotiations involve multiple issues, they offer opportunities to create and claim value through cross-issue trades. But to realize those potential gains and avoid confusion or deadlock, negotiators must carefully craft the agenda and parse it into promising subnegotiations. Because trade negotiations frequently involve many parties, the less powerful parties can increase their bargaining power by forming coalitions. But to avoid lowest-common-denominator agreements and neutralize potential spoilers, negotiators must cooperate. Because trade negotiations take place on multiple levels, they provide opportunities to build coalitions within the sides. But agreements must often be crafted to allow political leaders to save face. Because trade policy is made in negotiations that are linked in time, trades (or attempts to right perceived wrongs) can be made across multiple rounds. But the agreements that are made may ultimately prove to be insecure, either because they are abrogated outright or because their gains are whittled away during the incremental process of negotiating their implementation.

## Analyzing Process Dynamics

As the structure-strategy-process-outcomes model illustrates, each negotiation's structure strongly influences the strategies of the participating parties, and hence the emergent process. While multi-issue negotiations tend to stimulate cross-issue trading, giving rise to the negotiator's dilemma, single-issue negotiations obviously do not. Multiparty negotiations tend to promote coalition-building behavior, which has no place in two-party negotiations. Those engaged in multilevel negotiations tend to keep an eye on how their actions will be perceived on all levels of the game, while two-party negotiations require only that each negotiator send clear messages to the other. The parties in multiround negotiations, for good or ill, usually pay more attention to relationships and precedents than those in one-round interactions.

Though structure shapes strategy, individual players retain considerable scope to influence the process. In a negotiation, like a good soccer match, the overarching structure constrains and focuses the competition among players, who are themselves responsible for crafting and executing good plays.

Of course, the games of negotiation and soccer differ in fundamental ways. Not only is it possible for more than one side in a negotiation to

**Figure 2.4  Strategies in complex negotiations**

| | Accepting the structure: Working with existing parties, agendas, and linkages | Shaping the structure: Seeking to alter who participates and what the issues are |
|---|---|---|
| **At the table:** Advancing interests through agreement with other players | Learning and bargaining | Negotiating the game |
| **Away from the table:** Advancing interests through unilateral actions | Analysis and preparation | Unilateral game-changing moves |

win, but the boundaries of a negotiation are in several respects more fluid. In soccer, all play takes place on a field of specified size. In negotiation, strategic moves are not limited to the field—that is, established negotiating forums. On the field, parties seek to create and claim value by identifying complementary interests, proposing mutually beneficial trades, offering persuasive arguments, and committing themselves to favorable positions. Away from the field, they work, often in secret, to build coalitions, make side deals, and influence public opinion.

In soccer, moreover, the rules of the game are predetermined, and referees have the authority to enforce them. But in negotiation, the participants can influence the rules, changing the game even as they play it. Thus, while the structure of negotiation shapes strategy, strategy can also affect structure. The outcomes of trade negotiations are often strongly influenced, for example, by the moves preceding their formal start that set the agenda, determine the forum in which negotiations will take place, or establish procedural ground rules and substantive understandings. As the TRIPS negotiations will illustrate, early game-changing moves can be determinative.

The two-by-two matrix shown in figure 2.4 characterizes strategies in complex negotiations. One dimension distinguishes between moves to play the game—that is, to work within the established structure—and to change the game (for example, by shaping the agenda or influencing who participates). The other distinguishes between moves made at and away from the negotiating table. In superior negotiation strategies, players integrate a mixture drawn from all four cells of the matrix.

Many people associate *negotiating* with the at-the-table bargaining process in the upper left cell of the matrix. Perhaps the biggest revelation of this discussion is that such negotiation is only a small part of the process—possibly the least important. In fact, what happens at the table is largely predetermined by the efforts made by the parties, both at and away from the table, to prepare for the negotiations and to shape the game.

## Designing Negotiation Strategies

In order to achieve a favorable agreement, players craft negotiation strategies to shape how the other side or sides perceive their interests and alternatives. Sophisticated players of trade negotiation games draw from an established repertoire of seven tactical elements, all of which (in various combinations) are displayed in the cases explored in this volume.

1. *Organizing to influence:* creating, staffing, funding, and directing institutions in ways that influence the trade negotiation process.

2. *Selecting the forum:* identifying the most promising forum in which to pursue one's objectives and then ensuring that negotiations take place there.

3. *Shaping the agenda:* adding or removing issues from the agenda, dividing the larger agenda into modules for parallel negotiations, and establishing some high-level principles to govern the process.

4. *Building coalitions:* identifying potential winning and blocking coalitions and then devising plans for building supportive coalitions and breaking or forestalling opposing ones.

5. *Leveraging linkages:* linking and de-linking issues or sets of negotiations in order to create and claim value.

6. *Playing the frame game:* crafting and promulgating a favorable framing of "the problem" and "the options."

7. *Creating momentum:* channeling the flow of the negotiation process in promising directions by establishing appropriate stages to demarcate the process, as well as by instigating or taking advantage of action-forcing events.

### Element #1: Organizing to Influence

Lobbyists organize to influence and negotiate with their own government. Industry groups in one country may also organize to influence their counterparts in another country. Government negotiators themselves have to figure out how to organize their team, secure their mandate, and get instructions from their principals.

Sometimes entirely new organizations are created to help build coalitions, monitor the negotiation process, and develop strategy. Parties also seek to gain analyses and expertise by co-opting the resources of existing institutions, such as trade associations. Such organizations, if appropriately staffed, funded, and directed, can provide support that is essential to influencing the course of trade negotiations.

In the cases that follow, we will see that effective organizing to influence is key in shaping the outcome of trade talks. In the TRIPS negotiation, for example, a group of CEOs of US pharmaceutical, software, and entertainment companies created the Intellectual Property Committee (IPC) and staffed this new organization with people skilled both in working out policy positions and in playing the trade negotiation game. As a result, the IPC played a central role in developing the framework for the TRIPS agreement.

### Element #2: Selecting the Forum

Often, *where* a negotiation takes place strongly affects gains and losses. For this reason, vigorous jousting can occur as the forum for a particular set of trade talks is selected. That choice influences who will participate in the negotiation, the rules of the game, and how any resulting agreement will be enforced.

For example, supporters of strong intellectual property (IP) protection worked hard to include IP in the Uruguay Round of trade talks. The issue of international IP protection had been housed at the United Nations, whose lack of enforcement had frustrated many industry representatives; the WTO, they believed, would offer more recourse against a nation that failed to honor intellectual property rights. The failed negotiations for a Multilateral Agreement on Investment also underscore the significance of forum selection, for the decision to negotiate at the OECD, as opposed to the WTO or another institution, significantly shaped the direction of the talks and the challenges that ultimately led to their demise.

### Element #3: Shaping the Agenda

In tandem with selecting the forum, negotiators must establish the agenda for the talks. What issues will be negotiated and which will be set aside? Will the agreement be comprehensive and multisector, or will it focus on a specific issue (such as investment) or a single sector (such as steel)? Will parties have the ability to selectively embrace any provisions they choose (such as codes of conduct), or will they have to negotiate in order to opt out of or delay acceding to provisions they don't like? Will the implementation of an agreement be on the same schedule for all parties, or will it be staged over time (as, for example, in the Uruguay Round agreement)? Will parties make different levels of commitments, depending on such variables as their stage of development, or will all signatories make the same commitments?

In complex trade negotiations, those who control the agenda for the talks and the sequencing of issues strongly affect outcomes. Effective agenda setting involves defining the issues that will be covered in a negotiation and influencing the order in which they will be dealt with.[13] Negotiators typically undertake a "prenegotiation negotiation" over the agenda, attempting to define certain issues as "nonnegotiable" and to set preconditions.

For parties that seek an agreement, efforts at controlling the agenda focus on identifying bundles of issues that seem able to support value-creating trades. These parties also attempt to exclude or defer potentially toxic issues—those that could prevent agreement altogether. For deal spoilers, the goal is to undermine or delay decision making by turning the negotiation into a win-lose proposition. To that end, they may introduce or maintain toxic issues on the agenda. For example, in the negotiations to renew fast track, the question of whether labor and environmental issues belonged on the agenda of trade negotiations was a major potential stumbling block. In fact, the debates over fast track in the US Congress can be thought of as prenegotiations over the agenda for trade talks.

### Element #4: Building Coalitions

In negotiations involving more than two parties, in which none can unilaterally impose (or veto) the outcome, success in building coalitions can profoundly alter BATNAs. Building a winning coalition enables a negotiator to achieve the desired outcome; but if a blocking coalition forms, those plans may be frustrated.

Coalition building involves identifying groups with complementary goals, building alliances among them, and focusing their collective resources to shape a particular negotiation process. In essence, effective coalition building identifies and exploits alignments of interests.

Sometimes long-standing allies cooperate on a broad range of issues. One such industry coalition is USA Engage. Consisting of more than 600 corporations and associations—including Caterpillar, Boeing, Dow Chemical, General Motors, IBM, Motorola, USX, the US Chamber of Commerce, the American Petroleum Institute, the Business Roundtable, and the Environmental Export Council—it was created to promote international economic involvement by US business and discourage the imposition of unilateral trade sanctions by the US government for political purposes.

But coalitions need not be founded on shared goals and long-standing relationships; they may be short-term pragmatic alliances, based on mutually beneficial trades of support or of resources.

---

13. For a classic treatment of agenda setting in government, see Kingdon (1995).

Negotiators build coalitions by making sequences of moves that create momentum. By approaching the right people in the right sequence, they are able to reduce resistance. In part, such sequencing relies on patterns of deference, as mentioned above (see Lax and Sebenius 1991). Decision makers often defer to others whose opinions on a given set of issues they respect. For an effective sequencing strategy, it is therefore essential that negotiators analyze influence networks in complex negotiations and understand who defers to whom on crucial issues (see Krackhardt and Hanson 1993; on the psychology of interpersonal persuasion, see also Cialdini 1993, chapter 6).

Questions of sustainability also loom large in coalition building. Simply eliciting support is never enough, because allies can vanish in the night. Negotiators must also devote energy to buttressing the commitment of their supporters, as well as to expanding their own persuasive reach. In the words of Owen Harries (1984): "Preaching to the converted, far from being a superfluous activity, is vital. Preachers do it every Sunday. The strengthening of the commitment, intellectual performance, and morale of those already on your side is an essential task, both in order to bind them more securely to the cause and to make them more effective exponents of it."

### Element #5: Leveraging Linkages

Negotiators seek to advance their interests by linking or delinking potentially separate sets of negotiations. Standalone negotiations are rare. Typically, negotiators' perceptions of their alternatives are strongly influenced by linkages to other negotiations—past, present, and future—that can create barriers or open up opportunities (ideas developed in Watkins and Passow 1996). Negotiations can be linked in a number of common ways:

- *Synergistic linkages* combine sets of issues that could be negotiated separately in ways that enhance opportunities to create value.

- *Antagonistic linkages* poison the potential for agreement. Some toxic issues not only are impossible to settle but seriously complicate the settlement of other issues.

- *Sequential linkages* arise when past negotiations or the prospect of future negotiations affect current ones.

- *Competitive linkages* occur when only one negotiation can reach fruition as one party negotiates with two or more others.

- *Reciprocal linkages* occur when all negotiations must reach fruition for an overall deal to occur as one party negotiates with two or more others. In *conditional agreements*, each requires that agreement be reached in the others.

Linkages are a familiar feature of trade negotiations. Threats of sanctions in bilateral disputes, for example, can shape parties' perceptions of their interests and alternatives in multilateral processes and vice versa. Thus the United States used the club of potential section 301 actions to make a multilateral TRIPS agreement appear more attractive to developing countries. Bilateral or regional negotiations also can create useful precedents for subsequent multilateral processes. The TRIPS agreement was strongly shaped by an earlier bilateral agreement on intellectual property rights negotiated between the United States and South Korea. In another kind of linkage, US advocates of greater protection of human rights in China gained leverage by linking the issue to annual renewal of China's most favored nation (MFN) status.

Skilled negotiators also create and claim value by linking and de-linking issues within a particular negotiation. For example, although many developing countries were not enthusiastic about including intellectual property in the Uruguay Round, they were persuaded to include TRIPS in exchange for a phaseout of the Multi-Fiber Arrangement, which limited their opportunities for exporting textiles. A linkage can also be used to claim value; for example, a key issue can be held hostage until the other side shows willingness to make a concession. Negotiators therefore seek to identify synergistic linkages that combine issues in order to create value. At the same time, they work to neutralize antagonistic linkages; to the extent that toxic issues can be eliminated or deferred, agreement becomes easier to reach.

## Element #6: Playing the Frame Game

Public opinion shapes the positions of political leaders in trade negotiations. The parties to a negotiation will therefore often engage in a competition to frame the terms of the public debate. They do so by using arguments, analogies, and metaphors to define both the problem to be solved and the set of potential solutions in ways that favor their point of view.

Framing tactics work for two reasons: assessments of interests often crystallize only when people are confronted with the need to make choices or form opinions, and the "mental models" people use to make sense of a given situation depend on how that situation is presented (Johnson-Laird 1983). Mental models are conceptual frameworks; the products of formative experiences, professional training, and cultural heritage, they embody guiding assumptions and values, beliefs about cause and effect, and expectations of others' behavior (Goffman 1974). These frameworks are the crucial link between an individual's observations of external realities and conclusions about the nature of a problem. Moreover, they provide rules of thumb and scripts that guide actions (see Valley and Keros 2000).

Therefore, the art of framing is to define the problem and the options in ways that tap into particular preconceived beliefs and attitudes, elevating the importance of some and suppressing others. Effective framing has been called "a burning glass which collects and focuses the diffuse warmth of popular emotions, concentrating them on a specific issue" (Mitchell 1970, 111). Among the public, it promotes "right thinking"—that is, "right" in the eyes of those doing the framing—and discredits or provides counterarguments to possible "wrong thinking."

When two contending sides vie to sway public support, the contest is often primarily a language game. Each opponent tries to link its objective to the target audience's values and established beliefs about how the world works. In the TRIPS case, for example, the supporters of strengthening international protection of intellectual property rights succeeded in painting the developing countries as engaging in "intellectual piracy." Later, however, developing countries and NGOs applied the same term—*piracy*—to efforts by multinational companies to patent indigenous knowledge from developing countries. Likewise, in the MAI talks, opponents of the negotiations managed to frame the issue as an effort by large corporations to secretly take over the world, while proponents were unable to offer a compelling riposte.

### Element #7: Creating Momentum

Negotiations rarely proceed smoothly from start to conclusion. Instead, they ebb and flow; periods of deadlock or inaction are punctuated by bursts of progress until agreement is reached or a final breakdown occurs. Skilled negotiators recognize these patterns and work to build momentum in favorable directions, taking such actions as proposing a new formula for agreement or suggesting a face-saving compromise that breaks a logjam.

Skilled players often fashion *multistage processes* explicitly designed to build momentum in the desired direction. Initial agreements on basic principles shape preliminary negotiations over the basic framework of trades the parties will make. This framework, in turn, influences the course of the hard bargaining over details. By fashioning early successes, sophisticated negotiators create options for themselves and limit the choices of others.

*Action-forcing events* can also spur negotiations forward. They can be variously categorized: *internally imposed* (arising from the actions of the negotiators themselves) or *externally imposed* (arising from outside circumstances); *unilateral* (e.g., a threat tied to a deadline) or *consensual* (e.g., a mutual commitment to a deadline, perhaps as a spur to their internal decision making); and *macrolevel* (e.g., deadlines) or *microlevel* (e.g., meetings). All are break points at which negotiators must make a move to avoid incurring substantial and irreversible costs. For example, organizations' annual planning and decision-making cycles can force or delay negotiations. In international negotiations, key political events such as elections serve to drive or restrain action. Action-forcing events are important tools that impel counterparts (and even colleagues on the same side) to realize that hard choices are necessary.

Consider, for example, an action-forcing event in the Uruguay Round negotiations. Though the parties would have preferred to avoid confronting some issues, the impending expiration of US fast-track authority made the status quo untenable. Effective negotiators set up and use deadlines in order to create and claim value, on occasion even intentionally engineering impasses to increase the pressure on others to make concessions. To be sure, the use of action-forcing events sometimes backfires. In the case of PNTR for China, for example, the visit of Premier Zhu Rongji to the United States was intended to force the two sides to work out their remaining disagreements. But the gaps proved too broad to bridge; rather than gaining momentum toward agreement, the negotiations became deadlocked and descended into mutual recriminations.

## Guiding Questions

The cases that follow provide a rich base of data for exploring negotiation strategies. The following questions will be helpful in analyzing them:

- *Organization:* Who was better organized to influence the process, and why?

- *Forums:* What forum was selected for the negotiations? How did the forum influence the outcome?

- *Agenda:* Which parties exerted influence on the agenda, and how did they do it? How was the basic structure of the negotiation established, and who influenced the process?

- *Coalitions:* What coalitions were built (and broken), and which parties were most effective at coalition building?

- *Linkages:* How did the negotiations get linked to other negotiations, and which parties were most effective at using linkage to create and claim value?

- *Framing:* To what extent did public opinion influence outcomes, and which parties were most effective at playing the frame game?

- *Momentum:* Who was most skilled at channeling the flow of the negotiation process and in using action-forcing events to move it forward?

# 3

# Trade-Related Aspects of Intellectual Property Rights

## Making Trade Policy

The inclusion of intellectual property rules in the international trading system was a watershed event. Negotiated during the Uruguay Round, the 1994 Agreement on Trade-Related Aspects of Intellectual Property Rights (TRIPS) significantly broadened the reach of the trading regime. Prior to TRIPS, trade rules generally focused on "don'ts"—telling countries which practices to avoid or scale back. For example, General Agreement on Tariffs and Trade (GATT) members were told to eliminate quotas, to reduce tariffs, to avoid discriminating among GATT members (by mandating most favored nation, or MFN, status) and against foreign goods (by mandating national treatment), and, finally, to avoid standards and technical requirements that unnecessarily restricted trade. Provided that countries respected these don'ts, they remained free to adopt or reject any domestic policies they wished. For example, many countries chose not to enforce intellectual property rights—a perfectly acceptable policy under the GATT system.

*International Trade Meets Intellectual Property: The Making of the TRIPS Agreement* and *International Trade Meets Public Health—Patent Rules and Access to Medicines* are edited and revised versions of the cases with the same names originally written for the Case Program at the Kennedy School of Government. For copies or permission to reproduce the unabridged cases please refer to www.ksgcase.harvard.edu or send a written request to Case Program, John F. Kennedy School of Government, Harvard University, 79 John F. Kennedy Street, Cambridge, MA 02138.

## Depth

By contrast, the TRIPS agreement requires countries to "do" something. World Trade Organization (WTO) members are obliged to adopt policies that protect intellectual property in areas such as patents, trademarks, and copyrights. Though countries remain free to provide even more protection than TRIPS requires, the agreement sets minimum standards. These minimum standards represent a significant reduction in signatories' autonomy of national policy. Such policy constraints are binding because the Uruguay Round Final Act established a strong mechanism for dispute settlement that applies equally to TRIPS and the other rules governing trade in goods and services. In short, all WTO members are required to adhere to TRIPS, and those who fail to do so will suffer consequences.

The advocates of TRIPS rules achieved remarkable success: a far-reaching agreement in a forum that would work to ensure compliance. But the success of the TRIPS campaign has given rise to controversy. Some critics argue that intellectual property rules have no place in a trade agreement. Others worry about the implications of TRIPS for public health in developing countries. Issues relating to indigenous knowledge have also been controversial. Many observers also point out that TRIPS set a precedent by expanding the scope of issues covered in the WTO, opening the door to the inclusion of even more issues, such as labor and environmental standards.

## Coverage

The corporations supporting TRIPS made their case for trade policies enforcing intellectual property rights (IPRs) in moral terms. A failure to respect intellectual property (IP) rights, they argued, is tantamount to theft. But the analogy between IP and other kinds of property is not precise. For example, property rights are generally permanent, while patents and copyrights generally expire after a specific period. In addition, the time granted for exercising a patent differs from that granted for a copyright. Therefore, probably the most important policy question regarding such rights is not moral (whether they should exist) but practical—their optimal duration.

The economic case for protecting intellectual property rests on the tension between encouraging the efficient use of knowledge, on the one hand, and providing the appropriate incentive for its creation on the other. Knowledge is a classic public good. Its benefits are "nonrivalrous"—that is, the use of knowledge by one person does not detract from the ability of others to use it. Thus, the additional cost to society of using knowledge is zero. If there were nothing more to learn, the most efficient action would be to eliminate IPRs and make all knowledge available without charge. But our knowledge is not complete, and setting its price at zero would eliminate any financial incentive to seek more. One way to deal with this problem is to subsidize knowledge creation, and indeed most basic research is funded by national governments. But other mechanisms may also be required. Through intellectual property rights such as patents, an inventor is rewarded for his or her discovery for a certain length of time, after which the knowledge can be used without charge.[1]

Countries obviously differ in their ability to contribute knowledge. At one extreme, developing countries may have a strong interest in encouraging the diffusion of existing knowledge but little concern about stimulating the creation of new knowledge—and thus little interest in protecting intellectual property. In more technologically advanced countries, however, the need for new knowledge is generally much greater. Such national diversity may well warrant different national patent policies.

But because knowledge spills over national borders, a case can also be made for allowing inventors to capture some of the international benefits of their discoveries. Otherwise, countries would have an incentive to free ride on the discoveries of others and the world would spend too little on knowledge creation. On this argument, the provision of international IPRs would add to international innovation. Yet making knowledge expensive might limit its diffusion, even as the ability of innovators to operate abroad without fear they will be copied might encourage diffusion. Therefore, the overall net impact of international IPRs on global welfare is theoretically ambiguous.

But even if international IPRs are desirable, they may not belong in trade agreements. To be sure, the existence of such rules will affect what is traded. Producers of software, for example, will not be able to export their products and earn profits if foreign countries do not enforce IPRs and prevent other companies from copying the software without paying royalties. In this sense the failure to enforce IPRs, like a ban on imports, acts to inhibit trade and is therefore viewed as a trade barrier. However, a country that does not recognize such property rights will not grant the producers of such software the right to any returns. Moreover, as written in the WTO rules, TRIPS actually affects more than trade. Although the agreement's name is "Trade-Related Aspects of Intellectual Property Rights," countries are expected to enforce such rights throughout their own domestic economies. IPRs could therefore alter the returns earned by domestic producers in purely domestic transactions.

---

1. A second question in economics is relevant here: the relationship between monopoly and innovation. The prospect of having a monopoly might induce more innovation, but holding a monopoly could reduce the incentive to innovate. Providing a *temporary* monopoly reduces the dangers that a firm will rest on its laurels.

## Winners and Losers

Granting IPRs internationally has distributive implications, transferring income from knowledge users to knowledge producers. Indeed, its welfare consequences differ dramatically from those of trade. Under competitive conditions, both exporting and importing nations benefit from trade liberalization. IPRs, however, tend to create net winners and losers. Its differential impact makes IP a particularly controversial issue, especially in the area of pharmaceuticals.

Given this alignment of winners and losers, the introduction of TRIPS rules that heavily benefit high-technology corporations led to concerns about how power is distributed in the WTO. Though some developing countries saw IPRs as a mechanism for encouraging foreign investors to bring the latest technologies to their markets, most viewed the rules as reflecting the continuing dominance of firms based in developed countries.

## Enforcement

The motives of those seeking to introduce IP into the WTO were clear. If the Uruguay Round had focused only on IPRs, with the attendant creation of winning and losing countries, obtaining a binding multilateral agreement would have been difficult. But because the Uruguay Round dealt with a number of trade issues, the losers could be compensated with concessions in other sectors (such as the elimination of the Multi-Fiber Arrangement [MFA]). In addition, its dispute settlement mechanism made the WTO an attractive forum for IPR supporters. Countries found violating TRIPS could face the loss of benefits in other areas.

But inclusion in the WTO could boost the adoption and enforcement of many other systems of rules—as proponents of competition policy initiatives and of labor and environmental standards recognize. Indeed, a popular argument has been that if the trade rules provide intellectual property protection for companies, then they should also protect workers and the environment. For this reason, some see the inclusion of TRIPS as a dangerous precedent, fearing that the trade regime may become too overloaded to function effectively.

Other observers see TRIPS as quite different from labor and environment standards, arguing that the failure to provide IP protection constitutes a genuine trade barrier by depriving innovators of the ability to reap gains from trade. Producers of easily "pirated" commodities such as software, motion pictures, videocassettes, records, books, and pharmaceuticals are particularly vulnerable. But this argument assumes the existence of precisely those intellectual property rights not recognized by countries that refuse to enforce them.

## Participation

Before the Uruguay Round, the United States had sought—using its Special 301 legislation—to unilaterally introduce intellectual property protection in trade. The United States had also advanced IPRs in regional trade agreements, notably the North American Free Trade Agreement (NAFTA). But the idea of making IPRs part of the WTO was particularly attractive, because the organization has such broad membership and because it makes cross-retaliation possible.

## Developing Countries

The principle of special and differential treatment for developing countries is a pillar of the trading system. Its execution is fairly straightforward when border barriers are concerned: tariffs and quotas can be different for different countries. But applying such treatment to rules—which are either enforced or not—is not so easy. Thus, the preferential treatment of developing countries has been limited to the longer time periods they have been given to come into compliance with the agreement. But many developing countries lack an extensive IP regime, and their need to establish one consumes scarce administrative and legal resources.

As the second case study in this chapter elaborates, TRIPS has been especially controversial in its application to pharmaceuticals. Countries were particularly fearful that the agreement could be used to block their access to the medicines they required to deal with public health crises such as AIDS. TRIPS did provide for noncommercial use and compulsory licensing should such crises occur. It also made clear that nothing in the agreement barred the parallel importation of products legally sold in other countries. Nonetheless, developing countries (and others) felt it was necessary to clarify their rights under the agreement.

## Governance

Many WTO members did not enforce IPRs prior to the TRIPS agreement. Some members had partial enforcement; others had different systems from that outlined in TRIPS. For example, in some countries the entity that was first to invent a product was granted the patent; in others, it went to the first to file. In addition, they differed in what kind of knowledge could be patented and for how long. By setting minimum standards for all members, the WTO rules required many countries to change how their domestic IP regimes functioned. National governments could no longer implement new regimes that were less stringent than TRIPS, even when they believed it was in their interest to do so.

For many countries, the inclusion of intellectual property rules in the Uruguay Round Final Act effectively altered the internal political balance between supporters and opponents of intellectual property protection. By packaging IP rules with trade, IP supporters won gains they otherwise would not have been able to achieve. But these changes came at a price: the tactic antagonized and mobilized groups, both national and international, concerned about the impact of TRIPS. Most notably, many such groups organized to protest what they foresaw as one result of the agreement: the reduced availability of pharmaceuticals in developing countries. Eventually these groups formed coalitions that were able to bring their concerns to the Doha ministerial.

## CASE STUDY: International Trade Meets Intellectual Property—The Making of the TRIPS Agreement (TRIPS, Case 1)

As usual, it all comes down to sex, drugs, and rock 'n' roll.

The 1994 Agreement on Trade-Related Aspects of Intellectual Property Rights, or TRIPS, established the most comprehensive set of global trade rules for intellectual property—protecting everything from *Basic Instinct* to Prozac to Nirvana's *In Utero* (along with Roundup weed killer and Microsoft Windows). After seven years of negotiating, industries that rely on copyrights, patents, and trademarks received more protection than anyone had believed possible at the outset of the talks.

TRIPS was concluded in the context of the Uruguay Round of the General Agreement on Tariffs and Trade talks. GATT talks had usually been concerned with more conventional trade issues such as tariffs, and many countries initially had no interest in adding intellectual property protection to the Uruguay Round agenda; some were opposed to merely discussing IP under the auspices of the GATT. Moreover, even supporters— namely, the United States, Europe, and Japan—had serious disagreements about what constituted appropriate protection. Right up to the 1986 ministerial meeting that launched the negotiations, the interested parties had no idea whether intellectual property would be part of the round.

Although intellectual property protection was ultimately included in the ministerial declaration (i.e., the agenda for the round), the first two years of TRIPS talks showed little movement. As one US negotiator remembers, "There was no real discussion at all." Major rifts existed between developed and developing countries, and many of the negotiators had no previous experience with intellectual property. At the Uruguay Round midterm review in 1988, TRIPS was considered to be one of the "problem groups," lacking even a consensus on a framework for the negotiations.

The deadlock over TRIPS was broken in 1989, and negotiators began to discuss ways to protect, enforce, and settle disputes over intellectual property. However, because of the different legal traditions of protection in the United States, Europe, and Japan, the supporters' persistent disagreements soon intensified. If there were to be global standards, whose would they be? In the midst of this discussion, an impasse that developed in 1990 over agricultural subsidies brought the *entire* Uruguay Round to a halt.

Three years later, in December 1993, the Uruguay Round ended at last, after several sleepless nights of high-stakes negotiating. Officials emerged with more than 400 pages of detailed trade agreements and 22,000 pages of supplementary information and commitments. Among these documents was the final TRIPS agreement.

Many characterized the TRIPS talks as having been initiated and driven by US knowledge-based industries, particularly pharmaceuticals, entertainment, agrochemicals, and computer software. As one participant puts it, "It was a partnership between industry and government that had never existed before in an international trade negotiation." Some say this partnership led to "potentially the most important legal advance for the world trading system since the establishment of the GATT in 1947" (Ryan 1998, 1).

## What Is Intellectual Property?

Intellectual property can be defined as information with a commercial value. Intellectual property rights are a composite of "ideas, inventions, and creative expressions" and "the public willingness to bestow the status of property on them" (Sherwood 1990, 11; quoted in Braga 1995, 382). In the United States, the right to protect IP is recognized in the Constitution (Article I, Section 8).[2]

Economists generally believe in the need to protect intellectual property, arguing that free market forces alone do not provide sufficient incentive to create knowledge. An innovator cannot appropriate the full benefit of his or her innovation. Therefore, many economists maintain that the creation of knowledge must either be subsidized by the government or be protected through the creation of temporary monopolies, which can pay for the innovative activity. Policymakers must determine how much protection is needed to allow an adequate rate of return to stimulate innovation.

Policies to protect intellectual property include the granting of patents, trademarks, and copyrights. Patents protect inventions that are novel, not obvious to those in the field, and useful. A patentee has the right to exclude others from using, making, or selling the patented invention for

---

2. "The Congress shall have Power . . . To promote the Progress of Science and useful Arts, by securing for limited Times to Authors and Inventors the exclusive Right to their respective Writings and Discoveries." Harvard Law School professor William Alford notes in remarks to the author that Article I, Section 8, does not apply to trademarks.

a specified period of time. Trademarks are commercial symbols used to identify goods and services or their producers (e.g., Coca-Cola, Gucci). Copyrights protect works of authorship, such as books, from the time of their creation. Intellectual property protection is also often extended to trade secrets, industrial designs, layout designs of integrated circuits, and geographical indications that identify a product, such as wine, with a particular region (e.g., Chablis, Champagne).

The stakes in protecting intellectual property were high for many US companies. Not only is the cost of product development in the knowledge-based and artistic industries significant, but success is rarely guaranteed. The cost of imitating these products, however, is often relatively low. Before TRIPS was completed, the US International Trade Commission (ITC) estimated that American companies lost between $43 and $60 billion annually due to inadequate intellectual property protection abroad.[3] Pharmaceuticals, chemical products, films, software, publications, and sound recordings were among the products affected.[4]

International markets were of growing significance to the US film and television business. Hollywood was also important to the US economy; by 1991, the film and television industry generated an annual trade surplus of more than $4.5 billion, second only to the aerospace business.[5] But there were risks involved in making movies—two-thirds of all films did not recoup their production costs. As videocassette recorders became more readily available, allowing anyone to copy videotapes, the industry's problems with piracy abroad increased. The Motion Picture Association of America (MPAA) reported in 1989 that piracy accounted for some $1.2 billion in lost revenues. In 1990, the MPAA spent $20 million fighting film, videocassette, and cable TV "bandits."[6] "Keep in mind," remarked Jack Valenti, then president of the MPAA, "that the US film industry does about $24 billion a year. Forty-one percent of that comes from international markets, so it is increasingly crucial and important that those markets remain open and that our IP is protected from thievery. We are constantly vigilant because, like virtue, we are every day besieged."[7]

---

3. "Montreal Trade Talks; Intellectual Property Talks Stalled," *The Financial Times*, December 1, 1988, section I, 4. Debate continues over the actual value of foreign infringement of US intellectual property; critics note that USITC figures are based on data supplied by domestic industries.

4. In 1989, US IPR-related industries exported $58.8 billion in goods covered by patents, trademarks, and copyrights—about 16 percent of US merchandise exports (Maskus 1993, 15).

5. Bruce Stokes, "Tinseltown Trade Wars," *The National Journal*, February 23, 1991.

6. Faye Rice, "How Copycats Steal Billions," *Fortune Magazine*, April 22, 1991, 157.

7. Unless otherwise noted, all quotes from Jack Valenti are from an August 1997 interview with Charan Devereaux. According to industry sources, exports accounted for 22 percent of revenues in 1985, growing to 35 percent by 1989. See Bruce Stokes, "Tinseltown Trade Wars," *The National Journal*, February 23, 1991.

With respect to the pharmaceutical industry, experts note that only one commercially viable drug emerges from every 4,000 to 10,000 compounds screened in a process that often involves 10 years of testing and clinical trials (Ryan 1998, 5). In addition, to discover and develop a new medicine and bring it to market in the United States costs on average $500 million.[8] Given these tremendous costs, many US and European pharmaceutical companies argued that the copying and sale of patented drugs around the world diminished the amount of money available for further research. The drug company Merck & Co. found that global patent piracy cost the US pharmaceutical business about $6 billion in 1986, possibly reducing the industry's R&D investment by between $720 million and $900 million (USITC 1993, 9-3). In addition, Pfizer's chairman Edmund Pratt estimated that battles to defend his company's patents had cost over $100 million between 1981 and 1991.[9] US pharmaceutical companies were not getting "a fair shake," one Pfizer executive noted. For example, in six Latin American countries, Pfizer's sales of 12 patented drugs amounted to $24.6 million in 1984. Companies that copied these drugs, however, brought in $30.2 million in sales.[10]

The position of IP-based industries was not universally accepted, however. Many developing nations opposed the idea of strengthening international intellectual property rights. "And with good reason," says F. M. Scherer, professor of public policy and management at Harvard's John F. Kennedy School of Government. "In the US, we are lovely hypocrites. When we were a developing nation we systematically appropriated other people's technology. So that was the way we developed, but we don't want other people to appropriate our technology in order to develop. But of course we have no historical memory, so we don't even know we're being hypocritical."[11]

Nor were developing nations alone in their reservations. Some industrialized nations traditionally did not allow patents on foodstuffs and medicines, holding that monopolies should not be permitted on products so important to consumer welfare. Even Switzerland, home at one time to three leading pharmaceutical companies, offered no patent protection on drug products until 1977 (Scherer 1998, 6). As a result, some experts decried the characterization of copying products as "piracy," since such copying was often lawful under a country's legal system and existing in-

---

8. Ambassador Clayton Yeutter (United States Trade Representative, 1985–88) in the foreword of Gorlin (1999, ii). In addition, a number of PhRMA publications cite the $500 million figure (attributing it to a Boston Consulting Group study of January 1996).

9. Faye Rice, "How Copycats Steal Billions," 157.

10. Michael J. Zamba, "Going after Patent Pirates at Punta del Este," *Christian Science Monitor*, September 18, 1986, 22.

11. Unless otherwise noted, all quotes from F. M. Scherer are from a December 1998 interview with Charan Devereaux.

ternational agreements. According to Scherer (1998), use of the term was "a big public relations scam":

> There is a law of the seas that says "thou shall not steal merchandise from other people's ships." Doing so by force—taking another's ship and its property—is piracy and was mutually condemned by all nations. Some companies branded the activity of knocking off a drug that was patented in the United States, but not in India, or knocking off a piece of software that was copyrighted in the United States, but not in China, they branded that piracy. But the production of these products was perfectly consistent with the laws of the country in which the knocking-off firm was located. It was not violating any international law. Where was the law violation? So it's not piracy. But piracy has a terribly emotional impact and I'm sure the word was chosen deliberately in order to get the most public relations impact possible.

Other observers note that many developing countries had laws against copying certain products such as clothing and music, but often these laws were not enforced. In such cases, the charge of piracy made some sense, they said.

## International Intellectual Property Protection

The multilateral treaties on intellectual property that existed before the Uruguay Round—the most important being the Paris Convention for the Protection of Industrial Property (1883), relating to patents, trademarks, and industrial designs, and the Berne Convention for the Protection of Literary and Artistic Work (1886), an international agreement on copyrights—were administered by the World Intellectual Property Organization (WIPO). Established in 1967, WIPO joined the United Nations system in 1974, becoming one of 15 specialized UN agencies. WIPO was responsible for promoting the protection of intellectual property throughout the world, and its activities were largely devoted to helping less-developed nations draft and administer national IP laws (see www.wipo.int).

Many IP-related interests in the United States, Canada, and western Europe considered WIPO to be toothless. Membership in the existing conventions was not universal and no enforcement or dispute resolution mechanisms existed. According to one observer, this system was "largely incapable of disciplining even the most egregious forms of trademark and copyright infringement" (Maskus 1990, 168). For patents, the central tenet of the Paris Convention was *national treatment:* in its patent protection, a country had to treat foreign and domestic producers the same. This system "gave countries around the world a lot of discretion in designing their patent laws," says Arvind Subramanian, a former member of the GATT Secretariat's TRIPS group. "That's why you found in virtually all developing countries no protection for pharmaceutical or chemical products. This was legitimate under the Paris Convention."[12] For example, according to WIPO, of the 98 member nations of the Paris Convention, 49 excluded pharmaceutical products from protection and 22 excluded chemical products.[13]

With the support of US companies that relied on patents, especially Pfizer, the United States hoped to strengthen patent protection under WIPO by revising the Paris Convention. But the four conferences held between 1980 and 1984 failed, largely because the debates between the developed and developing countries could not be resolved. The United States and other industrialized countries argued that without patent protection, companies had no incentive to invest to create new and better drugs. Developing countries countered that they represented a very small slice of global market share. In addition, they said, most new drug innovations targeted the health problems of the *industrial* world—conditions such as ulcers and heart disease. In economic terms, increasing IP protection would bring the developing countries no significant dynamic gains but would inflict considerable static costs: increased prices, more royalties to foreigners, and harm to consumer welfare. Finally, the thriving generic drug industries in countries such as India, Brazil, and Mexico could be affected by increased patent protection. "The efforts in WIPO were unsuccessful because there was no scope for making trade-offs," Subramanian remembers. "Developing countries would say, 'If we were to do this, what would we get in return?' Apart from the fact that they were violently opposed to it at that stage, even if they were to concede the question was, What was the payoff for them?"

The inability to exercise leadership at WIPO frustrated some US government officials. "The fact that we were the number one market in the world and probably the best on intellectual property protection was often lost on everybody," recalls Gerald Mossinghoff, US ambassador to two of the sessions on revising the Paris Convention and later president of the Pharmaceutical Research and Manufacturers of America (PhRMA). "We were one vote among 150. I thought, 'This is crazy. What happened to the leadership role of the United States?'"[14]

---

12. Unless otherwise noted, all quotes from Arvind Subramanian are from a January 2000 interview with Charan Devereaux.

13. In addition, 45 members excluded animal varieties; 44, methods of treatment of the human or animal body; 44, plant varieties; 42, biological processes for producing animal or plant varieties; 32, computer programs; and 35, food products (WIPO 1988, annexes I, II, as cited in Drahos with Braithwaite 2002, 124).

14. Unless otherwise noted, all quotes from Gerald Mossinghoff are from an August 1997 interview with Charan Devereaux. After serving as chairman of the General Assembly of WIPO, Mossinghoff chaired the Subcommittee on Intellectual Property of President Reagan's Cabinet Council on Commerce and Trade. He was also Assistant Secretary of Commerce and Commissioner of the US Patents and Trademarks Office before becoming president of PhRMA.

## US Industry Frustrations

Industry groups had begun to approach the US government about what they viewed as piracy of their intellectual property in the mid-1970s. In particular, the agrochemical sector was frustrated by the copying of its products in Hungary.[15] Pesticides and other chemicals were extremely expensive to develop, test, and study—between $13 and $20 million per product, industry representatives said.[16] They argued that the chemicals manufactured in Hungary were sold in both domestic and international markets, including Brazil, India, and Taiwan, without the permission of the companies that developed them. The US National Agricultural Chemicals Association estimated that the United States stood to lose $150 million in exports in 1979 alone as a result of Hungary's efforts.[17] Jim Enyart, a Washington, DC representative of Monsanto, decided to do something about it. Together with representatives of two other agrochemical producers, FMC and Stauffer Chemical, Enyart approached officials in Congress, the Commerce Department, the US Trade Representative (USTR), and the US Patent and Trademark Office (USPTO) in an effort to gain some leverage in dealing with the Hungarians.

The agrochemical companies made the case that intellectual property should be treated as a trade issue and that its systematic theft therefore constituted an unfair trade practice. Enyart remembers the government's initial response. "At the time everyone said: 'Oh gee, patents are highly technical, very esoteric things. What do they have to do with trade?' And we pressed them and said: 'Look, intellectual property is property. It costs money and time to create; it has commercial value, and if people steal it, it's like stealing any other kind of property.'" This argument was a hard sell, according to Enyart, because "the minute you would say 'patent' everybody's eyes would glaze over."[18]

But in the end, the coalition found allies. In June 1979, the Commerce Department led a delegation to Hungary and leaned on local government officials to do something about the agrochemicals issue. Senator John Danforth (R-MO) of the Senate Subcommittee on International Trade was

---

15. These chemicals included Roundup weed killer (Monsanto), Furandan (FMC), and Eradicane (Stauffer Chemical).

16. Jack Early, President, National Agricultural Chemicals Association, testimony for a hearing before the subcommittee on International Trade of the Senate Committee on Finance, "Continuing the President's Authority to Waive the Trade Act Freedom of Emigration Provisions," 96th Congress, July 16, 1979, 77.

17. Bradley Graham, "Hungarians Respond to Senate Threat: Hungarian Trade Status in Doubt in Senate Panel," *The Washington Post*, August 4, 1979, D7.

18. Unless otherwise noted, all quotes from Jim Enyart are from a 1997 interview with Charan Devereaux.

also sympathetic. In hearings on Capitol Hill concerning renewal of most favored nation trading status for Hungary, Danforth questioned whether trade rights should be granted to a country that copied IP from US industries.[19] After hearing testimony from the chemical companies, committee chairman Senator Abraham Ribicoff (D-CT) declared that Hungary's MFN status was "in serious jeopardy."[20] This "kind of got the Hungarians' attention," says Enyart. Negotiations ensued between Hungarian officials, the chemical companies, the US Commerce Department, the USTR, and the USPTO. Days after the Senate hearing, Monsanto signed an agreement with the Hungarian agrochemical export trade organization that, according to a company official, would end Hungary's pirating of Monsanto's patented process.[21] Recalls Enyart: "We were slowly breaking down this idea that the whole range of intellectual property issues was just too complicated to deal with."

## Intellectual Property and the GATT

Having achieved some success in Hungary, the agrochemical companies wanted to join forces with other industries to further the cause of IP protection. Enyart hoped to work with companies that were looking to protect not only patents, as was his industry, but also copyrights and trademarks. The idea, says Enyart, was that "if we worked together to influence the government we could get a hell of a lot farther." Ultimately, Monsanto joined the Anti-Counterfeiting Coalition, a group led by Levi-Strauss that included other trademark-based companies such as Samsonite, Izod, Chanel, and Gucci.[22] One of the coalition's recent efforts had been an unsuccessful attempt to achieve trademark protection in the 1973–79 Tokyo Round of the GATT multilateral trade talks.

Intellectual property was not a major topic of negotiation during the first six rounds of GATT, for the original 1947 agreement did not require that

---

19. Those testifying at the July 19, 1979, hearing before the Senate Subcommittee on International Trade of the Committee on Finance, 96th Congress, 1st Session, "Continuing the President's Authority to Waive the Trade Act Freedom of Emigration Provisions," included Jack Early, president, National Agricultural Chemicals Association; Robert McLellan, vice president of international and government affairs, FMC Corp.; and Nicholas Reding, managing director, Monsanto Agricultural Products Co.

20. Quoted in Graham, "Hungarians Respond to Senate Threat," D7.

21. "Monsanto, Hungary in Agreement on Herbicide Marketing," Dow Jones News Service, July 25, 1979.

22. Founded in 1978, the International Anti-Counterfeiting Coalition had by 1997 grown to 180 members; among them were trademark-based companies, law firms, trade associations, and investment firms.

member countries adopt minimum standards of IP protection.[23] However, in the seventh round of talks, held in Tokyo, the Anti-Counterfeiting Coalition worked with representatives from the United States and the European Community to propose an anticounterfeiting code.[24] The code called for GATT signatories to intercept and dispose of counterfeit goods at international borders. "That effort started very late in the Tokyo Round," recalls TRIPS negotiator Mike Hathaway, who also worked on the 1979 code. "Even though we got a draft agreement, we didn't really achieve anything other than having a text out there for multilateral consideration. But it did serve to put IP on the GATT agenda."[25] A revised draft, supported by Canada and Japan, was submitted in 1982; though some responded positively to the anticounterfeiting code, it still was not put into effect.

## US Legislation: Section 301

Trademark industries and agrochemical companies were not the only IP-based industries distressed about intellectual property rights protection. Emery Simon, who was a US negotiator for the TRIPS agreement from 1986 until 1993 and was subsequently executive director of the Business Software Alliance, observes:

> In the immediate aftermath of the Tokyo Round we had a series of technological developments. One was the advent of videocassette recorders. That precipitated a specific video piracy problem. The second development was the increasing use of audiocassettes. We switched from 8-track to regular cassette tapes and there was widespread use of Walkmen. Those kinds of technologies led to music piracy. The third development was software. The PC became kind of a staple in the mid-1980s after IBM introduced its PC in 1982. So then we had a software piracy problem. Simultaneously, we have had a long-standing patent problem in that there were deficiencies in the Paris Convention which permitted a number of countries that were not party to it or which interpreted the convention very loosely to exclude

---

23. In the original GATT agreement, intellectual property is mentioned in Article XX, "General Exceptions":

> Subject to the requirement that such measures are not applied in a manner which would constitute a means of arbitrary or unjustifiable discrimination between countries where the same conditions prevail, or a disguised restriction on international trade, nothing in this Agreement shall be construed to prevent the adoption or enforcement by any contracting party of measures: . . . (d) necessary to secure compliance with laws or regulations which are not inconsistent with the provisions of this Agreement, including those relating to customs enforcement, the enforcement of monopolies operated under paragraph 4 of Article II and Article XVII, the protection of patents, trademarks and copyrights, and the prevention of deceptive practices[.]

24. In each round of talks following its inception, GATT produced new accords. World trade expanded dramatically during this period, from $60 billion in 1950 to approximately $4 trillion in 1991.

25. Unless otherwise noted, all quotes from Mike Hathaway are from a September 1997 interview with Charan Devereaux.

patentability of chemicals, including agricultural chemicals and pharmaceuticals. So markets developed for those [pirated goods] as well.[26]

Frustrated with *multilateral* approaches to IP protection (such as the Tokyo Round and WIPO), some US industries began to seek other means to address their IP concerns. One strategy was to increase *bilateral* pressure on countries that did not respect US companies' intellectual property rights. In 1982 the USTR conducted consultations with Korea, Mexico, Singapore, and Taiwan in an effort to strengthen patent, trademark, and copyright protection. In addition, Monsanto led an effort to make international violations of US IPRs subject to retaliation under US trade laws. US companies hoped that if trade actions were linked to a country's enforcement of intellectual property rights, protection for their products would increase.

Success was achieved when the Trade Act of 1984 made intellectual property rights actionable under section 301 of the 1974 Trade Act. Section 301 permits the US government to unilaterally raise tariffs against trading partners that maintain "unjustifiable or unreasonable" restrictions against US trade. Thus, for the first time, the US government was authorized to take retaliatory action against countries that failed to offer "fair and equitable provision of adequate and effective protection of intellectual property rights." Under section 301, companies and trade associations could petition the USTR to investigate countries for IPR violations. Congress also moved to make protection for US intellectual property a condition for continued eligibility under the Generalized System of Preferences (GSP), which granted concessional tariffs to imports from less-developed countries.[27] IPRs were clearly positioned on the US trade agenda.

Some observers credited the efforts of the US intellectual property industries with a pivotal role in developing this new powerful bilateral tool. "The IP industry in the US was extremely savvy and clever because they made intellectual property a moral issue," one explains:

> What happened in the US in the 1980s was that you had this growing momentum against those "pirates" and "robbers" out there, articulated by industry in a very moral tone. What developing countries were doing was seen as ethically objectionable. That's why the IP movement is a fascinating political economy story, because industry articulated this very, very cleverly. Their success was reflected in the fact that 301 got enacted in the United States. The rhetoric was translated into legislation.

---

26. Unless otherwise noted, all quotes from Emery Simon are from an October 1997 interview with Charan Devereaux.

27. The GSP provides preferential duty-free entry to more than 4,000 products (which otherwise be subject to customs duty) from about 140 designated beneficiary countries and territories. The program was instituted on January 1, 1976, under the Trade Act of 1974. See www.customs.ustreas.gov.

With the new legislation in place, the International Intellectual Property Alliance (IIPA) sought to inform the USTR about trade in intellectual property and the problems faced by the film, publishing, and recording industries.[28] In 1985, the IIPA wrote a report titled *Piracy of US Copyrighted Works in Ten Selected Countries*, which estimated US losses in those countries, including the Republic of Korea, at $1.3 billion annually (IIPA 1985, i).[29] Partly in response to this report and complaints from pharmaceutical makers, chemical companies, and the MPAA, the US government launched a section 301 case against the Republic of Korea in September 1985. After bilateral negotiations, the two countries reached an agreement in July 1986. Korea agreed to strengthen its copyright law and enforcement as well as to protect software and introduce product patents for pharmaceuticals and chemicals.[30] It also agreed to protect the trademarks of foreign firms and to give extensions to agricultural chemical patents. Jayashree Watal, a TRIPS negotiator for India, notes, "US trade negotiators, thus, achieved their first major victory on strengthening the protection of IPRs in a developing country using the threat of sanctions" (Watal 2001, 19). One negotiator calls the bilateral IP agreement between the US and Korea a model for TRIPS.

## Getting IP on the Uruguay Round Agenda

The Uruguay Round of GATT talks began under economic conditions substantially different from those when the Tokyo Round was completed. One obvious change was the large US merchandise trade deficit, which had grown dramatically since the late 1970s. In the face of West German and Japanese trade surpluses, many US government officials began to agitate for a new round of GATT talks to level the playing field. The notion of making a major push to include IP in the round was evolving at the same time.

Pfizer chairman Edmund Pratt and IBM chairman John Opel were instrumental in arguing that intellectual property should be included on the Uruguay Round agenda. Both executives served on the President's Advisory Committee on Trade Negotiations (ACTN) during the Carter and

---

28. Founded in 1984, the IIPA originally comprised five trade associations: the Motion Picture Association of America, the Recording Industry Association of America, the National Music Publishers' Association, the American Film Marketing Association, and the American Association of Publishers.

29. The other nine countries included in the study were Singapore, Taiwan, Indonesia, Philippines, Malaysia, Thailand, Brazil, Egypt, and Nigeria.

30. Some countries issued patents for the *process* of making a drug, and not for the *product*— the drug itself. Critics said that if only process patents were issued, companies could legally copy drugs by arguing they were using a different manufacturing process.

Reagan administrations, Pratt as the committee's chair and Opel as head of the IP task force.[31] "Both of them," according to one US TRIPS negotiator, "had problems with piracy and theft of their IP and they decided to get intellectual property into the trade venue where you had some teeth in the enforcement mechanism." Pratt and Opel displayed enthusiasm for the political process as well as the issues. As one of Pratt's colleagues recalls, "He liked Washington and he liked politics, as opposed to some chief executives who will do it, but only reluctantly. He loved the Washington world." "Pratt and Opel," remarks a US negotiator, "basically engineered, pushed, and cajoled the government into including IP as one of the topics for the negotiation."

In 1985, USTR Clayton Yeutter created the position of assistant USTR for international investment and intellectual property, a job filled by Harvey Bale. Working with Bale and Yeutter, Pfizer and IBM employees developed a position paper directed at White House staff; it prompted a presidential statement on the importance of intellectual property to the United States (Santoro 1992, 9).

As the former CEO of the maker of Yale locks, Commerce Secretary Malcolm Baldrige also had an interest in intellectual property; patents had been important to his company's business. After meeting with representatives of the motion picture, publishing, software, and recording industries in the summer of 1984, Baldrige committed to improve protection for US IP both at home and abroad. His commitment was translated into a major initiative under which two Commerce Department agencies, the International Trade Administration (ITA) and the USPTO, joined forces to combat the problem (Hill 1985, 4).

In addition, Baldrige established an intellectual property subcommittee of the Cabinet Council on Commerce and Trade and expressed interest in moving IP into a venue where the United States could exercise greater leadership. Gerald Mossinghoff, who became the chair of the IP cabinet council subcommittee, recalls: "There was a consensus that we would move the main push for multilateral intellectual property out of the WIPO, where typical UN procedures apply, into the GATT where we were accustomed to negotiating from a position of strength." Around the same time, Jacques Gorlin, a trade expert and consultant to IBM, wrote a paper described by one observer as "the first intellectual articulation of having broader IP standards plus an enforcement text in the GATT agreement."[32]

But not all US government and business interests wholeheartedly supported the idea of including a broad discussion of IPRs in the GATT. Many of the copyright-based industries were apprehensive. Protection for

---

31. The ACTN was created by Congress in 1974; Pratt was appointed by President Carter in 1979.

32. Jacques Gorlin's 1985 paper for IBM was titled "A Trade-Based Approach for the International Copyright Protection for Computer Software."

movies, recordings, and books was already fairly strong in the international arena, thanks to the Berne Convention.[33] Copyright industries were therefore concerned that they might *lose* ground if IP was brought into the GATT. Eric Smith, president of the IIPA, explains:

> Early on in 1985, when Jacques Gorlin wrote his paper for IBM, we were very wary of it. In 1985 and 1986, we had just begun the process of using the section 301 action. A 301 action had been brought against Korea and there was a lot of movement by the US government to improve protection on a bilateral basis. We were beginning to have very significant success. At that point, Singapore, Taiwan, Korea, and Indonesia—big pirate countries where we had no protection for copyrights—were beginning to move toward protecting US copyrights. . . . Of course, at this point the international standard in protection was the Berne Convention. The Berne Convention was accepted by everyone, even though the United States was not a member. We got Berne-level protection because the whole principle of the convention was national treatment. The bilateral mechanism was working very well and it looked like it would continue to work as well or even better than we had ever thought. So placing copyright standards into a trade negotiation, which is characterized by splitting the difference at the end of the day, now that made everybody nervous as hell.[34]

Some US government officials believed that the struggle should focus less on bringing IP into the GATT talks and more on getting the United States to agree to the principle of national treatment and sign on to the Berne Convention. Such an act, they maintained, would give the United States a better platform from which to argue that other countries should improve their copyright protection.

### The Proponents Organize

USTR Clayton Yeutter advised IBM's John Opel and Pfizer's Edmund Pratt to seek business allies in other industrialized countries to help overcome resistance to including IP in the GATT (Santoro 1992, 10). "We told them government couldn't do this alone," recalls one former trade official:

> We had to get business support in Europe and Japan to make this happen. So we would need them to get their European counterparts to go to their governments and say, "We want this." Japanese and Europeans—the Europeans particularly—are very conservative. . . . The US government over the years has tended to look at these issues in a business way: "We have a problem here, let's solve it." The European approach is more traditional. Their view is, "We have a problem here, but maybe there is no solution. The Indians and the Brazilians and the Argentineans, they're going to oppose all this and they outnumber us. It's only going to create a lot of friction. Besides we have a lot of other unfinished business." While the United States tends to bite off more than it can chew . . . the Europeans hardly want to bite off anything.

---

33. Although the United States was not a member of the Berne Convention until 1988, US companies benefited from its concept of national treatment.

34. Unless otherwise noted, all quotes from Eric Smith are from an October 1997 interview with Charan Devereaux.

In March 1986, Pratt and Opel founded the Intellectual Property Committee (IPC), a group of 13 CEOs committed to moving intellectual property onto the GATT agenda.[35] Jacques Gorlin, consultant to IBM and the IP taskforce of the President's Advisory Committee on Trade Negotiations, was hired to lead and staff the organization. "Our first task," Gorlin recalls, "was to go to Europe and Japan and work with the private sector within those countries to get them to put pressure on their trade ministries."[36] From June through August of 1986, IPC representatives traveled to Tokyo, Bonn, London, Paris, Brussels, and Copenhagen to make their case. Ultimately, the IPC formed a tripartite coalition with the European Union of Industrial and Employers' Confederations (UNICE, or Union des Industries de la Communauté européenne) and the Keidanren, a powerful private federation of economic organizations in Japan. These groups worked to convince their governments that intellectual property should be on the agenda for the GATT talks. Pratt noted that the joint action by US, European, and Japanese business groups was a significant breakthrough in the involvement of the international business community in trade negotiations (quoted in Drahos 1995, 13; cited in Sell 2003, 106).

Representatives of the IPC also traveled to Geneva to meet with officials at WIPO. The UN agency was run by Arpad Bogsch, who had been the US representative to the Paris and Berne Conventions in 1962 and had organized the conference that established WIPO in 1967 (he retired from WIPO in 1997). The organization was born and built from his vision.[37] Some intellectual property industries were dissatisfied with WIPO, viewing the protection offered by the regime it administered as insufficient. Enyart characterizes WIPO as "like many other UN agencies, kind of taken over by the developing countries"; it "spent enormous amounts of time talking about how everybody ought to have technology for free and governments were going to give it to everybody. Notwithstanding the fact that governments own no IP to speak of." (Other observers object to this characterization of WIPO, recognizing its value as a technical body.) The IPC nevertheless hoped to gain WIPO's support for including IP in the GATT talks. As Enyart tells it, Bogsch "invited us up to his penthouse overlooking Lake Geneva":

---

35. The IPC's 13 member companies were Pfizer, IBM, Merck, General Electric, Dupont, Warner Communications, Hewlett-Packard, Bristol-Myers, FMC, General Motors, Johnson & Johnson, Monsanto, and Rockwell International.

36. Unless otherwise noted, all quotes from Jacques Gorlin are from a September 1997 interview with Charan Devereaux.

37. Ryan notes that WIPO's story of institution-building leadership by one person is matched in the history of international governmental organizations only at the GATT and the International Labor Organization (ILO). Eric Wyndham White at the GATT and David Morse at the ILO each served as director-general for some 20 years beginning in 1948 (Ryan 1998, 127).

He fed us a multicourse lunch from his private dining room. It was concluded with cognac and cigars. . . . Finally, we said to him, "Look, Mr. Bogsch, we have found WIPO to be not constructive in the protection of IP and we are going to do something about it. You are either going to help out or we are going to go right around you." And he said, "Well, you can't do that, we are the only authorized organization." And we said, "Well, we are going to do it. You've got your choice; you either get on board or get left in the dust." . . . It turned out, when the negotiations started in GATT, Mr. Bogsch became very friendly and said that there was a great deal of expertise in WIPO and how there ought to be a huge role for WIPO in the TRIPS agreement. You will notice that the TRIPS agreement has a reasonably weak consultative role for WIPO.

Within the US government, Assistant USTR Bale became the point man for getting IP into the GATT talks. Bale and his colleague Emery Simon established an interagency process to promote a consensus for bringing the issue to the Uruguay Round. According to Simon, "It was not an easy process." The two also worked to convince America's major trading partners to support the inclusion of IP on the agenda. Discussion at that point focused not on details, specific industries, or standards, but just on the idea that the negotiation should take place. Although they worked closely with the IPC, Simon makes clear that "we were really doing two different jobs."

In the spring of 1986, six months before the Uruguay meeting, Bale met in Canada with the Friends of Intellectual Property, a group he organized. He recalls the government representatives from Europe, Japan, Australia, and Canada who gathered to discuss the issues displaying "a lot of curiosity, but not a lot of immediate support."[38] Soon thereafter Bale met with the GATT Secretariat to discuss the possibility of including IP in the Uruguay Round. According to Bale,

The reaction of the GATT Secretariat was, "Well, maybe there's a chance for counterfeiting to be addressed, but not other issues"—not copyright, not patents, not trade secrets. Their perception was that there was too much opposition coming from developing countries. There was too much of a North-South issue.

### The North-South Issue

Some developing countries did not agree that intellectual property should be protected like any other property. Technological innovation was not universally seen as a private capital good; many saw it as a public good that could be used to protect health or promote economic development. Indira Gandhi, for example, told the World Health Assembly in May 1982 that "the idea of a better ordered world is one in which medical discover-

---

38. Unless otherwise noted, all quotes from Harvey Bale are from a 1997 interview with Charan Devereaux. Bale worked at USTR from 1975 until 1987, when he became international trade manager at Hewlett-Packard; he became senior vice president international for the US Pharmaceutical Manufacturers Association (PMA, later renamed PhRMA) in 1989. In 1997, Bale became director-general of the International Federation of Pharmaceutical Manufacturers Associations (IFPMA).

ies will be free of all patents and there will be no profiteering from life and death" (quoted in Siebeck et al. 1990, as cited in Chaudhry and Walsh 1995, 88). Some developing countries viewed patents as a significant obstacle to technology transfer and believed managing and controlling patents to be key to development policy.

Developing countries that resisted the inclusion of IP in trade negotiations also cited the importance of protecting indigenous industries and controlling prices. Stronger IP protection was seen by many of these countries as a vehicle enabling foreign multinationals to exercise monopoly power and excessive control over technology, thereby forcing many domestic companies out of business and inflating prices. Finally, many developing countries argued that the Uruguay Round was not the appropriate venue for agreements on intellectual property. India was a strong proponent of this view, holding that IP was not "trade-related" and, hence, did not belong in the GATT structure. Inasmuch as GATT's mandate extended only to trade in tangible goods, IPR issues should continue to be addressed in the WIPO.

Nevertheless, some observers suggest that developing countries did not believe intellectual property to be the most threatening issue under consideration for the Uruguay Round. In the lead-up to Punta del Este, three so-called new issues were discussed: services, investment, and intellectual property. "On the developing countries' side, I think they were more focused on the services onslaught than the TRIPS onslaught," says former GATT Secretariat staff member Arvind Subramanian. "They were really, really opposed to liberalization of services. Some would say that the developing countries made a strategic mistake: they expended a lot of negotiating coinage trying to resist services and kind of overlooked TRIPS."

### A Decisive Moment

Right up to the GATT ministerial meeting in Punta del Este, the status of IP remained uncertain. Inclusion of intellectual property rights had been considered from the outset by the Preparatory Committee, established in November 1985 to discuss the next round of GATT negotiations. The committee's debates intensified through 1986; the United States raised the stakes by proposing that IPRs be covered in general rather than only in relation to trade in counterfeit goods. A group of 10 countries led by Brazil and India took a hard-line stance against the US position.[39] Even within the European Community, some believed that GATT was not an appropriate venue for IP; they feared that the complicated issue would overload the system, jeopardizing the whole negotiation. At the final preparatory meeting, Commerce Secretary Baldrige declared that President Reagan

---

39. The other eight countries were Argentina, Cuba, Egypt, Nicaragua, Nigeria, Peru, Tanzania, and Yugoslavia.

wanted intellectual property in the talks, and implied that the US would not move forward without it.

Baldrige and Agriculture Secretary Richard Lyng accompanied USTR Clayton Yeutter to the GATT ministerial meeting where Yeutter declared he would walk out of the talks unless four key US priorities were on the agenda for the new round. "We regard the issues of agriculture, services, investment and intellectual property as critical to the future of all GATT members," Yeutter said. "We cannot envision nor agree to comprehensive new trade negotiations that do not include these four issues on the agenda."[40] Pfizer's Edmund Pratt, who also attended the ministerial, noted that if the business community "doesn't get most of the new issues, our enthusiasm for the new round will go down substantially."[41] In the end, intellectual property was included in the September 1986 Punta del Este statement that launched the Uruguay Round—but the battle had just begun. "We wanted to get it on the agenda, get a foot in the door, but nobody knew where it was going to go from there," notes Bale. "Nobody had a clue what this agreement was going to look like."

## The TRIPS Negotiations

### The First Two Years

The TRIPS group, chaired by Lars Anell from Sweden, was one of 15 negotiating groups in the Uruguay Round of GATT. However, the presence of IPRs in the Uruguay Round process did not imply that there was any sort of international consensus on the issue, or even a mandate for broad discussion. The language of the ministerial declaration establishing the negotiation objective for IP, written by the Swiss and Colombian ambassadors, was somewhat ambiguous and general:

> In order to reduce the distortions and impediments to international trade, and taking into account the need to promote effective and adequate protection of intellectual property rights, and to ensure that measures and procedures to enforce intellectual property rights do not themselves become barriers to legitimate trade, the negotiation shall aim to clarify GATT provisions and elaborate as appropriate new rules and disciplines. Negotiations shall aim to develop a multilateral framework of principles, rules, and disciplines dealing with international trade in counterfeit goods, taking into account work already undertaken in the GATT.
>
> These negotiations shall be without prejudice to other complementary initiatives that may be taken in the WIPO and elsewhere to deal with these matters.[42]

---

40. Yeutter quoted in Mary Beth Franklin, "Protectionism Would Result in 'Suicidal' Trade War," United Press International, September 15, 1986.

41. Pratt quoted in Clyde H. Farnsworth, "US Rejects a European Trade Move," *The New York Times*, September 15, 1986, D10.

42. "Trade-Related Aspects of Intellectual Property Rights, Including Trade in Counterfeit Goods," in *WTO/GATT Ministerial Declaration on the Uruguay Round (Declaration of 20 September 1986)*, www.jus.uio.no.

Many developing countries understood the Punta del Este statement as limiting treatment of IP to the problem of trade in counterfeit goods, not as opening the negotiations to set global standards of protection for IPRs, raise the levels of such protection, or strengthen enforcement procedures. India and Brazil were among those resisting the notion that the statement should lead to a discussion of whether their own national legal systems offered foreign suppliers adequate IP protection.

Progress in the intellectual property group was consequently slow. With the United States emphasizing the need to set standards of protection and developing countries focused on having access to new technologies and balancing the interests of IPR owners and users, few points of agreement emerged. "The first two years was a depressingly familiar assertion and reassertion of everyone's positions," recalls Subramanian. US negotiator Mike Kirk concurs:

> The first two years were almost exclusively, to use the phrase of one of the guys involved, a Kabuki dance where we just talked in generalities. We would lob principles at the South and they would either sit there and ignore them or occasionally lob an idea back at us. But there was no real discussion. And since you're talking in the context of a trade negotiation, you've got primarily trade negotiators present, many of whom didn't have the foggiest idea of what the intellectual property issues were all about. . . . So you had this general discussion that went on for a couple of years as people became educated on what IP was.[43]

Many echoed Kirk's conclusion that participants' general lack of experience in IP slowed the negotiation process. The US team, in contrast, drew on a variety of federal agencies and included intellectual property experts as well as trade negotiators. Gorlin, the head of the IPC, emphasizes that difference:

> One of the things that the United States was very good about, which other countries were not, was the relationship between the Patent Office, the Copyright Office, and the USTR. USTR was the leader in the round because it was a GATT case. But the relationship between Mike Kirk at the Patent and Trade Office and Emery Simon and others who did IP at USTR was tremendous, a model relationship. It was especially good when Mike Kirk was there the last couple years. In some countries, the patent people weren't brought in by the trade people. But in the United States, it worked beautifully.

The US negotiating team attempted to make some progress. "We set up a negotiating group, including mostly the OECD [Organization for Economic Cooperation and Development] countries, and went through a substantive review of standards," recalls Mike Hathaway, the lead US negotiator until 1989. But despite these efforts, the first couple of years of the TRIPS talks were dominated by the North-South debate. Hathaway adds,

---

43. Unless otherwise noted, all quotes from Mike Kirk are from a September 1997 interview with Charan Devereaux.

We certainly had fun for two years, beating down arguments made by India. For example, patented products made up only 3 percent of all medicinals. The difference between the price a pharmaceutical pirate would charge and a legitimate producer would charge was at most around 15 percent. The pirates pretty much charged the same amount as the legitimate products; it was really the market, the ability to pay, that set the price. The difference to the consumer in terms of cost was almost nil, and think of the difference in what you get from a legitimate producer in terms of education, care, and reliability of product. No one could defend the existence of counterfeit birth control pills that were on the market. The advantages to the consumer of protecting legitimate products were really quite good even if you didn't count the biggest advantage, the market incentive to produce cures for illnesses.

The IPC founded by IBM and Pfizer was active during this period. According to Gorlin, preoccupation with the North-South debate blocked any "substantive negotiation . . . , so we took advantage of those two years." In November 1986, IPC IP specialists met with their counterparts at the Keidanren in Japan and UNICE in Brussels to begin drafting a framework for the round. Gorlin explains, "We basically wanted to come up with a book that said, 'This is what we want.'"

From the IPC's perspective, it was important that industry articulate the minimum acceptable standards for intellectual property protection. IPC representatives believed that the most relevant expertise on intellectual property was found in industry, where experts understood how any proposed standards would actually function. "You can be the top patent attorney with a tremendous amount of international experience in the Patent and Trademark Office," Gorlin maintains, "but if that is the only experience you've had, you will really not know the effect different laws and language will have on your ability to enforce a patent. So we basically said, 'Look, it is only the private-sector IP specialists who really know what types of minimum standards will help us.'"

Owing to their different IP systems, the Americans, Japanese, and Europeans did not always agree on what the minimum standards were. Instead of attempting to negotiate treaty language, industry officials tried to identify what baseline characteristics their patent, copyright, and trademark regimes shared. "For example," explains Gorlin, "we didn't say, in terms of patents, that it had to be a first-to-file system as opposed to a first-to-invent system. We just said that every country has to have a system for giving a patent." Such compromises were not always straightforward, however. He elaborates:

The negotiation of that basic framework was tough. We spent long hours. But we shared the same objective of trying to come up with an agreed text. In some areas, the biggest problems the Europeans and the Japanese had were not necessarily with the developing countries, but with the United States because we were their largest market. For example, the Japanese were very concerned about changing the US market because of all the Japanese electronic industries that were basically only exporting to the United States. So there were tensions. There were certain things we had to change and that we recommended. I mean, we were not government; we were industry. But our thrust was to create a set of minimum standards that would reflect the level of IP protection in those countries that had good IP protection.

The IPC also sought support from and consensus with US trade groups. While UNICE and the Keidanren represented all the employer industries in Europe and Japan respectively, the IPC represented only 13 companies. It therefore arranged meetings every six to nine months with industry associations; 30 to 40 would review drafts of recent work. Eric Smith, who represented the copyright industries through the IIPA, was invited to help develop the basic framework. He recalls that "the IPC people were pretty great. They welcomed us and they knew that we had the constituency that could help sell TRIPS in the United States and they didn't. So they invited us."

Completed in June 1988, the 100-page IPC report detailed minimum standards for an acceptable TRIPS agreement. It was viewed as the product of a unique collaboration among the US, European, and Japanese business communities. Hewlett-Packard president and CEO John A. Young characterized the undertaking as "unprecedented[,] . . . the first time that the international business community has jointly developed a document of this magnitude and such substantive detail for presentation to our government negotiators."[44] Delivered to the US negotiators, the document contributed significantly to the final agreement. According to one negotiator, "There were really two prototypes for what eventually became the TRIPS agreement. One was the IPC's basic framework and the other was a bilateral agreement the United States negotiated with Korea in the summer of 1986."

While the US government was interested in the coalition's position, other countries were not so receptive. Pfizer general counsel Lou Clemente remarked, "The European governments were less willing to adopt these views. Instead, they chose to emphasize the differences between the United States and Europe. The Japanese government was even less responsive to the document. In the Japanese culture there is a much different relationship between government and business. In Japan, it is the government which decides what is best for Japan and for Japanese business" (quoted in Santoro 1992, 12).

As the TRIPS effort continued, new trade legislation was passed by Congress that further strengthened the United States' ability to apply pressure on countries that denied IP protection to US firms. The 1988 Omnibus Trade and Competitiveness Act included a provision known as "Special 301," which required the USTR to submit an annual report to Congress identifying nations that denied adequate protection for IPR or that denied fair and equitable market access to US IPR holders—and to re-

---

44. IPC press release, June 14, 1988; quoted in Santoro (1992, 12).

taliate more quickly. The most serious violators were designated "Priority Foreign Countries"; other countries, placed on a "Priority Watch List," were subject to bilateral negotiations, while nations that merely required monitoring were put on a "Watch List."

The brainchild of TRIPS negotiator Mike Hathaway, Special 301 provoked great resentment among US trading partners and was denounced internationally. Yet from the perspective of US industry and many in Congress, threats of action under Special 301 succeeded in encouraging many countries to begin strengthening their intellectual property laws. In 1989, 25 countries were cited under Special 301, with Brazil, India, South Korea, Mexico, China, Saudi Arabia, Taiwan, and Thailand placed on the Priority Watch List. Brazil and India warned that US actions under 301 threatened the Uruguay Round and violated the GATT.

Under the 301 initiatives, USTR investigated Brazil's computer software protection and pharmaceutical patents. In response, Brazil created software copyright protection in its Software Law of 1987. But when the Brazilian government showed no commitment to increase process and patent protection for drugs, the United States increased tariffs to 100 percent on Brazilian exports of certain paper products, consumer electronics, and pharmaceutical products, affecting trade worth about $39 million. The tariff increases, which took effect October 1988, virtually prohibited Brazil from exporting these products to the US market during 1989 and the first half of 1990.[45] In its written submission to the TRIPS negotiating group in October 1988, Brazil argued that the group had a mandate to discuss "rigid and excessive protection of IPRs" (Watal 2001, 25).

In the end, the United States backed down from its section 301 retaliation when Brazil filed a complaint under the GATT. Following assurances by Brazil's president that patent protection would be extended to pharmaceutical products, USTR Carla Hills rescinded the tariffs (Brazil's legislation was not enacted until 1996). According to a former USTR official, Hills "didn't want to be found in violation of the GATT. When she rescinded the tariffs the Brazilians withdrew their complaint."

### The Mid-Term Review and Beyond

At the December 1988 Uruguay Round midterm review in Montreal, TRIPS remained among the problem groups, unable to arrive at a consensus for the framework of the talks. Mike Kirk recalls, "We were not ready for the midterm review, but it was a nice wake-up call. It told everybody, 'Okay, if we're going to achieve anything we've got to get a little bit more focused; we've got to come to grips with the issues a little bit better.'" Developing countries continued to block any discussion of substantive standards. In addition, Europe's official position was "far, far behind that of the United States," according to one US observer, who suggested that the

---

45. USTR, "Report to Congress on Section 301 Developments, January 1995–June 1996."

Europeans "were much more willing to provide exemptions that would have allowed India and Brazil to, in effect, gut any IPR obligations."[46]

The deadlock over TRIPS was finally broken in April 1989 at the Trade Negotiations Committee meeting in Geneva. "After April," according to Kirk, "we really got it together and started moving forward." Several US observers gave credit to the Association of Southeast Asian Nations for moving the talks along (at that time, ASEAN comprised Brunei Darussalam, Indonesia, Malaysia, the Philippines, Singapore, and Thailand). Former assistant USTR Bale explains, "The ASEAN countries were kind of middle-ground mediators. . . . India and Brazil were the most strenuous in their opposition to TRIPS, followed by Egypt and Pakistan. I'd say those were the four major opponents to the issue. But other countries that were far more interested in trade organization, like the ASEAN countries, felt it was essential that the United States have its way on TRIPS." Developing countries agreed to lift their block; India and Brazil were the last holdouts.[47] The negotiation objectives were clarified and the issues of adequate IPR standards and their enforcement were specifically identified as part of the talks. It was also agreed that the negotiations would take the developmental and technological concerns of developing countries into account. At last, US negotiators sighed, there was a framework for the TRIPS negotiations.

Why did developing countries agree to broaden the discussion? A number of observers believe that some nations were willing to trade support of TRIPS for improved access to industrial markets in agriculture, textiles, and light manufacturing products. "A negotiator from Argentina said that they didn't give a damn what was in the IP code as long as they got what they wanted in agriculture," notes Enyart. "Which shows you that these nontraditional GATT agreements [like TRIPS] would probably never make it if they weren't carried in a wider negotiation." As Simon puts it:

> One of the reasons why people try to get these issues onto the trade agenda is because there are cross-sectoral trade-offs. If you are negotiating on IP with Brazil and you say to the Brazilian, "If you don't protect US software, we won't protect Brazilian software in the United States," that is a meaningless threat. However, if you say to the Brazilians, "If you don't protect US software then we won't let you export coffee to the United States," then that is a meaningful threat. The big break after the midterm review was a much clearer engagement on agricultural issues. Developing countries in general wanted substantial liberalization on agricultural exports. So, suddenly, they had more of a stake in these negotiations. For us, the IP agenda was one of our big stakes. So, in return for being more forthcoming on agriculture, which really took another four and a half years, we got some greater forthcomingness on IP.

---

46. For example, European proposals excluded patents on plant and animal varieties and on biological processes for producing plants and animals.

47. India resisted until September 12, 1989, "when it announced it had accepted in principle the international enforcement of trade-related IP rights within the Uruguay Round context" (Sell 2003, 109).

The Uruguay Round agreement reduced agricultural tariffs and agricultural subsidies.[48] In addition, the Uruguay Round agreement phased out the MFA. Since 1974, the MFA had permitted discriminatory use of textile quotas, mostly applied by developed countries to products from developing countries (India also maintained high barriers under the MFA). Those expected to gain most from the MFA phaseout were low-income countries in South Asia as well as Hong Kong, South Korea, Taiwan, Singapore, and China (at the time, not a GATT member). Observers note that one of the key underlying bargains of the Uruguay Round was the acceptance of TRIPS by some developing countries in exchange for the end of such quotas. It was "a TRIPS-for-MFA deal," says one source.[49]

In addition to being attracted by the carrot of lower tariffs in textiles and agriculture, some developing countries threatened by the stick of section 301 saw TRIPS as the lesser of two evils. Under TRIPS, intellectual property conflicts would be subject to the WTO dispute settlement machinery. Though they strongly disliked "cross-sanctions"—reprisals on goods trade for breaches of TRIPS—developing countries found the prospect of answering exclusively to the United States even less appealing. In addition, many Latin American countries, including Chile and Mexico, were already strengthening their IP protections. Though these nations continued to hold their earlier positions on TRIPS, they were described as displaying a "marked lack of fervor" in pursuing those objectives (Watal 2001, 31). "Section 301 is really the ghost of this whole Hamlet story," according to Subramanian, "because it turned out to be key in shaping the eventual outcome. It had a huge influence in terms of changing developing countries' position on intellectual property."

Some developing countries also recognized that certain multinational companies increasingly viewed IP protection as decisive in attracting foreign investment. Providing IPRs had become one more way to vie for foreign capital in a competitive world. More generally, many developing countries, believing the GATT to be their best defense against stronger nations, viewed IP protection as the price they had to pay for the success of

---

48. Some argued that these changes would improve market access for developing countries, though others maintained that such benefits were overstated. Agricultural tariffs were reduced by an average of 36 percent in developed countries and 24 percent in developing countries. Because agricultural tariffs were to be reduced by 36 percent *overall*, developed countries could reduce tariffs in some areas while maintaining significant protections in other sectors.

49. Later, however, developing countries would be frustrated by the implementation process of the textiles deal. The MFA phaseout was "backloaded," meaning almost half of the textile products in question would not be liberalized until the very end of the 10-year implementation period. Many countries also worried that when textile quotas were eliminated, they would be replaced with other barriers.

the Uruguay Round. "There was a systemic issue at stake," Subramanian explains, "a real fear that if they didn't agree to intellectual property, the US would turn away from the Uruguay Round and that was not in the interest of developing countries."

## A Landmark

The break in the deadlock led to a flood of substantive proposals.[50] In general, submissions from developing countries favored looser standards and enforcement. The question of where to lodge the TRIPS agreement—in the GATT or in WIPO, as developing countries favored—also remained open. Jayashree Watal, then a negotiator for India, notes, "In retrospect, it appears that some developing countries paid more attention to this aspect than to taking coordinated positions on substantive norms and standards of IPRs" (Watal 2001, 28).[51]

Perhaps the most important proposal came from the Europeans, whose draft TRIPS agreement was forwarded in 1990. Subramanian calls it "a landmark in the process. . . . For some time, TRIPS had been seen as an exclusively US-led initiative. But when the EC tabled [i.e., submitted] its proposal, that signaled a change in the European position from one of being mildly in favor of an IP agreement to one that was almost as strong as that of the US. It changed the balance of power."

The Europeans had strategic as well as commercial reasons for becoming more assertive about pursuing TRIPS. Looking ahead to the final Uruguay Round agreement, the negotiators knew that changes in European agricultural policy were inevitable. In all likelihood, these changes would be most unappealing to France. The Europeans pushed for intellectual property rules related to geographical indications on wine as one method of satisfying the French, and thereby helping to sell the agreement as a whole.

As the negotiations moved through 1990, their focus shifted to disagreements between the countries that largely controlled IP. One negotiator recalls, "Increasingly it became a North-North debate, and everybody else was going along for the ride."

---

50. Legal drafts were submitted by the European Community, Argentina, Brazil, Chile, China, Colombia, Cuba, Egypt, India, Japan, Nigeria, Pakistan, Peru, Switzerland, Tanzania, the United States, Uruguay, and Zimbabwe.

51. Watal notes that the written submissions of Korea, Peru, and Brazil argued for a balance between the rights and obligations of IPR owners. In addition, Korea made a case for liberal compulsory licensing of patents. India argued that patents were linked to critical developmental priorities such as "food production, poverty alleviation, nutrition, health care, and disease prevention" (Watal 2001, 29).

### Negotiating Standards

Once a framework had been established for the negotiations, a variety of contentious issues needed to be resolved. Six of the differences between the United States, the European Community, and Japan were paramount.

**Geographical Indications.** The European Community and Switzerland wanted strong protection for geographical indications that "identify a good as originating in the territory of a Member, or a region or a locality in that territory, where a given quality, reputation or other characteristic of the good is essentially attributable to its geographical origin" (GATT, Article XXII). For example, such protection would apply to wines associated with specific regions, preventing US wineries from naming their products *champagne, bordeaux, chablis,* and so forth.

**Patents.** Disagreements continued about exceptions to patentable subject matter. For example, should plant and animal varieties be patented? Another area of dispute was the basis on which patents were awarded. While other countries used a first-to-file system, the United States granted patents to the first to invent a product—but insisted that foreign inventors seeking patents in the United States be the first to file. Therefore, it was possible for a US patent to be awarded to a US applicant rather than a foreign applicant who actually made the invention first.

**Pharmaceuticals.** In addition to ensuring protection for pharmaceutical patents more generally, the US pharmaceutical industry was especially interested in limiting compulsory licensing that could force patent owners to license their technologies to local domestic producers. The industry also wanted "pipeline" protection—that is, patent protection for pharmaceuticals that were in the research pipeline but not yet on the market.

**Software.** The United States wanted to accord software the same copyright protection as literary works, but the Japanese resisted.

**Moral Rights.** Europeans supported the inclusion of *moral rights,* which would protect an author's work by preventing others from claiming authorship of it or making deforming changes to it. US copyright law did not recognize moral rights.

**Rental Rights.** The US recording industry wanted to prohibit commercial rental of recorded works. In 1989, IIPA president Eric Smith drafted a preliminary 301 petition against Japan regarding the approximately 7,000 Japanese rental shops from which consumers could rent and then copy CDs.

One challenge in negotiating such issues was what one participant describes as "the all-or-nothing" nature of IP. "You can't split the difference," he explains. "It's not like you can have *half* of an exclusive right. You either have an exclusive right, or you don't." Most trade negotiators were accustomed to a more traditional system in which a middle ground could be negotiated and deals could be cut relatively quickly. "You go into a smoke-filled room with about 25 other countries and hammer out the deal, then you walk out, the white smoke lifts, and that's it. But you can't do that in IP. . . . TRIPS just did not fit the old paradigm."

Another problem with the negotiations, from the US perspective, was the perceived unwillingness of the Europeans to spend any political capital. During the TRIPS negotiations, one American recalls, "the Europeans traditionally would cater to and appear to side with the developing countries on certain issues, knowing the US had a common interest on the protection of IP and that the US was not going to cave in." Some observers go so far as to accuse the Europeans of getting a free ride through TRIPS on the back of US efforts. Others characterize it differently. According to one, "the EU negotiators were smarter than the US negotiators. The US goes for a sledgehammer approach to everything, which has its strengths and drawbacks. But the Europeans were much more subtle. If you work in the [European] Commission, which is a hotbed of intrigue, then it is a piece of cake handling the Americans. If you can manage a Commission process involving the Italians, the French, the Germans, and the Brits, then you can manage any negotiation. No problem."

More than politics and tactics separated the US and European teams. One difference was the consistency of the players. "This is one of the things that I think the EC has an advantage in," according to Kirk.

> In the trade directorate there, the folks that were involved in the TRIPS negotiation had been involved in this area for many years, and in the trade talks—the Tokyo Round, etc. They are still there, the same people. And in the US, there has almost been a complete turnover in the IP negotiating group. They started out with Harvey Bale who went to PhRMA, then Mike Hathaway who went into private practice, Bruce Wilson who went to the Hill, and then myself who left and came here [to the American Intellectual Property Law Association]. My concern about the future, and it's a serious concern, is that if we ever get into one of these things again who are you going to turn to? Who was there that really knew? We don't structure ourselves very well for this in the United States.

The US and European negotiating teams also approached their interactions with representatives of domestic industry very differently. "In terms of bringing industry input," recalls one observer, "the European Commission people were removed from the pressures of lobbying." EC officials communicated with representatives of the member states, but paid little attention to industry. In fact, European industry representatives often approached the US team in hopes of gaining more influence in the talks. In contrast, US negotiators met directly with industry representatives. Although these consultations slowed the US team in establishing an initial position, says one observer of the process, it enjoyed much better real-time information from the private sector.

### The Talloires Text and the Draft Composite Text

In order to counter the TRIPS proposals put forward by the US, Europe, and Japan, 14 developing nations created a common text with help from the UNCTAD Secretariat. The document became known as the Talloires text, after the picturesque French town where the delegations worked. Jayashree Watal notes that the Talloires process could have been a chance for interested developing countries to coordinate positions on each substantive issue, but because of their lack of technical expertise, time, and coordination, they "lost a crucial opportunity to put forward a more detailed text." However, the document did become the basis for negotiating a number of articles in the final TRIPS agreement (Watal 2001, 31–32).

Continued lack of overall consensus in the TRIPS group led Swedish ambassador Lars Anell, the group's chairman, to prepare a draft TRIPS text with his staff in June 1990. The document was essentially a summary of the issues and positions under debate. Anell combined the various legal proposals submitted by the negotiators, including alternate options in brackets in areas of disagreement.

Using the draft text as a baseline, the TRIPS negotiators followed the "Green Room" pattern of GATT talks. In the Green Room process, delegates from all the engaged countries face each other across a table to discuss and exchange texts. For six months, participants whittled away at the issues, trying to remove as many of the brackets as possible. "That period was the heart of the negotiating process," Subramanian remembers. "It was very technical, but the text was considerably streamlined." For example, many developing countries argued in favor of a rule permitting parallel imports—bringing goods into a country without the consent of the rights holder after those goods were placed on the market; the United States and Europe argued against it. (In the end, negotiators agreed that the exhaustion of intellectual property rights, the basis for parallel imports, could not be made an issue in any WTO dispute settlement.) The result of the overall negotiation process was the December 1990 "Draft Composite Text" presented at the Brussels ministerial meeting.

## The Uruguay Round Breaks Down

In December 1990, an impasse between the United States and the European Community over agricultural subsidies brought the entire Uruguay Round to a halt. At the time of the breakdown, tremendous progress was being made in TRIPS. "We were sitting there thinking we were doing some serious negotiating," recalls Kirk, "and the Argentine ambassador walked in and whispered in the ear of his negotiator at the table and the guy just stood up and said, 'We are walking out. This whole meeting is over.' And sure enough, everybody got up and walked out and it was over because agriculture fell apart."

In February, Bush administration officials, working through GATT staff, endeavored to resurrect the failed round. The Americans offered the Europeans an olive branch by abandoning their most prominent demand in farm trade policy—that the European Community commit to reduce its subsidized grain exports by 24 percent over six years.

## The Dunkel Draft

When the talks were restarted in early 1991, the TRIPS negotiation process continued, but little progress was made. Many issues from the year before remained unresolved, including moral rights, patents, the scope of protection for computer programs, the length of protection for sound recordings, trade secrets, dispute settlement, and transition periods for complying with the agreement. As GATT Director-General Arthur Dunkel explained at the time, "the reason why the list is essentially unchanged is that there has been a general reluctance to settle these issues until there is a perception that the Uruguay Round negotiations as a whole are in their final lap."[52] Jacques Gorlin remembers, "Since the remaining TRIPS issues were mostly political and related not only to each other, but also to concessions being made and received in other negotiating groups, the TRIPS negotiations proceeded at a snail's pace throughout most of [the] year" (Gorlin 1999, 5). Instead of leaving negotiators to work out language in face-to-face negotiations, Anell began to propose suggested text to the delegates.

The GATT Secretariat tried to break the continuing deadlocks in the overall Uruguay Round by presenting a comprehensive "Draft Final Act" for the entire negotiation in December 1991. The Dunkel Draft, which took its name from the GATT's director-general, paved the way for the completion of the talks. Instead of bracketing areas of disagreement, the Secretariat staff proposed its own text in consultation with the interested parties. According to longtime observers, this approach was unique in the history of the GATT, which traditionally had functioned as a kind of legal advising body to the member states. But the pending issues of agricultural and aircraft subsidies and of TRIPS, recalls one observer, drove the Secretariat to "put out a text on its own, which it never really had done before to such an extent with such controversial areas. It brokered the differences."

By some accounts, Dunkel had initially expressed doubts about including intellectual property on the Uruguay Round agenda, in large part because he was concerned about its implications for pharmaceuticals in developing countries. He had spoken publicly about the importance of

---

52. GATT document MTN.TNC/w/89/Add.1, 8 (dated November 7, 1991); quoted in Gorlin (1999, 2).

access to health care and the right of nations to regulate drug prices. From the point of view of some in the United States, such positions made him a tainted interlocutor.

The Dunkel Draft was nevertheless largely supportive of the US IP interests. Some observers believe that Dunkel recognized the GATT could not afford to lose the backing of companies such as Pfizer and IBM. In the United States, traditionally trade-bolstering industries such as steel and automobile manufacture were displaying less enthusiasm for free trade; the most aggressive support came instead from industries heavily dependent on intellectual property and high technology. Those industries were also seen as crucial for getting the GATT through Congress.

Others add that Dunkel himself had little to do with the TRIPS agreement draft. On this account, the TRIPS agreement was essentially a version of the December 1990 TRIPS Draft Composite Text, revised by Anell in consultation with interested delegations. "It was Lars Anell and his assistant Adrian Otten who sat through all of the negotiations," one observer points out. "It was the two of them who created that text. Ultimately they were working within fairly circumscribed parameters principally to do with what the negotiations had been all about." Participants in the TRIPS negotiations acknowledge that without the Draft Composite Text, there would have been no substantive TRIPS agreement: "we would have gotten little or nothing—just as it happened in investment and services," in the words of one. For that reason, several negotiators refer to Lars Anell as hero of the story, and of the GATT Secretariat (Ryan 1998, 112).

Ultimately, the Dunkel Draft's TRIPS agreement provided strong IP protection, but delayed its implementation for developing countries for five to ten years. US pharmaceutical companies were especially critical of these transition periods and also criticized the draft because it lacked pipeline protection for drugs under development. The entertainment industry complained that discriminatory practices in the copyright area were not explicitly addressed. But observers say these concerns must be put into perspective. For example, even longer implementation periods were under consideration—including a 15-year transition period for pharmaceuticals, proposed by the European Community and India. US negotiators were able to reduce that time frame.

## The End Game

By December 14, 1993, every item in the Uruguay Round had been decided except for elements of the entertainment industry's "audiovisual" issue (i.e., movies, television, and recordings). Stories in the *New York Times, Los Angeles Times,* and *Washington Post* chronicled the "culture war" being waged between Europe (primarily France) and the United States.

Differences between French and US filmmakers dated back to the industry's very beginnings, when the French credited the discovery of the cinema to the Lumière brothers of Lyons and the Americans to Thomas Edison.[53] In this case, Hollywood blasted the French as blatant protectionists, citing national policies that favored European films and television. The French accused the United States of cultural imperialism, with President Mitterand charging that Americans were trying to impose their "totalitarian" dominion over the minds of the world.[54] According to Pascal Rogard, the chief French film industry lobbyist, "French films are the cinema of creation. American films are products of marketing."[55]

The principal areas of disagreement fell under the purview of TRIPS and the agreement on trade in services. The French government taxed blank videocassettes and recorders, giving the proceeds to French filmmakers to compensate them for the illegal copying of their works that inevitably occurred. The Motion Picture Association of America argued that under the TRIPS principle of national treatment, US filmmakers should share in these levies. In the trade in services negotiations, the United States also pressed for changes in European laws that reserved 51 percent of local television programming for European productions. For their part, the French sought to make an explicit "cultural exception" part of the deal.

The US entertainment industry had commitments of support from both the Bush and Clinton administrations. President George H. W. Bush had said he would not sign a GATT that exempted audiovisual services from international trade rules. President Bill Clinton had told 16 top entertainment executives in October 1993 that he would not sign any agreement in which film, television, and video were "singled out for unacceptable restrictions."[56] The MPAA's Jack Valenti threatened to try and block congressional approval of the Uruguay Round if audiovisual services were exempted from the agreement. "I don't want there to be any ambiguity," he said. "If these quotas exist, this is Armageddon time. I'm on the Hill in a New York minute bringing out every Patriot missile, every F-16 in our armory, leading whatever legions we can find to oppose this agreement."[57]

---

53. Roger Cohen, "Aux Armes! France Rallies to Battle Sly and T. Rex," *The New York Times*, January 2, 1994, Section 2, 1.

54. Mitterand quoted in Charles Bremner, "Where Did French Films Go Wrong?" *The Times* (London), December 10, 1993, 18.

55. Rogard quoted in Charles Goldsmith and Charles Fleming, "The GATT Challenge—Big Picture," *The Wall Street Journal Europe*, November 23, 1993, 1.

56. Clinton, quoted in Karen Tumulty, "Europe's US Film Curbs Could Scuttle Trade Talks," *The Los Angeles Times*, December 4, 1993, A1.

57. Bruce Stokes, "Tinseltown Trade Wars," *The National Journal*, February 23, 1991.

Some felt that the US industry's rhetoric and posturing on these issues "certainly got the French riled up." One US official remembers:

> The French went to the European Commission and said very strongly, "Over our dead bodies will you make any concessions in these areas." I think we would have been better off if [US entertainment industry representatives] would have just shut up and sent some of their people to France to see what might be possible. How do you negotiate with somebody if you've got one of your team sitting over there across the ocean calling them a bunch of scumbags? It doesn't lead to progress, I think.

However, other observers note that the Uruguay Round package was already a big win for the MPAA, suggesting that Valenti and others decided to underplay the existing gains in order to bolster their position to demand those concessions they had yet to win.

The Uruguay Round negotiations were coming to a close. Initially, most countries considered June 1993—the expiration date for the US Congress's fast-track authorization—to be the final deadline for the completion of the GATT talks. A delay in the agreement would subject the Uruguay Round text to line-by-line scrutiny by US legislators rather than an up-or-down vote on the trade agreement's implementing legislation. It was widely held that such an outcome would doom the compromises reached over six years of negotiating to a death by a thousand cuts.

But Congress extended fast track, and the new deadline for completion of the Uruguay Round became midnight on December 15, 1993. USTR Mickey Kantor and EU negotiator Sir Leon Brittan sat down in Geneva one last time to hammer out a final agreement. The bottom-line US proposal, issued at 3 A.M., included further intellectual property protection for the record and movie industries. One by one, aides on both sides dropped away from the talks, exhausted. Jack Valenti, who also participated in the negotiations, claims to have gone three days without sleep and one without food. Finally, just before dawn in Geneva (and before midnight in Washington, DC), Kantor called President Clinton for approval to abandon the audiovisual issue in exchange for completing the rest of the global trade pact. Clinton agreed.

In the end, despite criticisms, the TRIPS Dunkel Draft became part of the Uruguay Round Final Act with only minor modifications (for example, developed countries managed to insert a clause tightening restrictions on compulsory licensing for semiconductors as well as protections for confidential test data). Negotiations closed and the Uruguay Round Final Act was adopted by the 117 members of GATT in Marrakesh, Morocco, in April 1994.

The Uruguay Round Final Act delineated the most sweeping changes to the world trading system since the original 1947 GATT agreement. Worldwide tariffs were slashed by more than a third and many nontariff barriers, such as quotas, were reduced as well. The agreement also set up a new body called the World Trade Organization to replace the GATT dispute resolution system. Many changes were required to bring US law into agreement with the terms of the act—changes that had to be approved by Congress.

## Getting the Uruguay Round Agreement (and TRIPS) Through Congress

After the heated battle in Congress over the North American Free Trade Agreement (NAFTA), some worried about the prospects for the Uruguay Round implementing legislation. The erstwhile NAFTA opponents rallying against the Uruguay Round agreements included former presidential candidates Ross Perot and Patrick J. Buchanan, Senator Jesse Helms (R-NC), consumer advocate Ralph Nader, and many environmentalists. Some believed that the proposed World Trade Organization would threaten US sovereignty, others emphasized the agreement's potential to harm American workers and the environment, and some decried the so-called favoritism being shown to big business.

US industry largely favored the Uruguay Round Agreements Act and worked to support its passage. Gerald Mossinghoff, then the president of PhRMA, recalls meeting "every morning when it was pending to decide who's doing what, who's seeing what congressman, who's weak, who's strong, where do we put an ad, and where do we find grass-roots support. It was a full-court press." PhRMA formed a coalition with other high-tech trade associations to work toward passage of the agreement. Ads were published in the *Washington Post*, the *New York Times*, the *Wall Street Journal*, and other newspapers, proclaiming "America's High-Technology Industries Need GATT."

Among those opposing the Uruguay Round Agreements Act were a group of Democrats led by Senate Commerce Committee Chairman Ernest Hollings (SC). Hollings delayed the bill by holding a series of hearings in which he criticized US trade policy. However, key members of the Democratic leadership—among them, Majority Leader Richard Gephardt (MO), House Speaker Thomas Foley (WA), and Senate Majority Leader George Mitchell (ME)—supported the Uruguay Round. In addition, in a pre-Thanksgiving agreement, Clinton guaranteed that Congress could back out of the new WTO if it arbitrarily began ruling against American interests. This assurance satisfied the great majority of Democrats and Republicans.

Meeting in a lame-duck session after the 1994 elections, just before Republicans assumed control of both houses, Congress passed the Uruguay Round Agreements Act—288 to 146 in the House and 76 to 24 in the Senate. Passage also required an additional vote to waive congressional rules against any bill that added to the federal deficit. Following this last action of the 103rd Congress, President Clinton signed the text into law on December 8, 1994. The enactment of the Uruguay Round and the passage of NAFTA the year before made trade a signal success of Clinton's first two years as president.

## US Industry Reaction to the Final Agreement

The principal provisions of the TRIPS agreement included

- protection of patents for 20 years after the date of filing, regardless of place of invention or manufacture;

- patent protection for pharmaceutical products;

- patent protection for life forms (with certain exclusions for plants and animals);

- protection of copyrights for at least 50 years, with extension of copyrights to software;

- exclusive rental rights to authors of computer programs and films as well as to performers and producers of sound recordings and broadcasts;

- recognition of "well-known" trademarks;

- protection of confidential test data;

- protection of semiconductor layout designs for 10 years;

- the scope of the enforcement obligation;

- supervision of the agreement under the WTO by a council on TRIPS; and

- submission of conflicts arising under TRIPS to the WTO's dispute settlement mechanism.

The US software industry was pleased that TRIPS accorded its products the same 50-year protection as literary works (the Japanese had rescinded their initial opposition to this provision). US pharmaceutical companies were satisfied that nations could no longer discriminate against them "by field of technology": that is, countries could not maintain laws that denied patents only to medicines. In Kirk's judgment, "The issues that were on the table in 1986 and 1987 when this thing got kicked off all got addressed fairly well. It was almost preordained that software would be protected as a literary work and pharmaceutical products would be patentable. . . . The pharmaceutical guys and the software guys started the round. They're the guys that drove the process. They had their oars in right up front."

The US record industry also made gains under the TRIPS agreement. Though many countries had no tradition of protecting sound recordings, they were now obligated to implement such protection. Moreover, its term was increased from 20 years (established under the Rome Convention) to 50 years. In addition, record companies were given the right to prohibit rental, subject to a grandfather clause that benefited Japan. Though the movie industry did not get everything it wanted, films and related products received improved IP protection under TRIPS. Because the Berne Convention was incorporated into the TRIPS agreement (see TRIPS Article 9), copyrights for films were enforceable through the WTO Dispute Settlement Understanding (DSU). Films also received protection under TRIPS Article 11 on rental rights.

Not all of the industry gains in the TRIPS agreement were concrete. When asked what had been achieved for the recording industry, Neil Turkewitz, senior vice president of the Recording Industry Association of America, replied: "Number one is not about the details, number one is the fact that the environment of the whole negotiating round, as well as the results, was a sign that intellectual property had risen to the forefront of consciousness of trade negotiators because of its prominence in global commerce. So I would start off with the recognition of the role of IP in the economic environment leading into the 21st century."[58]

To be sure, not all US companies were entirely satisfied with the agreement. Pharmaceutical companies' disappointment with the transition period for developing countries and lack of pipeline protection for their products had been softened by the inclusion of a "mailbox" provision that essentially allowed companies to file a patent in a country before it fully established a patent system (thereby giving some protection during the transition period). Agrochemical companies believed that their bioengineered plants were inadequately covered. Finally, US negotiators, who had hoped to end European demands that US winemakers cease using the names of French regions such as Chablis and Champagne to describe their products, expressed frustration that the issue had been put off for future discussion. Yet most industry representatives celebrated the agreement. Valenti reflects, "I think that TRIPS was one of the most important things that this trade association [the MPAA] and other IP trade associations have accomplished, certainly in the last decade or so."

Some observers add that while industry players complained loudly about a few issues, they were well aware that they had largely gotten their way. The protests of the pharmaceutical industry, for example, were "deliberately disingenuous," according to one analyst, who explains that "it's kind of a standard bargaining technique to say you are unhappy with the text. If you said you were happy, then the other side would say, 'Well, we've given him too much.' "

---

58. Unless otherwise noted, all quotes from Neil Turkewitz are from an October 1997 interview with Charan Devereaux.

## Conclusion

Intellectual property moved onto the GATT agenda largely through the efforts of American business interests. "As opposed to pretty much every other issue that was on the Uruguay Round," one business source observes, "IP was probably the one issue that was totally pushed by industry, first in the United States and then overseas."

Because the commercial stakes were so high, TRIPS became vital to the success of the round (for a TRIPS timeline, see appendix 3A). "There could not have been an Uruguay Round without intellectual property," says Subramanian. "The United States could not have come back with an agreement [that lacked] serious obligations on IP. Developing countries absolutely misread the evolution of TRIPS. They think they made a mistake by leaving the door slightly ajar. That's completely academic. The TRIPS juggernaut was really unstoppable."

Nevertheless, such important changes in international intellectual property protection would have been unlikely in the absence of a multilateral trade process such as the GATT. "In WIPO," Kirk emphasizes, "it is one-dimensional; it is all IP; there is nothing on the other side of the equation. . . . But for the fact that [TRIPS] was part of this big negotiation it never would have happened. It just flat-out would not have happened."

Although TRIPS' future impact was unclear at the time, one thing was certain: intellectual property would continue to grow in importance and complexity as information-based products and new forms of technology entered international commerce (Maskus 1990). By the mid-1990s, high-technology goods accounted for about one-quarter of all US goods and services sold in foreign markets (Good 1996, 853). If the TRIPS negotiations had succeeded in setting only minimum standards, then what would come next? Bonnie Richardson of the MPAA observes:

> Technology is changing so fast. And that's the trouble with the multilateral trading system: It takes 10 years to get an agreement like the Uruguay Round put together, maybe longer if you look at all the preliminary negotiations. And in 10 years the world changes completely in a high-tech industry like ours. So you are always playing catch-up; you are always writing the rules for what happened in the last 10 years. But if you write them right, at least it provides you guidance for the direction you are heading.[59]

## CASE STUDY: International Trade Meets Public Health— Patent Rules and Access to Medicines (TRIPS, Case 2)

The TRIPS agreement was the most comprehensive and far-reaching international agreement on intellectual property rights ever made. By rais-

---

59. Unless otherwise noted, all quotes from Bonnie Richardson are from an August 1997 interview with Charan Devereaux.

ing the recognition and enforcement of patents, copyrights, and trademarks from an area of national discretion to an international commitment, TRIPS represented the WTO's most radical departure from its predecessor, the GATT. Of course, negotiating the agreement was just the beginning of the TRIPS story—implementation came next.[60]

## Pharmaceuticals Take Center Stage

Perhaps the most widely discussed TRIPS-related issue was the debate over the impact of the agreement on efforts to improve public health in the developing world. When the Uruguay Round was launched in 1986, more than 50 countries did not confer patent protection on pharmaceuticals (UNCTAD 1996; cited in Correa 2000, 12). The TRIPS agreement obliged every WTO member to recognize patents in all fields of technology—including drugs. But some believed that by establishing or strengthening patent regimes in developing countries, TRIPS would increase the price and decrease the number of sources for pharmaceuticals, thereby restricting the access of the poor to affordable medicines. Concerns about TRIPS and health care intensified as the incidence of HIV/AIDS—which would become the leading cause of mortality worldwide for adults age 15–59—rose dramatically.[61] Though 95 percent of those infected with HIV lived in developing countries, fewer than 5 percent received the antiretroviral treatment.[62]

In nongovernmental organizations (NGOs), most worries about international IP obligations and affordable medicines began after the TRIPS agreement was negotiated. As James Love, who directs the Consumer Project on Technology,[63] remembers, in 1994 "there was virtually no awareness in the United States or European [NGO community] of the scope and importance of the trade effort to raise levels of patent protection on medicines" (Love 2002). Some countries, however, were already concerned about TRIPS. In Brazil, for example, a labor federation held an international meeting in São Paulo in 1994 to discuss the pressures to modify

---

60. Developed countries were directed to comply with TRIPS by 1996 and developing countries were to implement the agreement by January 1, 2000. Least-developed countries were given until 2005 to comply.

61. World Health Organization, *Facts and Figures: The World Health Report 2003*, 2.

62. WHO (2002, 1); WHO Press Release WHO/58, July 9, 2002.

63. The Consumer Project on Technology, a nonprofit organization started by Ralph Nader in 1995, focuses on intellectual property rights and health care, electronic commerce, and competition policy (see www.cptech.org).

Brazilian pharmaceutical patent laws. Similarly, debate was growing in the Argentinean National Congress over patents and health care.

The first major international NGO meeting on health care and TRIPS was held in Bielefeld, Germany, in 1996. Organized by Health Action International (HAI),[64] a nonprofit network of organizations from 70 countries, the meeting brought together a group of public health activists who would ultimately form the core of an NGO campaign to increase access to medicines in developing countries (Love 2002). That same year, the Indian National Working Group on Patents hosted government representatives and generic drug producers in New Delhi as they discussed TRIPS and health (Love 2003).

During the mid-1990s, HIV infection continued to rise—especially in southern African countries. In Zimbabwe, for example, less than 10 percent of the adult population was infected with HIV in 1985; in 1997, between a fifth and a quarter were believed to be HIV-positive. By the end of 1997, more than two-thirds of the world's 21 million people infected with HIV lived in Africa south of the Sahara Desert. This region also accounted for 83 percent of the world's AIDS deaths (UNAIDS/WHO 1998).

As HIV infections continued to rise in Africa, numbers of AIDS cases in many industrialized countries began to fall. By 1996, effective antiretroviral therapy—combinations of drugs that postpone the development of AIDS and prolong the lives of the HIV-positive—was widely available in nations that could afford the treatment (around $10,000 annually). In western Europe, new AIDS cases dropped by 38 percent between 1995 and 1997, a downturn that one report from the Joint United Nations Programme on HIV/AIDS (UNAIDS) and the World Health Organization (WHO) attributed primarily to the new antiretroviral drugs. Similarly, the United States saw its first-ever decrease in annual new AIDS cases in 1996 (UNAIDS/WHO 1998).

## Close-Up: South Africa

The debate over patents and access to medicines came into focus when a dispute over intellectual property rights and pharmaceuticals arose in the Republic of South Africa. With 1 in 10 South African citizens infected with HIV, and facing some of the highest drug prices in the world, the minister of health introduced an amendment to the South African Medicines and Related Substances Control Act of 1965. Dr. Nkosazama Zuma,

---

64. According to HAI Europe's Web site (www.haiweb.org), HAI "is a non-profit, global network of health, development, consumer and other public interest groups in more than 70 countries working for a more rational use of medicinal drugs. HAI represents the interests of consumers in drug policy and believes that all drugs marketed should be acceptably safe, effective, affordable and meet real medical needs" (accessed 2002).

variously described as "outspoken," "a lightning rod," "passionate," and "quirky," was not afraid of controversial positions and had the support of President Nelson Mandela, South Africa's first postapartheid president. Section 15(c) of the amended act began, "The Minister may prescribe conditions for the supply of more affordable medicines in certain circumstances so as to protect the health of the public"—conditions that applied to medicines under patent (see appendix 3B).

In addition to establishing a transparent pricing mechanism for AIDS drugs, Zuma's new provisions permitted parallel importing of medicines, compulsory licensing, and generic drug substitution. *Parallel importing* would enable South Africa to obtain patented drugs more cheaply by buying them from a foreign supplier rather than the manufacturer's local subsidiary. *Compulsory licensing* would permit the production of drugs without the patent holder's authorization in return for some compensation to the patent holder. Under *generic drug substitution* provisions, pharmacists were obliged to tell customers when a cheaper generic existed and to sell that medicine unless the doctor or the patient forbade it. Passed by the South African parliament, the South African Medicines and Related Substances Control Amendment Act of 1997 was signed into law by President Mandela.

In the United States, reaction from the pharmaceutical industry came swiftly. In May 1997, Aldridge Cooper of Johnson & Johnson and Harvey Bale of PhRMA wrote USTR officials and Commerce Secretary William Daley about their concerns.[65] Many other drug company representatives criticized the South African legislation, and 47 members of Congress signed a letter to USTR Charlene Barshefsky asking her to "pursue all appropriate action" against the law, which "effectively abrogates the intellectual property rights of foreign pharmaceutical companies."[66]

According to industry analysts, pharmaceutical companies were most worried that the Medicines Act could set a precedent of overriding pharmaceutical patents. PhRMA estimated that developing a new drug took on average 14 years and $500 to $800 million. In addition, the association argued that average returns from marketing new drugs had dropped by

---

65. Barton Gellman, "Gore in Conflict of Health and Profit," *The Washington Post*, May 21, 2000, A1.

66. The February 2, 1998, letter, whose signatories included the Republican chairman and ranking Democrat of the House Subcommittee on Africa, pointed to "at least two egregious provisions" in the new law: "First, it permits the parallel importation of patented products and second, it allows for the administrative expropriation of patented technology. Both provisions are violations of the TRIPS Agreement. Article 28 of the Agreement obligates member countries to prohibit parallel imports of patented products and Article 27 prohibits discrimination on the enjoyment of patent rights based on the field of technology" (see www.cptech.org).

approximately 12 percent since 1984.[67] According to industry leaders, strong intellectual property protection was crucial to maintaining vital and innovative research-based pharmaceutical companies. Should South Africa's Medicines Act be allowed to stand, other countries might follow, diluting patent protection and thereby reducing returns on the industry's investments. To be sure, the WHO's Michael Scholtz pointed out, lost profits from price cuts in Africa would amount to no more than "three days' fluctuation of exchange rates." But "If cheaper drugs in Africa put downward pressure on the global price, then the core markets of the pharmaceutical industry are at risk."[68]

In South Africa, the dispute between government and industry was characterized by mistrust on both sides. As the New York Times reported, "The dispute is bitter, and driven by deep suspicions. Virtually everyone interviewed quietly suggests—off the record—that the other side is hatching a plot." The South African Pharmaceutical Manufacturers Association (PMA) sponsored newspaper ads condemning the Medicines Act: they showed a crying baby under the headline "Health Warning! Remain Silent and the Unsafe Control of Medicine Could Cost You Forever." The ad contended the legislation would "ease the entry into established markets of counterfeit, fake, expired and harmful medicines." Members of both government and industry traded threats. The executive director of the PMA noted, "Health is a very emotive topic. When one party is totally unreasonable, the other becomes totally unreasonable. It becomes tit-for-tat. It's playground tactics, I'm afraid."[69]

In February 1998, a coalition of 39 Western pharmaceutical companies, represented by South Africa's PMA, filed a suit in Pretoria arguing that the Medicines Act was unconstitutional because it gave the health minister excessive power, that it violated TRIPS, and that it discriminated against the industry. Merck, the US-based drug company, backed away from a planned $10 million investment in South Africa, blaming the new law.[70]

The Republic of South Africa's Medicines Act was domestic legislation. However, officials and activists in other countries in the region also took the issue of access to medicines and TRIPS to the World Health Organi-

---

67. A number of PhRMA publications cite the $500 million figure (attributing it to a Boston Consulting Group study of January 1996); $800 million and the drop in return appear in PhRMA's submission to the US Federal Trade Division and the Department of Justice, Antitrust Division, of April 22, 2002, "Delivering on the Promise of Pharmaceutical Innovation: The Need to Maintain Strong and Predictable Intellectual Property Rights," page i.

68. Scholtz, quoted in Barton Gellman, "An Unequal Calculus of Life and Death," The Washington Post, December 27, 2000, A1.

69. Donald G. McNeil Jr., "South Africa's Bitter Pill for World's Drug Makers," The New York Times, March 29, 1998, section 3, 1.

70. Donald G. McNeil Jr., "South Africa's Bitter Pill for World's Drug Makers," section 3, 1.

zation, the United Nations health agency. In January 1998, Dr. Timothy Stamps, Zimbabwe's minister of health, introduced a draft resolution for a new WHO Revised Drug Strategy to ensure that "public health rather than commercial interests have primacy in pharmaceutical and health policies." Staff from HAI assisted in drafting the language of the resolution, which expressed concern about "the situation in which one third of the world's population has no guaranteed access to essential drugs, in which new world trade agreements may have a negative impact on local manufacturing capacity and the access to and prices of pharmaceuticals in developing countries." It also asked WHO members to review their options under TRIPS to safeguard access to essential drugs. The WHO Executive Board recommended the adoption of Stamps's proposal.

The ensuing meeting at the 51st World Health Assembly in May 1998 was contentious, with European and US delegations opposing the resolution. US delegates were concerned about the implications of the WHO involving itself in trade matters. With delegates unable to agree on language, WHO Director-General Gro Harlem Brundtland referred the matter back to the WHO's Executive Board. "The revised drug strategy resolution addressed many issues," she said, "such as national drug policies, drug regulation, quality assurance, drug prices, ethical drug promotion, and patient information. But it was the question of new trade agreements and pharmaceuticals which attracted the most attention."[71] Brundtland and WTO Director-General Ruggiero agreed to meet twice a year to discuss matters "related to world trade and health."

NGOs saw the World Health Assembly meeting as a turning point on the issue of TRIPS and access to drugs—"hugely important," according to James Love. "This whole debate in 1998 woke people up. It really got the attention of the public health community, which really started to get engaged at this point. It was what paved the way for the Doha Declaration— it was the Doha before Doha."[72] NGOs continued to organize around the issue of access to medicines. In September 1998, Thai NGOs staged a small demonstration outside the US Embassy in Bangkok to demand that the US administration stop pressuring Thailand to amend its pharmaceutical patent laws.[73] Also in 1998 a South African nonprofit called Treatment Access Campaign (TAC) was launched to mobilize national support for access to treatment by people living with HIV/AIDS; five years later,

---

71. Speech of WHO Director-General Gro Harlem Brundtland at the WHO Executive Board ad hoc working group on Revised Drug Strategy, Geneva (October 13, 1998); reprinted in WHO (1999, 69).

72. Unless otherwise noted, all quotes from James Love are from a 2002 interview with Charan Devereaux.

73. Anjira Assavanonda, "Health—NGOs Rally Against Patent Law Changes," *Bangkok Post*, September 5, 1998, 2.

the *Wall Street Journal* called it "one of the most effective activist organizations to arise in democratic South Africa."[74]

Activists also attributed the rapid escalation in concern about TRIPS to the tactic of using the Internet to organize. As early as 1995, James Love and other health activists began posting on the Web their worries about the agreement. Through these efforts an Internet newsletter known as *IP-Health* sprang up, covering intellectual property and health. "Even though the Web had been around for a little while, most people didn't really get Webbed up until 1996/1997," Love asserts. "Technically, we were using the Internet extremely early compared to most groups."

## The US Government Response

In the United States, the South African Medicines Act and the WHO debate over TRIPS were generally treated as trade issues. The office of the US Trade Representative and the Commerce Department pressed South Africa to change its law, which had yet to go into effect. In April 1998, USTR placed South Africa on the Special 301 Watch List, noting that South Africa's new law "appears to empower the Minister of Health to abrogate patent rights for pharmaceuticals. It also would permit parallel imports."[75] A State Department report later noted that South Africa was placed on the Watch List "based largely on the potential impact of Article 15(c), not only in the South African market but also due to its global precedent and the undermining of WTO principles."[76]

But not all agreed that the Medicines Act violated TRIPS. While some argued that Article 27.1 of TRIPS required that patent rights should be enjoyed without discrimination as to the field of technology (and thus special rules on compulsory licensing for pharmaceuticals would be discrim-

---

74. Mark Schoofs, "AIDS Activists Get Aggressive—South Africa's TAC Plans Civil Disobedience to Focus on Drugs," *The Wall Street Journal*, March 20, 2003, A16.

75. USTR press release, "USTR Announces Results of Special 301 Annual Review," May 1, 1998.

76. US Department of State, "US Government Efforts to Negotiate the Repeal, Termination or Withdrawal of Article 15(c) of the South African Medicines and Related Substances Control Act of 1965," February 5, 1999. The document adds: "The Administration understands the South African Government's wish to fulfill its commitment to make medicines more affordable for its people. Although Article 15(c), as it now stands, would authorize abrogation of pharmaceutical patents and would permit parallel imports, both WTO-inconsistent actions, the South African Government to date has not allowed parallel importation of a US patented pharmaceutical nor has it suspended any patents or other intellectual property rights held by US pharmaceutical producers. The US Government has nonetheless made clear that it will defend the legitimate interests and rights of US pharmaceutical firms. In our multilevel, broad-based discussions with the SAG, USG officials have explained that abrogating intellectual property rights of pharmaceutical firms is not a viable means of accomplishing SAG objectives to make medicines more affordable for South Africans."

inatory), others pointed out that flexibility had been built into the system. Article 31 permitted compulsory licensing of patents with some conditions (for example, the license should be "predominantly for the supply of the domestic market" with "adequate remuneration" for the patent holder). Some opponents of parallel importing maintained that Article 28 prevented third parties from importing patented products. But others countered that Article 6 clearly stated that the WTO would not resolve disputes over "exhaustion of intellectual property rights," the basis for allowing or preventing parallel importing. NGOs cited Article 6 in accusing some government officials and the pharmaceutical industry of mischaracterizing parallel importing as inconsistent with the TRIPS agreement (see appendix 3C). On the other side, PhRMA also argued that under TRIPS Article 39.3, pharmaceutical R&D data should be protected against disclosure, and under Article 41, WTO member countries are obligated to provide effective remedies to prevent the infringement of intellectual property rights.

The pharmaceutical industry and some members of Congress pushed the Clinton administration to increase pressure on South Africa. One US trade official recalls that when he asked PhRMA representatives what conditions would allow them to accept parallel importing, "They said no, we really just want you to hold the line and continue to pressure South Africa to terminate this law altogether."[77] Representative Rodney Frelinghuysen (R-NJ) inserted a provision into a congressional appropriations bill that cut aid to the government of South Africa until the State Department reported on its efforts to "negotiate the repeal, suspension, or termination" of the South African law.[78] The administration also decided to withhold preferential tariff treatment from certain South African exports under the Generalized System of Preferences until progress on IPR protection had been demonstrated. Despite such pressures, when South Africa passed a new medicines bill in November 1998, it included language identical to Article 15(c) of 1997, which had provoked so much debate.

In a February 1999 Binational Commission meeting, Vice President Gore reportedly told Deputy President Thabo Mbeki of South Africa, "I want to make you aware of the strong and growing domestic pressure being brought to bear in Washington. I'm concerned that, without significant progress toward a resolution, a single trade issue could overshadow our bilateral relationship."[79] For more than four years, Gore and Mbeki had cochaired the US–South Africa Binational Commission (established in March 1995 to facilitate bilateral cooperation between the United States and postapartheid South Africa), a forum for wide-ranging discussions on

---

77. Quoted in Barton Gellman, "Gore in Conflict of Health and Profit: Gore at Center of Trade Policy Reversal on AIDS Drugs to South Africa," *The Washington Post*, May 21, 2000, A1.

78. PL 105-277, Omnibus Consolidated and Emergency Supplemental Appropriations Act, 1999 (approved October 21, 1998).

79. Gore, quoted in Gellman, "Gore in Conflict of Health and Profit," A1.

such issues as expanding South Africa's rural electrification and privatizing telecommunications services. Observers say that Vice President Gore tried to ease the confrontation over drugs. Gore and Mbeki referred the dispute to a new trade council created by their Binational Commission, and in the spring of 1999 Gore dispatched a staff member to negotiate a solution with South African officials. In February, however, PhRMA recommended that USTR move South Africa to its Priority Watch List, a step closer to formal sanctions.[80] Gore's office pressured USTR not to do so.[81]

In April 1999, during its annual review of IPR violators, USTR once again placed South Africa on the 301 Watch List and scheduled a September out-of-cycle review of its progress. "The US is trying to get more than it got in [international] agreements," said Gary Hufbauer of the Institute for International Economics in Washington. "It's a little bit of bluff."[82] In addition to citing concerns about compulsory licenses and parallel imports, the USTR report noted that "South African representatives have led a faction of nations in the World Health Organization (WHO) in calling for a reduction in the level of protection provided for pharmaceuticals in TRIPS."[83] USTR also noted that copyright piracy and trademark counterfeiting was widespread.

One month later, the World Health Assembly unanimously adopted a Revised Drug Strategy Resolution (WHA52/19, May 1999) that gave the WHO a mandate to monitor the effects of trade agreements on public health. "When trade agreements affect health, WHO must be involved from the beginning," Brundtland told the 52nd World Health Assembly.[84]

## NGOs Organize

As these discussions were taking place, nongovernmental groups continued to organize to increase access to AIDS drugs. Until the end of 1998, concerns about the effects of IPRs on the availability of medicines in developing countries were raised mainly by a group of public health officials in southern Africa and by a few NGOs. While participating NGOs

80. Submission of the Pharmaceutical Research and Manufacturers of America (PhRMA) for the Special 301 Report on Intellectual Property Barriers, February 16, 1999.

81. Jonathan Weisman, "AIDS Protesters Track Gore on Campaign Trail: Activists Want Change in S. Africa Policy," *The Baltimore Sun*, June 23, 1999, 1.

82. Hufbauer, quoted in Bob Davis, "Gore Hopes New AIDS Pact Will Help Shake Protesters," *The Wall Street Journal*, August 12, 1999, A24.

83. USTR press release, "USTR Announces Results of Special 301 Annual Review," April 30, 1999. USTR cited industry estimates that between 1997 and 1998, US trade losses related to copyright piracy in South Africa had increased more than 35 percent.

84. World Health Organization, "WHO to Address Trade and Pharmaceuticals," Press Release WHA/13, May 22, 1999.

like Health Action International were well known in the public health community, their focus was on organizing health groups, not running wider media campaigns. But in 1999, Médecins Sans Frontières (MSF)—also known as Doctors Without Borders—launched an international campaign to improve the availability of "essential medicines," arguing that one-third of the world's population lacked access to much-needed drugs.

MSF kicked off its international Access to Essential Medicines Campaign with the release of a report on the lack of research and development of drugs for diseases that primarily affect the poor. To demonstrate the legitimacy of its campaign, MSF worked to publish articles in prestigious medical journals such as *JAMA: The Journal of the American Medical Association* and *Lancet*. As MSF's former worldwide director of press and campaigns Samantha Bolton puts it, "The first thing was to look at the real problems in the field and then try to get medical evidence so that we'd have credibility—not just be stating an opinion."[85] MSF also partnered with other NGOs, including HAI, the Consumer Project on Technology, and Oxfam International (Oxfam focuses on poverty by using research, lobbying, and media campaigns to influence policy). Finally, it used hooks to create greater public awareness about the problem of access to drugs. For example, in 1999 the staff organized events on World Tuberculosis Day at the European Commission and the European Parliament in Brussels.

In addition to lobbying for increased research and development into diseases affecting the poor, MSF paid close attention to intellectual property rights. While some antiglobalization protesters openly opposed the WTO altogether, MSF took a different public stance. The organization made statements supporting TRIPS, but expressing concern about the agreement's implications for health care. Intellectual property protection, the campaign organizers argued, should be balanced against health concerns. "MSF is not against patents and not against patent legislation," said the campaign's leader, Ellen 't Hoen. "True innovation deserves to be protected and to be awarded. We advocate a balanced IP regulation that takes into account the specific needs and priorities of developing countries and that follows the principles that are outlined in the TRIPS: patents should benefit the innovator and those who need access to the innovation."[86] In some ways, organizers point out, antiglobalization protesters who lobbied for the end of the WTO helped the Access to Essential Medicines cause. "Because they were so extreme, we seemed moderate in comparison," one NGO leader noted. However, some observers believe that the NGOs were much more anti-TRIPS than their public statements indicated. In March 1999, MSF cosponsored a conference in Geneva with HAI

---

85. Unless otherwise noted, all quotes from Samantha Bolton are from a 2002 interview with Charan Devereaux.

86. Statement by Médecins Sans Frontières (MSF) on TRIPS and affordable medicines, Geneva press briefing, June 19, 2001, www.accessmed-msf.org.

and the Consumer Project on Technology to examine compulsory licensing as a potential strategy to increase access to medicines. Campaign organizers also discussed TRIPS and public health with WHO representatives and with government officials—including ministers of health of many African nations.

The MSF Access to Essential Medicines Campaign grew out of not the AIDS issue specifically but tropical and infectious diseases more generally. For example, among infectious diseases, tuberculosis was the second leading killer in the world (after lower respiratory infections), responsible for two million deaths annually. The resurgence of sleeping sickness in sub-Saharan Africa and the problem of malaria in the developing world were also major challenges. In fact, organizers at MSF initially wondered if AIDS drugs belonged in their campaign at all. Bolton recalls,

> At one point we were deciding should we or shouldn't we include AIDS in the campaign because there are so many other organizations working on it—what could we add? But many of the other diseases we deal with, they're not sexy enough, they're not going to catch people's imagination because no one's ever heard of them. And AIDS was one of the biggest problems we were facing in the field. So we actually made a strategic decision to include it and figured the more voices that could join, the better.

According to observers, US and European AIDS activists had shown little engagement with the issue of access to medicines in developing countries up to this point. Instead, they focused their energies on AIDS treatment at home. The 1993 comment of David Barr of Gay Men's Health Crisis was typical: "I can't get AIDS medicine in the Bronx! Don't tell me about people in Africa."[87] However, harnessing the political power of the Gay Men's Health Crisis, ACT UP (the AIDS Coalition to Unleash Power), and similar groups was recognized as a key element in advancing the Access campaign. "The only way you'll change US policy," Love remembers being told by a US government official, "is by talking to the AIDS activists. They can do anything. You have no idea how powerful they are." Love and other Access to Essential Medicines Campaign organizers approached key AIDS groups (ACT UP among them) to discuss pharmaceutical patents, TRIPS, and the details of the South Africa case. With AIDS on the decline in the United States, activists turned some of their attention to South Africa.

In June 1999, Vice President Gore announced his intention to run for president over calls from AIDS protesters charging that "Gore's greed kills."[88] ACT UP dogged Gore's campaign trail, accusing him of "medical

---

87. Barr, quoted in Barton Gellman, "An Unequal Calculus of Life and Death: As Millions Perished in Pandemic, Firms Debated Access to Drugs," *The Washington Post*, December 27, 2000, A1.

88. Anne E. Kornblut, "Citing Family Values, Gore Announces Candidacy; Speech Distances Him from Clinton," *The Boston Globe*, June 17, 1999.

apartheid" in South Africa.[89] Though Gore worked to resolve the dispute, many believe that the protests added urgency to these negotiations. Other US government officials also responded to the demonstrations. In July 1999, the House Subcommittee on Criminal Justice, Human Resources, and Drug Policy of the Committee on Government Reform held a hearing on the role of the United States in combating the global HIV/AIDS epidemic, focusing on trade policy toward South Africa. Observers say the relationship between trade officials and drug industry representatives was also changing. For example, USTR Barshefsky was reportedly taken aback when several pharmaceutical executives argued that the problems with treating AIDS in Africa were not related to high pharmaceutical prices but the lack of health care infrastructure components such as computers. "I don't think you're suggesting a lack of computers is what's causing this pandemic?" she asked, according to people at the meeting.[90]

In September 1999, US trade negotiators eased their demands on South Africa. Instead of seeking the repeal of the Medicines Act, they asked South Africa to sign a statement pledging that the law would not violate TRIPS. A USTR press release declared, "The two governments have identified common ground with respect to South Africa's implementation of its so-called Medicines Act. The United States very much appreciates South Africa's assurance that, as it moves forward to bring improved health care to its citizens, it will do so in a manner consistent with its international commitments and that fully protects intellectual property rights." The South African Ministry of Trade and Industry sounded a concurring note, though with a different emphasis: "It is the express position of the South African Government that, in the implementation of provisions of the Medicines Act—which permits parallel importation and compulsory licensing of patents for pharmaceuticals—it will honour its obligations under the TRIPS Agreement."[91]

USTR removed South Africa from the Special 301 Watch List and also committed to implement GSP benefits that had earlier been withheld.[92] "We don't think very highly of either compulsory licensing or parallel imports," said one US trade official, "but in recognition of the fact they have

---

89. Lakshmi Chaudry, "US to South Africa: Just Say No," *Wired*, April 25, 2000.

90. Helene Cooper, Rachel Zimmerman, and Laurie McGinley, "Patents Pending: AIDS Epidemic Traps Drug Firms in a Vise: Treatment vs. Profits—Suit in South Africa Seeks to Block Generic Copies; US Reverses Its Policy—Activists Warn Mr. Papovich," *The Wall Street Journal*, March 2, 2001, A1.

91. USTR press release 99-76, "US–South Africa Understanding on Intellectual Property," September 17, 1999; Republic of South Africa, Department of Trade and Industry, "Joint Understanding Between the Governments of South Africa and the United States of America," September 17, 1999.

92. See USTR press release, "The Protection of Intellectual Property and Health Policy," December 1, 1999.

a major health care crisis there . . . we are also showing movement on this."[93] Drug makers showed some enthusiasm about the US–South Africa statement. PhRMA spokesman Jeff Trewhitt said South Africa's health minister appeared "very flexible" in working with the industry.[94] However, before the statement was released, US pharmaceutical industry officials noted that South Africa "would need to modify the law." Shannon Herzfeld, senior vice president for international affairs at PhRMA, said a statement "is not an acceptable outcome."[95]

Demonstrations by NGOs continued. In October 1999, two hundred protesters blocked traffic in front of USTR's offices in Washington, saying developing countries needed generic AIDS drugs. A few weeks later, a dozen protesters were arrested after occupying USTR offices where they chained themselves together at the wrists.[96]

In November, the Access to Essential Medicines Campaign took its TRIPS concerns to the 1999 WTO ministerial conference in Seattle, Washington. The WTO ministerial was intended to launch a new round of multilateral trade talks. At the conference the campaign's director, Dr. Bernard Pécoul of MSF, called for the formation of a WTO Working Group on Access to Medicines. That month, MSF was awarded the Nobel Peace Prize for its humanitarian work and donated the $1 million prize to support the Access Campaign. In addition to providing money, observers say, the Nobel Prize also helped legitimate the organization's efforts on this issue.

At the Seattle ministerial, President Bill Clinton announced, "Intellectual property protections are very important to a modern economy, but when HIV and AIDS epidemics are involved, and like serious health-care crises, the United States will henceforward implement its health care and trade policies in a manner that ensures that people in the poorest countries won't have to go without medicine they so desperately need."[97] Speaking on Global HIV/AIDS Awareness Day, Clinton promised that USTR and the US Department of Health and Human Services would work together to ensure that US trade policy was flexible enough to respond to critical public health crises.

The Seattle WTO conference collapsed amid controversy. Many attributed its failure to the lack of a clear agenda going into the talks. Some also

---

93. Quoted in "US, South Africa Strike Deal in TRIPS Fight over Drug Protection," *Inside US Trade*, September 24, 1999.

94. Ceci Connolly, "Deal Made on AIDS Drug Sales; US, South Africa Reach Agreement," *The Washington Post*, September 18, 1999, A11.

95. Herzfeld, quoted in Bob Davis, "Gore Hopes New AIDS Pact Will Help Shake Protesters," *The Wall Street Journal*, August 12, 1999, A24.

96. "Activists Protest Federal Policy on AIDS Drugs," *The Los Angeles Times*, October 7, 1999, 19A. Derrill Holly, "Protesters Arrested after Demonstration Against Patent Restrictions," Associated Press, November 19, 1999.

97. President Bill Clinton, address to the WTO in Seattle, December 1, 1999.

criticized President Clinton's commitment to include labor standards in trade agreements and his endorsement of sanctions to enforce such standards. This position, advocated by organized labor in the United States, was opposed by many developing countries; they argued that such provisions would function only to restrict their exports.

The WTO ministerial conference was also the target of large protests by environmental, consumer, and labor groups. Though many demonstrated peacefully, a minority of protesters vandalized property, leading to chaos in the streets. At the time, some analysts believed that the protests played a large role in the conference's collapse, but others held that the demonstrations merely drew attention to the ministers' failure to reach an agreement. Clinton and other officials were criticized for failing to more vigorously rebut the assertions made by anti-WTO protesters. For example, while many protesters claimed to defend the interests of developing countries, WTO supporters noted that with the collapse of the ministerial, poorer nations lost the chance to negotiate reductions in US, European, and Japanese agricultural subsidies and thereby to increase their agricultural exports. A *Wall Street Journal* editorial presented Seattle as an example of what happens when "business and politicians allow trade to become hostage to special interests."[98]

## South Africa Revisited

Despite the September 1999 US–South Africa joint statement on the Medicines Act, the issue continued to provoke political debate in the United States. In May 2000, Senator Dianne Feinstein (D-CA) threatened to filibuster a bill liberalizing trade with African and Caribbean countries because an amendment she had cosponsored with Senator Russ Feingold (D-WI) had been stripped out. The amendment, originally drafted with the assistance of Rob Weissman from the Consumer Project on Technology, would have prevented the United States from challenging laws or policies of sub-Saharan African countries that promoted access to AIDS drugs, as long as those laws or policies were consistent with the TRIPS agreement. A *Washington Post* editorial was sympathetic to her position, arguing that "pharmaceutical firms ought to concede that AIDS is an exceptional disease and that this justifies a limited weakening of intellectual property rules."[99] Feinstein insisted that affordable medications had to be made more available.

Heading off the potential filibuster, the Clinton administration issued an executive order on pharmaceuticals and AIDS similar to the amendment's

---

98. "While the WTO Burns" (editorial), *The Wall Street Journal*, December 2, 1999, A22.

99. "Good Deals for Africa" (editorial), *The Washington Post*, May 6, 2000, A18.

language.[100] The United States would keep its right to seek enforcement of the WTO's TRIPS agreement but forgo the pursuit of IPR commitments beyond TRIPS in this severe health crisis. According to USTR Barshefsky, Clinton's order gave the same treatment to sub-Saharan African countries that the United States had given South Africa, "strik[ing] a proper balance between the needs of African countries . . . and the need to ensure that basic intellectual property rights are protected."[101] But pharmaceutical industry representatives took strong exception to Clinton's action. "We recognize that AIDS is a major problem, but weakening intellectual property rights is not the solution," said Alan Holmer, president of PhRMA.[102]

At the same time, the pharmaceutical industry made a public commitment to supply lower-priced AIDS drugs to developing nations—especially in Africa. In a May 2000 event, five drug companies (Merck, Hoffmann-La Roche, Bristol-Myers Squibb, Glaxo Wellcome, and Boehringer Ingelheim) announced they would make AIDS medicines available to the poorest nations at deep discounts through the Accelerating Access Initiative, a public-private partnership with five UN organizations—the WHO (which took over leadership of the initiative in November 2001), UNAIDS, UNICEF, the World Bank, and the UN Development Program. Such a joint agreement by pharmaceutical companies was unprecedented. Peter Piot, director of UNAIDS, praised the effort: "It's the first time the companies are collectively willing to discuss a truly significant decline in prices." While some companies spoke of possible costs as much as 85 percent or 90 percent below those in the United States, or about one-fifth of the prices in some African nations, initially there were no announcements of actual reductions.[103] Instead, companies would negotiate prices with interested

---

100. Executive Order 13155, Access to HIV/AIDS Pharmaceuticals and Medical Technologies, May 10, 2000.

101. Barshefsky, quoted in Lisa Richwine, "US Pledges AIDS Drug Help for sub-Saharan Africa," Reuters News, May 10, 2000.

102. Holmer, quoted in Jim Abrams, "Senate Passes Africa Trade Bill after Decision on AIDS," Associated Press Newswires, May 11, 2000.

103. Information about Accelerating Access and Piot quoted in Michael Waldholz, "Into Africa: Makers of AIDS Drugs Agree to Slash Prices for Developing World—Five Firms' Pact with UN Will Still Leave Medicine Unaffordable for Millions—Black Markets and Generics," *The Wall Street Journal*, May 11, 2000, A1. The pharmaceutical industry also highlighted its efforts to assist those in need of medicines for other conditions. For example, since 1987, Merck has worked with aid groups to give away more than 600 million tablets of Mectizan to cure river blindness, a condition that affects millions of people in West Africa. Its pledge has led the United Nations to conclude that river blindness could be eradicated by 2007. GlaxoSmithKline, in what the company called "the largest drug donation program in history," agreed to donate its Zentel (albendazole) until the tropical disease lymphatic filariasis (more commonly known as elephantiasis) was eliminated—a 20-year commitment estimated at 5–6 billion tablets worth $1 billion. According to GlaxoSmithKline, by 2001, 26 million people had been treated in 22 countries (Karen Lowry Miller, "The Pill Machine; How Much

countries on a case-by-case basis, requiring assurances that the drugs would not be reexported elsewhere and demonstration of an adequate health care infrastructure.

The Accelerating Access Initiative held risks for the industry. The negotiations could reveal information about profit margins, which might lead to demands in the United States and Europe for domestic price reductions. Some feared that low prices could fuel a black market in AIDS drugs in wealthier countries. In addition, calls for lower-priced drugs and reduced patent protection might expand to include diseases other than AIDS. At the same time, companies worried that without price cuts, nations seeking cheap pharmaceuticals would turn to generic producers in countries such as India, Thailand, and Brazil—or engage in compulsory licensing. "If we don't solve the drug access problem, then our intellectual property is at risk," warned Raymond Gilmartin, Merck's chairman and CEO. Companies "need to demonstrate that intellectual property is not an obstacle" to access in developing countries.[104]

Some critics argued that the Accelerating Access Initiative was simply part of a larger strategy to make drugs available without threatening pharmaceutical patents. "Most of all, the drug companies wanted to squelch an increasingly damaging debate on prices and patents that the UN agencies had helped touch off," Barton Gellman concluded in a front-page *Washington Post* investigation of the program.[105] The activist Ralph Nader, founder of the Consumer Project on Technology, wrote to WHO Director-General Brundtland calling Accelerating Access "an ill-advised public relations effort" saying it would undermine compulsory licensing campaigns, pressure poor countries to adopt overly restrictive IP policies, and "undermine the success of Southern generics producers who have been the most effective agents in bringing down the prices of HIV drugs."[106]

Critics also noted that Accelerating Access was able to do no more than scratch the surface of the HIV/AIDS problem. A year after its launch, only 2,000 Africans had received cut-price drugs under the program. In comparison, they observed, in Brazil 115,000 patients received antiretroviral

Money Should Big Drug Firms Have to Lose to Treat the World's Poorest Patients?" *Newsweek International*, November 19, 2001, 46; see also GlaxoSmithKline press release, "10 Million People to Receive Free Medicines on One Day," July 25, 2003).

104. Gilmartin, quoted in Mark Schoofs and Michael Waldholz, "New Regimen: AIDS-Drug Price War Breaks Out in Africa, Goaded by Generics—Merck, Others Plan to Slash Costs of Key Medicines in Bid for High Ground—Weighing Patents and People," *The Wall Street Journal*, March 7, 2001, A1.

105. Barton Gellman, "A Turning Point that Left Millions Behind; Drug Discounts Benefit Few While Protecting Pharmaceutical Companies' Profits," *The Washington Post*, December 28, 2000, A1.

106. Ralph Nader, letter to Dr. Gro Harlem Brundtland, director-general of the World Health Organization, July 23, 2001, www.cptech.org.

drugs in 2001 alone through a government initiative. Raymond Gilmartin, chairman of Merck, defended Accelerating Access: "We were proceeding along the lines that you do in any market—like contracting with a managed-care organization or with Wal-Mart." Though such negotiations often take many months, the delay "was creating the impression that our offer wasn't real and that there were too many strings attached."[107] A year later, in March 2002, a total of more than 35,500 Africans had received reduced-price drugs.[108] Many viewed the negotiation process as too cumbersome and drug prices as still too high.

Some observers believed that regardless of the success of the Accelerating Access Initiative, simply lowering prices on drugs would not stop the AIDS pandemic in Africa. For effective treatment, patients had to be closely monitored by trained medical personnel—requiring a health infrastructure that was not always in place. Without such monitoring, inconsistent self-medication could lead to drug resistance, as had happened with tuberculosis. Governments, multilateral organizations, and major employers in Africa needed to address all the barriers to care. Moreover, critics of South Africa's ineffectual response to AIDS were growing louder, calling on the government to work harder to get drugs to the people. President Thabo Mbeki stoked the controversy further when he publicly questioned the safety and efficacy of standard HIV/AIDS medications. Mbeki was also skeptical of long-accepted conclusions about the nature of AIDS and refused to support giving antiretroviral drugs for pregnant women, despite research indicating that such medication could greatly reduce the chances of transmission from mother to child.

Pfizer chose not to join Accelerating Access; in December 2000, the company announced its own initiative in South Africa. Rather than simply lowering prices, Pfizer would *donate* $50 million worth of the drug Diflucan to help fight opportunistic fungal infections in South African HIV/AIDS patients.[109] Months before this announcement, ACT UP activists rallied at Pfizer's headquarters in New York demanding that the company reduce Diflucan's price or allow generic versions of the drug to be sold.[110]

---

107. Figure of 2,000 and Gilmartin quoted in Gardiner Harris, "Adverse Reaction: AIDS Gaffes in Africa Come Back to Haunt Drug Industry at Home—Price Cuts Abroad Deepen Domestic Trouble as Firms Reveal 'True' Cost of Pills—John le Carre's New Villain," *The Wall Street Journal*, April 23, 2001, A1.

108. Industry figure quoted in Ben Hirschler, "AIDS Drugmakers Say They're Boosting African Supply," Reuters, January 14, 2003.

109. Though Diflucan is not an AIDS drug, it effectively treats two serious opportunistic fungal infections associated with the disease, cryptococcal meningitis and esophageal candidiasis. Diflucan is also used in the treatment of vaginal yeast infections; worldwide, its sales in 1999 exceeded $1 billion. (See Steven Swindells, "Pfizer in AIDS Drug Deal with South Africa," Reuters, December 1, 2000.)

110. ACT UP New York press release, September 7, 2000.

In another move by activists, Zackie Achmat of South Africa's Treatment Access Campaign illegally brought a suitcase of a generic version of Diflucan from Thailand—where Pfizer's patent was not recognized—into South Africa; at a packed news conference, he pointed out that Pfizer's drug was 28 times more expensive.[111] South Africa's Medicines Control Council granted a legal exemption to the activists, allowing them to import the generic medicine.

Pfizer began its South African Diflucan donation program in April 2001, giving away the drug in public-sector clinics; the program later expanded to other countries, mainly in sub-Saharan Africa, giving away 4 million doses of the drug by March 2004.[112] But a spokesman for the Treatment Access Campaign warned that Pfizer's approach was not a sustainable solution: indeed, though the donations were "bettering the lives of a number of people," the program was really "a successful attempt to divert attention from patent questions and voluntary licensing."[113]

As such industry initiatives went on, prices for AIDS drugs continued to drop. In February 2001, the Indian generic drug maker Cipla promised to sell a combination of three AIDS drugs to African nations at $600 per patient per year—and to sell the drugs to MSF for only $350.[114] Several large pharmaceutical companies, including GlaxoSmithKline and Merck, announced another round of price reductions for AIDS drugs in Africa. Similarly, Bristol-Myers Squibb dramatically lowered the price of the antiretroviral d4T in South Africa—following pressure from a group of Yale law students (Yale University held the patent on d4T and exclusively licensed the drug to the company). John McGoldrick, executive vice president at Bristol-Myers, declared that the price cut was "not about profits and patents. It's about poverty and a devastating disease. We seek no profits on AIDS drugs in Africa, and we will not let our patents be an obstacle."[115] Drug companies urged governments of wealthy countries and private foundations to offer financing to African nations so that they could buy AIDS medicine.

Meanwhile, the pharmaceutical industry continued its effort in South Africa to challenge the Medicines Act. In March 2001, the suit brought by the 39 companies opened in Pretoria to international outrage. Activists

---

111. See Andrew Maykuth, "AIDS Drug Patent Issue Draws Drug Companies, South Africa into Conflict," Knight Ridder Tribune Business News, March 4, 2001. The daily cost of Diflucan (retail) in South Africa was between $13 and $17.

112. See Pfizer's Web site at www.pfizer.com.

113. Quoted in "S. African AIDS Groups Urge World Protest over Pfizer Drug Patent," Agence France-Presse, July 19, 2001.

114. "Medical Group Will Provide Free AIDS Drugs in 10 Countries," Chicago Tribune, February 25, 2001, 6.

115. McGoldrick, quoted in Melody Petersen and Donald G. McNeil Jr., "Maker Yielding Patent in Africa for AIDS Drug," The New York Times, March 15, 2001, A1.

framed the court battle as pitting the property rights of rich multinational corporations from the West against the attempts of the entire developing world to curb a major public health crisis. Celebrities such as Whoopi Goldberg, Carlos Santana, and the members of the band REM called for the case to be dropped. NGOs publicly questioned the industry's position that high drug prices supported further pharmaceutical research and development, pointing out to reporters that these R&D budgets were eclipsed by the amount of money spent on marketing. In addition, they emphasized that some of the funding for AIDS drug R&D was public. "The patents for important antiretrovirals such as d4T, ddI, and ddC are held by the US government or academic institutions," noted Achmat.[116]

Stories in the mainstream press were often critical of the pharmaceutical industry's tactics and sympathetic to NGO views (for a selection of press headlines over time, see appendix 3D). For example, a *New York Times* news analysis suggested that "the industry itself fueled the backlash by staunchly defending its intellectual property in the face of [the AIDS] pandemic." The high-profile case "painted the industry as greedy and uncaring," concluded an article in the *Financial Times*. Calling pharmaceutical companies "the pariah du jour," the *Wall Street Journal* pointed to their missteps: "in the last two years, the industry responded to international calls for lower AIDS-drug prices in poor nations with a series of gaffes that have tarnished its reputation, weakened its political positions and emboldened its adversaries in a host of battles in the US and abroad."[117]

By mid-April, the pharmaceutical companies had withdrawn their case against the Medicines Act, and South Africans celebrated in the streets. The industry was deeply frustrated by the press coverage of the suit, decrying its unfair and overly simplistic portrait of drug companies as the sole villain in the AIDS tragedy. Rick Lane, president of the worldwide medicines group of Bristol-Myers, felt that they had "underestimated the capacity to be made villains, as people without answers look for excuses." Jean-Pierre Garner, Glaxo's chairman and CEO, asked, "Do you want us to give these drugs away for free? Then there won't be any more drugs to treat AIDS or anything else. Isn't it ironic that the companies that brought the drugs to market are the ones being criticized for people dying?"[118] Pharmaceutical companies continued to argue that upholding patent protection was vital to maintaining R&D expenditures.

---

116. Joint MSF/TAC/Oxfam press release, "Voices Around the World Condemn Drug Industry Hypocrisy," April 17, 2001, www.accessmed-msf.org.

117. Andrew Pollack, "Defensive Drug Industry: Fueling Clash over Patents," *The New York Times*, April 20, 2001, A6; David Firn, "Patent Disputes and Litigation Take the Shine off of 2001," *The Financial Times*, December 17, 2001; Harris, "Adverse Reaction: AIDS Gaffes in Africa," A1.

118. Both Lane and Garner are quoted in Harris, "Adverse Reaction: AIDS Gaffes in Africa," A1.

## WTO Debates over TRIPS

A week before the pharmaceutical industry dropped its case in South Africa, the WTO and WHO held the Workshop on Differential Pricing and Financing of Essential Drugs (the government of Norway was a co-sponsor). On April 8–11, 2001, in Høsbjør, Norway, representatives from national governments, UN agencies, pharmaceutical companies, generic drug companies, and NGOs (including the Consumer Project on Technology, HAI, and MSF) came together to discuss differential pricing—the practice of charging different prices in different markets according to the buyer's purchasing power. Adrian Otten, director of the Intellectual Property and Investment Division at the WTO Secretariat, observed that while the WTO and WHO had held other joint meetings, this was "the first time that we have done anything together on this scale."[119]

In June 2001, the WTO TRIPS Council held a special session on intellectual property and access to drugs at the urging of the WTO's African members, who said that TRIPS faced a "crisis of legitimacy."[120] However, that view was not universal. Supporters of TRIPS noted that the agreement allowed a great deal of leeway for the use of compulsory licensing—not just in national emergencies but also in cases of public noncommercial use, as well as when patent rights were abused by their holder. In addition, TRIPS members could "adopt measures necessary to protect public health and nutrition . . . provided such measures are consistent with the provisions of this Agreement" (Article 8.1, a provision some NGOs called meaningless). Finally, under TRIPS, the WTO would not resolve disputes over "exhaustion of intellectual property rights," the basis for allowing or preventing parallel importing (Article 6). In the view of WTO Director-General Mike Moore, TRIPS thereby struck "a carefully-negotiated balance between providing intellectual property protection—which is essential if new medicines and treatments are to be developed—and allowing countries the flexibility to ensure that treatments reach the world's poorest and most vulnerable people. Countries must feel secure that they can use this flexibility."[121]

Some officials from the WHO countered, "The flexibility in the TRIPS agreement is not being used."[122] More than 100 NGOs attended the WTO TRIPS meeting and urged the WTO to address the concerns of developing

---

119. Adrian Otten, opening remarks, TRIPS: WHO/WTO Workshop on Differential Pricing and Financing of Essential Drugs, April 11, 2001, www.wto.org.

120. Frances Williams, "Battle over Cost of Pharmaceuticals Moves to WTO," *The Financial Times*, June 20, 2001, 12.

121. WTO press release, "Moore: Countries Must Feel Secure That They Can Use TRIPS' Flexibility," June 20, 2001.

122. Williams, "Battle over Cost of Pharmaceuticals Moves to WTO," 12.

countries by adopting a seven-point strategy, including an extension of the TRIPS implementation deadline for the least-developed countries. In addition, the NGOs argued, to ensure that health concerns were taken into consideration in TRIPS enforcement, developing countries should receive technical assistance on TRIPS not only from developed-country governments and the WTO TRIPS Council but also from health organizations.

NGOs also asserted that developing countries were being bullied by the pharmaceutical industry and threatened with trade sanctions by governments to discourage them from participating in parallel importing or compulsory licensing.[123] NGOs pointed to the United States as exemplifying the kind of pressure they were protesting. In April 2000, the United States had filed a challenge at the WTO against Article 68(1)(I) of Brazil's 1996 industrial property law, which called for "local working" as a condition of receiving patent protection—companies had the choice of manufacturing their inventions in Brazil within three years of obtaining a patent or being subject to a compulsory license. Though the law took effect in May 1997, it had never been enforced.

Activists and Brazilian officials called on the United States to drop its challenge, which they claimed would impede Brazil's ability to fight AIDS. Since 1997, Brazil had provided free HIV/AIDS drugs for patients who needed them, a policy that many NGOs viewed as a model for the developing world. Brazil's treatment program was controversial, however, since its cornerstone was the local production of generic equivalents of brand-name drugs. According to Brazil's health ministry, the country had brought down the price of AIDS drugs by 79 percent and had cut the number of AIDS-related deaths in half.[124] The country produced 7 of the 14 drugs it distributed, and health officials said that threats of compulsory licensing had enabled them to negotiate lower prices with global pharmaceutical companies for some of the remaining AIDS treatments. MSF warned that the US WTO challenge "might handicap the successful Brazilian AIDS program, which is largely based on Brazil's ability to manufacture affordable treatment. . . . The Brazilian patent policy has been key to the success of the strategies to offer universal access to HIV/AIDS medication in Brazil." Brazil's ambassador to the WTO, Celso Amorim, predicted that the US complaint "may prove politically disastrous."[125]

But US trade officials argued that the patent law cited in the WTO complaint did violate TRIPS and did not affect Brazil's AIDS policy, accusing

---

123. For example, in a February 2001 report calling for an overhaul of TRIPS, the UK NGO Oxfam noted, "The deeper problem lies in the unwarranted political influence of pharmaceutical corporations which leads to a subordination of trade policy to corporate goals, notably in the USA" (Oxfam 2001, 5).

124. Tina Rosenberg, "Look at Brazil," *The New York Times Magazine*, January 28, 2001, 26.

125. Quotations from Gary G. Yerkey and Daniel Pruzin, "Pharmaceuticals: United States Drops WTO Case Against Brazil over HIV/AIDS Patent Law," *WTO Reporter*, June 26, 2001.

NGOs of being misinformed about the case.[126] The Brazilian law was clearly proscribed by TRIPS Article 27 (reproduced in appendix 3C), which mandated patent protection without discrimination as to whether products were imported or locally produced. Nevertheless, after the WTO had acceded in February 2001 to its request to establish a panel to rule on its complaint, the United States dropped the matter in June 2001. The move came as the UN General Assembly opened discussions in New York on how to combat AIDS. Instead of pursuing the patent issue at the WTO, the United States sent the dispute to a newly created US-Brazil bilateral consultative mechanism.[127] Sources asserted that this backpedaling from the WTO panel reflected an unwillingness on the part of USTR Robert Zoellick to give opponents of trade liberalization an issue that appeared to give credence to the idea of the WTO interfering with poor countries' health policies.[128]

According to USTR, the new US-Brazil bilateral process would "permit more effective and less confrontational consideration of intellectual property issues and ensure that such discussions do not divert attention away from the shared goal of combating the spread of HIV/AIDS."[129] Under the terms of the agreement, Brazil would provide advance notice to the United States before utilizing the "local manufacturing" provision.[130] Zoellick praised the pact as "provid[ing] an early warning system to protect US interests," adding, "I stand four-square behind strong enforcement of the WTO rules on intellectual property. However, litigating this dispute before a WTO dispute panel has not been the most constructive way to address our differences, especially since Brazil has never actually used the provision at issue."[131]

## Anthrax and Accusations

The TRIPS issue, as well as a litany of other trade questions, would be discussed in the upcoming November 2001 WTO ministerial meeting in

---

126. The United States challenged Article 68 of Brazil's patent law but not Article 71, which allowed for compulsory licenses for medical emergencies and for the public interest ("US Rebuts Charges That IPR Panel Attacks Brazil's AIDS Policy," *Inside US Trade*, February 9, 2001).

127. USTR press release, "United States and Brazil Agree to Use Newly Created Consultative Mechanism to Promote Cooperation on HIV/AIDS and Address WTO Patent Dispute," June 25, 2001.

128. "US, Brazil End WTO Case on Patents, Split on Bilateral Process," *Inside US Trade*, June 20, 2001.

129. USTR press release, June 25, 2001.

130. Joint Communication, Brazil–United States, June 25, 2001.

131. USTR press release, June 25, 2001.

Doha, Qatar, which trade officials hoped would launch a new multilateral round of trade talks.

But the events of September 11, 2001, changed the context of the Doha ministerial dramatically. In the weeks that followed the terrorist attacks on New York and the Pentagon, fears increased as anthrax spores were sent through the US mail. In October, the Canadian health ministry ignored Bayer's patent rights on Cipro, an antibiotic used to treat anthrax, and commissioned a local manufacturer to produce one million tablets of the drug.[132] Bayer responded by donating Cipro to Canada and committing to deliver more in an emergency. As a result, Canada agreed to acquire Cipro exclusively from Bayer. The United States similarly decided to stockpile Cipro; in October, US Health and Human Services Secretary Tommy Thompson threatened to override Bayer's patent unless the German company lowered the price of the drug. Bayer assented to a price of 95 cents a pill, down from $1.77, and no action was taken to supersede the patent.[133]

However, activists and some developing-country officials seized on Thompson's threat. By even considering compulsory licensing, the United States was accused of judging pharmaceutical patents by a double standard. Four had died from anthrax; in the AIDS epidemic, millions had perished. "Tommy Thompson may not know it, but he became our ally when he threatened that patent," said Jose Viana, an adviser to Brazil's health minister, adding, "He did what he thought was in the best interest of his country. Why can't others do the same?"[134] James Love of the Consumer Project on Technology agreed: "The Cipro thing was timely. When the US did not like the price of a medicine, we were very fast to say we might override patent rights. When Brazil did the same thing (for AIDS drugs), they were savaged."[135] The incident "seriously weakened the industry's bargaining position" at Doha, concluded the *Financial Times*.[136]

As the Doha WTO ministerial approached, NGOs and developing-country officials led by Brazil and India continued to organize on the TRIPS issue, repeating their message to journalists that public health was under threat. Pharmaceutical industry representatives countered that not everyone involved in this movement was motivated solely by their concern for public health. Countries such as Brazil and India, they argued, hoped that the debate would lead to their own large generic drug in-

132. Amy Harmon and Robert Pear, "Canada Overrides Patent for Cipro to Treat Anthrax," *The New York Times*, October 19, 2002, A1.

133. Theresa Agovino, "US, Developing Countries Set to Clash over Patents Next Week," Associated Press Newswires, November 2, 2001.

134. Viana, quoted in Agovino, "US, Developing Countries Set to Clash."

135. Love, quoted in Sabin Russell, "US Push for Cheap Cipro Haunts AIDS Drug Dispute," *The San Francisco Chronicle*, November 8, 2001, A13.

136. Firn, "Patent Disputes and Litigation."

dustries producing patented pharmaceuticals with a freer hand. Mark Grayson, a spokesman for PhRMA, was blunt: "They've hijacked the AIDS crisis to hone their own industrial development."[137]

In addition, pharmaceutical industry representatives argued that in developing countries, poverty and weak health infrastructures threw up much more serious barriers to drug access than did patents (see Gillespie-White and Salmon 2000). "It is creating false hope to say if changes are made to TRIPS you'll get drugs to poor people," Grayson said.[138] In a controversial study published in the *Journal of the American Medical Association* and circulated by the industry, Harvard researcher Amir Attaran concluded, "It is doubtful that patents are to blame for the lack of access to antiretroviral drug treatment in most African countries" (Attaran and Gillespie-White 2001, 1890). In fact, according to the study, few antiretroviral drugs were patented in African countries at all. The real reason Africans could not buy drugs, Attaran said, was more simple—a lack of money. "Companies can offer a discount, a donation, but let's face it, it's not their job to build clinics or train doctors," he told a reporter. "It is, however, what foreign-aid agencies are supposed to do. And they're not doing it."[139]

## The Lead-Up to Doha

The United States went to Doha with limited objectives—its focus was on liberalizing trade in agriculture, industrial goods, and services.[140] European negotiators had broader goals, hoping to include four issues they had originally proposed at the 1996 Singapore ministerial: investment policy, competition policy, transparency in government procurement, and trade facilitation. EU negotiators were also focused on agriculture. The French in particular were strongly opposed to language that referred to phasing out agricultural export subsidies. Developing countries favored such a phaseout, which would make their own agricultural products more competitive in the European market.

Many developing countries wanted to include negotiations on antidumping measures in the Doha round. Some WTO members opposed these controversial policies aimed at protecting domestic industries from surges of cheap foreign imports. If imports were being sold at prices below their normal value or their cost of production, a levy could be imposed to bring the price up to that of domestic producers. Many countries were particularly angered by the United States' use of antidumping pro-

137. Grayson, quoted in Russell, "US Push for Cheap Cipro," A13.

138. Grayson, quoted in Agovino, "US, Developing Countries Set to Clash."

139. Attaran, quoted in Miller, "The Pill Machine," 46.

140. Guy de Jonquières, "All-night Haggling in Doha Ends in Agreement, WTO Meeting New Mood of Cooperation," *The Financial Times*, November 15, 2001, 11.

visions, which they viewed as disguised protectionism.[141] India, Pakistan, and other countries also wanted to increase the access for their textiles in such markets as the United States, the European Union, and Canada. India in particular strongly resisted negotiations on the new areas raised in Singapore until the "implementation issues" from the Uruguay Round were resolved.

The preparations for the Doha ministerial reflected some key organizational changes. "Since the Seattle ministerial there has been much greater emphasis on the need for 'transparency' and 'inclusiveness' in the WTO's institutional machinery," noted Stuart Harbinson, chairman of the WTO's General Council (Harbinson 2002, 3). As developing countries participated more fully in the WTO, more meetings were required to achieve results. In addition, rather than sending the trade ministers a document with various bracketed country proposals, as had been done before the Seattle ministerial, before Doha, Harbinson prepared a draft declaration to serve as the starting point of the negotiations.

Going into the ministerial, drug patents and TRIPS remained among the most difficult issues. "It's really proven a tough nut to crack," said one WTO official.[142] At a September 2001 meeting of the TRIPS Council, three draft proposals for a declaration on TRIPS were submitted. In their "Declaration on the TRIPS Agreement and Health," a group of 60 developing countries proposed that "nothing in the TRIPS Agreement shall prevent members from taking measures to protect public health." The pharmaceutical industry felt the statement was too broad. "That language is extraordinarily potent," Mark Grayson warned. "With that language, there might as well not be a TRIPS."[143] Activists from MSF, Oxfam, and other NGOs encouraged delegates from developing countries to demand that any TRIPS language not be limited to AIDS but instead address public health more broadly.

For its part, the United States appeared ready to make some concessions. In the lead-up to Doha, US officials proposed that the TRIPS implementation deadline for the least-developed countries be extended from 2006 to 2016 and suggested a moratorium on WTO challenges to African countries' efforts to fight AIDS and other pandemics for at least five years—concessions that would not apply to Brazil, India, and Thailand. The European Union did not support the two US proposals, objecting that neither would lead to a meaningful declaration spelling out the relationship between TRIPS and health.[144] In a press conference, EU Commis-

---

141. "Getting Close," *The Economist*, November 10, 2001.

142. Quoted in Paul Blustein, "Drug Patent Dispute Poses Trade Threat: Generics Fight Could Derail WTO Accord," *The Washington Post*, October 26, 2001, E1.

143. Grayson, quoted in Russell, "US Push for Cheap Cipro," A13.

144. "EU Criticizes US Position on TRIPS, Calls for Compromise," *Inside US Trade*, November 12, 2001.

sioner Pascal Lamy said the European Union would seek to strike a middle road between the contrasting US and developing-country positions. According to some sources, USTR Zoellick was irritated by how the European Union had handled the issue.[145]

## The Doha Ministerial

Participants began the WTO ministerial in Doha not only in the shadow of September 11 but also with clear memories of the failure to start a round of trade talks at the 1999 WTO ministerial in Seattle. Many delegates therefore came to Doha ready to work. WTO officials emphasized the importance of reaching an agreement to launch a new set of talks. WTO Director-General Mike Moore reminded the developing countries—three-quarters of the WTO's 142-nation membership—that without an effective multilateral body, the world would move toward regional trade agreements sure to favor the stronger economic players. "Everyone wants to do a free trade deal with Japan or with the United States," Moore said. "For the most marginal of our members, who's knocking on their door? Only us."[146]

The negotiations kicked off on November 9, 2001, without the protests of the Seattle ministerial (Qatar tightly limited the number of visitors). Much of the bargaining took place in six groups, focused respectively on agriculture, the environment, antidumping measures, implementation of the previous Uruguay Round agreement, investment and competition, and TRIPS.[147] Despite the importance of other areas, some saw the issue of drug patents as dominating the talks. Representatives from US, Swiss, and European drug companies were out in full force at the ministerial. "But," noted the *Wall Street Journal*, "unlike in 1993, when intellectual-property protections were first negotiated as part of the initial WTO pact, this time the lobbyists were matched by AIDS activists who proved to be a well-coordinated group of opponents."[148]

Developing-country negotiators knew that the United States and the European Union wanted a new round of trade talks—and that the Bush administration was anxious to keep the world on its side for the "war on terrorism." India's commerce and industry minister, Murasoli Maran, took a particularly hard-line approach. "India's Mr. Maran became the man to see

---

145. "Divisions on TRIPS Remain after Lamy, Zoellick Call on WTO Preparations," *Inside US Trade*, November 9, 2001.

146. Moore, quoted in "Doha Outcome Provides Crucial Boost to WTO," Agence France-Presse, November 15, 2001.

147. "Getting Close," *The Economist*, November 10, 2001.

148. Geoff Winestock and Helene Cooper, "How Activists Outmaneuvered Drug Makers in WTO Deal—Poor Nations Can Ignore Patents to Meet Public-Health Needs—'Our Expectations Were Fully Met,' " *The Wall Street Journal Europe*, November 15, 2001, A2.

at Doha," according to one report, "frustrating US and European efforts to get an agreement. He spent the first five days refusing to negotiate and the last day threatening to walk out of the talks." Maran's stance in part reflected pressure back at home: during the negotiations, 25,000 protesters marched in the streets of New Delhi in opposition to the WTO talks.[149]

The Doha negotiations ran well beyond their scheduled deadline of November 13. Though USTR Robert Zoellick was willing to compromise on TRIPS and talk about the use of antidumping measures, he refused to make concessions on textile imports. On the agriculture issue, EU Trade Commissioner Pascal Lamy agreed to negotiate open agricultural markets "without prejudging the outcome" and to reduce export subsidies "with a view to phasing [them] out," face-saving language that seemed to satisfy the French.

Even after the midnight deadline, India continued to hold out against negotiations on the Singapore issues, but some developing-country ministers were becoming frustrated with India's tactics. Only hours before the closing ceremonies were to begin, Kenya's trade minister attacked Maran for jeopardizing the TRIPS deal.[150] As it stood, the draft ministerial declaration read, "Negotiations [on Singapore issues] will take place after the Fifth Session of the Ministerial Committee on the basis of a decision to be taken, by explicit consensus, at that session on modalities of negotiation." The meaning of this language was uncertain, however. According to the European Union and the United States, the declaration clearly launched Singapore issue negotiations. Yet in a closed-door session that held up the conclusion of the talks, India obtained the following statement from the conference's chair, Qatari trade minister Youssef Kamal: "My understanding is that at that [fifth ministerial] session, a decision would indeed need to be taken by explicit consensus before negotiations on [Singapore issues] could proceed."[151] India interpreted his assertion as denying that negotiations on the Singapore issues would necessarily take place. On this interpretation Maran announced, "India is supporting the text" as other ministers at the closing ceremony cheered.[152] The issue would continue to be debated after the close of the ministerial.

At the end of the talks, USTR Zoellick was widely quoted as saying, "Today the members of the WTO have sent a powerful signal to the world—we have removed the stain of Seattle." Developing countries were

---

149. Helene Cooper and Geoff Winestock, "Poor Nations Win Gains in Global Trade Deal, as US Compromises," *The Wall Street Journal*, November 15, 2001, 1.

150. Cooper and Winestock, "Poor Nations Win Gains," 1.

151. "Chairman's Statement Casts Doubt on Final WTO Declaration," *Inside US Trade*, November 15, 2001.

152. Helene Cooper and Geoff Winestock, "WTO Reaches Agreement on New Round of Talks—But Years of Tortuous Wrangling Lie Ahead—Indian Filibuster Nearly Capsized Deal," *The Wall Street Journal Europe*, November 15, 2001, 1.

no longer complaining about being left out of crucial discussions. "Unlike in Seattle, Africa has been satisfied with all the stages of consultations," Nigerian commerce minister Mustafa Bello said.[153]

## The WTO Declaration on the TRIPS Agreement and Public Health

The Declaration on the TRIPS Agreement and Public Health emerged from the Doha Development Agenda as a separate document. Though not as strong as the developing-country proposal, it went beyond the narrower language initially advocated by pharmaceutical companies: "We agree that the TRIPS Agreement does not and should not prevent Members from taking measures to protect public health" (see appendix 3E). In addition, the TRIPS agreement was to be interpreted and implemented in a manner "supportive of WTO Members' right to protect public health and, in particular, to promote access to medicines for all." For the least-developed countries, the implementation of TRIPS was extended until 2016.

Some saw the final declaration as a triumph for developing countries. Activists believed the declaration on TRIPS represented a significant turning point at the WTO. The debate was reframed, now that public health was linked to intellectual property and trade. Brazil's foreign minister, Celso Lafer, described the text as an important step: "The declaration doesn't change the TRIPS agreement at all, but provides a new view of it which is public health-friendly."[154] Activists who had worked to achieve the declaration were thrilled. The Consumer Project on Technology's Love called it "the greatest moment of our entire campaign—we are euphoric. We could have written that declaration ourselves."[155] The WHO later noted, "The Declaration enshrines the principle WHO has publicly advocated and advanced over the last four years, namely, the re-affirmation of the right of WTO Members to make full use of the safeguard provisions of the TRIPS Agreement in order to protect public health and promote access to medicines."[156]

Pharmaceutical industry representatives also publicly welcomed the WTO's statement on TRIPS and public health. Some argued that it would have little impact. "The industry wanted to make sure that the final language of this declaration didn't expand or diminish the rights and obli-

---

153. Bello, quoted in "Doha Outcome Provides Crucial Boost to WTO," Agence France-Presse, November 15, 2001.

154. Lafer, quoted in "Doha Outcome Provides Crucial Boost to WTO."

155. Love, quoted in Gardiner Harris and Rachel Zimmerman, "Drug Makers Say WTO Setback Will Not Have Significant Impact," *The Wall Street Journal*, November 15, 2001, B5.

156. World Health Organization, "Statement by the Representative of the World Health Organization," WTO TRIPS Council, March 2002.

gations within world trade agreements," said PhRMA's president, Alan Holmer. "We are now satisfied that the language does not."[157] Brian Ager, director-general of the European Federation of Pharmaceutical Industries and Associations, agreed: "It's still very much a political declaration," not a legal change to the WTO rules.[158] Henry McKinnell, chief executive and chairman of Pfizer, described the battle in Doha as a public relations campaign by Indian generics manufacturers seeking to continue copying drug makers' discoveries. The Indian companies "make Napster look good," said McKinnell. But he insisted that the Doha Declaration would have "zero" effect on Pfizer's profit.[159]

Some observers pointed out that activists were most effective on issues in which their interests aligned with those of developing nations. "This week's [TRIPS] declaration showed how potent the alliance between the activists and developing countries can be," noted the *Washington Post*'s Paul Blustein.

> The activists' clout at the WTO is weakest when their goals aren't shared by developing country governments, whose citizens the activists purport to champion. That's often a problem for environmentalists, because trade officials in the Third World are leery of establishing international environmental standards. Such standards, they suspect, will be used as an excuse by protectionist-minded rich countries to restrict imports of goods made in poor countries. The issue of drug patents was one on which activists and developing countries saw nearly eye-to-eye.[160]

Even those in industry commented on the changes faced by business groups. Harvey Bale, the director-general of the International Pharmaceutical Manufactures Association, acknowledged the striking shift from the 1970s and 1980s, when the GATT was much more dominated by the "Quad" countries: the United States, the European Union, Japan, and Canada. Now, Bale said, developing countries are coming together and showing a greater readiness to use their muscle in the WTO, a change that "gives the activists fertile ground."[161] One news editorial summed up Doha as "a turning point": "It was not the radical climax for which some campaigners hoped, but it was a significant shift in the balance of power in global trade negotiations."[162]

---

157. Holmer, quoted in Harris and Zimmerman, "Drug Makers Say," B5.

158. Ager, quoted in Geoff Winestock and Helene Cooper, "Activists Outmaneuver Drug Makers at WTO— Poor Nations Can Ignore Patents to Meet Public-Health Needs," *The Wall Street Journal*, November 14, 2001, A2.

159. McKinnell, quoted in Harris and Zimmerman, "Drug Makers Say," B5.

160. Paul Blustein, "Getting WTO's Attention; Activists, Developing Nations Make Gains," *The Washington Post*, November 16, 2001, E1.

161. Bale, quoted in Blustein, "Getting WTO's Attention," E1.

162. "Power Shifts in the WTO: Developing Countries Flex Their Muscles" (editorial), *The Guardian* (London), November 15, 2001, 23.

## Continuing Controversy—Paragraph 6 and Beyond

Controversy continued, however, over the meaning and significance of the Doha Declaration on the TRIPS Agreement and Public Health. For example, it had left open one key issue: how poor countries with no pharmaceutical manufacturing capabilities could make effective use of compulsory licensing. Ministers appeared to agree that the poorest countries facing serious health threats should be allowed to buy generic drugs from manufacturers in other countries, but the details remained to be worked out. Paragraph 6 of the declaration read:

> 6. We recognize that WTO Members with insufficient or no manufacturing capacities in the pharmaceutical sector could face difficulties in making effective use of compulsory licensing under the TRIPS Agreement. We instruct the Council for TRIPS to find an expeditious solution to this problem and to report to the General Council before the end of 2002.

The negotiations over paragraph 6 were difficult. As one observer puts it, negotiators had to decide "which countries should be allowed to import which products, for what diseases, from which possible exporters, under what safeguards, and through which legal form this additional flexibility should be created" (van Thiel 2003, 13)—and positions on all these issues diverged widely. Predictably, developing nations and activists wanted to allow poorer countries to import a broad range of public health products—not just AIDS drugs, for example, but also diagnostic kits and equipment. One US trade official criticized NGOs for "trying to break patent protections on every conceivable health product, even X-ray machines."[163] In addition, activists believed it should be up to each WTO member to decide when it faced a public health problem. US delegates, in contrast, pushed to limit the agreement to include only drugs treating AIDS/HIV, malaria, tuberculosis, and infectious epidemics of comparable gravity and scale. "Broadening the solution to cover any public health problem, as some are advocating, would divert attention and resources away from these epidemics, at Africa's expense," wrote Assistant USTR for Africa Rosa Whitaker to African trade ministers on October 25, 2002, "and risks trivializing the gravity of these serious epidemics."[164]

Activists and developing countries viewed the limited disease coverage as too restrictive. Ellen 't Hoen of MSF argued that such limitations would mean that countries seeking to treat AIDS sufferers could import cheaper antiretrovirals, but would be barred from importing generic antibiotics to treat pneumonia or medicines to treat other opportunistic infections.[165]

---

163. Quoted in Neil King Jr., "Progress in Doubt on Drug Patents at WTO Summit," *The Wall Street Journal*, November 14, 2002, A11.

164. Letter reprinted in *Inside US Trade*, November 15, 2002.

165. 't Hoen, quoted in "Drug Companies Push for Limits on Disease Coverage in Drug Patent Deal," *Inside US Trade*, November 22, 2002.

Ultimately, TRIPS Council Chairman Eduardo Perez Motta proposed more ambiguous language that referred to "public-health problems afflicting many developing and least-developed countries, especially those resulting from HIV/AIDS, tuberculosis, malaria, and other epidemics." Some developing nations interpreted this as covering any public health problem.

On November 19, 2002, leading executives of 20 US research-based pharmaceutical companies sent a letter to USTR Robert Zoellick, urging him to ensure that WTO language be limited to medicines for serious epidemics and not to allow patents to be overridden for medicines treating diseases such as cancer, heart disease, or diabetes. "While we have been supportive of the Administration since Doha," the letter read, "it has become increasingly evident that some WTO countries with industries based upon copying medicines are pushing to expand the Doha frame of reference far beyond its original letter and spirit."[166] In addition, the writers emphasized that a solution should focus on the needs of patients in the "poorest countries" that "truly lack manufacturing capacity." PhRMA senior vice president for international affairs Shannon Herzfeld said that any agreement should require all but the least-developed countries to prove with "objective verifiable data" that they could not manufacture the drugs domestically, and must therefore issue a compulsory license for manufacture abroad.[167]

The negotiations on compulsory licensing ground to a halt in December 2002 when US officials rejected a draft text by Motta (see van Thiel 2003, 22). The United States was alone in rejecting the text; EU Trade Commissioner Pascal Lamy called US industry objections to the proposed WTO agreement "very stupid." Lamy also criticized NGO activists for trying to block a deal.[168] In the last-minute negotiations, in which WTO Director-General Supachai Panitchpakdi was directly involved, the United States insisted that any agreement must specify what diseases would be covered, but attempted to keep the negotiations alive by offering to expand that coverage to include 23 diseases.[169] This list, according to a USTR spokesman, was developed by the Department of Health and Human Services and the WHO to identify the "infectious epidemics of most concern to health pro-

---

166. Quoted in "Drug Companies Push for Limits on Disease Coverage." Signing the industry letter were CEOs and senior executives of Hoffmann-La Roche, Novartis Pharmaceuticals, Wyeth, AstraZeneca, Bristol-Myers Squibb, Bayer, Pharmacia, GlaxoSmithKline, Berlex Laboratories, Pfizer, Amgen, Genzyme, Johnson & Johnson, PhRMA, Schering-Plough, Aventis, Allergan, Eli Lilly, Schwarz Pharma, and Abbott Laboratories.

167. Herzfeld, quoted in "Drug Companies Push for Limits on Disease Coverage."

168. Lamy, quoted in Guy de Jonquières, "EU Condemns Stance of US Drug Groups: Cheaper Drugs for Poorer Nations," *The Financial Times*, January 21, 2003, 11.

169. "Consensus on TRIPS Unravels as US Blocks Deal on Scope of Diseases," *Inside US Trade*, January 3, 2003.

fessionals in the developing world."[170] But developing countries rejected the idea, favoring instead the more general deal proposed by Motta.

After talks broke down, the United States announced a unilateral moratorium on bringing WTO cases against countries that exported drugs to low-income nations under compulsory licenses, provided that those drugs were used to treat a limited set of infectious epidemics.[171] Despite US efforts to persuade other countries that such a moratorium would suffice, developing countries held out for a formal amendment to the TRIPS agreement as a permanent solution.

Soon after, in his State of the Union address, President George W. Bush noted that the price of antiretroviral drugs had fallen from $12,000 to $300 annually and asked Congress to commit $15 billion over five years toward AIDS in Africa. "More than 4 million require immediate drug treatment," Bush said. "Yet across that [African] continent, only 50,000 AIDS victims— only 50,000—are receiving the medicine they need. . . . A doctor in rural South Africa describes his frustration. He says, 'We have no medicines. Many hospitals tell people, you've got AIDS, we can't help you. Go home and die.' In an age of miraculous medicines, no person should have to hear those words."[172]

The failure to reach a TRIPS and health deal by the December 31, 2002, deadline marked another setback for the Doha Round, which faced other deadlines on agriculture, industrial market access, and services. WTO Director-General Supachai warned countries about the lagging pace of the overall negotiations, which he feared faced "imminent gridlock."[173] Trade negotiators were eager to reach agreement on the TRIPS issue before the September 2003 WTO ministerial in Cancún, Mexico, meant to serve as a midterm review of the Doha Round. Some officials worried that if the dispute remained unresolved before the meeting in Cancún, the medicines issue would cloud the overall negotiations.

In August 2003, just two weeks before the Cancún ministerial, the deadlock over paragraph 6 was broken. US negotiators ended their obstruction

---

170. One version of the footnote, obtained by *Inside US Trade*, reads: "This decision applies to public health problems arising from yellow fever, plague, cholera, meningococcal disease, African trypansimiasis, dengue, influenza, HIV/AIDS, leishmaniasis, TB, malaria, hepatitis, leptospirosis, pertussis, poliomyelitis, schistosomiasis, typhoid fever, typhus, measles, shigellosis, hemorrhagic fevers, and arboviruses and other epidemics of comparable gravity and scale including those that might arise in the future due to natural occurrence, accidental release or deliberate use." See "Consensus on TRIPS Unravels as US Blocks Deal on Scope of Diseases," *Inside US Trade*, January 21, 2003.

171. "Consensus on TRIPS Unravels, *Inside US Trade*, January 21, 2003."

172. President George W. Bush, State of the Union Address, January 28, 2003, www.whitehouse.gov.

173. Supachai Panitchpakdi, quoted in "TNC Fails to Advance Developing Country Implementation Demands," *Inside US Trade*, March 7, 2003.

when the chairman of the General Council added additional safeguards. In a statement accompanying the agreement that emerged, "Implementation of Paragraph 6 of the Doha Declaration on the TRIPS Agreement and Public Health, Decision of the General Council of 30 August 2003" (see appendix 3F), the chairman stressed that the 2002 TRIPS and health declaration should be implemented "in good faith to protect public health" and not to further "industrial or commercial policy objectives."[174] Measures to prevent the diversion of cheap drugs to Western markets, including special packaging or different-colored tablets, were also stipulated. In addition, most OECD members agreed to opt out of the system. The deal created a temporary waiver from specific TRIPS rules for pharmaceutical products until WTO members could create a formal amendment to the agreement. "This is a historic agreement for the WTO," Supachai said. "The final piece of the jigsaw has fallen into place, allowing poorer countries to make full use of the flexibilities in the WTO's intellectual-property rules in order to deal with the diseases that ravage their people."[175]

The activists were not so sanguine; some argued that the agreement on paragraph 6 was too complicated. A joint NGO statement labeled it "a gift bound in red tape" and urged that the waiver not be celebrated until it was seen to actually work.[176] A *Washington Post* editorial similarly cautioned, "While this agreement is fine in principle, many are still doubtful about how well it will work in practice. . . . Drug agreements may be hailed in Cancún, but what matters is whether they improve access to drugs in the poorest countries."[177]

Despite agreement on TRIPS, the talks in Cancún collapsed in September over disputes between developed and developing nations. A group of 22 developing countries, led by Brazil, China, and India, balked at a US-EU proposal on agriculture. In addition, developing countries refused to launch negotiations on the so-called Singapore issues (investment, competition policy, trade facilitation, and transparency in government procurement). "Compared with the past, the role of the developing countries has changed," said Hajime Ito, a senior director in Japan's trade ministry. "They have been able to achieve a homogeneous position that they could

---

174. The WTO, "The General Council Chairperson's Statement," August 30, 2003, www.wto.org.

175. Supachai Panitchpakdi, quoted in "WTO Votes to Bypass Patents on Medicines: Cheap Generics Go to Poor Nations," *The Washington Post*, August 31, 2003, A16.

176. MSF press release, "Joint NGO Statement on TRIPS and Public Health WTO Deal on Medicines: A 'Gift' Bound in Red Tape," September 10, 2003 (available at, e.g., www.epha. org); it was signed by ACT UP Paris, the Consumer Project on Technology, Consumers International, Essential Action, European AIDS Treatment Group, Health Action International, Health GAP, International People's Health Council, Médecins sans Frontières, OXFAM International, People's Health Movement, SEATINI, Third World Network, and Women in Development.

177. "The Task in Cancún" (editorial), *The Washington Post*, September 10, 2003, A18.

not in the past."[178] USTR Zoellick wrote in the *Financial Times* that the WTO had become "a forum for the politics of protest" and warned, "the US will not wait: we will move towards free trade with can-do countries."[179]

Though the Doha Round would eventually continue, some analysts worried that such ongoing disputes would spur the United States and the European Union to further accelerate bilateral and regional trade agreements rather than devoting effort to multilateral talks. They noted that the United States and EU were already working through bilateral and regional avenues to tighten intellectual property protections beyond TRIPS in developing countries. Such "TRIPS-plus" standards for IPRs included limiting compulsory licensing, requiring countries to join the International Union for the Protection of New Varieties of Plants,[180] extending patent terms, and implementing TRIPS early.

The continuing tensions over TRIPS were seen in provisions of the US Bipartisan Trade Promotion Authority (TPA) Act. In July 2002, Congress narrowly passed this legislation, which set priorities for US trade negotiators and ensured a quick vote on implementing legislation for trade deals. While TPA directed negotiators "to respect the Declaration on the TRIPS Agreement and Public Health" made at Doha, it also directed the USTR to ensure "accelerated" implementation of the TRIPS agreement and mandated that the IPR provisions of any multilateral or bilateral trade agreement entered into by the United States "reflect a standard of protection similar to that found in United States law."

MSF called on all WTO members to "reject any IP provisions more stringent than TRIPS requires (TRIPS-Plus), and to set the Doha Declaration as the ceiling on intellectual property protection for all bilateral and regional trade agreements."[181] Activists also wrote to members of Congress, criticizing the US-Singapore Free Trade Agreement, the US-Chile Free Trade Agreement, and the Central American Free Trade Agreement (CAFTA) for including "TRIPS-plus" patent protections and for delaying the introduction of generic drug competition. They had similar concerns about the Free Trade Area of the Americas (FTAA) negotiations.

---

178. Ito, quoted in Neil King Jr. and Scott Miller, "Trade Talks Fail amid Big Divide over Farm Issues—Developing Countries Object to US, EU Goals; Cotton as a Rallying Cry," *The Wall Street Journal*, September 15, 2003, A1.

179. Robert B. Zoellick, "America Will Not Wait for the Won't-Do Countries," *The Financial Times*, September 22, 2003, 23.

180. The International Union for the Protection of New Varieties of Plants (l'Union internationale pour la protection des obtentions végétales, or UPOV), an intergovernmental organization with headquarters in Geneva, is not mentioned in the TRIPS agreement. It was established by the UPOV Convention, adopted in Paris in 1961 (revised in 1972, 1978, and 1991) to bring new varieties of plants under the protection of IPRs. See www.upov.org.

181. MSF press release, "Doha Derailed: MSF Supports Developing Countries' Efforts to Implement the Doha Declaration," September 10, 2003.

## Return to South Africa

Meanwhile, South Africa announced a major shift in its AIDS policy, committing to undertake the world's largest AIDS treatment program by providing free antiretroviral drugs to its HIV-positive citizens. The plan took advantage of an October 2003 deal that the William Jefferson Clinton Foundation had brokered with Indian and South African generic producers. It lowered AIDS drug prices for a group of 15 African and Caribbean nations to $0.38 a day—a reduction of more than a third from already discounted prices.[182] South Africa's Department of Health estimated that in the first year of the program more than 50,000 people would receive drugs, a figure that would rise to more than one million by 2007.[183]

South African manufacturers of generics worked to get voluntary licenses for the antiretroviral drugs before going into production. In an out-of-court settlement, GlaxoSmithKline and Boehringer Ingelheim agreed to expand voluntary licensing of their patented AIDS medicines to the South African companies; the deal permitted the drugs to be sold in all 47 sub-Saharan African countries. In return, the South African Competition Commission, a government body, dropped a yearlong investigation into whether the companies had overcharged for their AIDS drugs.[184] In October 2003, the commission had ruled that the two companies had violated South Africa's Competition Act by "abus[ing] their dominant positions in their respective anti-retroviral (ARV) markets" through excessive pricing and "refus[ing] to license their patents to generic manufacturers in return for a reasonable royalty."[185] Though the drug makers held the complaint to be unfounded, GlaxoSmithKline senior vice president Peter Bains said the company was "pleased" to have escaped the months of negative publicity that might have accompanied hearings of the Competition Tribunal. Activists celebrated the agreement. "For us, this is an historic occasion," said Zackie Achmat, chairman of South Africa's Treatment Action Campaign. "It's come late, it's come at a cost of many thou-

---

182. The Clinton Foundation also struck a deal with five of the world's leading medical companies to deliver low-priced HIV diagnostic tests for sub-Saharan Africa, cutting costs by as much as 80 percent.

183. Nicol Degli Innocenti and John Reed, "Facing Up to AIDS: South Africa Plans to Treat 1M Patients, But Is It as Short of Political Will as It Is of Doctors?" *The Financial Times*, January 21, 2004, 17.

184. See Julia Flynn and Mark Schoofs, "Glaxo, Boehringer to Let Africa Make More Generics for AIDS," *The Wall Street Journal*, December 11, 2003, D4; "Glaxo, Boehringer Cut a Deal on AIDS Drugs," Reuters and Bloomberg, December 11, 2003.

185. South African Competition Commission Media Release no. 29, "Competition Commission finds pharmaceutical firms in contravention of the Competition Act," October 16, 2003.

sands of lives, but we now want to say to the drug companies, 'Let's put this behind us, and move on.' "[186]

But pharmaceutical companies, aware that large quantities of many types of drugs were stolen every year from South African state hospitals, worried that AIDS drugs would be smuggled to Western markets. "We are very concerned about unscrupulous importers," said Bains. "A clear condition of the voluntary licensing agreement is the inclusion of anti-diversion measures. The drugs must be distributed in sub-Saharan Africa only."[187]

## Negotiation Analysis of the Cases

The success of US intellectual property industries in getting TRIPS onto the Uruguay Round agenda and gaining a favorable agreement is a testament to their skill in negotiating. NGOs and developing-country delegations demonstrated similar skill in winning public health–related concessions on TRIPS at the Doha ministerial in late 2001. The TRIPS cases therefore offer an opportunity to see how actors with vastly different goals employ the same influence toolbox.

### Element #1: Organizing to Influence

The campaign to get TRIPS on the Uruguay Round agenda originated in the vision and commitment of just two people, both CEOs of major US corporations: Edmund Pratt of Pfizer and John Opel of IBM. Pratt and Opel, who represented companies with strong interests in strengthening international protections for intellectual property, educated and involved themselves in the issues, and then developed potent networks of connections with senior US government officials. They established the tone and secured the resources for an intense effort to influence key governments and the negotiation process itself.

By founding the Intellectual Property Committee, Pratt and Opel dramatically increased their leverage in two ways. First, they gained the support of like-minded CEOs in affected US companies. Second, and equally important, they staffed their new organization with highly committed and knowledgeable people, such as Jacques Gorlin, who had as much expertise on the issues as anyone in the US government. The resulting focus

---

186. Bains and Achmat are quoted in John Donnelly, "Deal Paves Way for Generic HIV Drugs: Drug Companies to Allow Sales in sub-Saharan Africa," *The Boston Globe*, December 11, 2003, A8.

187. Bains, quoted in Innocenti and Reed, "Facing Up to AIDS," 17.

and knowledge enabled the IPC to exert significant control over how the issues were framed and the agreements drafted. The IPC's 1988 position paper, for example, established minimum standards for IPR protection that were largely adopted in the TRIPS agreement.

The campaign to secure public health exemptions to TRIPS at the Doha ministerial likewise originated in the work of a small group of committed people. Health Action International, the nonprofit network of public health organizations, organized a key 1996 meeting in Germany that cemented the core coalition of activists who would help to lead the campaign. As the AIDS crisis escalated, South Africa became a focal point for organization, with activists working to get the issue on the World Health Organization and the World Trade Organization agendas.

## Element #2: Selecting the Forum

In both the TRIPS cases, efforts to select the negotiating forum proved decisive in shaping the outcome. The IPC decided to concentrate on getting intellectual property onto the Uruguay Round agenda, bypassing the World Intellectual Property Organization, which had several disadvantages from its point of view. First, WIPO was seen by industry as powerless to enforce agreements and punish violations. The GATT dispute resolution mechanisms would be further strengthened by the creation of the WTO, allowing for retaliation when trade rules were violated. Second, WIPO was a single-issue forum focused only on intellectual property, limiting the flexibility the United States in using threats, trade-offs, and other inducements to strengthen international IP protection. At the WTO, negotiations on IPRs would be part of a larger undertaking that included talks on many other sectors.

By getting TRIPS onto the agenda of the Uruguay Round negotiations, proponents of stronger international protection for IP opened up important opportunities for cross-sector and cross-issue trades. Key linkages were created among the issues of IP, textiles, agriculture, and light manufacturing products. The quid pro quo for the TRIPS agreement ultimately included concessions on textiles (phasing out the MFA) and agriculture. The linkage to the MFA was particularly important in winning the support of the ASEAN countries and in breaking the developing-country coalition opposing TRIPS.

The activists seeking to win exemptions from TRIPS for public health likewise concluded that their leverage would be greater if they negotiated in trade forums, specifically in the ministerial meetings that set the agenda for new rounds of WTO talks and in meetings scheduled to specifically focus on the medicines issue. However, activists and developing-country officials also brought their case to the World Health Organization, which was initially resistant to addressing the question of drug patents. But in an unprecedented event, the WTO and WHO cosponsored a workshop to explore the problem of access to medicines. The WHO's involvement increased pressure on the WTO to address the question of access to drugs.

## Element #3: Shaping the Agenda

Both the intellectual property industry coalition and the essential medicines coalition advanced their positions by threatening to block the start of new rounds of multilateral trade negotiations. The IPC was successful in persuading the US government, notably Commerce Secretary Malcolm Baldrige and USTR Clayton Yeutter, to make inclusion of IPRs on the agenda a precondition for launching the Uruguay Round.

Stealing a page from the IPC's playbook, the essential medicines coalition made public health–related concessions on TRIPS a precondition for launching the Doha Round of multilateral trade negotiations. Activists and developing-country negotiators knew that the United States and the European Union strongly desired a new round of trade talks. They also knew that the Bush administration was anxious to keep the world on its side for its war on terrorism. The failure of the Seattle ministerial had made Doha a make-or-break meeting, a circumstance that increased developing-country leverage. Rather than wait for the negotiations proper, they forced action at the Doha ministerial. Led by Brazil, developing countries succeeded in winning concessions on TRIPS.

## Element #4: Building Coalitions

In both TRIPS cases, effective multilevel coalition building proved to be pivotal. In the first TRIPS case, IPC leaders worked to build a network of relationships with senior US government officials and to convince them of the need to take stronger action on IPRs. Once key members of Congress and administration officials were on board, larger organizations were spurred to focus on the problem. Staff members of the IPC also advised the US delegation to the TRIPS talks throughout the process and even helped to draft some of the agreement's language.

Early on, the IPC also recognized the need to influence government officials in Europe and Japan to support the effort to get IP on the Uruguay Round agenda. However, the group lacked the requisite influence to successfully lobby these officials; nor could US government influence carry the day.

To overcome this barrier, the IPC launched a multilevel coalition building campaign. Because Japanese and European officials would be most likely defer to domestic business interests on IP issues, the IPC worked to build coalitions with influential organizations—UNICE and the Keidanren—representing European and Japanese businesses. At the same time, the US government engaged in talks with Japan and Europe. The result was a coordinated approach to influencing the "northern" governments to support common positions.

In order to maintain this coalition, the IPC focused on larger principles of protecting IP and establishing a framework for what would be acceptable, rather than focusing on details that could divide the group. By elevating principles and frameworks and suppressing details, the northern coalition could stay united until the battle was won, and only then focus on dividing the spoils.

Coalition building proceeded along similar lines in the second TRIPS case. The group of activists who had coalesced at a meeting organized by HAI made common cause with sympathetic officials in sub-Saharan Africa. Like the IPC in the first TRIPS case, this core coalition sought to broaden its support and weaken potential opposing coalitions. By taking the issue to the May 1998 meeting of the WHO and seeking a resolution on access to essential medicines, they succeeded in raising awareness of the TRIPS agreement in the international public health community.

The subsequent involvement of organizations such as Médecins Sans Frontières, Oxfam, and the Consumer Project on Technology situated concerns about TRIPS patent rules in the broader context of access to potentially lifesaving drugs in poor nations, and so further expanded the coalition beyond a limited group of health policy activists in NGOs. Like the IPC in the first TRIPS case, they engaged in multilevel coalition building. To build support in the professional medical community, NGOs both published articles in respected medical journals and launched a public influence campaign aimed at a more popular audience. MSF's 1999 Nobel Prize also enhanced its reputation, thereby strengthening its access to medicines effort.

The United States generally treated TRIPS-related issues, including language about pharmaceutical patents in the South African Medicines Act, as trade-related, with USTR taking the lead. Though Vice President Gore took the initiative to address questions about the Medicines Act in the US–South Africa Binational Commission, the US government continued to threaten action against South Africa, placing it on the Special 301 Watch List. But just as the IPC influenced European and Japanese governments by reaching "inside" and forming alliances with domestic business groups, so too did the essential medicines activists seek allies to increase their influence. By partnering with domestic AIDS groups such as ACT UP, which used their political power to organize protests at Gore's presidential campaign appearances, activists succeeded in pressuring the US government. This pressure worked to counteract the influence of the pharmaceutical industry, which was concerned that precedents set by the South African Medicines Act could weaken international IPR protection.

Outreach to government officials, industry executives, and WHO representatives in the lead-up to the 1999 Seattle ministerial broadened support still further. Momentum continued to build in the first WTO debate on TRIPS and affordable medicines in 2001, leading to the drafting of the Declaration on the TRIPS Agreement and Public Health at the Doha Ministerial.

## Element #5: Leveraging Linkages

Linkages between bilateral negotiations and multilateral negotiations were an important source of influence for the IPC in the first TRIPS case. Throughout the 1980s, US intellectual property industries sought to focus the administration's attention on international IPR protection and to provide officials with tools that would make possible greater bilateral influence over trading partners. The Trade Act of 1984 made intellectual property rights actionable under section 301 of the 1974 Trade Act. In addition, Congress made "adequate and effective" IP protection a condition for eligibility under the Generalized System of Preferences. In 1985, USTR created the position of assistant USTR for international investment and intellectual property, and the "Super 301" provision of the 1988 Omnibus Trade and Competitive Act further strengthened reporting requirements for intellectual property. India and Brazil, which were leaders of developing-country resistance to IPR protection, were specifically targeted under Super 301.

These efforts at linkage bore fruit in bilateral negotiations with Korea. After launching a section 301 case against Korea in 1985, the United States negotiated an agreement in 1986 that became a model for the eventual multilateral TRIPS agreement. The linkage between section 301 and the Uruguay Round was also important in achieving agreement with developing countries on TRIPS. Some developing countries far preferred TRIPS to Section 301.

In the second TRIPS case, the most powerful linkage was the one made by activists between TRIPS and the AIDS crisis in developing countries. Though hesitant at first to bring in an issue on which so many organizations were working, they decided that the inclusion of one of the biggest problems in contemporary world health made strategic sense. They were right: by linking TRIPS to the AIDS pandemic, activists were able to infuse their concerns about pharmaceutical patents with a certain moral imperative that resonated in the many press reports about the debate. At the same time, activists were careful to focus narrowly on public health issues and not to oppose TRIPS in its entirety. Their deliberate embrace of "reasonability" deprived their opponents in the drug companies of ammunition, for they could not be branded as impractical radicals. Claims (such as the following from MSF) that they were "not against patents and not against patent legislation," and that "True innovation deserves to be protected and to be rewarded," were critically important in preventing opposition from coalescing.

### Element #6: Playing the Frame Game

In the first TRIPS case, the IPC was successful in defining the debate in terms of "intellectual piracy" for the crucial domestic US audience, especially Congress. This description was potent because it evoked images of the worst forms of plunder and illegitimacy. The groundwork for this framing was actually laid earlier, notably in the 1985 IIPA report, *Piracy of US Copyrighted Works in Ten Selected Countries.* Its result was an increased willingness on the part of Congress to enact laws strengthening the administration's hand in international negotiations over IPRs.

But though copying of products was not in the interest of US IP companies, this act was not illegal if the country in question had no domestic IP protections—no laws were being violated. IPRs could have been framed differently, in accordance with the competing view that TRIPS would hinder development and allow IP industries to monopolize and withhold knowledge from those unable to pay for their products. For example, poorer countries might have labeled the situation "intellectual imperialism," a charge that would have resonated in the developing world. But the notion of intellectual piracy dominated the debate, and the IPC won the frame game.

The activists seeking to win concessions on TRIPS at Doha likewise proved highly skilled in playing the frame game. In the United States, ACT UP accused government officials of engaging in "medical apartheid" during their demonstrations. Most important, MSF and other NGOs framed their efforts as a campaign to make "essential medicines" more available to dying people in the developing world. The press often picked up this language, describing the debate as pitting dying people against corporate profits. In response, the pharmaceutical industry argued that patent protection was necessary to fund research and development for new cures. The industry also noted that access to AIDS treatment was blocked not by the high price of drugs but by lack of health care infrastructure and political will. However, these arguments did not prove as compelling as the NGOs' framing.

### Element #7: Creating Momentum

In the first TRIPS case, the IPC employed a potent sequencing strategy to excellent effect. Its approach can be summed up as follows: first unify the United States, then unify the North, next co-opt the middle, and finally isolate the implacable opponents.

The starting point for industry leaders was to build the coalition of IP businesses in the United States. The next step was to get IPRs on the US government's agenda, secure support, and set up coordinative mechanisms. With US support solidified, the IPC then turned to gaining support from the European and Japanese governments, first building coalitions with like-minded business groups and then encouraging them to influence their respective governments.

The IPC helped to craft a set "basic principles" to which all the northern countries could subscribe, and it explicitly pressed to defer "internal" negotiations over potentially divisive details. In this way, the northern countries succeeded in jointly creating value and claiming it as a group; they put off for later the question of how they should divide up the pie.

The next step was to expand the coalition, using linkages to market access for textiles, agriculture, and manufacturing products to win the support of ASEAN countries and to prevent the formation of a blocking coalition. This approach—combined with success in arguing that IP protection would be rewarded with increased foreign investment, that developing countries would have longer TRIPS phase-in periods, and that the United States would subject itself to the WTO dispute resolution mechanism—was sufficient to overcome the remaining opposition.

Efforts to build momentum had a decisive impact in the second TRIPS case as well. In part, activists similarly gained momentum by sequentially building their coalition. But they also made skilled use of action-forcing events. In the United States, for example, ACT UP used the upcoming presidential elections as an action-forcing event to push Vice President Gore to reduce US pressure on South Africa to overturn portions of its Medicines Act. As described above, the Doha ministerial also served as an action-forcing event. By in effect holding a new round of trade talks hostage, activists and developing-country officials sought concessions on TRIPS.

Finally, the pharmaceutical industry provided their opponents with a focal point for organizing by making a classic blunder: the decision by a coalition of Western companies to launch and pursue a lawsuit against South Africa's Medicines Act. Far from causing the South African government and local activists to back down, the court action stiffened resistance. Its opening in March 2001 provoked international outrage and extensive negative press coverage. These events provide a textbook example of *reactive coalition building*—the clumsy actions of a powerful player catalyzing the formation of an opposing coalition.

Rather than enter a losing argument over IP protection (and ultimately over prices and margins), the pharmaceutical industry would have been well advised to find a less damaging resolution. Though the companies did shift tactics—they lowered prices through the Accelerating Access Initiative—that initiative required them to negotiate distribution of the drugs with each interested country individually and to ensure that participating nations had a health care infrastructure able to administer the drugs. One alternative might have been to drop the South Africa case altogether and donate the drugs to the WHO or to set up a foundation. By doing so, they would have avoided opening up debates about true prices and margins; and because the WHO would have been responsible for distribution, the companies would have escaped criticism during the predictably challenging period of actually getting the drugs to sick people. This approach would have focused attention back on the policies of various African governments and the weakness of their public health infrastructures.

## Conclusion

The juxtaposition of the two TRIPS cases illustrates that the negotiation toolbox can be employed by any and all parties seeking to shape trade agreements: companies, NGOs, and governments. The parties that use these tools most effectively win a potentially decisive advantage. The cases also illustrate that the negotiation game never really ends. Gains made by the pharmaceutical industry in the first TRIPS case were partially lost in the second, and the story is ongoing. Both battles occurred in the context of a much longer war.

# Appendix 3A
## TRIPS: Timeline

| Date | Event |
|------|-------|
| 1883 | Paris Convention for the Protection of Industrial Property established. |
| 1886 | Berne Convention for the Protection of Literary and Artistic Work established. |
| 1967 | World Intellectual Property Organization (WIPO) established. |
| 1974 | WIPO joins the United Nations system. |
| Mid-1970s | Industry groups approach the US government about the "piracy" of their intellectual property. |
| 1978 | Trademark industries found the International Anti-Counterfeiting Coalition. |
| 1979 | The Anti-Counterfeiting Coalition works with negotiators to develop a proposed anti-counterfeiting code during the Tokyo Round of GATT talks. The code is not put into effect. |
| 1970–89 | Pfizer chairman Edmund Pratt and IBM chairman John Opel serve on the President's Advisory Committee on Trade Negotiations (ACTN) during the Carter and Reagan administrations. Pratt chairs the committee, and Opel is head of the IP task force. |
| 1980s | Software "piracy" begins to be identified as a problem (IBM introduced personal computers around 1982). |
| 1984 | The Trade Act of 1984 makes IPR infringement actionable under section 301 of the 1974 Trade Act. |
| Early 1980s | Jacques Gorlin, a trade expert and consultant to IBM, writes a paper described by one observer as "the first intellectual articulation of having broader IP standards plus an enforcement text in the GATT agreement." |
| 1985 | USTR Clayton Yeutter creates the position of assistant USTR for international investment and intellectual property. |
| 1986 | A bilateral IP agreement between the US and Korea (later used as a model for TRIPS) is reached. |
| March 1986 | Pratt and Opel found the Intellectual Property Committee (IPC), a group of 13 CEOs committed to moving intellectual property onto the GATT agenda. |
| 1986 | The IPC forms a tripartite coalition with the European Union of Industrial and Employers' Confederations (UNICE) and the Keidanren, a powerful private federation of economic organizations in Japan. |

*(timeline continues next page)*

# TRIPS: Timeline   *(continued)*

| Date | Event |
|---|---|
| September 1986 | Intellectual property is included in the Punta del Este statement that launches the Uruguay Round. |
| September 1986 | The Uruguay Round begins. |
| 1986–87 | The first two years of TRIPS negotiations are characterized by disagreements between developed and developing countries. |
| June 1988 | The IPC creates a report detailing the minimum standards for an acceptable TRIPS agreement. |
| 1988 | The US Omnibus Trade and Competitiveness Act includes a provision known as "Special 301" to bolster IP protection. |
| December 1988 | At the Uruguay Round midterm review, TRIPS negotiators reach no consensus for the framework of the talks. |
| April 1989 | The deadlock over TRIPS is broken. |
| June 1990 | Lars Anell, chairman of the TRIPS Working Group, prepares a draft TRIPS text. |
| December 1990 | The TRIPS Draft Composite Text is presented at the Brussels Ministerial Meeting. |
| December 1990 | The Uruguay Round breaks down. |
| December 1991 | The GATT Secretariat presents a comprehensive draft known as the Dunkel Draft. |
| December 15, 1993 | The Uruguay Round closes; the entertainment industry's audio-visual issue is left on the table. |
| 1994 | In the United States, as the last act of the 103rd Congress, the Uruguay Round Agreements Act passes, 288–146 in the House and 76–24 in the Senate. |

## Appendix 3B
## South African Medicines and Related Substances
## Control Amendment Act of 1997, Section 15C

The Minister may prescribe conditions for the supply of more affordable medicines in certain circumstances so as to protect the health of the public and in particular may:

(a) notwithstanding anything to the contrary contained in the Patents Act 1978 (Act No. 57 of 1978), determine that the rights with regard to any medicine under a patent granted in the Republic shall not extend to acts in respect of such medicine which has been put onto the market by the owner of the medicine, or with his or her consent;

(b) prescribe the conditions on which any medicine which is identical in composition, meets the same quality standard and is intended to have the same proprietary name as that of another medicine already registered in the Republic, but which is imported by a person other than the person who is the holder of the registration certificate of the medicine already registered and which originates from any site of manufacture of the original manufacturer as approved by the council in the prescribed manner, may be imported;

(c) prescribe the registration procedure for, as well as the use of, the medicine referred to in paragraph (b).

# Appendix 3C
# Excerpts from the TRIPS Agreement (1994)

### Article 6: Exhaustion

For the purposes of dispute settlement under this Agreement, subject to the provisions of Articles 3 and 4 nothing in this Agreement shall be used to address the issue of the exhaustion of intellectual property rights.

### Article 8: Principles

1. Members may, in formulating or amending their laws and regulations, adopt measures necessary to protect public health and nutrition, and to promote the public interest in sectors of vital importance to their socio-economic and technological development, provided that such measures are consistent with the provisions of this Agreement.

### Article 27: Patentable Subject Matter

Subject to the provisions of paragraphs 2 and 3, patents shall be available for any inventions, whether products or processes, in all fields of technology, provided that they are new, involve an inventive step and are capable of industrial application. Subject to paragraph 4 of Article 65, paragraph 8 of Article 70 and paragraph 3 of this Article, patents shall be available and patent rights enjoyable without discrimination as to the place of invention, the field of technology and whether products are imported or locally produced.

2. Members may exclude from patentability inventions, the prevention within their territory of the commercial exploitation of which is necessary to protect public order or morality, including to protect human, animal or plant life or health or to avoid serious prejudice to the environment, provided that such exclusion is not made merely because the exploitation is prohibited by their law.

### Article 28: Rights Conferred

1.  A patent shall confer on its owner the following exclusive rights:

(a) where the subject matter of a patent is a product, to prevent third parties not having the owner's consent from the acts of: making, using, offering for sale, selling, or importing for these purposes that product;

(b) where the subject matter of a patent is a process, to prevent third parties not having the owner's consent from the act of using the process, and from the acts of: using, offering for sale, selling, or importing for these purposes at least the product obtained directly by that process.

2. Patent owners shall also have the right to assign, or transfer by succession, the patent and to conclude licensing contracts.

**Article 31: Other Use Without Authorization of the Right Holder**

Where the law of a Member allows for other use of the subject matter of a patent without the authorization of the right holder, including use by the government or third parties authorized by the government, the following provisions shall be respected: . . .

(c) such use may only be permitted if, prior to such use, the proposed user has made efforts to obtain authorization from the right holder on reasonable commercial terms and conditions and that such efforts have not been successful within a reasonable period of time. This requirement may be waived by a Member in the case of a national emergency or other circumstances of extreme urgency or in cases of public non-commercial use. In situations of national emergency or other circumstances of extreme urgency, the right holder shall, nevertheless, be notified as soon as reasonably practicable. In the case of public non-commercial use, where the government or contractor, without making a patent search, knows or has demonstrable grounds to know that a valid patent is or will be used by or for the government, the right holder shall be informed promptly; . . .

(f) any such use shall be authorized predominantly for the supply of the domestic market of the Member authorizing such use; . . .

(h) the right holder shall be paid adequate remuneration in the circumstances of each case, taking into account the economic value of the authorization[.]

# Appendix 3D
# A Selection of Press Headlines on Intellectual Property Rights and TRIPS: What Can We Learn about How the Press Covers the TRIPS/IPR Issue over Time?

"Intellectual Piracy Captures the Attention of the President and Congress," by Bruce Stokes, *The National Journal*, February 22, 1986, 443.

"US Businesses Urge Trade Sanctions to Stop Piracy of Software in China," by Daniel Southerland, *The Washington Post*, April 11, 1989, E7.

"Waging War on Pirates," by Dave Savona, *International Business*, January 1995, 42.

"Protecting Intellectual Property: Strategies and Recommendations to Deter Counterfeiting and Brand Piracy in Global Markets," by Clifford Shultz and Bill Saporito, *Columbia Journal of World Business*, March 22, 1996, 18.

"Retribution for Reproduction," *The Economist*, May 18, 1996, 73.

"The Pill Machine; How Much Money Should Big Drug Firms Have to Lose to Treat the World's Poorest Patients?" by Karen Lowry Miller, *Newsweek International*, November 19, 2000, 46.

"Trial Opens in South Africa AIDS Drug Suit: Firms Seek to Block Law Allowing Generic Substitutes for Patented Medicines," by Jon Jeter, *The Washington Post*, March 6, 2001, A1.

"New Regimen: AIDS-Drug Price War Breaks Out in Africa, Goaded by Generics—Merck, Others Plan to Slash Costs of Key Medicines in Bid for High Ground—Weighing Patents and People," *The Wall Street Journal*, March 7, 2001, A1.

"Defensive Drug Industry: Fueling Clash Over Patents," by Andrew Pollack, *The New York Times*, April 20, 2001, A6.

"Lifting the Curtain on the Real Costs of Making AIDS Drugs," by Melody Petersen, *The New York Times*, April 24, 2001, C2.

"The Right to Good Ideas: Patents and the Poor," *The Economist*, June 23, 2001.

"A Bitter Pill for the Drug Makers: Instead of an Opportunity, the Anthrax Scare Has Raised Awkward Questions about Patent Protection," by Geoff Dyer and Adrian Michaels, *The Financial Times*, October 23, 2001, 27.

"Drug Patent Dispute Poses Trade Threat: Generics Fight Could Derail WTO Accord," by Paul Blustein, *The Washington Post*, October 26, 2001, E1.

"Software Pirates, Beware," by Stryker McGuire; with Richard Ernsberger Jr. and Tony Emerson, *Newsweek*, October 29, 2001, 68.

"'The Real Question Isn't Moral': Three Industry Analysts Wonder if Microsoft's War Against Software Piracy Is in the Company's Own Best Interests. Is It Fighting the Last War?" *Newsweek*, October 29, 2001, 68.

"Activists Outmaneuver Drug Makers at WTO—Poor Nations Can Ignore Patents to Meet Public-Health Needs," by Geoff Winestock and Helene Cooper, *The Wall Street Journal*, November 14, 2001, A2.

"Getting WTO's Attention; Activists, Developing Nations Make Gains," by Paul Blustein, *The Washington Post*, November 19, 2001, E1.

"US Seeks Tougher Cop on the Copyright Block," by Peter Goldstein, *Kiplinger Business Forecasts*, February 11, 2002.

"Pirates of the Information Age," *The Weekly Standard*, March 18, 2002, 1.

"Patently Problematic—Intellectual Property and the Poor," *The Economist*, September 14, 2002.

"US Flip on Patents Shows Drug Makers' Growing Clout—Political Donors Get Help in Reversing Policy on Poor Nations' Access to Cheaper Medicine," by Tom Hamburger, *The Wall Street Journal*, February 6, 2003, A4.

"Empty Shelves: As US Balks on Medicine Deal, African Patients Feel the Pain—Big Drug Makers, Protecting Their Patents, Seek Limits to a Global Trade Accord—Searching for Insulin in Chad," by Roger Thurow and Scott Miller, *The Wall Street Journal*, June 2, 2003, A1.

"Drug Patents Draw Scrutiny as Bush Goes to Africa—Laws to Protect Interests of Pharmaceuticals Companies May Be at Odds with Continent's Public-Health Dilemma," by Michael Schroeder, *The Wall Street Journal*, July 9, 2003, A4.

"Leading the News: Brazil to Stir Up AIDS-Drug Battle—Nation to Authorize Imports of Generics, Citing the Cost of Big Companies' Products," by Miriam Jordan, *The Wall Street Journal*, September 5, 2003, A3.

"Patents Out of Control? Growing Lawsuits Shake Up Internet Industry," Paul Davidson, *USA Today*, January 13, 2004, B1.

## Appendix 3E
## World Trade Organization
## WT/MIN(01)/DEC/2, 20 November 2001 (01-5860)

## Ministerial Conference, Fourth Session;
## Doha, 9–14 November 2001

### DECLARATION ON THE TRIPS AGREEMENT
### AND PUBLIC HEALTH
*Adopted on 14 November 2001*

1. We recognize the gravity of the public health problems afflicting many developing and least-developed countries, especially those resulting from HIV/AIDS, tuberculosis, malaria and other epidemics.

2. We stress the need for the WTO Agreement on Trade-Related Aspects of Intellectual Property Rights (TRIPS Agreement) to be part of the wider national and international action to address these problems.

3. We recognize that intellectual property protection is important for the development of new medicines. We also recognize the concerns about its effects on prices.

4. We agree that the TRIPS Agreement does not and should not prevent Members from taking measures to protect public health. Accordingly, while reiterating our commitment to the TRIPS Agreement, we affirm that the Agreement can and should be interpreted and implemented in a manner supportive of WTO Members' right to protect public health and, in particular, to promote access to medicines for all.

   In this connection, we reaffirm the right of WTO Members to use, to the full, the provisions in the TRIPS Agreement, which provide flexibility for this purpose.

5. Accordingly and in the light of paragraph 4 above, while maintaining our commitments in the TRIPS Agreement, we recognize that these flexibilities include:

   (a) In applying the customary rules of interpretation of public international law, each provision of the TRIPS Agreement shall be read in the light of the object and purpose of the Agreement as expressed, in particular, in its objectives and principles.

(b) Each Member has the right to grant compulsory licences and the freedom to determine the grounds upon which such licences are granted.

(c) Each Member has the right to determine what constitutes a national emergency or other circumstances of extreme urgency, it being understood that public health crises, including those relating to HIV/AIDS, tuberculosis, malaria and other epidemics, can represent a national emergency or other circumstances of extreme urgency.

(d) The effect of the provisions in the TRIPS Agreement that are relevant to the exhaustion of intellectual property rights is to leave each Member free to establish its own regime for such exhaustion without challenge, subject to the MFN and national treatment provisions of Articles 3 and 4.

6. We recognize that WTO Members with insufficient or no manufacturing capacities in the pharmaceutical sector could face difficulties in making effective use of compulsory licensing under the TRIPS Agreement. We instruct the Council for TRIPS to find an expeditious solution to this problem and to report to the General Council before the end of 2002.

7. We reaffirm the commitment of developed-country Members to provide incentives to their enterprises and institutions to promote and encourage technology transfer to least-developed country Members pursuant to Article 66.2. We also agree that the least-developed country Members will not be obliged, with respect to pharmaceutical products, to implement or apply Sections 5 and 7 of Part II of the TRIPS Agreement or to enforce rights provided for under these Sections until 1 January 2016, without prejudice to the right of least-developed country Members to seek other extensions of the transition periods as provided for in Article 66.1 of the TRIPS Agreement. We instruct the Council for TRIPS to take the necessary action to give effect to this pursuant to Article 66.1 of the TRIPS Agreement.

# Appendix 3F
## World Trade Organization

**IMPLEMENTATION OF PARAGRAPH 6 OF THE DOHA DECLARATION ON THE TRIPS AGREEMENT AND PUBLIC HEALTH**

### Decision of the General Council of 30 August 2003

The General Council,

Having regard to paragraphs 1, 3 and 4 of Article IX of the Marrakesh Agreement Establishing the World Trade Organization ("the WTO Agreement");

Conducting the functions of the Ministerial Conference in the interval between meetings pursuant to paragraph 2 of Article IV of the WTO Agreement;

Noting the Declaration on the TRIPS Agreement and Public Health (WT/MIN(01)/DEC/2) (the "Declaration") and, in particular, the instruction of the Ministerial Conference to the Council for TRIPS contained in paragraph 6 of the Declaration to find an expeditious solution to the problem of the difficulties that WTO Members with insufficient or no manufacturing capacities in the pharmaceutical sector could face in making effective use of compulsory licensing under the TRIPS Agreement and to report to the General Council before the end of 2002;

Recognizing, where eligible importing Members seek to obtain supplies under the system set out in this Decision, the importance of a rapid response to those needs consistent with the provisions of this Decision;

Noting that, in the light of the foregoing, exceptional circumstances exist justifying waivers from the obligations set out in paragraphs (f) and (h) of Article 31 of the TRIPS Agreement with respect to pharmaceutical products;

Decides as follows:

1. For the purposes of this Decision:

(a) "pharmaceutical product" means any patented product, or product manufactured through a patented process, of the pharmaceutical sector

---

This Decision was adopted by the General Council in light of a statement read out by the Chairman, which can be found in JOB(03)/177. This statement will be reproduced in the minutes of the General Council to be issued as WT/GC/M/82.

needed to address the public health problems as recognized in paragraph 1 of the Declaration. It is understood that active ingredients necessary for its manufacture and diagnostic kits needed for its use would be included;[1]

(b) "eligible importing Member" means any least-developed country Member, and any other Member that has made a notification[2] to the Council for TRIPS of its intention to use the system as an importer, it being understood that a Member may notify at any time that it will use the system in whole or in a limited way, for example only in the case of a national emergency or other circumstances of extreme urgency or in cases of public non-commercial use. It is noted that some Members will not use the system set out in this Decision as importing Members[3] and that some other Members have stated that, if they use the system, it would be in no more than situations of national emergency or other circumstances of extreme urgency;

(c) "exporting Member" means a Member using the system set out in this Decision to produce pharmaceutical products for, and export them to, an eligible importing Member.

2. The obligations of an exporting Member under Article 31(f) of the TRIPS Agreement shall be waived with respect to the grant by it of a compulsory licence to the extent necessary for the purposes of production of a pharmaceutical product(s) and its export to an eligible importing Member(s) in accordance with the terms set out below in this paragraph:

(a) the eligible importing Member(s)[4] has made a notification[5] to the Council for TRIPS, that:

(i) specifies the names and expected quantities of the product(s) needed;[6]

---

1. This subparagraph is without prejudice to subparagraph 1(b).

2. It is understood that this notification does not need to be approved by a WTO body in order to use the system set out in this Decision.

3. Australia, Austria, Belgium, Canada, Denmark, Finland, France, Germany, Greece, Iceland, Ireland, Italy, Japan, Luxembourg, Netherlands, New Zealand, Norway, Portugal, Spain, Sweden, Switzerland, United Kingdom and United States of America.

4. Joint notifications providing the information required under this subparagraph may be made by the regional organizations referred to in paragraph 6 of this Decision on behalf of eligible importing Members using the system that are parties to them, with the agreement of those parties.

5. It is understood that this notification does not need to be approved by a WTO body in order to use the system set out in this Decision.

6. The notification will be made available publicly by the WTO Secretariat through a page on the WTO website dedicated to this Decision.

(ii) confirms that the eligible importing Member in question, other than a least-developed country Member, has established that it has insufficient or no manufacturing capacities in the pharmaceutical sector for the product(s) in question in one of the ways set out in the Annex to this Decision; and

(iii) confirms that, where a pharmaceutical product is patented in its territory, it has granted or intends to grant a compulsory licence in accordance with Article 31 of the TRIPS Agreement and the provisions of this Decision;[7]

(b) the compulsory licence issued by the exporting Member under this Decision shall contain the following conditions:

(i) only the amount necessary to meet the needs of the eligible importing Member(s) may be manufactured under the licence and the entirety of this production shall be exported to the Member(s) which has notified its needs to the Council for TRIPS;

(ii) products produced under the license shall be clearly identified as being produced under the system set out in this Decision through specific labeling or marking. Suppliers should distinguish such products through special packaging and/or special colouring/shaping of the products themselves, provided that such distinction is feasible and does not have a significant impact on price; and

(iii) before shipment begins, the licensee shall post on a website[8] the following information:

—the quantities being supplied to each destination as referred to in indent (i) above; and

—the distinguishing features of the product(s) referred to in indent (ii) above;

(c) the exporting Member shall notify[9] the Council for TRIPS of the grant of the licence, including the conditions attached to it.[10] The information provided shall include the name and address of the licensee, the product(s) for which the license has been granted, the quantity(ies) for which it has been granted, the country(ies) to which the product(s) is (are) to be supplied and the duration of the license. The notification

---

7. This subparagraph is without prejudice to Article 66.1 of the TRIPS Agreement.

8. The licensee may use for this purpose its own website or, with the assistance of the WTO Secretariat, the page on the WTO website dedicated to this Decision.

9. It is understood that this notification does not need to be approved by a WTO body in order to use the system set out in this Decision.

10. The notification will be made available publicly by the WTO Secretariat through a page on the WTO website dedicated to this Decision.

shall also indicate the address of the website referred to in subparagraph (b)(iii) above.

3.  Where a compulsory license is granted by an exporting Member under the system set out in this Decision, adequate remuneration pursuant to Article 31(h) of the TRIPS Agreement shall be paid to that Member taking into account the economic value to the importing Member of the use that has been authorized in the exporting Member. Where a compulsory license is granted for the same products in the eligible importing Member, the obligation of that Member under Article 31(h) shall be waived in respect of those products for which remuneration in accordance with the first sentence of this paragraph is paid in the exporting Member.

4.  In order to ensure that the products imported under the system set out in this Decision are used for the public health purposes underlying their importation, eligible importing Members shall take reasonable measures within their means, proportionate to their administrative capacities and to the risk of trade diversion to prevent re-exportation of the products that have actually been imported into their territories under the system. In the event that an eligible importing Member that is a developing country Member or a least-developed country Member experiences difficulty in implementing this provision, developed country Members shall provide, on request and on mutually agreed terms and conditions, technical and financial cooperation in order to facilitate its implementation.

5.  Members shall ensure the availability of effective legal means to prevent the importation into, and sale in, their territories of products produced under the system set out in this Decision and diverted to their markets inconsistently with its provisions, using the means already required to be available under the TRIPS Agreement. If any Member considers that such measures are proving insufficient for this purpose, the matter may be reviewed in the Council for TRIPS at the request of that Member.

6.  With a view to harnessing economies of scale for the purposes of enhancing purchasing power for, and facilitating the local production of, pharmaceutical products:

> (i)  where a developing or least-developed country WTO Member is a party to a regional trade agreement within the meaning of Article XXIV of the GATT 1994 and the Decision of 28 November 1979 on Differential and More Favourable Treatment Reciprocity and Fuller Participation of Developing Countries (L/4903), at least half of the current membership of which is made up of countries presently on the United Nations list of least-developed countries, the obligation of that Member under Article 31(f) of the TRIPS Agreement shall be

waived to the extent necessary to enable a pharmaceutical product produced or imported under a compulsory license in that Member to be exported to the markets of those other developing or least-developed country parties to the regional trade agreement that share the health problem in question. It is understood that this will not prejudice the territorial nature of the patent rights in question;

(ii) it is recognized that the development of systems providing for the grant of regional patents to be applicable in the above Members should be promoted. To this end, developed country Members undertake to provide technical cooperation in accordance with Article 67 of the TRIPS Agreement, including in conjunction with other relevant intergovernmental organizations.

7. Members recognize the desirability of promoting the transfer of technology and capacity building in the pharmaceutical sector in order to overcome the problem identified in paragraph 6 of the Declaration. To this end, eligible importing Members and exporting Members are encouraged to use the system set out in this Decision in a way which would promote this objective. Members undertake to cooperate in paying special attention to the transfer of technology and capacity building in the pharmaceutical sector in the work to be undertaken pursuant to Article 66.2 of the TRIPS Agreement, paragraph 7 of the Declaration and any other relevant work of the Council for TRIPS.

8. The Council for TRIPS shall review annually the functioning of the system set out in this Decision with a view to ensuring its effective operation and shall annually report on its operation to the General Council. This review shall be deemed to fulfill the review requirements of Article IX:4 of the WTO Agreement.

9. This Decision is without prejudice to the rights, obligations and flexibilities that Members have under the provisions of the TRIPS Agreement other than paragraphs (f) and (h) of Article 31, including those reaffirmed by the Declaration, and to their interpretation. It is also without prejudice to the extent to which pharmaceutical products produced under a compulsory license can be exported under the present provisions of Article 31(f) of the TRIPS Agreement.

10. Members shall not challenge any measures taken in conformity with the provisions of the waivers contained in this Decision under subparagraphs 1(b) and 1(c) of Article XXIII of GATT 1994.

11. This Decision, including the waivers granted in it, shall terminate for each Member on the date on which an amendment to the TRIPS Agreement replacing its provisions takes effect for that Member. The TRIPS

Council shall initiate by the end of 2003 work on the preparation of such an amendment with a view to its adoption within six months, on the understanding that the amendment will be based, where appropriate, on this Decision and on the further understanding that it will not be part of the negotiations referred to in paragraph 45 of the Doha Ministerial Declaration (WT/MIN(01)/DEC/1).

## Annex

### Assessment of Manufacturing Capacities in the Pharmaceutical Sector

Least-developed country Members are deemed to have insufficient or no manufacturing capacities in the pharmaceutical sector.

For other eligible importing Members insufficient or no manufacturing capacities for the product(s) in question may be established in either of the following ways:

(i) the Member in question has established that it has no manufacturing capacity in the pharmaceutical sector;

OR

(ii) where the Member has some manufacturing capacity in this sector, it has examined this capacity and found that, excluding any capacity owned or controlled by the patent owner, it is currently insufficient for the purposes of meeting its needs. When it is established that such capacity has become sufficient to meet the Member's needs, the system shall no longer apply.

# 4

# The Multilateral Agreement on Investment

## Making Trade Policy

In 1998, a two-year effort to negotiate a multilateral agreement on foreign investment ended in frustration and without a treaty (Graham 2000). The talks, sponsored by the Organization for Economic Cooperation and Development (OECD), aimed to create a set of global rules that would protect investors, remove governmental barriers and controls on foreign investment, and establish an effective system for settling disputes. Participants dealt not only with the challenges of the negotiations themselves but also with being made the target of a global network of protestors.

The attempt to create a Multilateral Agreement on Investment (MAI) raises questions about foreign direct investment (FDI)—cross-border ownership of companies, property, or production facilities—and its role in the world's integrating economy. Who gains and who loses from FDI? What impact does international investment have on developing countries? Should international trade agreements cover FDI?

### Coverage

The rationale for free trade is that countries gain from trading because they can specialize in the activities they do comparatively well. FDI offers

*A Virtual Defeat? Stalling the Multilateral Agreement on Investment* is an edited and revised version of the case with the same name originally written for the Case Program at the Kennedy School of Government. For copies or permission to reproduce the unabridged case please refer to www.ksgcase.harvard.edu or send a written request to Case Program, John F. Kennedy School of Government, Harvard University, 79 John F. Kennedy Street, Cambridge, MA 02138.

similar benefits: Host countries gain technological know-how and management skills from the foreign firms that invest within their borders, and home countries benefit because their firms are able to conduct more business abroad. Nevertheless, foreign investment can raise concerns and foreign firms are sometimes viewed with hostility. Critics fear that such firms have little interest in contributing to domestic economic development and will merely exploit a host country's resources.

Trade agreements have attempted to address FDI because FDI is often complementary to trade. For example, a firm wishing to export products or services to another country often finds it more efficient to establish a foreign presence. Thus manufacturers will set up operations to market and service their products. Rules covering foreign investment can provide a predictable playing field for investors and host countries alike. However, such rules are sometimes seen as being skewed toward protecting the investor and unduly constraining the domestic sovereignty and policy autonomy of the host country. In addition, some believe that trade agreements should not cover investment issues at all.

A country might try to simply obtain the benefits of FDI by enacting policies that create a friendly environment for foreign investors, but without a history of implementing such policies it might have trouble convincing investors that the future will be any different. By signing an international agreement, a country may make its policy commitments appear more credible. International agreements may also provide foreign investors with recourse against expropriation, requirements relating to local content and technology transfer, and the like, thereby making them more willing to invest. While some countries have tried to inhibit foreign investment, others have sought to attract it by offering tax holidays and other inducements. This competition between countries to attract foreign investment can lead to a costly race to the bottom that erodes their tax base; an international agreement might help host countries by establishing limits on such competition (Encarnation and Velic 1998, Moran 1998).

## Depth

The Uruguay Round Final Act included an agreement on Trade-Related Investment Measures (TRIMs). The TRIMs agreement prohibits host countries from requiring foreign investors to use local content. But the rules in TRIMs are limited—even some investment provisions that specifically affect trade are not covered in the agreement. Some therefore believe that further negotiations are needed that will increase discipline on domestic policies that distort trade and provide additional rights for foreign investors regarding establishment, national treatment, and profit repatriation. Some of these proposed rules—for example, limiting a country from taking actions against foreign firms that it is permitted to take against domestic firms—are controversial.

## Participation

Investment agreements have appeared not just in the TRIMs provisions in the multilateral World Trade Organization (WTO) but also as essential parts of regional trading arrangements. The European Union guarantees all European firms national treatment and rights of establishment. The North American Free Trade Agreement (NAFTA) requires free investment, with the exception of a few sectors. The Asia Pacific Economic Cooperation forum (APEC) countries negotiated a nonbinding agreement on investment in 1993. In addition, hundreds of bilateral investment treaties (BITs) were signed between developed and developing countries in the last quarter of the twentieth century.

What did not exist was a broad, multilateral agreement on investment. In 1995, the (mainly developed-country) members of the Organization for Economic Cooperation and Development (OECD) decided that they would attempt to negotiate such a treaty. The OECD had already concluded agreements on capital movements and guidelines for multinational behavior. Most analysts believed that OECD members, with their generally liberal investment regimes, would be able to establish a set of rules that would represent the state of the art for investment agreements. Once a MAI was concluded, non-OECD members could subscribe to it, or it could serve as the basis for an agreement in the WTO, or both.

This approach, as it turned out, created considerable problems. For one thing, the prospective benefits from an agreement among countries that already had liberal investment regimes were rather limited. Moreover, negotiators were often unwilling or unable to make significant new concessions, because the remaining exceptions usually reflected strong political or strategic considerations. In addition, some were unwilling to make concessions that would further liberalize service industries, fearing that such a move could affect their negotiating position in future WTO talks.

## Enforcement

If the purpose of investment agreements is to lend more credibility to domestic liberalization measures, then logically they should be binding (because the measures will then be most credible). Foreign firms dealing with sovereign governments would also welcome the greater protection afforded to investors by the ability to appeal to binding arbitration.

Enforcement is one element that makes the prospect of including investment rules at the WTO so attractive to investors, for the WTO holds out the promise of cross-sectoral retaliation when an investment rule is broken. Thus, if a country were to violate the TRIMs, its concessions might be suspended in areas other than investment. For example, it could face tariff increases on some of its key exports. Cross-sectoral retaliation is particularly appealing to multinationals operating in countries where little other FDI is present, since retaliation in the investment sector would have negligible impact.

## Developing Countries

Why should developing countries sign an agreement that would constrain their ability to control foreign investors? After all, both developed and developing countries have tried to use market access as a bargaining tool to induce foreign firms to transfer technology and to add to local employment. To be sure, as developing countries have reduced their trade barriers and become more open to international competition, the rents that foreign firms can earn by producing behind these barriers have been reduced. This reduction in turn lessens the ability of governments to persuade foreign firms to comply with such requirements. In any case, the role of these requirements remains controversial (for an analysis arguing that they are counterproductive, see Moran 2002).

## Distribution

Clearly, multinational firms that seek to engage in FDI will benefit if their rights are enhanced. In addition, host countries could benefit if the agreements are successful in bringing them more FDI. The impact on workers in the home country and on capitalists in the host country is more uncertain, however. On the one hand, if trade and investment are complementary activities, and if FDI abroad boosts domestic exports, then workers in the home-country export industry could gain. On the other hand, if FDI and trade are substitutes and FDI reduces home-country exports, workers in the export industry could lose. In general, FDI increases the demand for workers in the host country, but it may also mean more competition for the country's own local firms. But spillovers of knowledge to the local economy can bring gains to domestic producers in the host country. Similarly, if FDI leads to increased exports, domestic suppliers to the foreign firms may also benefit.

Opponents of globalization generated considerable opposition to the MAI negotiations and ultimately claimed victory for the failure of the talks. Protesters viewed them as proof that multinational corporations have a controlling influence on trade negotiations. They also argued that such agreements would harm developing countries. Ironically, the protesters' success in contributing to a breakdown in the talks demonstrates that the ability of private firms to dominate trade negotiations had its limits. In addition, since there are only three developing countries in the OECD (Turkey, Korea, and Mexico), the MAI negotiated at the OECD would have had little initial impact on developing countries, except insofar as it became a model for later agreements with an expanded membership.

## Governance

Providing foreign investors with an extensive set of rights is controversial, since doing so constrains governments from enacting policies they might otherwise prefer. For example, a guarantee on the repatriation of profits may limit the ability of a government to control capital outflows. Agreements to limit requirements on foreign firms may also limit a government's ability to impose such requirements on its own domestic firms. These limits are particularly contentious if they provide foreign investors with better than national treatment (i.e., rights that domestic firms do not enjoy). A noteworthy example that became important in the MAI negotiations occurred as a result of NAFTA. In NAFTA's Chapter 11, investors are guaranteed protection from expropriation without compensation at fair market value (for a more complete discussion, see Graham 1999). Chapter 11 was invoked by a foreign firm to demand compensation as a result of costs incurred by changes in domestic environmental regulations—so-called regulatory takings. Similarly situated domestic firms would not necessarily have such rights. Environmentalists have voiced concerns that the need to provide such compensation could leave countries less able to implement strict environmental policies. More generally, agreements covering foreign investment will deepen the scope of international agreements and thus further limit the choices available to those making domestic policy.

# CASE STUDY: A Virtual Defeat? Stalling the Multilateral Agreement on Investment

When a group of officials from the most affluent countries sat down to pen an agreement on foreign investment in September 1995, hopes were high. "The time is ripe to negotiate a multilateral agreement on investment (MAI) in the OECD," read a report from the Organization for Economic Cooperation and Development (OECD 1995). Negotiators aimed to create a set of global rules that would protect investors, remove governmental barriers and controls on foreign investment, and establish an effective system for dispute settlement. In short, they hoped to achieve for investment what had been done for international trade in goods and services at the General Agreement on Tariffs and Trade (GATT) and the WTO. The MAI would become the new model governing international investment worldwide, replacing about 900 bilateral investment treaties.[1]

Foreign direct investment (FDI)—cross-border ownership of companies, property, or production facilities—was growing dramatically. When the MAI talks began in 1995, global flows of FDI were more than $315 billion annually, up from around $60 billion in 1985, and the total value of outward FDI stock exceeded $2.6 trillion.[2] In fact, foreign investment was growing even faster than international trade in goods and services.[3] The United States was the largest FDI recipient and investor, with $60 billion of investment inflows and $95 billion in outflows in 1995 alone.[4] The United States was also the nation lobbying most actively for an MAI.

But the proposed MAI sparked fury around the world, becoming, in the words of a European MAI negotiator, "the focal point for fears about globalization." Indeed, according to some observers, the MAI protests marked the beginning of the international antiglobalization movement (though many protesters object to that characterization, preferring to be called pro–fair trade and investment). The MAI negotiations were targeted by hundreds of grassroots environmental, consumer, and development organizations and condemned by critics ranging from labor union leaders to movie actresses, all voicing concerns about the harmful impacts of global economic integration.

Opponents of the MAI painted apocalyptic pictures of a future under the agreement, denouncing it as "the biggest power play yet of the megacorporations" (Deal 1998, 7A). A top union official called the MAI "the next big international issue for the labor movement."[5] Nongovernmental organizations (NGOs) leveraged the resources of cyberspace to create a cascade of opposition to the MAI, charging that it would threaten democracy, national sovereignty, the environment, human rights, and economic development. "The opponents' decisive weapon is the Internet," noted Guy de Jonquières of the *Financial Times*. More than 600 organizations in nearly 70 countries expressed disapproval of the talks, many organizing and com-

---

1. There were around 900 BITs as of mid-1995 (UNCTAD, *World Investment Report 1995*, overview, 3).

2. WTO, *Annual Report 1996*, 44; UNCTAD, *World Investment Report 1995*, overview, table 1.

3. Over the period 1973–95, the estimated value of annual FDI outflows multiplied more than 12 times (from $25 billion to $315 billion) while the value of merchandise exports multiplied 8.5 times (from $575 billion to $4,900 billion) (WTO, *Annual Report 1996*, 46).

4. UNCTAD, *World Investment Report 1996*, Investment, Trade and International Policy Arrangements, overview, 6. See also USTR, *Annual Report 1996*, section V, "Other Multilateral Activities."

5. Peter Beinart, "The Next NAFTA," *The New Republic*, December 15, 1997, 4.

municating through e-mail and Web newsgroup postings.[6] In the MAI postmortem, some observers accused NGO "network guerrillas" of "ambush[ing]" the negotiations.[7]

But the role played by NGOs and their well-organized campaign in the demise of this effort was only part of the story. Many observers say that the difficulties of the talks themselves were just as—if not more—significant. For one thing, negotiators had substantive disputes about what the MAI should achieve. In addition, the participating governments were often unready or unable to make the commitments necessary to reach agreement, proposing hundreds of pages of exceptions to the general rules. As a result, the draft text of the MAI became watered-down, "a pale imitation of the document originally envisaged," noted *The Economist*.[8] Because of such challenges, some say the NGO protests were merely the final shots into an already sinking ship. "The MAI was a wake-up call," concluded Mike Moore, who would later head the WTO; "this is how *not* to do things."[9]

Regardless of the degree to which the NGOs were responsible for ending the talks, the fight invigorated and empowered many organizations, as seen in the 1999 protests against the WTO in Seattle, Washington. Yet even after the close of the MAI negotiations, the effort to create a global agreement on investment remained alive. Indeed, some believe that portions of the MAI may ultimately serve as a model for a WTO accord.

## International Investment

The MAI was largely aimed at establishing rules on FDI.[10] FDI occurs when an investor based in one country acquires an asset in another country with the intent to manage that asset. Such investment, a key pursuit of multinational corporations, includes mergers and acquisitions as well as "greenfield" investments (the creation of new facilities). Multinational enterprises invest abroad to get closer to their markets, acquire new technologies, form strategic alliances, and enhance competitiveness by integrating production and distribution. As Larry Bossidy, chairman and

---

6. According to NGOs, more than 600 organizations from over 70 countries signed a February 1998 joint statement opposing the MAI. Public Citizen, Friends of the Earth, and the Sierra Club press release, "International Coalition Launches Campaign Against the MAI," February 12, 1998, www.citizen.org.

7. Guy de Jonquières, "Network Guerrillas," *The Financial Times*, April 30, 1998, 20.

8. "The Sinking of the MAI," *The Economist*, March 14, 1998, 81.

9. Moore, quoted in Guy de Jonquières, "Convert to Free Trade Who Sees 'Liberalization Fatigue,'" *The Financial Times*, November 25, 1998, 7.

10. Its rules were meant to cover all types of international investment, including portfolio investment, real estate, intellectual property rights, rights under contract, and rights conferred by permits.

CEO of Allied Signal, explains: "To succeed in today's markets . . . a company cannot hope to sit back home in Dubuque making widgets and then export the finished goods to buyers abroad. . . . Either through affiliates or joint venture partners you need to be there, on the ground with local facilities. . . . To gain a foothold in an overseas market, you need to invest."[11]

Economists generally argue that FDI brings benefits to the countries that welcome it, such as technology transfer, higher wages for domestic workers, savings and capital formation, increased efficiency in production, lower prices, and higher-quality goods and services. Expanding from $25 billion annually worldwide in 1973 to more than $315 billion in 1995 when the MAI talks began, FDI is considered a critical engine of economic growth.[12] For example, in 1994, FDI in the United States supported nearly five million jobs. In addition, exports from US parent companies to their foreign subsidiaries accounted for approximately 25 percent of all US merchandise exports.[13]

The MAI rules were meant to be liberalizing—to remove existing government barriers and controls on foreign investment. Proponents of the MAI saw such liberalization as part of a global trend, as evidenced by 95 percent of the 599 changes to national regulatory FDI regimes over the period leading up to the talks (1991–96). These changes mostly involved opening industries that were previously closed to FDI, streamlining or abolishing approval procedures, and providing incentives for FDI.[14] However, many countries had done more to liberalize their trade regimes than their FDI policies.[15]

The idea of creating rules to protect FDI was not a new one. As already noted, more than 900 bilateral investment treaties had been signed throughout the world when the MAI negotiations began in 1995.[16] Most of these agreements were made between European and developing countries—fewer than 10 of the agreements were between two OECD nations. Indeed, as one observer noted, "Between OECD members, there are virtually no such agreements, since they are viewed as unnecessary" (Henderson 1999, 12).

---

11. Bossidy, quoted in US Council for International Investment, *A Guide to the Multilateral Agreement on Investment* (1996), as cited in Canner (1998, 658).

12. WTO, *Annual Report 1996*, 44. See also UNCTAD, *World Investment Report 1996*, xiv.

13. USTR, *1997 Trade Policy Agenda and 1996 Annual Report of the President of the United States on the Trade Agreements Program*, 142.

14. UNCTAD, *World Investment Report 1997*, overview, 10.

15. UNCTAD, *World Investment Report 1995*, overview, 3.

16. BITs are also known as investment promotion and protection agreements; 385 had been completed at the end of the 1980s. By the end of the 1990s, there were 1,857; at the end of 2002, 2,181 (UNCTAD 2000, iii; UNCTAD, *World Investment Report 2003*, overview, 7).

**Table 4.1  Growth in total number of bilateral investment treaties**

| End of year | Total number |
| --- | --- |
| 1959 | 1 |
| 1969 | 72 |
| 1979 | 165 |
| 1989 | 385 |
| 1999 | 1,857 |
| 2002 | 2,181 |

*Sources:* UNCTAD (2000, iii); UNCTAD, *World Investment Report 2003*, overview, 7.

Originating in Europe in the late 1950s, BITs covered market access and investor protection. Over the years, each developed country evolved its own model BIT. Generally, the host government (usually the developing country) agreed to treat foreign investors no less favorably than its own domestic investors, extending what is known as *national treatment*. The host government was also prohibited from discriminating among its foreign investors, as all were extended *most favored nation* (MFN) treatment. However, some BITs provided only MFN and not national treatment, allowing the host country to favor its own domestic firms over foreign investors.

In addition, BITs often included certain mandates for dealing with foreign investors, such as absolute protections against *performance requirements*—obligations placed on investors or their investments. For example, a government might impose a local content requirement, demanding that investors use a certain percentage of domestic inputs to achieve their output. BITs also provided guidelines on financial flows and guarantees on *expropriation*—the circumstances under which a government can deprive investors of their property. By the mid-1990s, European countries had completed more BITs than the United States, but US BITs were generally more comprehensive.[17]

The number of new bilateral investment treaties surged throughout the mid-1980s and into the 1990s as foreign investment continued to grow (see table 4.1). The pattern of these treaties began to change, as increasingly the agreements were made between two developing countries. Of the 180 BITs concluded in 1996, nearly a third were between developing countries, led by China, Chile, Algeria, and the Republic of Korea.[18]

---

17. The United States did not start its bilateral investment treaty program until 1982. According to Deputy USTR Jeffrey Lang, the United States had negotiated more than 40 BITs by 1998 (Lang 1998, 457). The US treaties dealt with both pre- and postestablishment issues, while European BITs generally covered only postestablishment issues.

18. UNCTAD, *World Investment Report 1997*, overview, 11.

In addition to these *bilateral* approaches to protect international investment, detailed *regional* investment provisions were featured in the 1992 North American Free Trade Agreement—negotiated by Canada, Mexico, and the United States. NAFTA's Chapter 11 was the first investment agreement involving more than two parties. As the OECD's Pierre Sauvé emphasizes, "NAFTA achieved a level of comprehensiveness in investment rule making that had never been done before, and it achieved that in a trade policy setting, affirming the close links between trade and investment—market access and market presence—in an integrating world economy."[19] NAFTA's Chapter 11 established an "investor-to-state" system of dispute settlement and banned a list of performance requirements, including export quotas. "From the perspective of an international investor," notes Stephen Canner of the United States Council for International Business, "NAFTA rules on investment were a quantum leap forward" (Canner 1998, 664).

Furthermore, NAFTA introduced a new dynamic to international investment talks: negotiation between two developed countries. Both the United States and Canada wanted to develop rules for their investments in Mexico, but in order to do so, they had to agree to abide by those same rules themselves. According to former USTR deputy general counsel Daniel Price, one of the principal US negotiators of NAFTA's investment provisions, "One of the interesting features of NAFTA is that it was really the first time that two developed countries—namely Canada and the United States—were forced by the negotiating dynamic to make the same commitments to each other that they had traditionally demanded of developing countries bilaterally."[20] To be sure, the United States and Canada had taken some steps toward investment liberalization in their free trade agreement of 1988, but the measures in NAFTA were more far-reaching.

Another regional initiative that reduced restrictions on FDI occurred in the context of efforts toward European integration.[21] The 1957 Treaty of Rome, which established the European Community, largely freed investment flows within Europe. Its rules permitted investors from European member states to establish and conduct business in other member states on a national treatment basis (see Chapter 2, Articles 43–48). The 1986 Single European Act further reduced barriers to intra-European investment,

---

19. Unless otherwise noted, all quotes from Pierre Sauvé come from a 2000 interview with Charan Devereaux.

20. Unless otherwise noted, all quotes from Daniel Price are from a 2000 interview with Charan Devereaux. Price co-chaired the US delegation with Bill Barreda, the Treasury Department's deputy assistant secretary for trade and investment.

21. Regional investment agreements were also under discussion among non-OECD countries. For example, talks about investment were part of the negotiations for the Mercosur agreement between Argentina, Brazil, Paraguay, and Uruguay.

and the 1992 Maastricht Treaty on the European Union gave the European Union new responsibilities over capital movements and treatment of new third-country investors.

Though NAFTA and the European agreements succeeded in making regional investment rules, attempts at developing a more global, *multilateral* approach toward FDI had not produced comprehensive results. The 1947 Havana Charter included provisions on foreign investment, but it never entered into force.[22] More recently, in 1992 the World Bank and the International Monetary Fund (IMF) completed a set of Guidelines on the Treatment of Foreign Direct Investment that endorsed national treatment and nondiscrimination among foreign investors. States and corporations thereafter regularly invoked the World Bank Guidelines as the standard for how developing nations should treat foreign capital to encourage investment, but they were not binding and did not rise to the level of a formal international agreement (Ratner 1998).

The idea of creating broad, enforceable, multilateral international investment rules was broached during the Uruguay Round of the GATT multilateral trade talks (1986–93), negotiations that included more than 100 countries. Initially, the United States had ambitious goals for investment issues in the Uruguay Round and hoped to establish comprehensive rules on FDI as a part of the talks. "Indeed," says the economist Edward M. Graham, "the original TRIMs proposals, originating in the US Treasury, were for an agenda almost as large in scope as that of the MAI."[23] However, developing countries were opposed to including such a broad discussion of investment.[24] They were suspicious of efforts to formalize investment rules, fearing that any binding policies would benefit wealthier nations and impinge on their own domestic sovereignty. Many developing countries saw the proposed international investment rules as potentially more intrusive than traditional trade rules. "Think about trade rules," says one US observer:

---

22. The 1947 Havana Charter was intended to create the International Trade Organization, but for various reasons (including its failure to be ratified by the US Congress) it never took effect. Instead, the GATT was born.

23. Unless otherwise noted, quotes from Edward M. Graham are from comments to Charan Devereaux, August 2003.

24. For example, in the lead-up to the March 1986 Punta del Este ministerial meeting that kicked off the Uruguay Round, the United States proposed the following investment text for the ministerial declaration: "the Contracting Parties should 1) seek to increase discipline over investment measures which divert trade and investment flows at the expense of other contracting parties, in contravention of a major objective of the GATT, i.e., 'the elimination of discriminatory treatment in international commerce,' and at the expense of sustainable economic growth and liberalization and 2) explore a broad range of investment issues in the negotiations, including: national/MFN treatment for new and established direct investment and the right to establish an investment" (GATT Doc. No. Prep. Com. 86/W/35, June 11, 1986; quoted in Gibbs and Mashayekhi 1998, 4).

Trade rules started as regulating border measures—namely, tariffs. You were free to regulate your domestic economy as you wished as long as you didn't discriminate at the border (i.e., MFN). What the Uruguay Round did was to bring international rules to bear on some areas of internal regulation (e.g., intellectual property, technical standards, and services). Countries were reluctant to do this in the area of investment, however, because investment rules—at least in the perception of the developing world—potentially affected a much broader range of economic issues.

Developing countries were especially nervous about investment rules that included strong dictates about national treatment. In a weaker version of national treatment, foreign investors, once established, would receive the same treatment as locally owned enterprises. Proponents of stronger provisions believed that foreign investors should have the same right to establish a business as local investors. Manmohan Singh, the finance minister who began India's economic liberalization in the early 1990s, explained that though several BITs had been signed granting national treatment to foreign investors, "We are not ready as yet for right of establishment. You have to remember our history as a colony. The East India Company came here as a trader and ended up owning the country."[25]

In the end, the Uruguay Round dealt with investment on a limited basis, primarily in the Agreement on Trade-Related Investment Measures (TRIMS) and the General Agreement on Trade in Services (GATS). A brief agreement (reproduced in appendix 4A), TRIMs applies only to "trade-related" investment measures in the context of manufactured goods. In other words, the agreement was designed to prevent governments from implementing investment policies that would create trade restrictions or distortions. To that end, TRIMs emphasizes that each member government must refrain from applying measures inconsistent with GATT Articles III and XI.[26] For example, according to the agreement, it is inconsistent with GATT Article III for governments to impose local content requirements on investors, such as requiring them to use a minimum level of local inputs.

---

25. Singh, quoted in "Does the WTO Need Special Rules for Foreign Direct Investment? Trade by Any Other Name," *The Economist*, October 3, 1998, 10.

26. GATT Article III, Paragraph 4: "The products of the territory of any contracting party imported into the territory of any other contracting party shall be accorded treatment no less favorable than that accorded to like products of national origin in respect of all laws, regulations and requirements affecting their internal sale, offering for sale, purchase, transportation, distribution or use. The provisions of this paragraph shall not prevent the application of differential internal transportation charges which are based exclusively on the economic operation of the means of transport and not on the nationality of the product."

GATT Article XI, Paragraph 1: "No prohibitions or restrictions other than duties, taxes or other charges, whether made effective through quotas, import or export licenses or other measures, shall be instituted or maintained by any contracting party on the importation of any product of the territory of any other contracting party or on the exportation or sale for export of any product destined for the territory of any other contracting party."

Developing countries were given five years to comply with TRIMs, and least-developed countries seven years.

Many say the TRIMs agreement proved to be "little more than an affirmation and modest strengthening of the status quo of the 1947 GATT" (Trebilcock and Howse 1999, 358). Indeed, most BITs were far more comprehensive than TRIMs. "This failure to engage on a wider set of issues during the Uruguay Round was one reason why the United States later insisted on the OECD as the venue for the MAI," says Graham (for background on the TRIMs negotiations, see Graham and Krugman 1999).

The second Uruguay Round agreement to deal with investment was GATS. According to the WTO, GATS is among the organization's most important agreements (WTO 2001, 1). It is the first and only enforceable set of multilateral rules covering trade and investment in the service sector—the largest and fastest-growing sector of the world economy. (Examples of services include banking, insurance, accountancy, telecommunications, tourism, health, and construction.) Trade in services was considered a "new issue" for GATT talks. Many developing countries initially opposed the inclusion of services in the Uruguay Round, because they viewed it as actually a means of bringing investment within the scope of GATT disciplines.[27] As one preparatory document noted,

> [S]ervices delivery, that is to say, trade in the sector, normally requires some form of investment in the place where the service is to be delivered. Consequently, an international trade regime on trade in services also implies a consideration of matters related to investments. This has in fact been one of the main reasons why the developing countries have been opposed to the inclusion of the services issue in the negotiations.[28]

The term *investment* is used sparingly in the text of GATS. One observer described the word as "pretty much taboo." Instead, the agreement refers to supplying a service through a "commercial presence"—that is, "any type of business or professional establishment" (Article XXVIII). Though establishing a commercial presence is recognized as one means by which services can be traded, members are not obliged to open all service industries to all comers. GATS is a "bottom-up" agreement, in that it applies only to activities specified in the agreement. (In contrast, a "top-down" agreement applies to all sectors unless they are listed as exceptions.) Developing countries were expected to liberalize in fewer sectors and types of transactions than the more industrialized countries. According to the WTO, it was this flexibility that put an end to the North-South controversy over services that marked the early years of the negotiations (WTO 2001, 7).

---

27. Developing countries that did not oppose discussing trade in services in the Uruguay Round included Jamaica, Chile, and Singapore.

28. Latin American Consultation Meeting on Multilateral Trade Negotiations, GATT Doc. No. PREP.COM (86)/W/44/Add.1, p. 33, as quoted in Gibbs and Mashayekhi (1998, 20, n. 8).

In the concluding phase of the GATS negotiations, conflict broke out between developed countries—more specifically, between Europe and the United States. Europeans proposed that cultural industries such as magazine publishing, motion picture production, and television broadcasting be exempted from provisions such as national treatment. They argued that such exemptions were vital to maintaining national cultural identity. The Americans refused to accept a cultural exception, arguing that Europe was merely trying to protect its own industries by discriminating against foreign firms.

In the end, GATS contained a number of obligations important to foreign investors, including national treatment, MFN status, and requirements to publish government rules on trade in services. Investors' concerns were not fully addressed, however; GATS did not contain a number of provisions found in most BITs. For example, national treatment in GATS applies only to the sectors listed in the agreement—and even in the listed sectors, further exceptions to national treatment can be made. In addition, GATS allows developing countries to impose performance requirements on investors. For these and other reasons, some investors found GATS unsatisfactory.

Given how investment fared in the Uruguay Round, the United States had little appetite for anchoring a new investment negotiation at the World Trade Organization. US officials feared that attempting to negotiate with more than 100 WTO members would stymie the process and result in a weak agreement. As US NAFTA Chapter 11 negotiator Daniel Price explains,

> The Uruguay Round demonstrated the difficulty of getting developing countries to sign off multilaterally on things that they had agreed to many times bilaterally. So the US negotiators were convinced—and I think they were right in this—that if they started the process in the WTO, they would not have ended up with the type of high-standards investment agreement that would have been very effective or that the business community as well as the governments would be happy with.

But if not at the WTO, where would investment discussions take place?

The International Monetary Fund, a specialized UN agency set up to promote the health of the world economy, was one possibility. In fact, the IMF tried to promote itself as a host for investment talks in the mid-1990s. As the central institution of the international monetary system, the IMF was the logical venue for any agreement that had bearing on capital flows, some officials argued. The IMF had little experience as a negotiating venue, however. Another possible home for the talks was the UN Conference on Trade and Development (UNCTAD). Established in 1964, UNCTAD aims at the development-friendly integration of developing countries into the world economy. But UNCTAD, too, had limited experience as a negotiating venue and was seen by some as a "hotbed of antimultinational fervor." A third potential host was the Organization for Economic Cooperation and Development.

## Enter the OECD

The Paris-based Organization for Economic Cooperation and Development was best known for providing research and analysis to its member countries on a variety of economic issues. Member countries included most of the developed world and a few developing countries—25 nations in all.[29] Originally formed to administer American and Canadian aid to Europe under the Marshall Plan after World War II, the OECD was a quiet organization of about 2,000 staff members and rarely claimed a role in the public spotlight.[30] "It was a talk shop," summarizes one observer.

In addition to other activities, the OECD worked to foster agreement on foreign investment issues, mostly through its Codes of Liberalization. The Code of Liberalization of Invisible Transactions was first adopted in 1951. In 1961, the OECD developed the Code of Liberalization of Capital Movements, an investment commitment that provided market access on a non-discriminatory basis for direct investments from one OECD country to another.[31] The responsibility for overseeing and further developing these two codes lay with the OECD Committee on Capital Movements and Invisible Transactions (CMIT).

In addition to the codes, the OECD Declaration on International Investment and Multinational Enterprises had been in place since 1976. While the codes were legally binding, the declaration was not. The declaration addressed the issue of national treatment, stating that foreign enterprises

---

29. As of 1994, the OECD members were Australia, Austria, Belgium, Britain, Canada, Denmark, Finland, France, Germany, Greece, Iceland, Ireland, Italy, Japan, Luxembourg, Mexico, the Netherlands, New Zealand, Norway, Portugal, Spain, Sweden, Switzerland, Turkey, and the United States. By 2001, OECD membership had increased to 30 countries with the addition of the Czech Republic (1995), the Republic of Korea (1996), Poland (1996), Hungary (1996), and the Slovak Republic (2000). Members share a commitment to the market economy, belief in pluralist democracy, and respect for human rights. See www.oecd.org.

30. The OECD was originally founded as the Organization for European Economic Cooperation (OEEC); the name was changed in 1961. According to the history of the OECD on its Web site, since then its "vocation has been to build strong economies in its member countries, improve efficiency, hone market systems, expand free trade and contribute to development in industrialised as well as developing countries" (see www.oecd.org).

31. Over time, the range and scope of the codes have increased. For example, the range of transactions subject to the Capital Movements Code was extended through successive revisions in 1964, 1984, and 1989. The Code of Liberalization of Current Invisible Transactions was extended in 1989. The MAI, if realized, would have superseded the codes and the Declaration on International Investment and Multinational Enterprises.

already established within a member's borders must be treated no less favorably than domestic enterprises. Further development of the declaration and other issues concerning the treatment of established foreign investors were overseen by the OECD Committee on International Investment and Multinational Enterprise (CIME). As one European analyst put it, "The OECD played a major role in the formation of international law with respect to investment" (Juillard 1998, 478).

Though they were wide-ranging, the OECD codes and the declaration had limitations. For example, some argued that the claim of the codes to be "legally binding" was rather hollow. Because they lacked dispute settlement mechanisms or enforcement procedures, members generally relied on peer pressure to encourage adherence to the codes. Moreover, they did not bind members to specific measures or programs of liberalization—it was up to each country to determine how, when, and how far to liberalize. As the codes evolved, member governments also retained the right to enter reservations to specific items, thereby limiting the degree to which they would put those commitments into effect.[32] Thus Canada exempted transport, energy, culture, telecommunications, and fisheries sectors from the codes (Dymond 1999, 27). Another limitation was that the codes applied only to national governments—for example, only to the federal and not the state or local government in the United States. And even at the federal level, they were binding in the United States only by executive order. Thus, any law that was enacted could override the OECD's codes. Finally, national treatment was addressed only in the OECD's Declaration on International Investment and Multinational Enterprises, which (as already noted) was not legally binding.

To address the last of these problems, in 1991 the CIME attempted to achieve a binding National Treatment Instrument (NTI). The discussions failed to produce an agreement, in part because some European governments insisted that the NTI cover law and policy at the level of subnational (provincial, state, and local) as well as national governments. The US CIME representatives opposed this, because any agreement binding state governments would meet resistance back at home. Another source of conflict was the insistence of some countries on excluding cultural industries—such as motion pictures and publishing—from the agreement.

The failed NTI talks left the CIME needing to find a new approach. The group began to explore the possibility of creating a broader instrument for investment protection, initiating a three-year feasibility study in June 1992. Involving a wider range of issues, delegates reasoned, would offer more opportunities for trade-offs and thus a better chance of success. Some note that by this logic, perhaps the entire investment agenda would

---

32. Where reservations were not in place, members committed to remove restrictions (in a "rollback"); they also agreed to a "standstill"—i.e., to rule out the introduction of new restrictions.

be more reasonably negotiated in the WTO, which provides an even broader set of issues for trade-offs (on the NTI, see Graham 2000, 20–22).

In 1995, the CIME and the CMIT committees prepared a report for the OECD Council's ministerial meeting. It argued that an MAI was "needed to respond to the dramatic growth and transformation of foreign direct investment (FDI) which has been spurred by widespread liberalisation and increasing competition for investment capital" (OECD 1995).

The country most actively lobbying for further OECD investment talks was the United States. "It was really a US initiative," says one observer. One of the US MAI negotiators, USTR's Joseph Papovich, recalls the rationale for pursuing negotiations at the OECD.

> Developing countries weren't willing to agree to the kinds of investment protection that should be provided to investors. The United States suggested to the Europeans that it would be a good idea to try to reach an agreement of like-minded countries on investment that was at a very high level, similar to what we seek in our bilateral investment treaties. That high-level standard investment agreement might then be used as a model for negotiating a multilateral investment agreement with developing countries.[33]

Many European countries were also interested in negotiating an OECD agreement. As some point out, institutional dynamics played a role in the OECD's appeal: EU member states may have favored a negotiation in that forum, where they could bargain on their own behalf, rather than at the WTO, where the European Union was represented as a single entity by the European Commission. In addition, an MAI made sense for a variety of substantive reasons. "With European bilateral agreements saying nothing about preestablishment and little on investment in the regional agreements that the EU had concluded, the EU saw real benefit in negotiating something on liberalization and investment in a multilateral agreement," one Austrian MAI negotiator remembers. "Because it was not possible in the Uruguay Round, they settled for the OECD as the second-best solution."

In short, the idea of negotiating an investment agreement at the OECD made sense to many participants, not least because OECD members were so deeply involved with foreign investment—the source of 85 percent of all FDI and home to 65 percent of the inflows.[34] OECD member governments also had a record of progressively freeing cross-border capital flows and reducing restrictions on inward FDI through agreements such as NAFTA and EU 1992. Moreover, OECD negotiations would not be constrained by the need to be trade-related, as they had been at the WTO. The

---

33. Unless otherwise noted, all quotes from Joseph Papovich come from a 2000 interview with Charan Devereaux.

34. Robert Ley, "The Multilateral Agreement on Investment: Some Questions and Answers," *Special Edition of the OECD Observer from the WTO Ministerial Conference in Singapore*, December 1996, 28.

OECD itself perceived a need to negotiate an MAI—the CIME and CMIT concluded in their report, "Foreign investors still encounter investment barriers, discriminatory treatment and uncertainties" (OECD 1995)—and had already laid the foundations for sponsoring it. Hosting the talks, wrote Robert Ley, head of the OECD's Capital Movements, International Investment and Services Division, "was a logical step to consolidating and completing the existing OECD instruments which had helped promote international investment and economic cooperation for many years."[35] Observers also note that the liberalization of external investment had generally progressed without arousing serious political opposition. The extensions made to the OECD Codes of Liberalization over the years had interested only a circle of experts.

Furthermore, some see broader, institutional concerns behind the OECD's interest in investment negotiations. An official closely involved in the talks points out that the MAI came at a time when the institution was going through "a bit of a midlife crisis" and was looking for a new project to reaffirm its legitimacy and relevance. In addition,

> The OECD was under a lot of stress on the budget front and the US had led discussions to slash the budget. One of the things the OECD decided to do was push the MAI, which was initially championed by the US government, and put a lot of resources into this as a way to perhaps endear itself to the government that had the greatest influence over its budgetary future.

Not all observers are persuaded by such institutional explanations, however—especially because OECD efforts are initiated when the representatives of member governments agree on a project, not at the will of the organization. It is not the Secretariat's role to have an opinion on whether to negotiate an agreement: Its role is to provide support for work pushed by member countries.

Some business groups came out early in support of an OECD investment agreement. The US Council on International Business (USCIB),[36] which is the US representative to the OECD's Business and Industry Advisory Council (BIAC), urged the OECD to move toward negotiating a wider investment instrument. In March 1995, the USCIB released a statement outlining what US businesses sought in an MAI. "For multinationals, investment was becoming as important, if not more important, than trade as a means of market access," says Steve Canner, USCIB's vice president for investment and financial services.

> Even though countries openly court foreign investment, many sectors are still closed. In addition, once you get into a market, you often find that governments

---

35. Ley, "The Multilateral Agreement on Investment," 28.

36. Founded in 1945 to promote an open world trading system, the USCIB had a membership of about 300 global corporations, professional firms, and business associations.

do things that make it inefficient and more expensive for corporations to operate. For example, a government might say to a corporation, "You have to produce your widgets here or you can't sell them in the local market" or "You must agree to export a certain amount from this facility which you otherwise would have exported from another facility." That disrupts your business plan. Many government mandates of performance requirements get in the way of doing business efficiently. Addressing these concerns was the key attraction to negotiating an MAI.[38]

Yet business community support for OECD investment talks did not run very deep, according to some observers, including Pierre Sauvé (described by some as an "internal critic" of the talks). At the time of the MAI negotiations, he was at the OECD's International Trade Directorate. "What makes the MAI such a fascinating story," says Sauvé, "is that the bureaucracies were proposing an agreement that the private sector in most countries was not necessarily calling for. The whole initiative could be described as a solution in search of a problem. Even in the private sector, almost the only business group that took an interest in the MAI was the USCIB, a business grouping with strong ties to both the State Department and the US Treasury (both of which tended to take the lead in international investment matters, with USTR traditionally assuming a secondary role) and the OECD." For example, before he became president of the USCIB in 1984, Abraham Katz had for three years served as the US ambassador (and State Department representative) to the OECD.

## The Lead-Up to the MAI Negotiations

A mandate to negotiate a Multilateral Agreement on Investment was expected to be approved by OECD ministers, but a statement was needed to kick off the talks. The wording of this report would frame the goals of the negotiations. The proposed agreement would focus on three areas: a broad multilateral framework of rules for investor protection, the liberalization of investment regimes, and the creation of effective procedures for dispute settlement. Unlike the previous OECD codes, the MAI was to be a freestanding international treaty "open to all OECD Members and the European Communities and to accession by non-OECD Member countries" (OECD 1995).

Disagreements arose over the draft report—some of the arguments were familiar. One EU-US conflict centered on the coverage of subfederal governments, such as those in US states and localities, Canadian provinces, and Australian states.[39] Another controversial issue was the treatment of

---

38. Unless otherwise noted, all quotes from Steve Canner are from a 2000 interview with Charan Devereaux.

39. "US Blocks OECD Investment Recommendation over Coverage Dispute," *Inside US Trade*, April 28, 1995.

regional economic integration organizations (REIOs), such as the European Union.

In April 1995, the United States refused to endorse the report kicking off the MAI negotiations, charging that it tilted too far toward the European Union on these issues; it gave its support after changes were made. OECD negotiators also agreed to a US request to change the name of the agreement from the Multilateral Investment Agreement (MIA) to the Multilateral Agreement on Investment (MAI). As one American put it, the abbreviation *MIA* has "unfortunate associations" with soldiers missing in action.[39] (Observers later commented that in Italian, the word *mai* means "never.") The CIME and CMIT report calling for the MAI negotiations specified that its goals were to

a)  set high standards for the treatment and protection of investment;

b)  go beyond existing commitments to achieve a high standard of liberalization covering both the establishment and postestablishment phase with broad obligations on national treatment, standstill, rollback, nondiscrimination/MFN, and transparency, and apply disciplines to areas of liberalization not satisfactorily covered by the present OECD instruments;

c)  be legally binding and contain provisions regarding its enforcement;

d)  apply these commitments to all parties to the MAI at all levels of government;

e)  deal with measures taken in the context of regional economic integration organizations;

f)  encourage conciliation and provide for effective resolution of disputes, taking account of existing mechanisms;

g)  take account of member countries' international commitments with a view of avoiding conflicts with agreements in the WTO such as GATS, TRIMs, and TRIPS; and with tax agreements; and similarly seek to avoid conflicts with internationally accepted principles of taxation. (OECD 1995)

In May 1995, with the approval of OECD ministers, officials announced the decision to begin talks on a Multilateral Agreement on Investment. Sir Leon Brittan, the European Commission's top trade negotiator, said the future agreement was the "biggest single step we can take to encourage growth and international economic relations" (quoted in Patel 1995, 2A). Attending the OECD meeting as an observer, WTO Director-General Renato Ruggiero privately cautioned ministers against bypassing the WTO.

---

39. "US Agrees to OECD Investment Mandate After Report Is Changed," *Inside US Trade*, May 5, 1995.

The MAI would not be truly multilateral, he said, unless non-OECD members were able to take part in drafting the document. Some suspected that developed countries would create an agreement that did not take the views of developing countries into account. OECD Secretary-General Jean-Claude Paye stressed that the ultimate objective of OECD members was to draw up an accord that could be universally accepted, an aim that implied the need to coordinate with the WTO "in due course," as well as to consult with non-OECD countries.[40]

US officials noted that their goal for the MAI was to get "high standards" through the OECD and then to "spread [the agreement] to countries in transition and developing countries, starting with dynamic Asian and Latin American countries." But European delegations insisted that they must be careful not to present a fully negotiated text to non-OECD countries on a take-it-or-leave-it basis.[41] "Rule number one of negotiating an agreement," emphasized one European observer, "is that you have to give all parties a sense of ownership over the process." As Brittan put it, "Our approach has always been that there should be parallel discussions in the WTO in order to involve the developing countries and not to present a treaty to them as a fait accompli."[42] Canada was supportive of such parallel talks, but European officials reported that the idea was cold-shouldered by the United States.

Some US observers countered that in fact, investment rules penned by richer countries in the form of BITs had frequently been signed by developing nations seeking to attract greater flows of international investment. "Some people nevertheless thought that developing countries would not agree to the same rules if they were packaged as part of the MAI," recalls US NAFTA investment negotiator Daniel Price. "I think that argument is a red herring. It has been demagogued both by developing countries and by critics of the MAI process, but it's really a false argument. The truly mistaken premise was that the like-minded countries would be able to reach agreement. By that I mean that divisions within the capital-exporting, developed world led to the demise of the MAI, not objections by developing countries."

---

40. Ruggiero's aides and Paye quoted in Jan Kristiansen, "OECD States Set Negotiations on Investment Treaty," Agence France-Presse, May 23, 1995.

41. US and European officials quoted in Jan Kristiansen, "OECD States Consider Investment Treaty," Agence France-Presse, May 23, 1995.

42. Brittan, quoted in "OECD Investment Pact 2: Accord Will Involve Non-Members," Dow Jones International News, May 23, 1995.

## The MAI Talks Begin

The MAI talks began in September 1995. Negotiators were aiming to draft the treaty by the May 1997 OECD ministerial (less than two years away), a deadline that would enable the MAI to be integrated into the 1999 WTO ministerial. A progress report on the negotiations would be issued at the 1996 OECD ministerial.

The negotiators met every six weeks or so at the OECD Secretariat in Paris. Frans Engering of the Netherlands Economic Affairs Ministry, described by one observer as "a consensus-seeking individual," served as chairman of the MAI Negotiating Group. The two vice chairs were Akitaka Sakai, from the Japanese Foreign Ministry, and Alan Larson, assistant secretary of state for economics and business at the US State Department. Sakai and Larson managed the process between meetings and made proposals to the negotiation group. Some viewed the two as representing the extreme positions in the OECD on investment liberalization, noting that "the US has been the strongest champion of open doors in investments while Japan is often criticized for being inhospitable to such flows."[43]

MAI working groups were established on a variety of investment-related issues, covering market access, investment protection, dispute settlement, institutional questions (such as the relationship with non-OECD members), special topics (such as privatization and monopolies), and financial matters. Composed of representatives from each OECD member country, each working group reported back to the MAI Negotiating Group. Most OECD committees had working groups, so this pattern was familiar, though some participants felt that the MAI talks involved an unusually heavy program of discussions.

A WTO representative attended all the meetings of the MAI Negotiating Group as an observer, and representatives of the IMF and the World Bank were sometimes present. MAI negotiators also met with members of the OECD Business and Industry Advisory Group "just about every negotiating session," according to USCIB's Steve Canner, usually just before the actual talks began. "We also had informal discussions," he adds; "occasionally we would submit papers, but it was basically an informal give-and-take." OECD officials also met with the OECD Trade Union Advisory Committee (TUAC), which is the interface for labor unions with the OECD and, like the BIAC, had consultative status with the OECD and its committees.

The core principles of the MAI were national treatment and MFN status. Because the MAI was a top-down agreement (unlike GATS, which was bottom-up), any investment area not specifically listed as an ex-

---

43. "OECD Mulls Multilateral Pact on Investments," *The Asian Wall Street Journal*, November 9, 1995, 1.

ception would automatically be subject to the MAI disciplines. In other words, exceptions would establish which MAI rights and obligations each country would adhere to. Country-specific exceptions would also be subject to "standstill" (i.e., exceptions could not be added later), and "rollback" (i.e., each member would phase out their exceptions over time).

Outside of this basic architecture, the visions of how the agreement would accomplish its goals diverged. Notably, European and US negotiators had different ideas about how to remove government controls and barriers on foreign investment and thereby liberalize it. As USCIB's Steve Canner recalls,

> From the outset, the US wanted to liberalize barriers. The Europeans, on the other hand, started out with the notion that liberalization might happen somewhere down the road, but initially you'd just follow the OECD model and freeze existing stuff into place. Liberalization would be a second phase of this exercise. This difference didn't come out immediately, but about a year into the negotiations. There was never any agreed model of how to do this. Do you follow the WTO trade model or the OECD model? So the whole concept of liberalization, how to achieve it, what time frame to use, and how to negotiate it was not well thought out or well planned. That was the first sign of trouble.

In addition, though OECD members were often referred to as "like-minded" countries, in fact their investment practices differed. Negotiators were not always willing or able to agree to changes in their own domestic policies; not surprisingly, each negotiating party wanted *other* countries to change or revise discriminatory practices, while leaving its *own* domestic laws and policies unaltered. "If any large negotiation is a matter of give-and-take," writes the economist Edward Graham (2000, 25), "the MAI negotiating parties seemed, almost from the beginning, prepared only to take, and to give nothing of substance in return." For example, as noted above, US negotiators worried that possible REIO exceptions in the MAI would become the basis for eroding the rights of US-based firms operating in Europe.[44] But their hopes to change this practice did not increase their willingness to discuss modifying US practices. One frustrated observer complained, "The United States was not about to change any of its own laws or regulations. So how could they expect others to liberalize?"

Another challenging issue was taxation. In January 1996, the MAI negotiators formed an expert group to determine what tax-related provisions should be included in the agreement. Ultimately, they chose to carve taxation issues almost completely out of the MAI (OECD 1996b, 2), deciding instead to "carve in" a small number of tax issues that could impede investment. Business was not happy with this choice. The International Chamber

---

44. Conversely, Europeans have repeatedly charged over the years that EU-based firms often do not receive as favorable treatment under US law as do US-based firms under EU law.

of Commerce (ICC) released a statement urging that these issues be included to prevent governments from using tax measures to circumvent MAI obligations: "Without the inclusion of taxation, or at least an anti-abuse clause, the MAI would set a lower standard than that of many existing bilateral investment treaties" (ICC 1998). The European-American Business Council, an association of 80 US and European companies, similarly declared its disappointment "that MAI negotiators have chosen to carve taxation issues almost completely out of the agreement. If the MAI does not require national treatment in taxation policy, governments will be able to use discriminatory tax measures to circumvent their MAI commitments. Without disciplines, taxation can effectively become expropriation."[45]

During the MAI talks, the passage of the US Helms-Burton Act created even more controversy. Formally known as the Cuban Liberty and Democratic Solidarity Act, the legislation was meant to tighten the economic noose around Cuba's President Fidel Castro by discouraging foreign investment in Cuba.[46] It was signed into law by President Clinton on March 12, 1996, after being overwhelmingly approved in both houses of Congress (74–20 in the Senate, and 336–86 in the House). The month before, Cuban MIG fighters had shot down two US civilian airplanes owned and piloted by members of a Miami-based Cuban exile group called Brothers to the Rescue, killing four.[47] Leading Republicans—including Majority Leader Robert Dole (KS), who led the fight for Helms-Burton in the Senate—had criticized Clinton for being too soft on Castro.

Helms-Burton allowed US nationals to sue in US courts foreign companies that "trafficked" in property expropriated by the Castro regime after it took power in 1959. In addition, US visas would be denied to individuals (and their families) who "trafficked" in expropriated property, including executives of foreign corporations with interests in that property.[48] Helms-Burton also barred certain products from entering the United States unless they were certified as non-Cuban in origin. US officials composed a statement to the MAI delegations that described how Helms-Burton would be implemented and enforced; it also noted that "The Pres-

---

45. The European-American Business Council, "Policy Statement on the MAI," March 1998.

46. Its sponsors were Senate Foreign Relations Chairman Jessie Helms (R-NC) and House International Relations Western Hemisphere Subcommittee Chairman Dan Burton (R-IN). The 1996 Iran-Libya Act, which penalized foreign companies that invested in Iran's or Libya's petroleum sector, also came under discussion at the MAI talks.

47. Brothers to the Rescue had earlier been the subject of two actions by the Federal Aviation Administration for violating Cuban airspace, contrary to FAA regulations; at least one incident involved an aircraft buzzing Havana and dropping anti-Castro leaflets.

48. Unusually, Helms-Burton defined expropriation retroactively. Thus Cuban Americans who were US nationals at the time the law entered into force could sue under Helms-Burton regardless of their nationality at the time their property was expropriated.

ident recognized the need to take strong measures after the recent downing of unarmed US civilian aircraft by the Cuban Government" and that the deadly incident "greatly increased the bipartisan sentiment on Congress to pass this tough legislation."[49]

Helms-Burton had a powerful impact on the MAI negotiations. Though President Clinton was able to waive some of the law's most controversial provisions, Europeans, Canadians, and many others were angered by its attempt to impose US laws on other nations and their companies. Such extraterritorial reach was antithetical to the US position regarding the MAI, they said. A spokesperson for Canada scolded the United States, "the leading proponent for an investment agreement with the highest possible standards," for having "taken actions, and ha[ving] incorporated into its law further measures that strike at the very core of these negotiations."[50] According to an observer, efforts by the chief US negotiator, Alan Larson, to argue that Helms-Burton was a legitimate security exception further chilled the talks as a whole. Canada called on negotiators to incorporate into the MAI language prohibiting boycotts of firms that invested in third countries. Most OECD members supported the Canadian proposal, but in the face of US opposition negotiators opted only to have an expert-level group study the issue. "Helms-Burton now seems to have become the political football in this negotiation," said one official. "It will come back to haunt us."[51]

The European Union, which had a complaint against Helms-Burton at the WTO, halted the action with the understanding that the law would be addressed in the MAI negotiations. However, it reserved the right to renew the case if necessary. "The Europeans were quite clear that despite the fact that they wanted to conclude the MAI, there had to be a solution on Helms-Burton either as part of the MAI or concomitant to it," says USTR's Joseph Papovich. The law kept on provoking debate and bad feeling as the talks continued. "Helms-Burton was incompatible with both the letter and the spirit of the MAI," Pierre Sauvé emphasizes. "This was a real problem throughout the negotiations. It provided a lot of ammunition against the US."

Another contentious debate arose concerning the treatment of cultural industries. In June 1996, France proposed a general exception for any measure that regulated foreign investment in order to preserve and promote cultural and linguistic diversity (Dymond 1999, 35). Without such

49. "United States Statement on the Helms-Burton Act," reprinted in *Inside US Trade*, March 22, 1996.

50. Quoted in "Canada Takes Initiative Against Cuba Sanctions in NAFTA, MAI," *Inside US Trade*, March 15, 1996.

51. "Canada Proposes OECD Disciplines on Extraterritorial Measures," *Inside US Trade*, July 5, 1996.

an exception, France worried that it would no longer be able to protect its domestic arts (through subsidies to filmmakers, for example) without being obliged to offer the same kind of help to nationals of all countries. Canada similarly favored insulating the cultural sector from MAI disciplines. US entertainment and media interests made the idea of a general exception unacceptable to the United States; one US official called it "a deal breaker."[52] Japan also objected to the cultural exception.

Despite these disagreements, the MAI talks pressed forward. In April 1996, in its report to the OECD Ministerial Council, the MAI Negotiating Group concluded, "Overall, the negotiations are on course. Most substantive issues have been examined and a framework for the MAI is evolving. . . . However, much remains to be done. . . . Some difficult choices remain" (OECD 1996a, 3). It reported that work on investment protection was proceeding rapidly, with key provisions on national treatment, MFN status, and transparency "well advanced"; the outline of a dispute resolution mechanism was likewise "in an advanced state of development."[53]

OECD ministers responded with a communiqué calling on the MAI to "aim at achieving a higher level of liberalization" and "engage in an intensified dialogue with non-member countries, in particular those interested in acceding to the MAI."[54] Brazil, China, and Lithuania were among the non-OECD countries that were invited to watch the negotiations. Before the talks ended, Argentina, Chile, Estonia, Hong Kong, Latvia, and the Slovak Republic would also participate as observers in the MAI Negotiating Group (Geiger 1998, 474). The question of the WTO's involvement in the process also continued to create debate. At the urging of France, Germany, and other nations, the OECD ministers affirmed their interest in examining investment issues in the WTO, committing to "begin an examination of trade and investment in the WTO and work towards a consensus which might include the possibility of negotiations."[55]

At the ministerial, observers noted that the United States had not yet paid its 1996 share of the OECD budget and owed about $50 million from 1995 (having paid only one-third of the total due). "One member country, and not the least member country, has not paid its dues," OECD Secretary-General Paye noted. "If mandates are given to the [OECD], then the means should come with it." The United States and other coun-

---

52. Quoted in "US Draws Hard Line Against Blanket Cultural Carve-Out in MAI," *Inside US Trade*, November 1, 1996.

53. OECD (1996a, 3), and William H. Witherell, director of financial, fiscal, and enterprise affairs at the OECD, "An Agreement on Investment," *OECD Observer*, 1996, 8.

54. OECD, "Communiqué: Meeting of the Council at Ministerial Level," Paris, May 21–22, 1996, in *OECD Observer*, June 16, 1996.

55. OECD, "Communiqué."

tries were also seeking a 2.5 percent reduction in the OECD budget for the 1996 fiscal year. [56]

By January 1997, the OECD Secretariat had produced a first draft consolidated text of the MAI that captured the state of the negotiations after 15 months of work.

## The Opposition Organizes

The North American Free Trade Agreement—specifically Chapter 11— was used as a point of reference in the MAI talks. "The MAI took its investment model from NAFTA," says Georgetown University Center for Public Interest Law's Robert Stumberg, a consultant to anti-MAI governors and members of Congress. "It was maybe 10 percent broader than NAFTA's Chapter 11."[57] NAFTA's importance to the MAI story extends beyond its contents, however. In the United States and Canada, a number of NGOs organized against NAFTA. The US Congress passed the agreement, but not without a heated battle that left environmental, labor, and consumer groups more engaged on the issues of trade generally (though not Chapter 11 specifically). North American NGOs apparently chose to focus this energy on the emerging MAI: "NAFTA on steroids" was one of the buzz phrases used to rally opposition to the agreement.

In February 1997, a citizen's watchdog group called the Council of Canadians procured a working draft of the MAI that was not intended for public distribution.[58] Some believe that this vanguard of the anti-NAFTA crusade in Canada was given the document by a Canadian government official. Many NGOs heralded the dissemination of the draft as the first step in tearing down the wall of secrecy cloaking the talks. Negotiators, though concerned, did not panic at the leak. According to one,

> It wasn't an enormous betrayal of confidence or devastating to the negotiating process. More than anything, it was embarrassing. The OECD, like the WTO, has

---

56. Quote from Paye and information about the OECD budget, "OECD Ministers Move Toward Trade and Investment Talks in WTO," *Inside US Trade*, May 25, 1996. As decided in 1994, OECD Secretary-General Jean-Claude Paye was replaced by Canadian Donald Johnston on June 1, 1996.

57. Unless otherwise noted, all quotes from Robert Stumberg are from a 2000 interview with Charan Devereaux.

58. According to the organization's own Web site, www.canadians.org, the group, founded in 1985, "is Canada's pre-eminent citizens' watchdog organization, comprised of over 100,000 members and more than 70 Chapters across the country. Strictly non-partisan, the Council lobbies Members of Parliament, conducts research, and runs national campaigns aimed at putting some of the country's most important issues into the spotlight: safeguarding our social programs, promoting economic justice, renewing our democracy, asserting Canadian sovereignty, advancing alternatives to corporate-style free trade, and preserving our environment."

a policy of restricting certain documents, and who knows, maybe the days are numbered for that process. So suddenly, this document appeared on the Internet—everybody had a copy. It was complicated by the fact it did not remain the right version for long. At each monthly meeting, pieces of the text were renegotiated intensively while the NGOs were still wanting to talk about this document that was no longer relevant.[59]

The groups opposing the agreement included Friends of the Earth, the Preamble Center for Public Policy, the International Forum on Globalization, the Third World Network, Oxfam, Amnesty International, the Sierra Club, and Global Trade Watch, a division of Public Citizen. Some labor unions and politicians began to take note of the negotiations. Pat Buchanan called the MAI the next great economic struggle, and Ross Perot's Reform Party opposed the plan.[60]

One of the primary tools employed in the organizing effort against the MAI was the Internet. In addition to creating a profusion of Web sites— more than 1,000 protesting the MAI—NGOs built electronic mailing lists and used e-mail to drum up support among their constituencies. "Being able to organize this way was tremendously important," says Margrete Strand of Public Citizen's Global Trade Watch. "It provided ways for meeting and connecting our activists. It helped organize the movement."[61]

Even as news about the MAI ricocheted across the Internet, it was barely noticed in the elite US press. Though stories appeared in the *Financial Times*, the *Journal of Commerce*, and the *Economist* during the lead-up to the MAI talks and the first two years of the negotiations, the *New York Times*, the *Washington Post*, the *Christian Science Monitor*, *USA Today*, the *Wall Street Journal*, and the *Los Angeles Times* mentioned the negotiations briefly if at all.[62] In response to the lack of coverage, the International Forum on Globalization (IFG) raised money to purchase full-page ads in the *International Herald Tribune* and the *New York Times* asking the bold question, "Top Secret: New MAI Treaty, Should Corporations Govern the World?" Strand reflects,

59. The OECD has since made available a large quantity of documents related to the MAI negotiations. See www.oecd.org.

60. Peter Beinart, "The Next NAFTA," *The New Republic*, December 15, 1997, 4.

61. Unless otherwise noted, all quotes from Margrete Strand are from a 2000 interview with Charan Devereaux.

62. This description of news coverage is based on Lexis-Nexis and Factiva database searches. A story about FDI in *The Christian Science Monitor* mentioned the MAI talks (David Francis, "Business Goes Global as Investment Booms," November 17, 1996, 1), and two short articles appeared in *The Wall Street Journal* (Eduardo Lachica, "OECD Nations Ask Outsiders to Join Investment Treaty," November 9, 1995, A17; "EU Official Proposes Talks on Global Investment Pact," February 1, 1995, A7).

Part of what we had to face was that the big papers and the large media did not cover the MAI at all. They didn't even mention that it was being negotiated or that there was all this activity going on against it. So we had to find a way to get to people and inform them about what was gong on. Which is why the Internet became so important—because people couldn't just pick up a copy of the local paper and read about it.

In other countries, the MAI was covered more widely. In Canada, for example, a front-page headline declaring "Treaty to Trim Ottawa's Power" ran in the Toronto *Globe and Mail* in April 1997, just before elections.[63]

Perhaps the most politically charged accusation made by the NGOs was that the talks were not inclusive—that they were taking place largely in secret, without public participation or scrutiny. This argument gathered force and was repeated by the mainstream press. Lori Wallach of Public Citizen was quoted as saying that there was no way the MAI would pass "the Dracula test," because it couldn't stand the light of day.[64] NGOs were incredulous that the business community had been involved in the talks all along, while representatives of nonprofits and other interest groups had no role at all. Strand explains, "The fact that business had a seat at the table and we didn't—I think it raised the stakes and got both NGOs and activists incredibly angry. Whatever happened to democracy?"

To underscore the lack of a democratic process, NGO representatives and Web sites often cited a characterization of the MAI attributed to WTO Director-General Renato Ruggiero: "We are writing the constitution of a single global economy." If such a sweeping document was under negotiation, MAI opponents said, why was participation limited? Ruggiero's quotation was picked up by journalists, appearing in the *Wall Street Journal*, the *Nation*, the *Jakarta Post*, the *Toronto Star*, the *Guardian*, and elsewhere.[65] The WTO responded in February 1998 with a press release:

> In recent days a number of news organizations have run stories containing an erroneous quote linking WTO Director-General Renato Ruggiero with the negotiations for a Multilateral Agreement on Investment. This erroneous statement has been supplied by a number of special interest groups which oppose the MAI. . . . On 16 January in London, Mr. Ruggiero gave a speech at Chatham House in which he quoted John Jackson, the highly respected law professor from the University of Michigan. "John Jackson has described the multilateral trading system

---

63. Laura Eggertson, "Treaty to Trim Ottawa's Power," *The Globe and Mail* (Toronto), April 3, 1997, A1.

64. For example, see Paul Magnusson and Stephen Baker, "The Explosive Trade Deal You've Never Heard Of," *Business Week*, February 9, 1988, 51.

65. For example, see George Melloan, "Crony Capitalists Will Cheer for the Seattle Zanies," *The Wall Street Journal*, November 2, 1999, A27 ("MAI, in case you missed the excitement last year, refers to the Multilateral Agreement on Investment, once described by former WTO Secretary General Renato Ruggiero as 'the constitution for a global economy' ").

as a 'constitution' for the world economy." At no point in that speech, nor in any other, did Mr. Ruggiero make a reference to the MAI and its role in the global economy.[66]

According to an UNCTAD press release, in an October 1996 speech to the UNCTAD Trade and Development Board, Ruggiero said of the multilateral trade order, "We are no longer writing the rules of interaction among separate national economies. We are writing the constitution of a single global economy."[67] But he was speaking of the multilateral trade order, not the MAI.

Not just concerned about secrecy and democracy, NGOs criticized the MAI generally as dramatically skewed toward protecting investors. They argued that through their right to sue national governments under the agreement's investor-to-state dispute settlement procedures, corporations would gain power and threaten domestic laws. Robert Stumberg notes that for this and other reasons, the MAI "makes previous sovereignty debates look like parlor conversations."[68]

Environmental groups were particularly fearful that corporations could use the MAI to strike down environmental laws and regulations. A frequently invoked example was a complaint brought against the Canadian government under NAFTA's Chapter 11. The Ethyl Corporation of Richmond, Virginia, claimed that a bill passed by the Canadian parliament banning the gasoline additive MMT (methylcyclopentadienyl maganese tricarbonyl) violated NAFTA and was tantamount to expropriation. Because Ethyl's Canadian business consisted of importing MMT into Canada, blending it with fuel, and then distributing that blend nationally, the ban effectively prevented the company from conducting its business. Though the impetus for the bill came from the Canadian Environmental Ministry, the parliament did not impose an outright ban on the use of MMT on environmental grounds; instead, it disallowed interprovincial trade of the additive. Technically, the Ethyl Corporation could have manufactured MMT in each of the Canadian provinces, but the costs of doing so were prohibitive. In addition to its NAFTA complaint, Ethyl brought a Canadian court case arguing that the ban violated the country's laws that govern interprovincial

---

66. WTO press release, Press/91, "WTO Denies Claims by Special Interests Linking Ruggiero to MAI," February 17, 1998. For the speech, characterizing the multilateral trading system as intended to increase the scope of national treatment and MFN status, see Renato Ruggiero, "The Multilateral Trading System at 50," address to the Royal Institute of International Affairs, London, January 16, 1998.

67. UNCTAD press release, "UNCTAD and WTO: A Common Goal in a Global Economy," TAD/INF/PR/9628, October 8, 1996, www.unctad.org.

68. Peter Beinart, "The Next NAFTA," *The New Republic*, December 15, 1887, 4.

commerce and seeking $251 million in restitution. In July 1998, before the NAFTA complaint could enter the dispute settlement process, the Canadian government settled with Ethyl for $13 million (for a thorough discussion of the case, see Soloway 1999). More important, in the eyes of many observers, the MMT ban was repealed.

Though the case was not formally decided in Ethyl's favor, a number of MAI opponents saw the case as a harbinger of things to come. The MAI, they argued, would allow foreign investors to seek compensation for "regulatory takings"—when a host government reduced the value of an asset through regulation. In the words of a Friends of the Earth policy paper, the MAI "empowers foreign corporations with a new avenue for challenging environmental laws" (Vallianatos 1998, 14). Opponents argued that the agreement would undermine health and safety laws around the world: Countries would resist banning dangerous products out of fear they could be sued by foreign companies hurt by such regulations.

Some observers—including Daniel Price, who negotiated Chapter 11—point out that the mere lodging of the Ethyl complaint does not demonstrate that the case was legitimate or that the NAFTA rules were problematic. Price says, "The possibility that a case can be brought against the United States or Canada can't be used as an indictment of the rule. Cases—even frivolous cases—are brought all the time in the domestic legal system. The rules are sufficient to separate meritorious claims from frivolous claims." He adds, "The track record under NAFTA to date hardly demonstrates that arbitration tribunals have overstepped their bounds in protecting the rights of investors. To the contrary, the evidence to date shows that tribunals have taken a reasonable, balanced, and judicious approach in interpreting and applying the NAFTA investment provisions."

Even those with substantive criticisms of the MAI questioned the deployment of the Canadian case to illustrate the agreement's dangers. Stumberg faults "the American NGOs," which "went off citing this as the death of democracy in the United States. You don't get that from the Ethyl case." US officials also found the campaign troubling. As Papovich remembers:

> We thought that the concerns being expressed by NGOs were exaggerated and that view was confirmed when the Canadians settled the Ethyl case in provincial litigation and NGOs blamed NAFTA. In our view, even if there had been no NAFTA, Canada would have settled because they had acted in a manner inconsistent with their own interprovincial rules. That was the basis of the decision. NAFTA was irrelevant except that the complainant had chosen also to bring a corresponding complaint under the NAFTA "investor-to-state" dispute settlement provision. So, I believe the NGOs were grossly exaggerating or even distorting the situation.

Nevertheless, the core question—how the MAI would ensure that governments could exercise their standard regulatory powers without being charged with expropriation and then sued for compensation—continued to cause debate.[69]

NGOs brought up a host of other worries about the MAI as well, including its potential implications for human rights. Though few human rights organizations were involved in the initial campaign, some criticized the MAI for increasing investor rights without adding to investor responsibilities. The MAI would spell an end to boycotts and trade sanctions against countries that violated human rights standards, opponents declared. "Had the MAI been in force in the early 1980s," argued a Sierra Club publication, "there would have been no international sanctions against South Africa under apartheid, and Nelson Mandela might still be in jail."[70] MAI supporters found such claims incredible.

In addition to NGOs, some US states' rights groups, state attorneys general, and, most notably, the Western Governors' Association expressed concerns about the MAI. Robert Stumberg coauthored the MAI report for the Western Governors' Association, and he recalls that when he first read the draft text of the MAI, he "was just astonished. . . . It embodied a breathtaking scope of constitutional reform." The Western Governors' Association concluded that while the MAI might foster investment activity, it "may also have the effect of eroding the sovereignty of state governments."[71] According to Stumberg's report, the agreement had the potential to limit state policies favoring local businesses and to limit state use of investment incentives and performance requirements (Stumberg, Singer, and Orbuch 1997).

The early NGO efforts were largely a North American phenomenon. As the organizing effort against the MAI became more international, the lead NGOs created smaller, private electronic mailing lists for the core organizers of the various country-based campaigns. Again, according to Margrete Strand, the cyberconnection was essential: "That's where we would do our strategizing. Conference calls and international meetings are really expensive and hard to organize. It was cheaper and more effective to do it through the Internet." Some note that these acts of international coordination were unusual—NGOs have traditionally worked in their own domestic spheres.

---

69. Cases brought under NAFTA's Chapter 11 continued to cause controversy after the MAI talks had ended. In the most publicized case, Methanex, a Canadian methanol producer, sought nearly $1 billion over a California decision to ban the use of its methanol-based gas additive as harmful to the environment.

70. Paul Rauber, "All Hail the Multinationals: The Secret Trade Deal That Corporations Hope You Never Hear About," *Sierra Magazine*, July/August, 1998, 16.

71. See Western Governors' Association, Resolution 97-010 on the Multilateral Agreement on Investment and Implementation of Trade Pacts, June 24, 1997.

## The OECD's Response

The reaction to this growing protest was surprise and, according to many, disbelief. The scale of the international grassroots fight was unprecedented against an economic agreement, observers said. While NGO-led protests had previously occurred domestically and regionally around trade and investment (as seen with NAFTA), international efforts (such as the Uruguay Round of GATT talks) had never been targeted with such ferocity.

The OECD was unprepared for such vehement NGO opposition; its officials did not expect to have to sell the MAI politically. "I think they thought it was going to be a slam dunk," says the USCIB's Steve Canner. "The OECD had been working on this stuff for years. They were all like-minded countries. What was there to worry about?" Previous OECD work on investment had been more akin to academic exercises, drawing the attention of only a circle of experts. Moreover, OECD officials believed they were undertaking an important, valuable exercise and were surprised by the angry response. As Papovich explains, OECD negotiators and officials "tend to be lawyers and economists who believe free trade is good for countries and investment liberalization is similarly good. Most trade negotiators were unprepared for dealing with people who fundamentally opposed what they did."

One way they responded to the NGOs was by opening up the MAI process to some extent. The first groups to oppose the OECD investment talks were Canadian. When the Canadian MAI negotiators approached Negotiating Group Chairman Frans Engering about the protests back at home, he took the situation seriously. Engering convened a meeting to discuss the appropriate response. At the May 1997 OECD ministerial, the initial target date for completion of the MAI, the talks were extended for one year with special instructions to consult with "civil society." In October 1997, the OECD held an informal consultation with representatives of about 50 NGOs.

In hindsight, one European negotiator believes that the OECD NGO consultations harmed the MAI effort because the meeting became an opportunity for protesters to make contacts and organize further. Indeed, he suggests that

> involving the NGOs may have been what sank the MAI. One personal feeling I have is that by inviting them to Paris in [the fall of] 1997, many of them met for the first time. They exchanged their cards. We helped them establish the connections, the network that in the end would bring down the MAI. When they came together nobody knew the other guys. I saw them in the antechamber saying, "Oh, that is you."

During the consultation, OECD officials and negotiators found many NGO arguments unfair. For one thing, OECD officials objected to their characterization of the talks. "Negotiations were not conducted in secrecy," insists Rainer Geiger, the OECD's deputy director for financial, fiscal, and enterprise affairs. "Ministers, not bureaucrats, decided to launch the process. Public information was available early in the process and business and trade unions were informed and consulted through their advisory bodies at OECD. Nonmember countries were aware of the MAI negotiations through regular briefings after each meeting of the Negotiating Group and were consulted through regional meetings held in Latin America, Asia, and Africa" (Geiger 1998, 474).

In addition, the outset of the talks had been announced with press conferences and public statements, though few press outlets had chosen to report on them. "Contrary to what has been alleged," one negotiator stresses, "the possibility that such negotiations would take place in the OECD, as also the decision to launch them, were entirely public. Although it can now be seen that a wider process of publicity and consultation would have been advisable, neither the governments concerned nor the OECD engaged in concealment at any stage" (Henderson 1999, viii). Many of the NGOs' allegations about the substance of the MAI were also viewed as hyperbolic and lacking any analytical rigor. However, MAI participants say that more reasonable NGO positions were taken into consideration. Consultations with environmental and consumer groups "helped identify critical issues and improved the draft," according to one observer.

Though some NGO representatives were interested in proposing changes to make the MAI more environmentally friendly, most apparently were not. Negotiators and other officials were frustrated by what they saw as an outright effort to kill the talks rather than to improve the agreement with productive suggestions. One observer remembers a US NGO representative telling negotiators, "We killed fast track and we're going to kill the MAI."

NGO leaders agree that the aim of many protesters was to stop the talks. "The majority of the NGOs decided to take a hard-line position saying 'We oppose these negotiations altogether,' " says Public Citizen's Margrete Strand. After meeting with OECD officials, the NGOs released a joint statement in October 1997; the signatories, about 600 organizations from around the world, called for the negotiations to be suspended while a comprehensive assessment of the social, environmental, and development impact of the MAI was conducted and meetings and hearings were held for the public.[72] The OECD made an attempt to continue the discussions, suggesting another meeting in January 1998, but NGO representatives declined the invitation.

Domestically, US government negotiators also met with NGO representatives—and continued to do so regularly, usually once every three months. Their discussions, which typically lasted a few hours, took place

---

72. Joint NGO Statement on the Multilateral Agreement on Investment (MAI), NGO/OECD Consultation on the MAI, Paris, October 27, 1997.

at the USTR or the State Department. The group sometimes included officials from the Commerce Department, the EPA, and the Justice Department as well. Outside of the meetings, Friends of the Earth and Public Citizen's Global Trade Watch hosted a US NGO working group on the MAI. Strand stresses their cooperation; when preparing for the government consultations, "We would always try to get members of the working group to go so that we could show the power as a coalition to the State Department and USTR. Obviously, it was better if we had the AFL-CIO, the Sierra Club, and other big groups in the room with us." Among the other NGOs that attended the meetings were the Alliance for Democracy, the Defenders of Wildlife, the Center for International Environmental Law, the Preamble Center, the Center of Concern, the National Family Farm Coalition, and the National Wildlife Federation.

None of the participants found the US domestic consultation process to be completely satisfying, however. On the NGO side, many felt the discussions were disingenuous. The government representatives were "very straightforward, as much as they could be," Strand says. "They're nice, friendly people. It's not like the meetings were hostile. It was a collegial forum where they pretended to seek our advice and get our input. Despite the friendly nature of the meetings though, it was clear that they didn't plan to take into account any of our concerns." On the government side, officials felt that the NGOs had little constructive advice to offer on modifying the agreement. Joseph Papovich (whose friendly and open demeanor won him the nickname "Uncle Joe" from the NGO representatives) describes the consultations as

> a very interesting process. The NGOs were very negative. They had a great deal of antipathy towards the MAI, so they really wouldn't give us much advice. They would ask us questions, some substantive questions, but they would rarely say, "We don't think you should do this," or "We don't think you should do that." It was a very strange consultation process[;] . . . they weren't interested in telling us, "Well, if you remove this provision the agreement might be more tolerable." They didn't want there to be an MAI—period!

In the meantime, US NGOs continued to organize public demonstrations against the MAI in Washington, DC, including rallies on Capitol Hill. In March 1998, the US House International Relations Subcommittee on International Economic Policy and Trade held a hearing on the MAI. Chairwoman Ileana Ros-Lehtinen (R-FL) commented that "for the last two years, there has been little, if any, substantive consultation with the Congress" on the negotiations.[73] In fact, as Graham notes, "the executive

---

73. Prepared statement by Representative Ileana Ros-Lehtinen, "Multilateral Agreement on Investment: Win, Lose, or Draw for the US?" hearing before the Subcommittee on International Economic Policy and Trade of the House Committee on International Relations, 105th Congress, 1st session, March 5, 1998.

branch established no process for consultation with Congress on the desirability of MAI negotiations" before the talks got under way. As a result, a number of legislators first learned about the MAI from NGOs (Graham 2000, 19).

MAI proponents continued to be frustrated by the lack of a coherent response to the charges levied by the NGOs. In the opinion of Canner,

> that was absolutely critical to the demise of the MAI. Most important and discouraging was that when the NGOs would make these silly statements—and I'm being generous in saying silly—there was no pushback from governments. They could have posted something on the Web. They could have had administration spokesmen dealing with this in the daily press briefings by the USTR and the State Department. But they chose not to take them on head-on.

Political controversy over the MAI was also growing in France. In French, the agreement is abbreviated AMI, which also means "friend." Opponents of the agreement mocked the acronym as a misnomer, saying "L'AMI c'est l'ennemi" (The friend/MAI is the enemy). One focus of criticism in France was the MAI's effect on culture. The French cultural minister, Catherine Trautmann, called the MAI

> shocking because it considers artistic works only as investments and not as creations. The mechanism the MAI would put into place would end up dismantling national policies supporting the arts and torpedo the creation of a European cultural policy. If MAI is applied to culture, it would upset everything—the system of supporting artistic works, distribution subsidies, the quota system for visual and musical works, and bilateral agreements we have signed with many other countries.[74]

## Back at the Table

Some say that even before the NGO effort had peaked, the MAI was already facing the beginning of the end. "The growing pressure from civil society simply exacerbated the differences of opinion within the OECD," observed an official of the Belgian Foreign Trade Ministry (Kobrin 1998, 97). For example, disagreement had surfaced concerning how to introduce MAI provisions to safeguard environmental and labor standards. Pushed by the United States, Austria, and Britain, labor and the environment became major issues by the end of 1997. Opponents to incorporating these matters into the MAI included Australia and New Zealand as well as South Korea and Mexico. Some consensus emerged in the form of an agreement to maintain domestic environment and labor standards, an ap-

---

74. Trautmann, quoted in "France Wants Culture Out of OECD Investment Accord," *Reuters News*, February 14, 1998.

proach modeled on NAFTA.[75] But disputes over a central issue—whether this commitment not to lower standards would be a binding obligation—continued.

Further complicating the talks was the continuing absence of clarity regarding the most basic goals of the MAI effort. "Even through the final 12 months there were differing views about the ultimate objective," recalls one negotiator. Some parties wanted to focus on improving the standard of investment protection among OECD countries. Others believed that the negotiations should concentrate on creating a model agreement for developing countries, not on the investment relationship among OECD members.

According to some government officials, the negotiations also suffered from a lack of assistance from business. While business leaders thought the MAI was a good idea, some say, actual support for the agreement was anemic at best. As one European negotiator notes,

> In contested situations, governments are only effective if they are seen as being between different sides of the argument. If you have business on one hand calling for liberalization and if you have civil society on the other saying, "We want nothing but regulations on the environment," then government can say, "We'll try and find a middle ground." But with business saying nothing, we had only the concerns of civil society. So government came by definition to be seen taking an extremist view from the point of view of what was expressed in the public.

Others, including Daniel Price, see this as an unfair mischaracterization of business's role: "The business community was solidly behind the effort to negotiate the MAI. The fact is that international investment rules had never been particularly controversial. There was an expectation that the United States would strongly advocate the same position that it had during the negotiation of bilateral investment treaties and NAFTA. The business community believed that this was well-trodden ground not requiring any special advocacy on their behalf."

Yet after a few years of MAI negotiations, business clearly was questioning what kind of benefits the agreement could offer. At a January 1998 consultation, members of the Business and Industry Advisory Committee to the OECD criticized the proposed MAI as watered-down, pointing out that OECD members were refusing to liberalize their investment restrictions, that taxation should be included in the agreement, that environmental and labor standards were problematic, and that protections for expropriation were insufficient. While noting that business "was very interested

---

75. A 1998 OECD press release declared, "Ministers note the increased convergence of views on the need for the MAI to address environmental protection and labor issues, and the broad support for including a strong commitment by governments not to lower environmental or labor standards in order to attract or retain an investment." Press release, OECD Meeting at Ministerial Level, Paris, April 27–28, 1998, Ministerial Statement on the Multilateral Agreement on Investment (MAI), www.oecd.org.

in seeing this project succeed," the chairman of the BIAC delegation, Herman van Karnebeek, said that there were disturbing signs that many elements business hoped to see in the final agreement might not be attainable: "What then, we are beginning to ask ourselves, is in the MAI for us?" (ICC 1998). There were also worries that the agreement might create costly new barriers to FDI.[76] "With all the opposition [from environmentalists and states' rights activists] the question was, 'why expend all this energy?' " one business adviser asked (Maggs 1998, 3A).

Within the lead US government agencies, too, the purpose of the MAI was being debated. State Department officials envisioned the MAI as a freestanding agreement administered by the OECD, but USTR had concerns about this vision: For example, how would dispute settlement really work at the OECD? USTR was also concerned that the MAI would not attract the support needed to win approval in the US Senate. European negotiators noted the growing tensions between the State Department and USTR.

Some wondered if the MAI was truly a priority of the US administration. "That's really the first question to ask," says one observer. "Were they ever serious about this negotiation?" While the MAI was cleared by the White House and organized and monitored through an interagency process, critics held that no senior official ever really owned the negotiation and that the administration never geared up its lobbying effort. One source has the sense that "there was really no commitment from the top." In France, the MAI—especially its effect on culture—was the subject of widespread public debate. The Communists and the Green Party were especially vocal, and actors as well as members of political groups spoke out against the agreement. Some believe that the extent of the opposition to the MAI surprised and disconcerted political leaders. "It led them to question a commitment, and a process, which in the earlier stages they had barely noticed," says one MAI participant (Henderson 1999, viii).

Others suggest that the lack of high-level involvement was a reflection more of institutional arrangements at the OECD than of domestic leadership. The MAI talks took place among mid-level civil servants who, unlike more senior officials, did not have the authority or political power needed to make broad concessions and trade-offs. In addition, they did not have the ability to sell the MAI politically back at home. As Graham notes, "Most of the persons involved in the preparations for the talks were fairly junior and lacked experience with multilateral negotiations. Many were investment specialists in various ministries. . . . Often these specialists did not have easy access to higher-level officials inside their own governments." Indeed, the lack of commitment and participation of top political

---

76. Guy de Jonquières, "Worries over Planned Investment Accord," *The Financial Times*, Janu-ary 19, 1998, 5.

leaders "may have been critical to the outcome of the MAI negotiations" (Graham 2000, 17).

The OECD did hold a key MAI negotiation with senior officials. This high-level meeting was held in February 1998—just a few months before the annual OECD ministerial. In the lead-up to the talks, one European negotiator explains, participants knew that the MAI "was rather bogged down, but everybody thought we had a fighting chance. This was the last window of opportunity to get it through. Everybody tried to come up with some compromises, ways of creating value, or third ways to overcome the problems." Many negotiators hoped the meeting would help drive the MAI to completion by the upcoming ministerial.

But in a press conference just before the February meeting began, USTR Charlene Barshefsky declared, "We do not envision signing onto any agreement this April." Barshefsky called the MAI "unbalanced" and "prejudicial," saying it would require "very substantial, very substantial work to make it something the US will sign." "It's just not good enough yet," Barshefsky told reporters. "We have shown no hesitation in walking away from agreements that aren't very good."[77] Barshefsky noted that other OECD countries might proceed without the United States to try to wrap up a deal. But Prime Minister Lionel Jospin of France said there would be "no agreement" on the MAI if the French film industry was not given protection from US imports.

Despite these strong statements, OECD Secretary-General Donald Johnston said he remained "optimistic" that agreement would be reached by the OECD ministerial as planned.[78] But when officials arrived in Paris for the February meeting, the talk was about Barshefsky's press conference. "Have you heard what Barshefsky said?" one European Commission representative was overheard saying. "This thing is gone." Barshefsky's statement "overshadowed this last window of opportunity," according to an observer. Work continued, however. In the summary report of the February 16–17 meeting, the "Chairman's Conclusions" note: "The High Level Meeting made progress on the issues of political importance. . . . Delegations are ready to intensify their efforts to reach agreement on all outstanding issues" (OECD 1998a, 5).

In March 1998, Frans Engering announced that he would no longer serve as chairman of the MAI Negotiating Group as of May 1 (OECD 1998b, 3).

---

77. Barshefsky is quoted in a number of wire reports of February 13, 1998; see, e.g., "France Says Not Certain of OECD Deal by April," Reuters News; "US Barshefsky Says US Not Ready to Sign MAI by April Deadline," AFX News; "USTR Barshefsky—2: MAI 'Not Good Enough' and 'Unbalanced,' " Dow Jones Newswires; "USTR Barshefsky—3: Pact with Philippines on Pork, Poultry," Dow Jones International News.

78. Jospin and Johnston quoted in Sue Kendall, "Increasing Pessimism Over International Investment Accord," Agence France Presse, February 13, 1998.

Engering said that the pressure of his responsibilities as a senior official of the Dutch Foreign Ministry made it impossible for him to continue.[79]

In April 1998, the OECD ministerial began, and on the 27th hundreds of activists staged an entire day of protest. Inside the meeting, OECD representatives agreed to a six-month "period of assessment and further consultation" at the request of France, Canada, and the United States. "We were not prepared to drive to a conclusion," remembers USTR's Papovich. Some remarked on the unusual alliance. "It was really quite fascinating to see France sit on the same side of the table as the United States," notes one observer. "All the European member states were on the other side, furious with the French." The MAI negotiations would begin again in October. This delay in the talks was hailed by the NGOs as a triumph for civil society and a direct result of the public opposition to the MAI (Human Rights Clinical Program 1999, 3).

Despite the claims of victory from NGO representatives, some observers say that the MAI would have stalled in any case. "NGOs captured the process to some extent," says Pierre Sauvé.

> But what they captured was a process teetering on the edge, with much of its body already over the cliff. All they did was nudge it into free fall. The MAI would have failed, in my view, even without an NGO crusade against it, because there were many profound contradictions in the draft itself. There's no doubt that NGOs used the MAI as target practice. It was a way for them to internationalize—to transnationalize. They realized that if they could create a dynamic of cooperation at the international level, they would have far more influence than by mounting a series of domestic opposition campaigns.

## The End of the MAI

The MAI negotiations were scheduled to reconvene on October 20, 1998, after the six-month hiatus. In the meantime, the French government commissioned Catherine Lalumière, a member of the European Parliament, and Jean-Pierre Landau, the inspector general of finances, to prepare a report on the MAI. Observers note that Lalumière and Landau were not players in the MAI negotiations, nor were they particularly familiar with the OECD. While supportive of international investment rules and liberalization, their document—commonly known as the Lalumière Report—was critical of the structure and substance of the MAI. It concluded that the OECD was not created to serve as a forum for negotiating major international economic agreements and negotiations should not resume on the existing basis. The report also noted that "for the first time, we are witnessing the emergence of a 'global civil society' represented by nongovernmental organizations, which are often active in several countries and communicate across borders" (Lalumière and Landau 1998). The Lalumière report was released in September 1998.

---

79. Guy de Jonquières, "Axe Over Hopes for MAI Accord," *The Financial Times,* March 25, 1998, 5.

In the lead-up to the October negotiations, anti-MAI forces ramped up their efforts. NGO representatives from 23 countries gathered at a strategy meeting in Geneva, and the AFL-CIO also issued a statement condemning the agreement. A rally was held outside UNCTAD headquarters that featured musicians, MAI opponents, and celebrity speakers.

On October 14, 1998—less than a week before talks were scheduled to resume—France announced that it was pulling out of the MAI negotiations, citing the Lalumière report to justify its withdrawal. France could not support "abandoning sovereignty to private interests under the pretext of an international investment code," Prime Minister Jospin told the national assembly. "France will not take part in the OECD negotiations on October 20. We want the negotiations to resume on a totally new foundation and in a framework that includes all participants, that is all countries, including developing nations." Jospin added that the proposed accord was of limited interest to French companies and that the right framework for the talks was "quite naturally that of the WTO."[80]

The manner of the French withdrawal—a sudden and public exit—was viewed as unusual for a multilateral negotiation. Parties generally negotiated how a set of talks would close. Observers suggest that Jospin may have used the dramatic departure to shore up his domestic support and prevent the controversy surrounding the MAI from aiding the Green Party and the Communists.

Following Jospin's statement, a spokeswoman for the OECD said there were no plans to cancel the October 20 relaunch of the negotiations, declaring, "You can't cancel a meeting just because one sovereign state pulls out."[81] However, the OECD downgraded the scheduled two-day "negotiation" to one day of "consultation." Ultimately, without France, EU member states would not continue the negotiations; and without the European Union, there could be no talks (Dymond 1999, 25). Still vigilant, NGOs released a joint statement in November titled "A Call to Reject Any Proposal for Moving the MAI or an Investment Agreement to the WTO."[82]

On December 3, 1998, following efforts by the OECD Secretariat to resuscitate the MAI, the OECD released a statement: "Negotiations on the MAI are no longer taking place."[83]

---

80. Jospin, quoted in David Pearson, "France Torpedoes OECD Talks on Global Investment Accord," "France/OECD Talks—2: Wants to Shift Talks to WTO," "France/OECD Take 3: Third World Groups Criticize Talks," Dow Jones International News, October 14, 1998.

81. Quoted in Pearson, "France/OECD Talks—2: Wants to Shift Talks to WTO," Dow Jones International News, October 14, 1998.

82. This letter is widely available on the Web; see, e.g., www.citizen.org.

83. Christopher Noble, "OECD Admits Global Investment Treaty Dead," Reuters News, December 4, 1998.

## Conclusion

Some believe that the downfall of the MAI represents the first major victory by the civil society groups that would later gain force in protesting economic globalization and international trade efforts by the WTO, the World Bank, and the IMF. On this view, the MAI campaign is particularly significant in providing the momentum for the protests during the 1999 WTO ministerial in Seattle.

Others insist that what really sank the MAI was the initial decision to negotiate an agreement between countries with well-established foreign investment policies—and the subsequent choice of the OECD as a negotiating forum. While many assumed that OECD countries could easily assemble a high-quality agreement, some believe that the talks lacked enough substance for a productive negotiation. In the end, says one participant, the MAI's "fatal weakness" was that "OECD countries had few investment barriers whose removal was negotiable or worth the effort." Therefore, negotiators came to the table "determined to offer nothing beyond the maintenance of current regimes" (Dymond 1999, 26).

As the talks progressed, the MAI faced both internal and external problems. Internally, various issues proved more contentious and difficult to negotiate than had been expected. Externally, anti-MAI NGOs organized an international movement against the agreement, and the OECD, a traditionally low-profile organization, was forced into the public eye in a way it had not anticipated. Some believe that as each of these challenges grew stronger, the two dynamics became mutually reinforcing and overwhelmed the MAI effort (Henderson 1999, 21).

The demise of the MAI talks did not signal an end to interest in negotiating a multilateral investment agreement, however. In a Working Group on Trade and Investment was founded at the WTO during the Singapore Ministerial Conference. Other major new "Singapore issues" introduced during the ministerial were transparency in government procurement, competition, and trade facilitation. In the run-up to the 1999 Seattle ministerial, the European Union, Japan, and several developing countries strongly urged that what they called "modest investment negotiations" be initiated at the WTO. "It's interesting," reflects one observer. "While I feel that the MAI was a US idea, the mantle has now been picked up by the European Union and Japan."

But any movement on investment issues at the WTO would be hard-won. Discord surrounded the implementation of the TRIMS agreement signed during the Uruguay Round. Although developing countries were to come into compliance by 2000 and the least developed countries by 2002, several countries submitted requests for deadline extensions, saying they needed more time to make the substantial policy reforms required by the agreement.

Controversy over multilateral investment rules persisted at the 2001 WTO ministerial in Doha, Qatar, which kicked off a new round of trade talks. In September 2003, WTO negotiations broke down at the Cancún ministerial when developing countries refused to talk about investment and the other Singapore issues put forward by Europe and Japan. Brazil, India, and China led an "unlikely coalition" of more than 20 developing nations that banded together to argue that EU and US agricultural proposals fell far short of their expectations.[84] With few assurances that developed nations would slash their $300 billion in domestic farm subsidies, developing countries had little interest in pursuing new rules such as those on investment. "Developing countries do not have the capacity to deal with the new issues. We are still grappling with [WTO negotiations] on agriculture and non-agricultural products," noted Indonesia's trade minister, Rini Mariani Sumarno.[85] "We wanted to negotiate issues that are essential for us—agriculture subsidies, closed markets," said Yashpai Tandon, a delegate from Uganda. "Why would we now add investment? It is too much."[86]

## Negotiation Analysis of the Case

Failure often is instructive, and the MAI negotiations therefore provide an opportunity for learning. Some have credited a strong campaign by nongovernmental organizations with torpedoing the MAI effort; but though energetic opposition from NGOs played a role in the demise of the negotiations, the groundwork for failure was laid much earlier. As the analysis below elucidates, fundamental weaknesses in the structure of the talks, the selection of the OECD as the negotiating forum, and the design of the process raised formidable barriers to agreement.

### Element #1: Organizing to Influence

While the extent of their impact on the negotiation process can be disputed, the NGOs did a brilliant job of mobilizing global opposition to the MAI. Their campaign is a dramatic example how the Internet has enabled previously fragmented groups to be knit together into a powerful movement. The NGOs successfully used the Internet as an *influence lens*, a tool

---

84. Scott Miller and Neil King Jr., "Poor Countries May Hold Sway in WTO Session—Group Opposed to Supports for Rich-World Farmers Wields Newfound Clout," *The Wall Street Journal*, September 11, 2003, A11.

85. Sumarno, quoted in Guy de Jonquières and Frances Williams, "WTO Talks Collapse Without Agreement," *The Financial Times*, September 15, 2003, 1.

86. Tandon, quoted in Elizabeth Becker, "Poorer Countries Pull Out of Talks over World Trade," *The New York Times*, September 15, 2003, A1.

that can gather diffuse rays of support and focus them on key points. The NGOs also had a clear, simple goal: They sought to stop the negotiations altogether, not to incorporate certain issues or language into the agreement. Some have criticized the NGOs for lacking substantive knowledge about investment and for disseminating misinformation (including misquotes), but these groups were undeniably very effective in getting out their core message and rallying support for their cause.

At the same time, proponents of the MAI failed to organize to influence key constituencies and decision makers. They handled public relations poorly (as discussed in the section on framing below), and their efforts to build momentum were undermined by the failure of the participating governments to claim ownership and be involved at sufficiently high levels. Bureaucratic politics within the US administration also played a role in undermining the talks, as did lackluster support by the business community. The NGOs may have only put the nails in the MAI's coffin, but they were able to claim a victory that gave them momentum as they planned protests for the WTO ministerial in Seattle.

## Element #2: Selecting the Forum

One reason for the selection of the OECD, an organization of mostly developed countries, as the forum to host the MAI negotiations was the perception that efforts to address investment issues within the WTO had fallen short because of resistance from developing nations. The OECD had a long history of facilitating the making of investment codes, particularly within its Committee on International Investment and Multinational Enterprise. The OECD thus had the requisite technical expertise and institutional credibility to host the talks; moreover, some groups within the OECD had advocated for such an agreement.

Besides, there were simply not many plausible alternatives to the OECD. The International Monetary Fund might have been a candidate, and indeed in the mid-1990s it had argued that because FDI is capital flow, it was the logical place to negotiate the agreement. But the Fund had limited organizational experience as a negotiating forum. The United Nations Conference on Trade and Development, another possibility, had little experience with organizing negotiations and, perhaps more important, was seen by some as a hotbed of antimultinational fervor. The only other option would have been to create an entirely new forum.

Unfortunately, the choice of the OECD proved highly problematic. First, the OECD lacked the process expertise needed to run a complex, multiparty negotiation. Because of its technical and research mindset, the OECD was insufficiently sensitive to process design and seemingly unprepared to conduct the public diplomacy required to support negotiations over such a contentious set of issues.

In addition, its selection both reflected and exacerbated internal political struggles within the US administration over the making of trade policy—historically the purview of USTR, while international investment policy had been under the control of the Departments of Treasury and State. To the extent that investment was subsumed into a multilateral trade agenda and negotiated in the WTO, the USTR gained influence. By anchoring negotiations over investment in the OECD, Treasury and State remained in charge. But this control came at the cost of internal consensus within the United States and even of opposition by some elements in USTR.

### Element #3: Shaping the Agenda

The MAI talks were explicitly designed to involve a limited set of parties (developed countries) negotiating over a limited set of issues (investment rules), a structure motivated by two primary factors. The first was the logic of sequencing. Many believed that OECD members would generally agree on what investment rules were desirable. Once they had negotiated an agreement, they could put forward the MAI as the model for a broader agreement to which developing countries would accede in time.

However, there were significant differences in developed countries' investment rules, shaped largely by domestic political realities, which were not easy to overcome. These included variation in the treatment of cultural industries, the power of subfederal governments (e.g., the ability of US states to create their own investment incentives), and the treatment of industries deemed critical to national security and development. In negotiations with a broader agenda such differences might have been welcome grist for cross-issue or cross-sector trades, but at the OECD they simply became blocks to agreement. The top-down agreement design, which made it difficult to opt out of provisions, only exacerbated the tension.

The MAI agenda also intended to hit a sweet spot in its breadth and complexity. By focusing on the full range of investment issues, negotiators hoped to craft an agreement broad enough to permit trades across issues, but not so broad that it couldn't be negotiated in a reasonable amount of time. But the focus on investment forestalled the creation of linkages to a wider range of trade-related issues. For example, a country could not make a concession on investment in exchange for a desired outcome in agricultural tariffs.

The negotiators therefore had great difficulty making value-creating trades. The talks were further complicated by the reluctance of each party to concede anything, while insisting on concessions from others. This dynamic grew out of the inadequate negotiating authority of the MAI participants, who were generally midlevel civil servants without the power to commit to many domestic policy changes.

## Element #4: Building Coalitions

This case is really all about coalition building (and breaking). For the reasons described above, the facilitators and participants in the MAI process were not able to build a winning coalition and reach a final agreement. The MAI's opponents, in contrast, successfully organized a vocal coalition and helped to catalyze France's departure from the negotiations, precipitating the breakdown of the process. Negotiation organizers even unwittingly provided opportunities for the MAI's implacable foes to meet and make connections beyond their efforts on the Internet. Providing such an opportunity for opposition efforts to coalesce is a classic mistake.

## Element #5: Leveraging Linkages

The organizers of the MAI negotiations may have thought they had learned the needed lessons from prior failures and successes in negotiating investment agreements. Because bilateral investment treaties had yielded a patchwork of agreements between developed and developing countries, MAI proponents believed that the time had come to more broadly harmonize international rules on investment. But they might also have observed that business interests seemed largely satisfied with the BIT process, suggesting that no dramatic groundswell of business support for negotiating improved protections could be expected.

Lessons had also been gleaned from linked efforts to advance the investment agenda in the GATT. Developing countries were resistant to including investment in the GATT, fearing that by doing so they would lose control of a key lever of domestic and development policy. Though some progress on investment had been made in the Uruguay Round through the TRIMs and GATS negotiations, these agreements were seen as incremental and watered-down. Therefore, proponents of a multilateral investment agreement viewed negotiating outside of the WTO as the best plan. But another important lesson from GATT efforts was that developed countries had their own disagreements over issues such as investment in culturally sensitive industries.

At the same time, prior efforts to negotiate narrow investment-related agreements at the OECD offered their own lessons. The OECD had created Codes of Liberalization, but they lacked any binding enforcement mechanism—and the one attempt by the OECD to negotiate a binding National Treatment Instrument had ended in failure in 1991. Negotiators therefore deduced that the agenda for future negotiations needed to be broadened to encompass the full range of investment issues, apparently failing to observe that closing the remaining gaps in investment policy between OECD members would not be easy.

Lessons had also been learned from NAFTA. Proponents of the MAI saw NAFTA's Chapter 11 as a success story: investment rules worked out in the context of a regional agreement. Because the United States and Canada had made investment commitments to each other, Chapter 11 was understandably held up as a model for what could be achieved through negotiation between developed countries. This model made plausible the notion that negotiating a broad investment agreement among a set of developed nations would move the investment liberalization agenda forward. Some argue, however, that such a conclusion overlooks an important factor in NAFTA: that Canada and the United States had entered into the negotiation more motivated to liberalize investment with Mexico than with each other.

In short, some lessons from past linked investment negotiations were noted by MAI proponents, but other lessons were disregarded.

## Element #6: Playing the Frame Game

When it came to the frame game, participants in the MAI process essentially left the field, giving the NGOs and other opponents free rein. The NGOs employed framing tactics very effectively to mobilize other activists, painting the agreement as "NAFTA on steroids" and "the biggest power play yet of the global mega-corporations." At the same time, they succeeded in shaping broader public perceptions by accusing MAI negotiators of secrecy and conspiracy. Opponents used evocative language such as "the Dracula test" to drive home their concerns, and they also played up potential risks to national sovereignty. The ads about a "top-secret" agreement, the leaked MAI draft, and the spinning of the Ethyl case all contributed to the mainstream press picking up the story in ways that favored the opponents' interpretation of the negotiations.

Some government officials believed that business did not push hard enough for the MAI in the public arena. Such public support from business was needed, they argued, for negotiators to be seen as mediating between the two competing sides (business and NGOs). For their part, some business representatives claimed that government officials did not do enough to counter the arguments of the NGOs. The meeting between officials and NGO organizers to discuss substantive issues, for example, was in fact counterproductive, for in reality the NGOs had no desire to modify the agreement, only a wish to stop it. Government officials might have been better served by taking their arguments to the general public. OECD organizers, coming from a culture in which the benefits to society of their efforts were assumed to be obvious, were similarly unprepared to argue their case publicly. MAI proponents thus failed to create a public relations strategy to help educate the press and key publics about the MAI process and the benefits of the agreement.

## Element #7: Creating Momentum

Finally, MAI organizers failed to create the momentum necessary to reach agreement. A potentially powerful logic of sequencing underpinned the design of the MAI process, but that potential was not realized. The expectation was that developed countries would first negotiate among themselves to create a common position, thereby setting high standards for subsequent negotiations with developing countries. The agreement would include an accession mechanism to entice developing countries interested in attracting investment. The result would be a "race to the top," increasingly isolating most developing countries that were opposed to the agreement. Association with the WTO would come in due course—that is, when momentum toward agreement became unstoppable.

In addition, the MAI process was designed to move from negotiations over a framework to negotiations over details. The agenda was divided into six groups of issues, and working groups (patterned on the standard OECD structure) were established for each issue. Each working group was intended to develop common understandings as a prelude to constructing the broader framework. One weakness with this process strategy was that an initial phase of negotiations on goals and principles was not fully undertaken. Therefore, the most fundamental question about the goal of the MAI—whether it should establish an initial lowest-common-denominator agreement or instead push forward liberalization dramatically, beyond even Chapter 11 of NAFTA—was never answered. A related problem was that key decision makers and major political figures had not sufficiently bought into the process. As a consequence, the working groups fostered only parallel discussions of narrow sets of issues with inadequate overall integration.

The MAI negotiations also provide numerous examples of the strategic use of action-forcing events by opponents and participants. Charlene Barshefsky's public comments about the negotiations and the French exploitation of the Lalumière Report as an excuse to withdraw from the talks demonstrate how participants can deploy action-forcing events to slow or end negotiations.

## Conclusion

Before we close the book on the MAI, we must remember that negotiations are linked in time. A number of parties are still interested in creating multilateral rules on investment. How the MAI experience will inform future efforts remains to be seen.

# Appendix 4A
# Agreement on Trade-Related Investment Measures (1995)

*Members,*

*Considering* that Ministers agreed in the Punta del Este Declaration that "Following an examination of the operation of GATT Articles related to the trade-restrictive and distorting effects of investment measures, negotiations should elaborate, as appropriate, further provisions that may be necessary to avoid such adverse effects on trade";

*Desiring* to promote the expansion and progressive liberalisation of world trade and to facilitate investment across international frontiers so as to increase the economic growth of all trading partners, particularly developing country Members, while ensuring free competition;

*Taking into account* the particular trade, development and financial needs of developing country Members, particularly those of the least-developed country Members;

*Recognizing* that certain investment measures can cause trade-restrictive and distorting effects;

Hereby *agree* as follows:

## Article 1: Coverage

This Agreement applies to investment measures related to trade in goods only (referred to in this Agreement as "TRIMs").

## Article 2: National Treatment and Quantitative Restrictions

1. Without prejudice to other rights and obligations under GATT 1994, no Member shall apply any TRIM that is inconsistent with the provisions of Article III or Article XI of GATT 1994.

2. An illustrative list of TRIMs that are inconsistent with the obligation of national treatment provided for in paragraph 4 of Article III of GATT 1994 and the obligation of general elimination of quantitative restrictions provided for in paragraph 1 of Article XI of GATT 1994 is contained in the Annex to this Agreement.

## Article 3: Exceptions

All exceptions under GATT 1994 shall apply, as appropriate, to the provisions of this Agreement.

## Article 4: Developing Country Members

A developing country Member shall be free to deviate temporarily from the provisions of Article 2 to the extent and in such a manner as Article XVIII of GATT 1994, the Understanding on the Balance-of-Payments Provisions of GATT 1994, and the Declaration on Trade Measures Taken for Balance-of-Payments Purposes adopted on 28 November 1979 (BISD 26S/205-209) permit the Member to deviate from the provisions of Articles III and XI of GATT 1994.

## Article 5: Notification and Transitional Arrangements

1. Members, within 90 days of the date of entry into force of the WTO Agreement, shall notify the Council for Trade in Goods of all TRIMs they are applying that are not in conformity with the provisions of this Agreement. Such TRIMs of general or specific application shall be notified, along with their principal features.

2. Each Member shall eliminate all TRIMs which are notified under paragraph 1 within two years of the date of entry into force of the WTO Agreement in the case of a developed country Member, within five years in the case of a developing country Member, and within seven years in the case of a least-developed country Member.

3. On request, the Council for Trade in Goods may extend the transition period for the elimination of TRIMs notified under paragraph 1 for a developing country Member, including a least-developed country Member, which demonstrates particular difficulties in implementing the provisions of this Agreement. In considering such a request, the Council for Trade in Goods shall take into account the individual development, financial and trade needs of the Member in question.

4. During the transition period, a Member shall not modify the terms of any TRIM which it notifies under paragraph 1 from those prevailing at the date of entry into force of the WTO Agreement so as to increase the degree of inconsistency with the provisions of Article 2. TRIMs introduced less than 180 days before the date of entry into force of the WTO Agreement shall not benefit from the transitional arrangements provided in paragraph 2.

5. Notwithstanding the provisions of Article 2, a Member, in order not to disadvantage established enterprises which are subject to a TRIM notified under paragraph 1, may apply during the transition period the same TRIM to a new investment (*i*) where the products of such investment are like products to those of the established enterprises, and (*ii*) where necessary to avoid distorting the conditions of competition between the new investment and the established enterprises. Any TRIM

so applied to a new investment shall be notified to the Council for Trade in Goods. The terms of such a TRIM shall be equivalent in their competitive effect to those applicable to the established enterprises, and it shall be terminated at the same time.

## Article 6: Transparency

1. Members reaffirm, with respect to TRIMs, their commitment to obligations on transparency and notification in Article X of GATT 1994, in the undertaking on "Notification" contained in the Understanding Regarding Notification, Consultation, Dispute Settlement and Surveillance adopted on 28 November 1979 and in the Ministerial Decision on Notification Procedures adopted on 15 April 1994.

2. Each Member shall notify the Secretariat of the publications in which TRIMs may be found, including those applied by regional and local governments and authorities within their territories.

3. Each Member shall accord sympathetic consideration to requests for information, and afford adequate opportunity for consultation, on any matter arising from this Agreement raised by another Member. In conformity with Article X of GATT 1994 no Member is required to disclose information the disclosure of which would impede law enforcement or otherwise be contrary to the public interest or would prejudice the legitimate commercial interests of particular enterprises, public or private.

## Article 7: Committee on Trade-Related Investment Measures

1. A Committee on Trade-Related Investment Measures (referred to in this Agreement as the "Committee") is hereby established, and shall be open to all Members. The Committee shall elect its own Chairman and Vice-Chairman, and shall meet not less than once a year and otherwise at the request of any Member.

2. The Committee shall carry out responsibilities assigned to it by the Council for Trade in Goods and shall afford Members the opportunity to consult on any matters relating to the operation and implementation of this Agreement.

3. The Committee shall monitor the operation and implementation of this Agreement and shall report thereon annually to the Council for Trade in Goods.

## Article 8: Consultation and Dispute Settlement

The provisions of Articles XXII and XXIII of GATT 1994, as elaborated and applied by the Dispute Settlement Understanding, shall apply to consultations and the settlement of disputes under this Agreement.

## Article 9: Review by the Council for Trade in Goods

Not later than five years after the date of entry into force of the WTO Agreement, the Council for Trade in Goods shall review the operation of this Agreement and, as appropriate, propose to the Ministerial Conference amendments to its text. In the course of this review, the Council for Trade in Goods shall consider whether the Agreement should be complemented with provisions on investment policy and competition policy.

## ANNEX
### Illustrative List

1. TRIMs that are inconsistent with the obligation of national treatment provided for in paragraph 4 of Article III of GATT 1994 include those which are mandatory or enforceable under domestic law or under administrative rulings, or compliance with which is necessary to obtain an advantage, and which require:

   (a) the purchase or use by an enterprise of products of domestic origin or from any domestic source, whether specified in terms of particular products, in terms of volume or value of products, or in terms of a proportion of volume or value of its local production; or

   (b) that an enterprise's purchases or use of imported products be limited to an amount related to the volume or value of local products that it exports.

2. TRIMs that are inconsistent with the obligation of general elimination of quantitative restrictions provided for in paragraph 1 of Article XI of GATT 1994 include those which are mandatory or enforceable under domestic law or under administrative rulings, or compliance with which is necessary to obtain an advantage, and which restrict:

   (a) the importation by an enterprise of products used in or related to its local production, generally or to an amount related to the volume or value of local production that it exports;

   (b) the importation by an enterprise of products used in or related to its local production by restricting its access to foreign exchange to an amount related to the foreign exchange inflows attributable to the enterprise; or

   (c) the exportation or sale for export by an enterprise of products, whether specified in terms of particular products, in terms of volume or value of products, or in terms of a proportion of volume or value of its local production.

# 5

# Fast Track/Trade Promotion Authority

## Making Trade Policy

Trade promotion authority (TPA), known until 2001 as fast track, plays a major role in determining US trade policy. In the United States, the president has the constitutional authority to negotiate international trade agreements. But if a trade agreement requires changes in US statutory law, Congress must approve the implementing legislation. From 1974 to 1993, Congress granted the president fast-track authority—that is, in return for being consulted regularly by the administration, it committed to an expeditious yes-or-no vote on such legislation, with no amendments. Beginning in the early 1990s, however, fast track became the subject of fierce political debate and a focal point for concerns about global trade liberalization—especially in connection with labor and environmental issues.

The fast-track/TPA case provides insight into the role of the US Congress in international trade negotiations. It also highlights the erosion of political support for trade liberalization in the United States, particularly among Democrats in the House of Representatives, and raises the central question of what issues should be covered in trade agreements.

---

*Fast Track Derailed: The 1997 Attempt to Renew Fast-Track Trade Legislation* is an edited and revised version of the case with the same name originally written for the Case Program at the Kennedy School of Government. For copies or permission to reproduce the unabridged case please refer to www.ksgcase. harvard.edu or send a written request to Case Program, John F. Kennedy School of Government, Harvard University, 79 John F. Kennedy Street, Cambridge, MA 02138.

## Governance

Foreigners often view the United States as a single rational actor—typically embodied by the president. But US trade policymaking occurs through an intricate process in which the Congress plays a key role. Indeed, the Constitution of the United States gives Congress the power to regulate international commerce, leaving the president only the power to negotiate. Therefore, the relationship between the president and the Congress is that of agent and principal, where there is an expectation that the agent (the president) will act on behalf of the principal (Congress). It is a problematic arrangement: The classic principal-agent problem arises when the agent's objectives differ from those of the principal and the agent can pursue hidden actions. The fast-track/TPA case exemplifies how complicated such relationships can become, as we see Congress trying to exert control over the actions of the president.

Economic theory suggests that trade liberalization provides benefits to a nation as a whole, while at the same time creating individual winners and losers. The president, whose constituency is the entire nation, is likely in the best position to internalize these costs and benefits and to represent the overall national interest in open trade. By contrast, members of the House of Representatives have constituencies whose opinions about trade are largely determined by the fate of a few local industries or organizations. Representatives from districts that are hurt by trade will find it difficult to support liberalization despite the potential benefits to the nation as a whole. Senators, who generally must answer to more numerous and more diverse voters, will typically adopt an intermediate perspective. It is thus no surprise that enthusiasm for trade liberalization usually comes from presidents and resistance to it from the House.

Congress is aware of its propensity to favor special interests; ever since the disastrous adoption of the Smoot-Hawley tariffs in the 1930s, it has sought to restrain this tendency by delegating more power over trade to the president. Starting in 1934, and renewed at three-year intervals, the Reciprocal Trade Agreements Act gave the president temporary authority to negotiate and implement reciprocal tariff reductions without the need for further congressional approval. Congress, while never giving up its constitutional authority, thus showed its willingness to constrain its behavior for the sake of promoting the national interest.

Once trade agreements began to cover nontariff measures, it became clear that a new arrangement was needed between Congress and the president. Indeed, after the Kennedy Round (1964–67), Congress refused to implement the round's antidumping rules and an agreement on US customs procedures, rejecting the argument that the president had the power to make such commitments without congressional oversight.

The failure of the United States to deliver on important parts of the Kennedy Round agreement naturally caused problems with negotiating partners in the General Agreement on Tariffs and Trade (GATT). To deal with the difficulty, fast-track procedures were developed in 1974. Under fast track, Congress was restricted to an up-or-down vote on trade-implementing legislation within a specific time limit. By forfeiting its ability to amend trade agreements, Congress was again shifting power to the president. As a result, the president could strategically frame the agenda for any particular trade agreement. For example, the president could bundle many issues under one negotiation, increasing the chance for agreement on certain measures that might never be accepted if considered in isolation. Such power clearly increased the need for trust between the president and Congress—a factor that would loom large when it became necessary to renew fast-track legislation.

## Coverage and Depth

Fast track worked well as long as there was consensus on which issues should be covered by trade agreements and how they should be dealt with. However, debate over the inclusion of labor and environmental standards came to the forefront when the North American Free Trade Agreement (NAFTA) was being considered. These issues are highly controversial. On the one hand, organized labor and most environmental groups believe that provisions on core labor standards and environmental standards should be included in trade agreements; on the other hand, many business representatives would like to see such provisions excluded or limited solely to measures that are strictly trade-related. In addition, many in Mexico and other developing countries resist having these standards enforced by a trade agreement.

There are compelling arguments on both sides of this argument. One concern is that these standards could be used as a means of protecting domestic markets. For example, if one nation decides to trade only with countries that meet certain environmental regulations, then its domestic firms will not face as much foreign competition. The worry that protectionism may be disguised as regulation is not new: Such fears prompted Tokyo Round negotiators in the 1970s to design a code that dealt with standards and technical barriers to trade. While the code did not seek to enforce particular standards, it did lay out requirements that had to be met. For example, standards that "create an unnecessary obstacle to international trade" were not permitted. These requirements, in turn, raised concerns among environmental groups that trade was being allowed to trump other important policy considerations. Environmentalists argued that trade agreements should explicitly redress this imbalance.

Proponents of including both labor and environmental standards in trade agreements point to the precedent set by the Agreement on Trade-Related Aspects of Intellectual Property Rights (TRIPS). If the trade regime is used to enforce intellectual property rights that benefit corporations, they argue, then it should also be used to enforce other basic rights and standards. Many labor and environmental groups worry that without such measures, trade could result in a race to the bottom as countries seek to use lax labor and environmental standards to gain competitive advantage. In particular, they point to the development of special export-processing zones in which national labor and environmental rules are not enforced. Labor standards proponents also stress that they do not seek to establish a global minimum wage that would price developing countries out of world markets; instead, they ask only for the enforcement of the core International Labor Organization (ILO) standards, which entail four principles: nondiscrimination, the right to unionize and bargain collectively, prohibitions on exploitative child labor, and prohibitions on forced labor.

## Enforcement

Although most international agreements are enforced by international law, signatory countries that violate the terms of their agreements are not necessarily penalized, aside from their loss of face in the court of public opinion. But a country found in violation of a trade agreement may well suffer consequences. In the World Trade Organization (WTO), for example, a country that refuses to come into compliance may find that its trading partners "suspend concessions" and raise tariffs. This superior enforcement mechanism was the key factor in making the inclusion of TRIPS in the WTO so attractive to its proponents—and in increasing the desire of proponents of labor and environmental standards to have their issues similarly incorporated into trade agreements.

## Developing Countries

Opponents of introducing labor and environmental standards into trade agreements fear that developing countries could be required to implement rules that are inappropriate for their level of development. While many developing countries favor international labor standards, they do not support including these issues at the WTO, because only developed countries generally have large enough economies to resort to trade sanctions against violating nations. Instead, they believe the ILO to be the most appropriate forum. In addition, many developing countries voice concern about the competence of trade officials to deal with questions of labor and environmental policy.

## Winners and Losers

George H. W. Bush was the first president to struggle with this debate over labor and environmental standards, and its attendant difficulties have been integral to the controversy of fast track ever since. Between 1993 and 2001, the relevant players in almost every conceivable alignment failed to mobilize sufficient support for fast track's passage. In 1994, the Clinton administration tried to work with House Democrats in a pro-labor alignment and found inadequate support. In 1995, House Republicans sought a probusiness formulation without the administration's support and failed. In 1997, the administration worked with the Republicans and failed. In 1998, the Republicans acted independently and failed. Only in 2001 was a Republican president able to achieve passage of the desired authority in the House by abandoning efforts at bipartisanship: With Republican support, he won by the narrowest of margins.

The basic problem is that Congress in recent years has been highly polarized and evenly balanced between the two major parties. If the fast-track/TPA language includes stronger labor and environment provisions, more Democrats become supporters but Republicans drop out; if the language is weakened to attract more Republicans, support from Democrats erodes. The case also highlights the growing opposition to trade liberalization and globalization in the Democratic Party more generally, a trend that made it essential for the president to work with Republicans to obtain negotiating authority.

Such challenges raise the question of whether fast track/TPA is really necessary. The successful passage of China's permanent normal trade relations (PNTR; see chapter 6) and of the US-Jordan Free Trade Agreement indicates that bilateral deals can be negotiated without fast-track legislation. But conventional wisdom (and the early experience with the Kennedy Round) suggests that in negotiating multilateral agreements, fast track/TPA is more important. Certainly, a US president who is not equipped with this authority will be unable to extract the best foreign offer, because other countries know that any commitments made at the table could be altered or rejected by Congress.

In June 2002, President George W. Bush was able to obtain trade promotion authority. This achievement raises the question of whether the problems faced by President Clinton were related to strategic failures by him and his administration or were instead structural, suggesting that future granting of TPA will require the particular alignment of a Republican president and a Republican Congress.

## CASE STUDY: Fast Track Derailed— The 1997 Attempt to Renew Fast-Track Trade Legislation

At 1:15 A.M. on November 10, 1997, President Bill Clinton telephoned House Speaker Newt Gingrich (R-GA) and asked him to cancel the vote on fast-track trade authority scheduled for later that morning. The Clinton administration and the Republican leadership had intensely lobbied members of the House of Representatives for days in an attempt to secure its renewal, but the effort was over. The head count had come up short of the 218 votes needed for passage: Republicans, who controlled the House, had lined up more than 150 votes, but reportedly no more than 45 Democrats supported the fast-track legislation.

At a time when the United States was the world's largest exporter, the US economy was booming, and the unemployment rate was at its lowest in seven years, the failure of an effort to facilitate international trade negotiations might seem surprising.[1] But labor unions, many Democrats, environmentalists, and certain right-wing groups were not convinced that most Americans would benefit from competition in the international economy. In the aftermath of NAFTA's passage, many US workers felt threatened by the prospect of jobs moving overseas, where labor costs were lower. In the end, many observers attributed fast track's defeat to domestic anxiety about the impact of globalization on labor and the environment, giving rise to disagreement about the extent to which trade agreements should incorporate labor and environmental protections.

Other issues raised by the fast-track debate had proven divisive as well. To what degree should Congress participate in the formulation of US trade policy? Who should set goals for international trade negotiations? Should the president be entrusted with fast track? Is fast track necessary? In addition to these substantive concerns about the legislation came a host of political considerations. For example, some Democrats felt that Clinton had worked out the details of the 1998 budget with Republicans, essentially cutting his own party out of the process. As a result, some Democrats were unwilling to hand the president a victory on fast track. Ultimately, fast track came to exemplify the increasing politicization of trade.

---

1. In 1996, unemployment fell as low as 5.2 percent. USTR, *1997 Trade Policy Agenda and 1996 Annual Report*, 1.

## What Is Fast Track?

The president has the constitutional authority to negotiate international trade agreements. If a trade agreement requires changes in US statutory law, however, Congress must approve the implementing legislation. The key to fast track, originally passed in 1974, is that it restricts Congress to an expeditious yes-or-no vote on the legislation to implement trade agreements; no amendments or changes are allowed. But the executive branch can't simply negotiate any trade agreement it pleases: Congress sets guidelines, and negotiation objectives are specified in advance. In addition, the executive branch has to meet certain requirements, such as consulting with congressional committees and private-sector advisers. In practice, Congress also played an active role in drafting the implementing bills during informal sessions known as "non-markups," though such sessions were not codified as part of the fast-track process.

Proponents of fast track argued that without such authority, the power of the United States was blunted in trade negotiations. Other countries would know that any commitments made at the table could be altered or rejected by Congress. According to former White House Special Assistant Jay Berman, the Clinton administration's point man on fast track, "Fast track is important because it's very hard to see how trade negotiations can go on without it. Other countries would be very unlikely to put their final best offer on the table if, each time they did so, Congress had an opportunity to go back and say, 'That's not enough' or 'We're going to change it.' "[2] Without fast track, supporters said, the United States' traditional leadership role in the global trade arena was compromised.

President Clinton and others cited the growing importance of trade to the American economy. The United States, they argued, was the world's largest exporter, sending more than $848 billion in goods and services worldwide in 1996.[3] One in every five jobs in America was supported by international trade, and almost 33 percent of overall US growth in GDP between 1985 and 1994 came from exports (Destler 1997, 30). Trade accounted for nearly a quarter of the US economy in 1997, up from 10 percent in 1970.[4] And this trend would only continue. The Office of the US Trade Representative (USTR) estimated that by 2010, trade would be responsible for 36 percent of US GDP.

---

2. Unless otherwise noted, all quotes from Jason Berman are from a March 1998 interview with Charan Devereaux.

3. US Bureau of the Census, Foreign Trade Division, 1996.

4. David Sanger, "Trade Fight Was Battle of Perception Against Analysis," *The New York Times*, November 16, 1997, sec. 1, 26.

## The History of Fast Track

Until 1934, Congress imposed tariffs on specific imports as a way of protecting domestic industries and generating income. US tariffs were subject to change only by an act of Congress. However, during Franklin D. Roosevelt's first administration, Congress conceded authority to the president for making product-specific trade law. Believing that high tariffs had contributed to the Great Depression, Congress passed the 1934 Reciprocal Trade Agreements Act, which authorized the president to negotiate reductions in US tariffs in exchange for concessions by US trading partners. Congress typically limited how much tariffs could be lowered and how long negotiations could last. Once the reductions were negotiated, the president issued an order declaring the new tariff rates, and they became US law—no implementing legislation was needed. This arrangement persisted through the 1940s, 1950s, and 1960s, with Congress reauthorizing the 1934 act through 11 successive Trade Agreement Extension Acts (see Shapiro and Brainard 2003). Average US tariffs fell from around 60 percent in 1930 to 5.8 percent by 1975 (Dobson 1976, 34; cited in Destler 1997, 6).

By 1970, however, trade negotiations were increasingly focused on nontariff barriers to trade, such as subsidies, technical standards, discriminatory procurement practices, and barriers to service exports. US officials could not negotiate credibly on these issues, because they lacked the power to implement any required changes in US law. This impotence became clear after the Kennedy Round of multilateral trade talks in 1967, when Congress refused to pass two nontariff measures agreed on by negotiators. With this precedent in mind, the Senate Finance Committee reached agreement on fast track as part of the Trade Act of 1974, signed by President Gerald Ford in 1975. Through this mechanism, Congress attempted to balance its insistence on review and approval of trade agreements with some guarantee that US negotiators had a good chance of securing congressional approval in a timely manner (Shapiro and Brainard 2003). Fast track was subsequently the mechanism under which major trade agreements were negotiated (on this subject generally, see Destler 1997, 6–7). These agreements included the Tokyo Round (1979) and the Uruguay Round (1994) of the GATT, the Canada-US Free Trade Agreement (1988), and NAFTA (1992).

The 1979 Tokyo Round implementing bill included an eight-year extension for fast track, and the legislation was again extended in 1988. In 1991, as described below, the debate was contentious, but the authority was ultimately renewed for another two years. In 1993, fast track was extended for less than a year in order to allow completion of the Uruguay Round of trade talks; in 1994, it lapsed. A powerful force in the unfolding fast-track saga was concern about NAFTA.

## The Shadow of NAFTA

On June 11, 1990, President George H. W. Bush and President Carlos Salinas of Mexico declared that they planned to negotiate a US-Mexico trade agreement. Bush formally notified Congress of his plans in September 1990. After months of discussions, the administration announced in early 1991 that Canada would also join the US-Mexico talks. The goal would be a North American free trade agreement that would eliminate many tariff and nontariff trade barriers within 10 years, liberalize restrictions on foreign investment, and strengthen protection for intellectual property rights.

On March 1, 1991, President Bush requested a renewal of fast track. The 1988 Trade Act had reauthorized fast track until 1991, but an additional extension was permitted if neither the House nor the Senate objected. Congress had until June 1, 1991, to block fast track; barring congressional action, it would be extended automatically for two years.

Never before 1991 had Congress voted on fast track alone, rather than as part of a larger, complex trade bill (as in 1974, 1979, 1984, and 1988). The 1991 fast-track vote became an early referendum on the yet-to-be-negotiated NAFTA agreement. Fast track would also cover continuing talks in the multilateral GATT Uruguay Round, which were stuck in a quarrel over agriculture. However, it was largely the controversy over trade with Mexico that fueled the ensuing three months of congressional debate.

The AFL-CIO strongly opposed extending fast track. Labor organizations argued that the free trade agreement would pave the way for jobs to be exported to Mexico, and they made the defeat of fast track a top priority. It was a long-standing position of several powerful unions—the Teamsters, the Steelworkers, the United Auto Workers (UAW), the textile and apparel workers union (UNITE, the Union of Needletrades, Industrial, and Textile Employees), and the Oil, Chemical, and Atomic Workers union (OCAW)—that worker rights must be addressed in trade negotiations. UAW political director Alan Reuther cites his union's objections to fast-track negotiating authority as far back as 1977.

Public Citizen, a consumer group founded by Ralph Nader, also opposed fast track, raising a number of worries about the Mexico deal—including its implications for food safety. In addition, US fruit and vegetable growers expressed concern about competition from Mexican producers.

Environmental groups were split on fast track. Though the Sierra Club, Friends of the Earth, and Greenpeace opposed it, the president of the National Wildlife Federation wrote a letter to the *Washington Post* tentatively supporting it.[5] The Environmental Defense Fund, the Nature Conservancy,

---

5. Jay D. Hair, "An Environmental Vote," *The Washington Post*, May 22, 1991, A20.

the Natural Resources Defense Council, and the National Audubon Society also expressed cautious support. A few leaders of environmental groups met with President Bush to discuss trade with Mexico, a move that fast-track opponents blasted as "selling out."[6]

Though initially undecided about fast track, Democratic House Majority Leader Richard Gephardt (MO) eventually supported the extension. "I sympathize with labor's concerns," Gephardt said. "But I think we should try to do a treaty [with Mexico]. We retain the right to amend or reject it if it's not agreeable to us."[7] Some of his constituents were far from happy with Gephardt's position—union members and farmers picketed his St. Louis office.[8] Fast track was supported by other powerful Democrats as well, including House Ways and Means Chairman Dan Rostenkowski (IL), Speaker Thomas Foley (WA), and Senate Finance Committee Chairman Lloyd Bentsen (TX).

The Bush administration fiercely lobbied for fast track, seeing the vote as a major test of presidential authority. The administration's chief lobbyist in the House, Nicholas Calio, devoted almost all of his time to fast track and postponed plans to leave the administration for the private sector until after the House vote. "We've not left a lot to chance here," Calio said.[9]

Business support for fast track was broad and included the US Chamber of Commerce, the Business Roundtable, and the National Association of Manufacturers. On the team of lobbyists were leaders from American Express, Eastman Kodak, General Electric, Procter & Gamble, and many other companies. "We've never had a trade issue that has been this hot," said Harry Freeman, a former American Express executive who was lobbying for the bill. "It's a pan-business effort," said Calman Cohen of the Emergency Committee for American Trade. "I've never seen a larger grouping from the private sector." According to some observers, however, the effort was slow to start until Representative Dan Rostenkowski bluntly warned 20 business leaders two months before the vote, "If you want to win this thing, move your ass."[10] Mexico and Mexican business interests also hired lobbyists to generate support in Congress for fast track.

Many commented on the wide range of players in the fast-track controversy. "For the first time," said one advocate, "different social groups

---

6. As described in Gary Lee, " 'Fast Track' Sprint: Frenzied Lobbying on a Treaty Not Yet Written," *The Washington Post*, May 23, 1991, A21.

7. Gephardt, quoted in Lee, " 'Fast Track' Sprint," A21.

8. Philip Dine, "Gephardt's Trade Stance Draws Labor Protesters," *The St. Louis Post-Dispatch*, May 14, 1991, 8A.

9. *Congressional Quarterly Almanac* (1991), 119.

10. All quoted in Jill Abramson, "US-Mexico Trade Pact Is Pitting Vast Armies of Capitol Hill Lobbyists Against Each Other," *The Wall Street Journal*, April 24, 1991, A16.

have been brought into the negotiations over a trade pact. . . . Trade has become a public issue."[11] A turning point came on May 1, when the administration submitted an 80-page "action plan" on the US-Mexico free trade agreement to Congress. The plan addressed labor and environmental issues prominently, including a commitment to worker adjustment assistance and a pledge to negotiate safeguards to protect US producers from sudden import surges. Observers say the document persuaded more Democrats to support fast track.

On May 23, 1991, the House of Representatives voted 231 to 192 to defeat a resolution to deny fast track, giving President Bush a victory; 91 of 268 Democrats voted with the majority. The Senate also voted to extend fast track, 59 to 36 (23 Democrats joined 36 Republicans allowing the extension). Representative Byron L. Dorgan (D-ND), sponsor of the House resolution to deny fast track, said, "I'm obviously disappointed that the leadership of our caucus is not close to the caucus itself on this issue."[12] However, Democratic leaders Gephardt and Rostenkowski sponsored a nonbinding "sense of the House" resolution (H. Res. 146) calling on the Bush administration to pay close attention to environmental, labor, health and safety, and other matters during the NAFTA negotiations. The measure passed 329 to 85.

Some fast-track opponents complained that lobbyists for the AFL-CIO had conceded defeat several weeks before the vote and were not active in the final fight. The AFL-CIO's Bill Cunningham noted that the unions "cared only about the Mexico free trade agreement" and felt that fast track for Mexico could have been defeated if it were somehow separated from fast track for the Uruguay Round, a trade negotiation more popular in Congress.[13]

The NAFTA negotiations concluded in August 1992, and President Bush signed the agreement in December 1992. As he ran for president in 1992, Bill Clinton had initially delayed taking a position on NAFTA; he ultimately voiced his support, with the stipulation that additional protections should be negotiated for labor and the environment.[14] After defeating George Bush in the election, Clinton became US president in January 1993.

In 1993, the Clinton administration requested an extension of fast track in order to complete the GATT Uruguay Round negotiations. Labor leaders indicated they would not fight a short-term extension limited to the

---

11. Quoted in Lee, " 'Fast Track' Sprint," A21.

12. Dorgan, quoted in Guy Gugliotta, "House Vote Backs Bush on Trade; President Seeking 'Fast Track' Talks for Pact with Mexico," *The Washington Post*, May 24, 1991, A1.

13. Cunningham, quoted in Gugliotta, "House Vote Backs Bush on Trade," A1.

14. See remarks by Governor Bill Clinton at the student center at North Carolina State University, Raleigh, North Carolina, Federal News Service, October 4, 1992.

Uruguay Round and Gephardt supported it. Fast track passed in the Senate 76–16 and in the House 295–126 (145 Democrats voted for the extension; 102 were opposed).[15]

Also in 1993, the Clinton administration began to negotiate with Canada and Mexico on labor and environmental standards, relying on side agreements to supplement NAFTA without reopening the negotiations as a whole (the trade deal had already been signed). The effort found little support among Republicans, some of whom opposed any linkage of trade with labor and environmental issues—especially if sanctions could be used to enforce the agreed-on standards. Many Republicans also felt that the process of negotiating side agreements endangered NAFTA's passage in Congress because it gave the opposition time to mobilize. Brian Bieron, legislative assistant to "fierce free trader"[16] Representative David Dreier (R-CA), recalls:

> People who were going to lead the fight for NAFTA [in Congress]—Republicans like Archer, Dreier, Kolbe, and Gingrich—opposed reopening NAFTA. They also opposed any kind of side agreements that allowed the use of trade sanctions to enforce what they considered to be domestic policy considerations [i.e., labor and the environment]. The administration's method of dealing with the Republican members was basically just to tell them what they were going to do. Republican members would say, "We don't want you to do that." Then the administration would go and do it anyway. In fact, what we heard from the Canadians and Mexicans was that the administration was attempting to portray Congress as demanding side agreements that were enforceable by sanctions. For much of that year, Republican members actually consulted more closely with the Mexicans and the Canadians than they did with the Clinton administration. The staff members were having meetings saying "Don't believe [the administration]."[17]

Yet the negotiations resulted in two side agreements that, Bieron said, "Republicans could live with . . . because neither of them really had sanctions involved."

These agreements earned support from some environmental groups (six major organizations said they would back NAFTA) but not from labor unions, which continued to totally oppose NAFTA.[18] Thelma Askey, chief

---

15. The deadline for notifying Congress of the president's intent to enter the Uruguay Round agreement was extended to December 15, 1993, and it had to be signed by President Clinton by April 15, 1994. (Fast track had been set to expire March 1, 1993.)

16. Amy Borrus and Richard S. Dunham, "Tech: The Virtual Third Party," *Business Week*, April 24, 2000, 74.

17. Unless otherwise noted, all quotes from Brian Bieron are from a March 1998 interview with Charan Devereaux.

18. The six environmental groups were the National Wildlife Federation, the Natural Resources Defense Council, the Environmental Defense Fund, the World Wildlife Federation, the National Audubon Society, and Conservation International. "Six Environmental Organizations Back NAFTA, Denounce Opponents," *Inside US Trade*, September 17, 1993.

of staff of the House Ways and Means Subcommittee on Trade, reflected on Clinton's frustrations: "First he was in a big hole because he spent a [long time] negotiating the side agreements, rather than building support for implementation. Then he got into a bigger hole because the side agreements weren't making organized labor come on board."[19] Labor unions and some environmentalists criticized the side agreements as a half-hearted effort whereby the United States, Mexico, and Canada merely agreed to fully enforce their own domestic labor and environmental regulations.

The NAFTA debate in Congress was fierce, and initially some analysts predicted that the agreement would never pass. Many observed that anti-NAFTA forces were better organized and more vocal than NAFTA's business-minded advocates, who, some complained, never launched an effective grassroots campaign.[20] Opponents to the agreement formed an unlikely coalition that included former presidential candidate Ross Perot, conservative commentator Patrick Buchanan, consumer activist Ralph Nader, many Democrats, some environmental groups, and a good number of labor unions. Perot's most-quoted statement about NAFTA was that the agreement would create a "giant sucking sound" as jobs left the United States for Mexico.[21] Many Democratic lawmakers shared Perot's view that American manufacturers would relocate to take advantage of less expensive Mexican labor. Notably, two members of the House Democratic leadership—Majority Leader Richard Gephardt and Majority Whip David Bonior (MI)—strongly opposed the agreement. Bonior came out early against NAFTA and spearheaded the opposition.

Among NAFTA's proponents were President Clinton, many Republicans, much of the business community, and every living ex-president. Some environmental groups and key Democrats such as Representative Robert Matsui (CA) also supported NAFTA. Moreover, almost every American Nobel laureate in economics and 41 of 50 state governors endorsed the agreement. NAFTA supporters worried that defeat would signal that the United States was turning inward, abandoning its leadership on international trade. NAFTA would increase exports and create new jobs, they argued. "We have to decide whether we're going to participate in a global economy. . . or turn our backs," said Representative Rick Lazio (R-NY).[22]

---

19. Unless otherwise noted, all quotes from Thelma Askey are from a March 1998 interview with Charan Devereaux.

20. Martin Kasindorf and Susan Page, "The NAFTA Vote: Clinton Comeback as in Budget Vote, a Run from Behind," *Newsday*, November 18, 1993, 4.

21. Ross Perot in the October 19, 1992, Presidential Candidates Debate, Wharton Center, Michigan State University, East Lansing, Michigan.

22. Lazio, quoted in Bob Davis and Jackie Calmes, "The US House Passes NAFTA," *The Asian Wall Street Journal*, November 19, 1993, 1.

The White House devoted two months to a final massive lobbying campaign. The administration's tactics included setting up a "war room" to monitor the issue and bringing in a NAFTA czar from outside of Washington—Chicago businessman William Daley. The effort culminated in a debate between Vice President Al Gore and Ross Perot that Gore was widely judged to have won. Yet even two days before the vote in the House, the outlook remained uncertain. Many described the intense end of the battle as messy and a frenzy of deal cutting. The most crucial bargains protected the producers of sugar, citrus, tomatoes, asparagus, and sweet peppers.

NAFTA was approved in November 1993, and Clinton shared credit for the victory with an unlikely ally, Newt Gingrich. The House Republicans' deputy leader delivered a dozen more votes than expected. The final count was 234 to 200 in the House (with 102 of the 258 House Democrats supporting the agreement) and 61 to 38 in the Senate.

But NAFTA cast a long shadow over later attempts to renew fast track. In its aftermath, many Democrats committed themselves to the pursuit of labor and environmental goals more specifically through trade agreements. Mike Wessel, Gephardt's trade adviser, explains: "The side agreements were unacceptable to Mr. Gephardt, which is why he opposed the final passage of NAFTA. So having that history under our belt, we then wanted to make sure that the fast-track language in 1994 and thereafter was much more specific about what constituted an acceptable conclusion."[23]

Some Republicans, by contrast, saw NAFTA as the model for how labor and environmental issues should be handled in the trade arena. Don Carlson, chief of staff for Bill Archer (R-TX, and chair of the House Ways and Means Committee after the 1994 election), articulates this position: "We have contended all along that there is no reason to have [labor and environmental provisions] in fast-track legislation, because the administration already has the authority to negotiate labor and environmental agreements. It's only trade agreements that they don't have the authority to negotiate. We can do the same thing as in NAFTA where those issues were handled outside the scope of the actual treaty."[24]

NAFTA also influenced how Congress and the administration interacted over subsequent trade issues. As Republican legislative assistant Bieron recalls, "NAFTA really established the mental framework among Republicans as to the administration's attitude on labor and environment, as well as what USTR consultations really meant. The feeling was that consultations with these guys were not worth a dime, because of what

---

23. Unless otherwise noted, all quotes from Mike Wessel are from a March 1998 interview with Charan Devereaux.

24. Unless otherwise noted, all quotes from Don Carlson are from a March 1998 interview with Charan Devereaux.

happened during the consultations over the NAFTA side agreements." Thus when the Clinton administration's efforts to renew fast track began in 1994, many Republicans already had a stance. Bieron explains,

> The Republicans saw the administration threaten the entire passage of NAFTA by delaying five months trying to squeeze the Canadians and Mexicans into a trade sanction process [for labor and environmental standards]. So that made us think, "Gosh, those guys are very serious about labor and the environment—to the point where they are willing to endanger a good free trade agreement that we all like." That lesson was behind the way some Republicans members reacted to the administration. They wanted a very, very tight reading of how labor and environment was to be included in fast track. There was very little personal or ideological trust.

## The 1994 Attempt to Pass Fast Track

Soon after the passage of NAFTA, USTR Mickey Kantor completed negotiations for the Uruguay Round of GATT, the seven-year, 124-nation multilateral trade deal that, among other accomplishments, lowered tariffs, strengthened intellectual property rules, and established the World Trade Organization. The Uruguay Round, like NAFTA, required the passage of implementing legislation. Hoping to avoid another battle, the Clinton administration undertook lengthy consultations with Congress to develop the legislation and smooth the way.

Because fast track would expire in 1994, the implementing bill for the Uruguay Round was expected to contain an extension. The fast-track draft produced by the administration in June 1994 included a new element: trade-related labor and environmental issues. These were included among the fast-track negotiating objectives, the specific goals that the administration would try to achieve during trade talks. This position had been developed in consultation with labor unions. As AFL-CIO policy analyst Thea Lee recounts, "There were extensive discussions between the AFL-CIO, Mickey Kantor, and other people in the administration in order to work toward some consensus or agreement that we all could live with."[25]

But the administration's fast-track draft provoked hostility among some Republicans and many in the business community. According to Thelma Askey of the House Subcommittee on Trade, Kantor "wanted to propel labor and the environment into the same category as trade violations, which could be enforced by trade sanctions. That worried the business community. It worried our members." Such a policy would lead to retaliation and challenges in the WTO, opponents argued. They also worried that traditional trade goals would take a back seat to these new preoccupations.

---

25. Unless otherwise noted, all quotes from Thea Lee are from a March 1998 interview with the author.

As one Republican insider complained, "It would divert resources. Instead of focusing on the traditional objectives about what should be achieved in a trade agreement, Kantor would spend a lot of time trying to achieve unachievable goals. We didn't believe that there was enough consensus for labor and environment in order to make that step." In August 1994, the House Ways and Means Committee approved draft fast-track language that did not include labor and environmental standards in the principal negotiating objectives.

Meanwhile, the debate over the Uruguay Round Agreements was starting to heat up. Republicans worked to delay the vote on the bill until after the midterm 1994 elections, not wanting to give the Clinton administration a legislative victory before the elections. In addition, Senator Ernest Hollings (D-SC) held the bill in committee for the full 45 days permitted under fast track as a way of registering his opposition to US trade policy.[26] The leadership of both parties committed to voting on the Uruguay Round before the end of the year, however.

Worried that fast track would endanger passage of the entire Uruguay Round Agreement, two influential members of the Senate Finance Committee—the chairman, Daniel Patrick Moynihan (D-NY), and the ranking minority member, Robert Packwood (R-OR)—made known their reluctance to include language renewing the authority.[27] At a September meeting of the National Economic Council, Treasury Secretary Lloyd Bentsen declared that the administration lacked the votes for fast-track extension (Destler 1997, 19). The White House was convinced, and the bill implementing the Uruguay Round—approved overwhelmingly by Congress in a special December lame duck session—contained no new fast-track authority. The vote was 288 to 146, with 86 House members casting their vote after being defeated in the elections or choosing to retire; 167 of 256 Democrats supported the agreement.

Despite the setback on fast track, President Clinton was soon taking steps toward new free trade commitments. In December, the president played host to the heads of 32 other Western Hemisphere nations, meeting at the Summit of the Americas to discuss trade issues. Latin American nations, especially Chile, had hopes of expanding NAFTA beyond Mexico and Canada, and therefore "the Latins were aghast when fast track was pulled off the table," said one observer.[28] Another attempt to renew fast track was imminent.

---

26. See "Moynihan Announces Deal for Senate GATT Vote in December," *Inside US Trade*, September 30, 1994.

27. "Moynihan, Packwood Urge Clean GATT Bill, Better Funding Options," *Inside US Trade*, September 2, 1994.

28. Quoted in Linda Robins, Jack Epstein, Tim Zimmerman, David Bowermaster, and Matthew Cooper, "Reaching for New Heights Latin Leaders Will Push for Free Trade at the Summit of the Americas," *US News and World Report*, December 12, 1994, 68.

## The 1995 Attempt

In early 1995, fast track was back on the legislative agenda with an important change in the dynamic. In the 1994 elections, Republicans gained control of the House for the first time in 40 years; they also controlled the Senate.

Republicans took the lead on the fast-track issue. Republican members of the Ways and Means Committee developed a proposal and consulted with the administration, but no House Democrats were involved in the process. "By their own choice, Democrats on the committee never participated," Thelma Askey recalls. "This was always an effort between the administration and the House Republicans." The Ways and Means fast-track proposal was quite restrictive in its treatment of labor and the environment. While not excluding all references to these issues, it required any labor or environmental objective to be "directly related" to trade. By this, Republicans meant that only labor and environmental measures that *impeded* trade could be considered under fast-track authority (Destler 1997, 21).

In August 1995, the House Ways and Means Trade Subcommittee postponed action on fast track until September. A few days later, Subcommittee Chair Phil Crane led a nine-member US congressional delegation to Santiago, Chile. Negotiators from Chile, Mexico, Canada, and the United States had kicked off the first round of talks on Chile's entry into NAFTA, and Crane wanted to discuss the possibilities. Eduardo Aninat, Chile's finance minister, noted that Chile wouldn't negotiate any crucial points without fast track for fear that any agreement would be open to major amendments in the US Congress. "What Chile is not going to do is negotiate twice," Aninat said.[29]

Back in the United States, the Ways and Means committee passed a version of fast track lacking the labor and environmental provisions favored by the administration. It also limited bills implementing trade agreements to provisions "necessary" to carry out those agreements, as opposed to more permissive prior fast-track language that allowed "necessary and appropriate" provisions. According to Askey, the new language attempted to clarify that no "extraneous matters" could be included in implementing legislation.[30] The House Ways and Means fast-track bill was opposed by USTR Mickey Kantor, who criticized it as more limited and less flexible than the authority given to past administrations.[31] But the news of the Ways and Means bill dominated the front pages of Chilean newspapers.

---

29. Aninat, quoted in Christopher Chazin, "US Congress Delegation in Chile to Discuss NAFTA," *Emerging Markets Report,* August 7, 1995.

30. "House Ways and Means Approves GOP Version of Fast-Track Bill," *Inside US Trade,* September 22, 1995.

31. Robert S. Greenberger and Nancy Keates, "Fast-Track Bill on Trade Is Backed by Panel in the House," *The Wall Street Journal,* September 22, 1995, A6.

The fast-track bill was dropped from an upcoming budget reconciliation measure after the administration and Ways and Means Republicans failed to reach an agreement. Moreover, some Democrats announced they would oppose the budget bill if it included fast-track language. In a final blow, presidential aspirant Bob Dole declared in November that "it would be a mistake to extend new fast-track authority at this time." Dole further asserted, "I do not believe Congress should extend new fast-track authority until we've had an adequate cooling-off period following the two recent major trade agreements [GATT and NAFTA]."[32] As one senior House Republican aide noted, "That speech was the death knell for fast track."

## The 1997 Fast-Track Effort

In his 1997 State of the Union speech, President Clinton once again called on Congress to renew fast-track negotiating authority. The United States, Clinton said, "must act to expand our exports, especially to Asia and Latin America, two of the fastest-growing regions on earth, or be left behind as these emerging economies forge new ties with other nations."[33] A few weeks later, he repeated his commitment during a visit from the president of Chile.

Clinton wanted to be armed with fast-track authority because the United States faced a variety of upcoming trade talks, among them new discussions on including Chile in NAFTA, creating a hemisphere-wide Free Trade Area of the Americas, and creating an Asia-Pacific free trade zone. The president also wanted to build on the Information Technology Agreement (ITA) that had eliminated $5 billion in tariffs on IT products.[34] Finally, the administration argued that it could not successfully participate in planned WTO negotiations—on intellectual property in 1998, agriculture in 1999, and trade in services in 2000—without fast track.[35] At the same time, according to some observers, the administration lacked an explicit negotiating agenda and none of the prospective talks was urgent; when fast-track renewal was at issue in 1974, 1988, and 1993, by contrast, a global round of trade talks was under way. Did the administration really *need* fast track?

---

32. Dole, quoted in his statement on the Senate floor, Congressional Record, 104th Congress, 1st Session, Vol. 141, No. 173, November 3, 1995.

33. President William J. Clinton, address before a Joint Session of the Congress on the State of the Union, February 4, 1997.

34. Under the ITA, the United States and 43 other countries agreed to eliminate tariffs, with a few exceptions, by the year 2000.

35. Stuart Eizenstat, testimony at a Hearing of the International Economic Policy and Trade Subcommittee, House International Relations Committee, 105th Congress, 1st session, September 24, 1997.

The president's endorsement of fast track was not immediately followed by a legislative proposal. As one Republican staffer noted, "[Clinton] made a very good statement on fast track in his State of the Union address. However, it was not reflected in anything of substance." Some senior administration officials were unenthusiastic about fast track; they worried about the political costs of pursuing the legislation and the difficulties of securing its passage. Thelma Askey of the House Trade Subcommittee agrees that the administration was divided:

> I think the president was solidly behind it. Beyond the president, I think you'd find a range of views or even resistance. You have some individuals like [Clinton's boyhood friend and senior adviser Thomas "Mack"] McLarty and [White House Chief of Staff Erskine] Bowles who I think personally were very supportive of fast track. . . . You'd find as many people, if not more, who thought it was not a good idea politically. They weren't looking at it from a policy point of view. They just thought politically it did not address their base. And, in fact, it was objectionable to a significant part of their base—organized labor. So the president's strong commitment to fast track was never adequately or consistently reflected in how the administration pursued it.

Of course, fast track was not the only legislative issue the administration faced that spring. Securing passage for the fiscal 1998 federal budget was crucial. One senior House Republican aide remembers the administration's being "unwilling to move forward [on fast track] while the budget deal was being hammered out because it would split Democrats. The administration needed all the Democrats it could get on the budget." Another priority for the administration was the controversial renewal of China's most favored nation (MFN) trading status (see chapter 6). Some Democrats did not want to side with business and Republicans on both China's MFN status and fast track.

On April 1, 1997, the sequence in which these legislative issues should be handled was discussed in a meeting of cabinet members; also attending was Charlene Barshefsky, Clinton's nominee to replace Mickey Kantor as the US Trade Representative. No final determination was made.[36] As Barshefsky remembers, "Basically, the division in the White House at the time was this: Some of us were saying, 'We should go for fast track early in the spring;' others were saying, 'No, no, no, we have budget negotiations going on in the spring.' It turned out we were right. We should have pushed ahead on fast track in the spring."[37]

---

36. "Administration Wrestles with Timing, Substance of Fast Track Bill," *Inside US Trade*, April 4, 1997, 1.

37. Unless otherwise noted, all quotes from Charlene Barshefsky are from a March 2001 interview with Charan Devereaux.

## Labor and Fast Track

One major force attacking fast track was organized labor, whose opposition had been stiffened by the battle over NAFTA. Many union members essentially viewed NAFTA as a 1,000-page agreement aimed at protecting US investments in Mexico. Labor had fought hard against NAFTA, and the loss was infuriating. "There was a lot of pent-up resentment over NAFTA," the AFL-CIO's Thea Lee acknowledges, "having lost the battle as narrowly as we did." Even some staunch supporters of NAFTA admit that the agreement was probably oversold to Congress and the American public, with promises that it would create 200,000 jobs in its first two years and alleviate pollution along the border with Mexico, among other benefits. Three years after the enactment of the agreement, labor remained unconvinced. According to Bill Klinefelter of the United Steelworkers of America, "NAFTA was the key. We saw actual job loss and we knew which plants were closed because of that agreement. The steelworkers could point out very accurately that we had lost about 7,000 jobs since NAFTA had gone into effect."[38] The collapse of the Mexican peso and reports of worsening environmental degradation along the border fueled labor's charge that NAFTA was a failure. Fast track, labor insisted, should protect workers as well as investors. As the United Auto Workers' Alan Reuther put it, "We saw NAFTA as having been a disaster. We did not want to see NAFTA expanded, which was the whole point of fast track."[39]

Even so, insiders report that the AFL-CIO, a 78-union labor federation representing 13.1 million workers, initially resisted embarking on a fight against fast track. In a February 1997 Executive Council meeting, a few AFL-CIO staff members balked at the idea of mobilizing to oppose the legislation. Observers attribute this resistance to the close relationship between the AFL-CIO and the Clinton administration.

Vice President Gore reportedly attended the February 1997 Executive Council meeting in an effort to dissuade AFL-CIO leadership from a full-scale battle over fast track, but the leaders of the Steelworkers, the Autoworkers, and OCAW were unconvinced. After a contentious meeting, the council issued a strong statement opposing any "grant of fast track negotiating authority . . . that does not include provisions and enforcement mechanisms for addressing worker rights, labor standards and environmental protection. These provisions must be part of the core agreement."[40]

---

38. Unless otherwise noted, all quotes from Bill Klinefelter are from a March 1998 interview with Charan Devereaux.

39. Unless otherwise noted, all quotes from Alan Reuther are from a March 1998 interview with Charan Devereaux.

40. AFL-CIO Executive Council, "Fast Track Trade Negotiating Authority," Portland, OR, February 19, 1997, www.aflcio.org.

## Union Arguments for Opposing Fast Track

Labor's essential argument was that international trade does not help everyone. A globalized economy benefits the wealthier member of society, labor maintained, while middle- and lower-income citizens are often left behind. US companies often move their operations to, or purchase products from, countries where workers cost less to employ. These lower labor costs were sometimes attributable to unfair, even inhumane labor practices and lax environmental protection. Labor also claimed that US companies often threatened workers at the negotiating table by emphasizing their freedom to relocate abroad. Thea Lee explains:

> It is a universal experience among workers that globalization is used as a threat. It's used as a tool to bring their wages down. To frighten them. To cow them. And this is the contradiction that people who live in Washington, who sell free trade for a living, don't understand. Managers across the country are beating workers over the head with the threat of globalization. Sometimes it may be just a bluff— maybe the company has no intention of moving overseas. That doesn't matter, because if they threaten to move overseas and workers believe the threat, they'll take a 50 percent pay cut. Then trade has had an impact on their wages without any trade having taken place.

Many fast-track supporters suspected that what unions really wanted was to block international trade. They interpreted efforts to insert language on labor and the environment into fast track as thinly disguised protectionist attempts to limit trade altogether. "It's a poison pill designed to scuttle trade agreements," said Julius Katz, the Bush administration's chief negotiator for NAFTA (quoted in Kosterlitz 1997, 2076). Another fast-track supporter charged, "We think what [labor] has done is to try and establish conditions for trade agreements which they know are not achievable so they can avoid the US entering into trade agreements." Unions wanted to turn back the clock, some fast-track advocates argued, to a time when trade was less important.

Labor interests countered that they were not motivated by protectionism, nor were they capable of stopping the trend toward globalization. "We can't put the genie back in the bottle. We're not trying to block trade," says Thea Lee. "But we do want to change the rules under which international trade and investment take place." Not enough was being done, labor argued, to help US workers adversely affected by trade. To be sure, assistance and training were available for some—for example, through Trade Adjustment Assistance (TAA), which was created in 1962 to assist workers and firms hurt by imports.[41] But labor called such programs

---

41. In the Tokyo Round of trade negotiations, Congress liberalized TAA eligibility requirements and enriched the TAA package. As part of the legislation granting trade-negotiating authority for the Uruguay Round of trade talks, Congress enacted the Economic Dislocation and Worker Adjustment Act of 1988.

inadequate. Those who lost their jobs because of global trade faced rough times. Among American manufacturing workers whose jobs were permanently eliminated, 20 percent were still out of work a year later. The average length of unemployment was five months and those who succeeded in getting a job took on average a 10 percent pay cut (Stokes 1998, 9).

For their part, fast-track advocates argued that trade should not be blamed for unemployment and the growing income inequality in the United States. They pointed to interest rates set by the Federal Reserve and rapid technological change as having a far greater impact on wages and employment levels, and they insisted that in the long run, holding the American economy hostage by opposing fast track would only hurt workers and consumers. After all, export-related employment accounted for 23 percent of private-industry new job growth in the United States between 1990 and 1995 (Stokes 1998, 6). "Let's be realistic about this," said USTR spokesman Jay Ziegler. "The choice is: Are we going to make progress, or disengage from the rest of the world? We would prefer to advance trade—and labor and environmental goals—in a realistic framework, rather than to set a standard that prevents us from making any progress" (quoted in Kosterlitz 1997, 2076).

In response to organized labor's argument that low wages abroad often reflected unfair practices by governments and companies, fast-track supporters retorted that the *imposition* of labor and environmental standards through the vehicle of trade agreements was not an appropriate remedy. Indeed, suggests Don Carlson, trade itself may be the solution:

> Frankly, we believe that increased trade and the involvement of American business in many of these countries has a far greater impact in raising standards within those countries. How American businesses operate overseas ethically and legally, and the way they treat their workers, raises the standards within these countries by example. We operate in a far different manner than . . . the French and the Italians, and many of the other trading countries in the world. We have a great deal to offer by example.

Furthermore, some claimed, trade-generated wealth is a more powerful vehicle for change than forcing standards on a nation. "If you look at Korea, Taiwan, Chile, and Argentina, these are the models for how you raise the standards for average people," says Republican congressional staffer Brian Bieron. "The transition toward a more free economy ends up empowering people. As a country gets wealthier and wealthier, they invest in worker rights and cleaner technologies."

In part, the fast-track debate centered on determining the best place to negotiate and enforce agreements on labor standards. Many fast-track supporters believed that labor talks belong at institutions like the International Labor Organization, an independent agency of the United Nations whose "main goal is to promote decent work for all men and women" (see www.us.ilo.org). Unions disagreed, noting that workers have no leverage at the ILO because the organization lacks the power to enforce its conventions.[42] The only way to ensure enforcement, the AFL-CIO argued, was to link violation of labor standards to economic consequences—and thus the best forum is a trade negotiation. "We want the same kind of binding dispute settlement for our concerns that business gets for things like intellectual property rights and investment rules," says Thea Lee. "Businesses understand, as we do, that you use the leverage of a trade agreement to obtain promises from your trading partners to improve their laws."

Labor also portrayed addressing worker rights in trade negotiations as a matter of fairness. Lee notes, "If you look at NAFTA, the GATT, these are sets of rules that look like they were written by businesses. That's because they *are* written by businesses. All we're really asking for is to have equal weight for the concerns of American workers and the environment." Inviting in more participants would indeed make the policy process messier, Lee acknowledges, but "democracy can be inconvenient."

## Labor Organizes

The time seemed right for labor to marshal its arguments. Labor's frustrations over NAFTA had already hurt Democrats in Congress. They "felt disenfranchised about what happened on NAFTA," says one congressional staff member. "And they didn't show up to vote [in 1994]—a lot of folks didn't. And it hurt Democrats at the polls." In the aftermath of NAFTA, many Democrats were ready to listen to their labor constituencies about trade.

According to labor representatives, they were able to oppose fast track outright in 1997 before language was drafted because the administration had signaled from the start that it would not be able to meet labor's demands. Compromise was not possible. "We had many conversations with the White House and USTR and various other people, where they told us they were not going to address our concerns," recalls Thea Lee of the AFL-CIO. "That's why we were willing to go out early, we didn't have to wait to see the bill."

Organizing on fast track at labor's grassroots level soon gathered steam. Post-NAFTA, unions recognized the need to reenergize their members. And so, Bill Klinefelter explains, they tried new strategies:

> After the 1994 elections, steelworkers decided that we really needed to change the way we communicated with our membership—mainly because we weren't communicating with our membership. In 1994 what was being discussed in the plants and in the shops were not worker's issues, were not economic issues, were not social issues, but wedge issues like abortion and prayer in the public schools. We

---

42. In addition, the United States has signed only two of the ILO's eight core conventions.

decided that in order to better communicate with our membership, we had to devise a grassroots program.

Coordinators trained local union leaders to recruit 4 percent of their members into this new program, called "Rapid Response." Once the recruits were in place, local leaders received a fax machine and became a part of a communication loop. Klinefelter continues:

> So now we could communicate with a large percent of our membership almost instantaneously and make things happen. We put out a series of informational faxes on fast track that prepared them for action. We looked at the data from the NAFTA adjustment assistance program and saw where we had lost members. Then we talked to those people at the local plant level, got their stories and said, "What we would like you to do is sit down, write a letter and write your story. What happened to you, what happened to your family." And we sent them to the White House. This was before any Hill action began.

Some Republican leaders charged that the strong-arm tactics of "Big Labor" doomed fast track, but other observers disagree. Responsibility lies not with the leaders, they say, but with the tens of thousands of members who took action. "When the AFL-CIO's grassroots and communications department got involved, they were excellent," says Lori Wallach of Public Citizen's Global Trade Watch, a nonprofit consumer advocacy organization founded by Ralph Nader. "But all of the formative and much of the most important grassroots work were rallies of Teamsters. Letters and visits of Steelworkers. UAW folks on the ground."[43] The apparel workers' union ran ads in Spanish-language newspapers to spread the word. And the Teamsters broadcast anti-fast-track ads on radio stations popular with truckers. Members of the Steelworkers union alone sent 160,000 handwritten letters to Congress.[44] Many members of Congress noted the grassroots nature of the union effort. As one Democratic staffer reflects: "I would say from the labor perspective, this is one of those issues that is really from the bottom up. This is an issue that gets their membership all over America very fired up. It's a very grassroots-driven type of an issue, and what the unions did was a reflection of what all their membership thinks. This is a bottom line for them."

## Strange Bedfellows—Other Fast-Track Opponents

Labor was hardly fast track's only opponent in 1997. In fact, an unusually diverse coalition of interests mobilized to fight the legislation. Though

---

43. Unless otherwise noted, all quotes from Lori Wallach are from a March 1998 interview with Charan Devereaux.

44. Jill Abramson and Steven Greenhouse, "The Trade Bill: Labor Victory on Trade Bill Reveals Power," *The New York Times*, November 12, 1997, A1.

some environmental organizations had supported fast track's reauthorization in 1991 and NAFTA in 1993, most now opposed fast track. One such group was the National Wildlife Federation (NWF), America's largest not-for-profit conservation organization. Steven Shimberg, NWF's vice president for federal and international affairs, told Congress:

> We recognized the potential of trade as an instrument to enhance environmental protection, and believed that NAFTA was a good first step toward the integration of trade and environment. . . . Based on our experience with NAFTA and with other trade and investment agreements, we now know we can no longer rely solely on side agreements to achieve our environmental objectives, or on fast track rules which do not state explicit goals for environmental protection.[45]

Another fast-track opponent was Public Citizen's Global Trade Watch, which published three reports charging that NAFTA had compromised food safety, promoted environmental degradation in Mexico, and failed to facilitate job creation. For Global Trade Watch, fast track became a referendum on NAFTA. Other foes included conservative populist Pat Buchanan, who argued that protecting US national interests was more important than free trade; he also urged withdrawal from the WTO. Some Republicans opposed fast track on constitutional and political grounds, arguing that it was a mistake to grant any type of extra executive authority to the president. Others simply didn't trust Clinton to negotiate agreements they would support. Representative Dana Rohrabacher (R-CA) declared, "I would predict that the president is going to have a difficult time getting fast track through this Congress. I mean, after all, he's relying on Republican votes and, quite frankly, we Republicans, at least this Republican, doesn't trust the president. . . . I feel like I was betrayed the last time I gave up that authority."[46] Other Republicans had concerns specific to their districts, such as worries about how certain agricultural and textile sectors would be affected.

## Gephardt Mobilizes

Union and environmentalist apprehension about trade intersected with many traditional Democratic values, and House Minority Leader Dick Gephardt moved early to oppose fast track. Gephardt's office reportedly had five separate meetings with the White House on fast track beginning

---

45. Steven J. Shimberg (vice president for federal and international affairs, National Wildlife Federation), testimony to the House Subcommittee on Trade of the Ways and Means Committee, 105th Congress, 1st Session, September 30, 1997.

46. Rep. Dana Rohrabacher, speaking at a Hearing of the House Subcommittee on International Economic Policy and Trade of the International Relations Committee, 105th Congress, 1st Session, September 24, 1997.

in late 1996, two of them one-on-one sessions between Gephardt and Clinton. Gephardt's position was clear, says his trade adviser Mike Wessel:

> Gephardt had supported fast track in the past and was prepared to do so again. But we would publicly organize around the Democratic Leader's views and we would not sit idly by while [the administration] moved forward, therefore diminishing our effectiveness at the end of the day. We did that during the NAFTA fight, which is in part why we lost. We did not organize opposition to NAFTA until it became clear that we could not work these issues out. Gephardt said that he would not make that same mistake again, of sitting in negotiations where it was clear that the other side was not acting in good faith but was already organizing and had already made up their minds. We began very serious organizational activities to enhance the Leader's effectiveness.

In February 1997, Gephardt wrote a 12-page "Dear Colleague" letter to House Democrats denouncing NAFTA and voicing disapproval of any fast-track proposal that lacked protections for labor and the environment. Gephardt opposed relegating labor and environmental issues to side agreements, as in NAFTA, and called for their inclusion in the body of trade pacts "equal in stature and force and linked to provisions on investment and trade . . . fully enforceable with access to trade sanctions where necessary" (Gephardt 1997).

Gephardt's colleague, House Minority Whip David Bonior, also organized early. Bonior's office led regular meetings on the fast-track issue for members of the House. "We started in March, meeting every week," says one staff person active in the anti-fast-track effort, "to educate ourselves and the rest of the caucus about what happened in NAFTA and to what extent it was relevant to fast track. We had blue dogs, we had new members, the tomato folks, Hispanic Caucus members, members who had supported NAFTA, it was really a cross section of the Democratic Caucus that was active."

In March, the *Washington Post* obtained a copy of a Clinton administration memo to Stuart Eizenstat, undersecretary of commerce for international trade, which made clear that the executive would try to push a fast-track bill over the objections of Gephardt and Bonior.[47] Many administration officials believed that there was no room for compromise with Gephardt because his position was doomed to political failure. Some said the Minority Leader himself knew that a fast-track bill with provisions he favored stood no chance of getting out of the Republican-led Ways and Means Committee.

Some critics accused traditional Democrats of siding with the labor unions for financial reasons. Union money had become increasingly important for House Democrats, whose financial support from business de-

---

47. Paul Blustein, " 'Fast Track' Trade Plan Pits White House Against Top Congressional Democrats," *The Washington Post,* March 22, 1997, A11. Also see "Confidential Memo Reveals Administration Strategy on Fast Track," *Inside US Trade,* March 28, 1997.

creased when the Republicans won control of Congress in 1994. By 1996, contributions from labor's political action committees accounted for 48 percent of PAC donations to House Democrats, up from 33 percent in 1992. Furthermore, in 1997, the Democratic Party was $15 million in the red. "The Democratic Party is bankrupt, everyone knows that," said Thomas J. Donohue, president of the US Chamber of Commerce, "and the only money these guys can get is from the unions."[48]

While acknowledging the decline in business support for the Democratic Party, union officials are skeptical about the degree to which it influenced the fast-track battle. As one observes:

> A lot of people talked about union money. What people said was that since the Republicans took over Congress, businesses stopped giving as much to Democrats and so labor money became more important than ever. And that is why Democrats couldn't afford to vote [yes on fast track]. I think that is putting way too much emphasis on the money and not giving members of Congress credit for having brains and constituents and being able to read the bill themselves and to draw their own judgments.

Finally, presidential politics was also a variable. Many press accounts of the fast-track fight pointed to the presidential ambitions of both Gephardt and Gore. Pundits wondered if the prospect of the upcoming presidential race in 2000 increased Gephardt's fervor in campaigning against fast track in order to secure union support for his potential candidacy. Participants in the anti-fast-track campaign scoff at this interpretation. "It is the lazy reporter's way of explaining what happened," says one senior Democratic staffer. "The political story is much more interesting than the mundane trade debate. You know, two titans of the Democratic party fighting over an issue that divides the party. It's good drama, but it was not that relevant to the process."

## The House Ways and Means Trade Subcommittee: Republicans Push for Action

Even as labor and the traditional Democrats mobilized against it, Republicans on the House Ways and Means Trade Subcommittee were pushing fast track as an idea whose time had come. Ways and Means Chairman Bill Archer and Trade Subcommittee Chairman Phil Crane (R-IL) wanted to move the legislation during the spring of 1997. Fast-track supporters from Ways and Means were eager for Charlene Barshefsky to be confirmed as the next US trade representative, succeeding Mickey Kantor. Barshefsky was expected to be fast track's most ardent supporter in the

---

48. Figures on labor's PAC contributions and Donohue, quoted in Abramson and Greenhouse, "The Trade Bill," A1.

administration and a catalyst for momentum on the issue. Don Carlson, Archer's chief of staff, recalls, "From the first announcement of Charlene's nomination, she indicated that her highest priority was fast track, and we kept hoping that the nomination would move. But all of the nominations stalled. So there was no movement whatsoever."

During the spring, Trade Subcommittee Republicans and the administration exchanged language on the substance of fast-track legislation. In late April, Republicans rejected an administration proposal to eliminate negotiating objectives from fast track on the grounds that doing so would allow the administration to pursue trade agreements with no limits at all. On May 13, House Republican staff presented a proposal to administration officials to allow the inclusion of labor and environmental issues in future trade agreements only if they were "directly trade-related," language similar to the 1995 proposal. Generally, Republicans felt that the inclusion of labor and environmental objectives could hurt US businesses, as nations would simply choose to trade elsewhere. Carlson explains their position:

> One of the big tensions in international trade is the tension between major companies for advantage in developing markets. There is a fight between the major trading nations to develop positions of advantage in opening markets. The underlying issue in almost all of our trade relations is, To what extent are American businesses placed at a disadvantage with regard to their foreign competitors? Will America get access to the markets that we helped to force open, or will others take advantage of these efforts? That's one of the big issues that we've got to deal with.

Business interests echoed these concerns. "Let's not delude ourselves into thinking that we are bestowing a special favor on other countries by letting them buy our goods and services," says lobbyist Gail Harrison of the Wexler Group. "American businesses and farmers face very stiff competition in overseas markets."[49]

Ways and Means Republicans continued to press the administration on the timing of fast track. Thelma Askey of the House Trade Subcommittee told the *Washington Post* that Republican members had informed the White House of a possible meeting on May 15 to draft the legislation. This move was criticized by the White House and Representative Robert Matsui, the ranking Democrat on the Trade Subcommittee, as premature. Askey said, "What we're telling the administration now is that this is a window of opportunity that shouldn't be lost."[50]

---

49. Unless otherwise noted, all quotes from Gail Harrison are from a March 1998 interview with Charan Devereaux.

50. Askey, quoted in Blustein, "Republicans Urge Clinton to Join Trade Fast Track; Some on Hill Say There Is a Window of Opportunity for Legislation to Speed Treaties," *The Washington Post*, May 14, 1997, D9.

On May 14, White House spokesman Mike McCurry commented that the Clinton administration expected to renew fast-track authority in time for the Second Summit of the Americas, which was to be held in Santiago in early 1998.[51] Partly in response to this remark, Archer wrote a letter to the president the next day accusing the administration of paying lip service to fast track without taking action: "Although voicing strong support for fast-track authority, no concrete steps have been taken by your Administration to reach our objective of enacting trade negotiation authority. . . . Every month that goes by means more lost contracts and more job opportunities forgone for Americans."[52] Archer warned that the administration's failure to agree to a May 15 markup endangered the chances for passage of the bill in 1997.

The reaction of many Democrats to the proposals coming out of Ways and Means was far from enthusiastic. As one Democratic congressional staffer active in the anti-fast-track coalition remarks, "Obviously, no Democrats had any role in the drafting process. So from our point of view, what they put in it was relatively trivial because they never really tried to meet our concerns. It's not as though we had a give-and-take." David Bonior and other House Democrats paid attention to the activity in the Ways and Means Committee mainly to glean "clues about timing"—to figure out how long they had before a vote. The same staffer continues:

> The only people fooled, to be honest, were some of the opinion leaders in the media. They thought that because the Republicans were talking about labor and environmental issues that would mean the problems were solved. Newt Gingrich made a speech saying he endorsed this approach, and there were some stories written about how Gingrich was allowing these environmental issues to be considered in fast track, and this was going to save it. When you actually looked at what it was all about, it was a joke.

## A Long Hot Summer

On May 21, President Clinton decided to delay action on fast-track negotiating authority until September. The decision was made at a meeting attended by Vice President Gore, National Security Adviser Sandy Berger, National Economic Council Director Gene Sperling, Treasury Secretary Robert Rubin, Deputy Treasury Secretary Larry Summers, and USTR Charlene Barshefsky.[53] During the meeting, Barshefsky argued that the

---

51. "White House, Republicans Trade Charges Over Timing on Fast Track," *Inside US Trade*, May 16, 1997, 33.

52. "Archer Letter on Fast Track" reprinted in *Inside US Trade*, May 23, 1997.

53. "Administration Decides to Delay Fast Track until September," *Inside US Trade*, May 23, 1997.

administration should move ahead with fast track as soon as possible. As she recalls:

> The president announced in the State of the Union address at the end of January that he wanted fast track. But the real effort, the muscle that the White House would bring to bear, didn't come along until the end of the following September. And in the intervening period, the opposition to fast track was allowed to grow essentially unchecked. It was a terrible mistake. Terrible. Sandy Berger, Larry Summers, and I were the most vocal people saying, "Do it now. Don't wait. The longer you wait, the more this is going to be like NAFTA. We almost lost the NAFTA because of the hiatus over the August recess. You're going to risk loss again."

Despite these arguments, other members of the administration were convinced that it was unwise to expend political capital on fast track when Congress faced votes on both the budget and the renewal of China's MFN status. Mike McCurry announced the decision: "The President has come to the conclusion that we should push hard for fast-track authority beginning in the fall, in September, and use the time between now and then to really help educate the American people on all the benefits that free trade has brought to this country."[54] Action on fast track thus was postponed. "[But] we probably don't want to do it on Labor Day," a White House aide wryly noted (quoted in Simendinger 1997, 1338).

In July, the administration appointed Jason Berman, longtime president of the Recording Industry Association of America, to coordinate the campaign on fast track. The choice of someone outside the administration did not come as a total surprise. As Berman points out, "It was a system that [the administration] had used to some extent in NAFTA when [Chicago businessman] Bill Daley worked with Mickey Kantor. In addition, there were some internal issues that needed to be resolved. Some people [in the administration] weren't so interested in going forward on fast track and, therefore, if you took it out of the normal process, you might avoid having to deal with that." Berman was well known on the Hill; according to a senior House Republican aide, "He knew a lot of members and had a very good relationship with them. He had been associated with free trade for a long time. He was from a very popular industry and was good at what he did. It was a long struggle to find someone and the administration had been talking about naming a fast-track czar for some time."

As the summer continued, the administration attempted to generate more support among Democrats for fast track. President Clinton met with more than 60 Democrats in late July and early August to make the case for the legislation. According to a congressional source, Democrats told Clinton that they would take "a lot of heat" if they supported fast track. Mc-

---

54. McCurry, quoted in "Key House Supporter Sees Speedy Action on Fast Track This Fall," *Inside US Trade*, May 30, 1997.

Curry said members told the president there needed to be "sufficient protection" for US workers, as well as attention to the needs of workers in other countries and to the environment.[55]

In July, 14 Hispanic House members, led by Representative Esteban Torres (D-CA), wrote a letter to President Clinton saying that for Latinos, African Americans, and women, NAFTA had cost more jobs than it had created. The legislators added that they could not support fast-track extension until improvements were made, such as strengthening the Trade Adjustment Assistance program that helped US workers who lost their jobs.

The administration downplayed NAFTA in discussions of fast track. USTR Barshefsky, speaking to members of the Business Roundtable in late June, emphasized that the goal of fast track was not expanding NAFTA but promoting trade with Asia and agricultural trade with the European Union.[56] The Clinton administration "did not want to support NAFTA during this process," says Thelma Askey. "A number of times they tried to take NAFTA off the table in spite of the fact that we told them their efforts would be fruitless. As we warned, they couldn't ignore NAFTA because labor was always going to bring it up."[57]

In fact, playing up the relationship between NAFTA and fast track was a key aspect of labor's strategy. As an AFL-CIO pamphlet argued in boldface type: "Fast Track brought us *NAFTA*, and look where that got us. . . . Now, big *corporations* want to extend the NAFTA deal to other countries. In today's world, America needs *fair* balanced trade—*not more NAFTAs*" (AFL-CIO pamphlet, 1997).

Labor kept up its campaign against fast track, as Thea Lee of the AFL-CIO explains:

> The lobbying effort, as you can imagine, slows down in the summer. Congress was on recess, so there wasn't very much going on. But we started with a postcard campaign. We sent out almost a million tear-off postcards to our members and through affiliates letting them communicate with their members of Congress. We were also organizing district visits as well as Washington visits to members of Congress. We targeted members of Congress that we knew were undecided.

Gephardt's office was said to have met with labor representatives to persuade them not to target Democratic members of Congress. Though Gephardt himself opposed fast track, as Minority Leader he was not eager to see fellow Democrats threatened by labor.

---

55. Congressional source and McCurry quoted in "Administration Considering New Policies to Win Passage of Fast Track," *Inside US Trade*, August 1, 1997, 18.

56. "Barshefsky Promises Start of Fast-Track Campaign in Early September," *Inside US Trade*, July 4, 1997.

57. A congressionally mandated three-year review of NAFTA, due in July, was delayed; the report was ultimately delivered in the fall.

Labor's growing effectiveness frustrated Ways and Means Chairman Archer, as Don Carlson remembers: "We were very discouraged, particularly because of the long August recess, because the opposition kept targeting members in their districts. And as they put people into the 'no' column, they went out and targeted others. So the universe in which we could potentially get our votes was constantly shrinking. And the passage of time played clearly against us and into the hands of the opponents."

## The Role of Business

The business community had kept a low profile during the maneuvering, but in July the Business Roundtable, a lobbying group made up of the nation's 200 largest corporations, organized and funded the America Leads on Trade (ALOT) Coalition. ALOT's mission was to build support for a version of fast-track legislation capable of attracting bipartisan endorsement. TRW chaired the trade and investment task force of the Business Roundtable, and thus became the lead company in the effort. Ultimately, the coalition was joined by more than 550 trade associations and companies, including the National Association of Manufacturers and the US Chamber of Commerce. ALOT did not favor any particular fast-track bill. "At the time ALOT was formed, the administration had not yet proposed, and Ways and Means Committee leadership had not reacted to, detailed legislative language," says Gail Harrison, who lobbied on behalf of ALOT. "The coalition was therefore not in the position to endorse a specific bill."

In fact, business had been asked to withhold its support for fast track until the administration and Ways and Means Republicans had come to agreement on a fast-track version. "That was coming from the [Ways and Means] Committee leadership and the House [Republican] leadership," says one source in the business community. "The signal from the Republican side to the business community was 'Do not do this until we're agreed on the language.'" Reportedly, pressure from Republicans continued through July and August and into September. One senior House Republican aide recalls:

> We were afraid that the administration would co-opt the business community by getting them so intent on having fast track that they would agree to the administration's version. Then the administration could use the business community to put pressure on [Ways and Means]. . . . But at the same time, we wanted some general advocacy of the concept of fast track by the business community to Members. It was just very difficult for the business community to straddle that line because the companies were being asked in their meetings which version of fast track they supported. So they basically just held off. The administration sent us its proposal on September 21, and then that began a two-week negotiation period between us and the administration, culminating in the Ways and Means markup on October 8. Then the business community came out strongly in support of fast track, but by that point we really only had a month left.

Some observers also point to the lack of a clear motivation for business to put its weight behind fast track. One member of Congress said that the executives who came to lobby her characterized fast track as a "nice opportunity" rather than a dire necessity.[58] Jay Berman, the administration point man, says of the business effort:

> The word *mobilize* would cause some people to cringe compared to the effort we saw on NAFTA. NAFTA was a country-specific set of circumstances. Companies had the ability to say, "If we do a NAFTA deal, this is what's going to happen in terms of our business with Mexico." It was much more direct and concrete, whereas just getting fast-track authority was more generic. Business didn't make the same level of effort over a sustained period of time. But most importantly, they bought into the Republican strategy which was to say, "Don't come out for fast track, don't negotiate the terms of this deal with the administration. We will do that. Once we've done the deal and you look at the bill, then you can decide what you want to do."

The administration, for its part, was signaling the business community that action during the spring and summer was crucial. According to one observer, the administration "hoped the business community would rally and convince Congress like they always had." But, as some House leadership and Ways and Means Republicans had counseled, business did not rally until late in the game.

## The Administration Floats a Proposal

On September 4, USTR Barshefsky met with House Ways and Means Committee Chair Bill Archer and Senate Finance Committee Chair William Roth (R-DE) to discuss the upcoming administration legislative proposal on fast track.[59] On September 8, the White House delayed the introduction of its fast-track proposal until the following week. The decision was largely prompted by Senate Democrats, who demanded that the administration lay out what role Congress would play in trade negotiations. Some wanted more specific language about how the administration would consult with legislators during trade talks. As Senate Finance Committee member Bob Kerrey (D-NE) pointed out, "Members very much involved with these [trade negotiations] over the years . . . are of the opinion that consultations have not occurred . . . in a meaningful way."[60] Some Democratic senators advocated formal consultations with Congress before a negotiation was complete—when it was initialed but not signed.

---

58. Steven Pearlstein, "US Trade on Fast Track of Its Own; Upcoming Legislation on Treaties Is Expected to Have Little Effect," *The Washington Post*, November 7, 1997, D1.

59. "Archer Sees Good Prospects for Passage of Fast-Track Authority," *Inside US Trade*, September 5, 1997.

60. Kerrey, quoted in "Senate Democrats Prompt Delay of Fast-Track Bill Until Next Week," *Inside US Trade*, September 12, 1997, 24.

On September 16, the administration floated its fast-track proposal. "We put in what you would have predicted given the fact that Republicans controlled both the Senate and the House," says Jay Berman. Bruce Stokes, a senior fellow at the Council on Foreign Relations, concurs: "This was clearly a bill that was designed to placate the Republicans and the business interests in the Democratic Party."[61] Labor's reaction was predictable, as Thea Lee makes clear:

> We hated it. We were pretty dismayed because it was even worse than we had imagined it would be. It was a step backwards from previous fast tracks in the Reagan and Bush era. This fast-track authority we read as very restrictive. It limited the president's ability to negotiate anything that looked like upward harmonization, where other countries might be forced to improve their labor standards or the United States might actually be subject to any requirement that it enforce its own laws or improve its labor standards to be in compliance. And the same thing with environment. So it was a big disappointment to us.

## The Response

On the day that the administration offered its proposal, the AFL-CIO announced it would target 13 undecided House members and the entire California market in a $1 million television and radio advertising campaign against fast track.[62] One day later, the ALOT Coalition unveiled a large-scale media effort in support of fast-track renewal: The four-week advertising campaign would target 103 congressional districts, and its television ads alone would cost $2 million. The coalition also drew a who's who of the Washington lobbying community into the fight. ALOT did not explicitly endorse the Clinton proposal, however. Jim Christy, ALOT's coordinator and TRW's chief lobbyist, said that coalition members found Clinton's proposal "constructive" but agreed that it wouldn't pass as proposed (Stone 1997, 1903).

On September 22, an AFL-CIO convention in Pittsburgh turned into a protest rally against fast track. Nine hundred union delegates vowed to fight even harder against fast track than they had against NAFTA. The delegates jumped to their feet when Richard Gephardt said, "If intellectual property and capital deserve protections in the core free-trade treaties, with trade sanctions to enforce it, so do labor laws and environmental laws, on an equal basis."[63] President Clinton was given a cool reception when he told the crowd, "We cannot create enough good jobs and

---

61. Stokes, quoted in Ronald Brownstein, "Clinton Trade Agenda Draws Steady Barrage from the Left, Right," *Los Angeles Times*, September 25, 1997, A4.

62. By November the AFL-CIO had spent $1.5 to $2 million on advertisements, according to Denise Mitchell, an AFL-CIO spokeswoman (Abramson and Greenhouse, "The Trade Bill," A1).

63. Gephardt, quoted in Steven Greenhouse, "AFL-CIO Turns Energy Against Pacts on Free Trade," *The New York Times*, September 24, 1997, A22.

increase wages if we don't expand trade."[64] Clinton also urged labor not to let the trade issue create a rift between unions and Democrats.

Many trade proponents felt that the unions left no room for a compromise. Asked about the administration's strategy for dealing with labor, Berman responded:

> There was no need to have a strategy. Labor announced very early on that they were going to be against any fast track that didn't have [certain labor and environmental objectives] in it. And anything that had [such objectives] in it was guaranteed not to move. So we had to make a decision. We agreed to have a gentlemanly disagreement about it and then they went out and did what they had to do and we tried to do what we had to do. There was no mystery to this. This was not complicated, given how stark the choices were.

## Trouble in Congress

House Republicans faulted the administration's fast-track draft for giving the president too much flexibility in negotiating trade agreements. For one thing, the language did not obligate the president to bring back trade agreements that reflected *only* the negotiating objectives stated in the fast-track authority. The use of the phrase "necessary or appropriate" to describe what could go into implementing legislation drew further opposition; Archer's bill, by contrast, allowed only provisions "necessary" to implement the agreement.[65] Finally, Republicans also criticized the "undue vagueness" of the proposed bill's labor and environment provisions.

The difficulty of building a congressional majority for fast track was widely recognized. "Obviously, if you go anywhere close to the minimally acceptable position for labor, you won't get Republican support," said I. M. Destler, a trade expert at the University of Maryland. "If you don't include anything on labor and the environment, you are going to give the Democrats an excuse to take a walk. . . . That leaves you with a fairly narrow line."[66] With protectionist sentiment growing in the GOP, Republican supporters needed some Democrats on board to pass fast track. They had little choice, observed one administration official: "If they want to make it a total Republican bill, fine, they should come up with the 218 Republican votes [the bare majority needed in the House]; but they don't have the 218 Republican votes."[67]

---

64. Clinton, quoted in Ronald Brownstein, "Clinton Trade Agenda Draws Steady Barrage from Left, Right," *Los Angeles Times*, September 25, 1997, A4.

65. Carter Dougherty, "House Republicans Preparing New Version of Fast-Track Legislation," *Inside US Trade*, September 19, 1997, 1.

66. Destler, quoted in Brownstein, "Clinton Trade Agenda Draws Steady Barrage," A4.

67. Ronald Brownstein, "Clinton Trade Agenda Draws Steady Barrage," A4.

The continued opposition of some Democrats could be blamed in part on their disgruntlement at the recent budget negotiations. The administration had delayed the fast-track vote in order to get the budget through Congress, and many Democrats claimed that Clinton had worked more closely with Republicans than with Democrats to reach a deal. "Many of us feel left out," said one House Budget Committee member.[68] Representative Charles Rangel (D-NY) denounced the accord as "a Republican's budget."[69] Some Democrats were left in no mood to do the administration's bidding. ALOT lobbyist Gail Harrison reflects:

> I think fast track was sort of a payback for the budget agreement that curbed funding for some of the [traditional Democrats'] domestic priorities. A share of the Democrats were not going to give this [fast-track] victory to the president after the budget agreement. If you look at the way the votes were breaking out toward the end of the period, you had quite a number of members on the Democratic side who in the past had voted for trade, who were sending a message back to the administration. It may have been that the unstated message was, "We didn't like the budget agreement, and you're not doing enough for the cities and the districts that are economically disadvantaged."

Former USTR Barshefsky believes that the impact of the budget negotiations on Democrats may have been one of the most important elements in the fast-track story:

> Bill Clinton had worked out the budget with the Republicans and informed the Democratic Caucus of the outcome. What really went on with fast track more than anything else was captured by the views of most members of the Democratic Caucus which said to Bill Clinton, "You cut us out of budget negotiations and other legislative initiatives and now you're telling us you need our vote on fast track? No way." This was in large measure a personal rebuke to President Clinton, payback; Democrats felt that the president worked with the Republicans to effect compromise, rather than with the Democratic Caucus. The president understood the depth of these feelings. It was very painful for him. In addition, however, there was substantial pressure brought to bear on Democrats by anti-fast-track unions. It was a very nasty campaign.

## Pressure for a Vote

On October 1, the Senate Finance Committee approved a version of fast track. The bill declared that labor and the environment were two of four "international economic policy" objectives that would not be covered by

---

68. Quoted in Gerald F. Selb and Greg Hitt, "Budget Pact Seems Headed for Approval— Clinton Shows Optimism on Reaching an Accord on the Tax Component," *The Wall Street Journal*, May 19, 1997, A2.

69. Rangel, quoted in James Pinkerton, "The GOP Will Really Have Its Budget Day," *Newsday*, May 8, 1997, A53.

fast-track rules. In order to comply with the constitutional requirement that the House vote first on revenue legislation, the House now needed to vote on fast track before the Senate could act.

The House Ways and Means fast-track markup session went long into the night, but agreement on language was finally reached at 2:00 A.M. on October 7. Fast track cleared the committee by a vote of 24 to 14; of the panel's 16 Democrats, only 4 (Matsui among them) supported the measure. Congress promptly adjourned for its October recess. When the members returned, only about three weeks would remain in the legislative session.

Still, the administration hoped that a vote on fast track would be taken in 1997. According to some observers, the White House wanted to keep the fast-track fight inside the Beltway. An argument across the nation would have put Democrats at the center of a controversy just when they needed to prepare for the 1998 midterm elections. Reportedly, House Speaker Gingrich initially suggested a vote in the spring. "When the Speaker mentioned to the president, 'We really think we might not win, what do you think about doing it in the spring?' the president and his people said, 'We would rather you vote now and lose. We do not want to push this thing off to the spring,'" says Republican staffer Brian Bieron. The administration "figured that as long as you have a quick bloody battle, win or lose, the important thing at the end of the day, was [for Democrats] to kiss and make up. That was their ultimate desire."

On October 22, the chairman of the House Ways and Means Committee indicated that he did not want to bring the fast-track bill to the floor until the president could provide a list of 70 Democrats who would vote for the legislation. Archer's letter came after a Republican leadership meeting concluded that Democrats were "not even close to 70 votes."[70] In addition, some Republicans had mixed feelings about the bill, viewing the passage of fast track as an outcome that would strengthen a Democratic president.

Business interests lobbying for fast track pressed for a prompt vote. The issue was so controversial, they argued, that many members would not commit to either side unless a vote was imminent. In an October 28 letter, a group of 40 CEOs called on Clinton and the congressional leadership to hold the vote before adjournment. They believed that scheduling a vote would force the administration and Republicans to make the deals that were necessary to pass the legislation.

At the end of October, Gingrich met with pro-fast-track Democrats led by Robert Matsui. Participants said a vote was needed to convince undecided Democrats to support the measure. "If they don't think they're

---

70. "Archer Presses for Democratic Fast-Track Support Before Setting Vote," *Inside US Trade*, October 24, 1997, 1.

going to have to vote, there's no reason to take a position," noted Matsui.[71] Gingrich also met with the president for almost two hours. In the end, according to one observer, "The Speaker said, 'Let's go for it.' " On October 29, the Republican leadership scheduled a fast-track vote for November 7, the day the House hoped to adjourn.

## The Final Push

The House fast-track vote was only nine days away. These days were characterized by intense arm-twisting by the Clinton administration and Speaker Gingrich. Passage of the legislation required 218 votes; Gingrich hoped to produce 150 Republicans for fast track, but internal GOP counts had the party evenly split, 93–93.[72] To gain more Republican support, the Speaker cut deals ranging from agreeing to make fund-raising appearances to lowering Mexican tariffs on exported wine.[73] The Clinton administration also made a broad array of commitments in exchange for votes, many of them outlined in an amendment drafted by the House Ways and Means chairman. Archer's draft included 18 specific provisions, ranging from enforcing an antidumping suspension agreement for Mexican tomatoes (crucial for the Florida delegation) to agreeing to a new section 301 provision that would address trade barriers to US agricultural exports.

The administration dispatched the entire cabinet to Capitol Hill to lobby for fast track. USTR Barshefsky spoke individually with more than 350 members of the House. The president also brought UN Ambassador Bill Richardson back to Washington to press his former House colleagues. Dozens of corporate CEOs walked the halls of Congress seeking votes. ALOT reported that it spent about $5.5 million in television and radio advertisements and lobbying between Labor Day and the end of the fast-track campaign. "It was a sale like I've never seen before," said Representative Sonny Bono (R-CA).[74]

As the battle continued, the media was generally pro–fast track. The *New York Times,* the *Washington Post, Los Angeles Times, Chicago Tribune,* and the *Boston Globe* all backed the legislation, as did many other major

---

71. Matsui, quoted in John E. Yang and Helen Dewar, "House Sets Trade Authority Vote for Nov. 7; Deadline May Clarify Legislators' Positions on 'Fast Track' Power," *The Washington Post,* October 30, 1997, A10.

72. David Rogers, "Gingrich Says GOP Right Will Torpedo Fast Track Without Deals on Other Bills," *The Wall Street Journal,* November 3, 1997, C27.

73. Juliet Eilperin and Jim Vande Hei, "Despite Yanking Fast Track Vote, GOP Vows to Deliver on Promises to Members," *Roll Call,* November 17, 1997.

74. Bono, quoted in Guy Gugliotta, "Wheeling and Dealing and Keeping Score on the 'Fast Track'; Legislators Put Promises from Clinton in Writing," *The Washington Post,* November 26, 1997, A17.

newspapers. *USA Today* summed up the general consensus: "To keep the US economy, jobs and stocks on the fast track, Clinton needs fast-track authority to bring trade barriers down."[75] Labor's concerns were acknowledged, but generally viewed as outweighed by the benefits of free trade. "Many overseas workers are exploited, it's true," a *Washington Post* editorial remarked, but "economies that are open to trade and foreign investment grow more quickly and lift their populations out of poverty more quickly than economies that are closed."[76] Fast track also had the support of almost every major academic economist and dozens of former high-level public figures. Former national security adviser Brent Scowcroft wrote in the *Washington Post*, "If America does not lead on international trade, it will be harder to lead on security and political issues. . . . Fast-track authority is essential to being able to lead on trade."[77]

Despite such support and the administration's lobbying efforts, fast-track proponents had a hard time lining up votes for the measure. Some members told stories about plants in their districts that had been forced to close because of foreign competition. Labor's efforts had paid off, with more than a million pieces of mail sent to union households and months of visits to representatives by the end of the fast-track battle.

A week before the vote, Gingrich told a group of business representatives that if fast track were voted on that day, it would lose by 50 votes. If business did not raise the intensity of their lobbying campaign, Gingrich said, they should not bother to seek his assistance "for the next couple years."[78] Over the next six days, fast-track supporters narrowed the gap to victory. On November 5, GOP leaders could count 112 Republicans committed to fast track—an increase, but still short of the goal of 150 Republican votes. "We have a long, uphill struggle," said Republican Whip Tom DeLay of Texas. "If they [the White House] want to win it, they're just going to have to work very hard to deliver 70 Democrats."[79] On November 6, however, White House allies could only count 42 backers out of 206 Democrats—one in five.[80] When November 7 arrived, the president and the Speaker believed they still lacked the necessary support. Gingrich rescheduled the vote for Sunday, November 9, and Clinton and Gingrich continued their efforts.

---

75. "To Keep the Economy on Fast Track, Let Clinton Trade," *USA Today*, September 11, 1997, 14A.

76. "The Fast-Track Fight" (editorial), *The Washington Post*, September 12, 1997, A24.

77. Brent Scowcroft, "Say Yes to Fast Track," *The Washington Post*, October 19, 1997, C9.

78. Gingrich, quoted in "House, Senate Gearing Up for Votes on Fast Track Bills Next Week," *Inside US Trade*, October 31, 1997, 1.

79. DeLay, quoted in Hitt and Davis, "Lobbying Pace Quickens on Fast Track," B18.

80. Bob Davis and Greg Hitt, "White House Scrambles to Avert Defeat in House of Fast-Track Trade Measure," *The Wall Street Journal*, November 7, 1997, A3.

## The Mexico City Provision

In the lead-up to the vote, some Republicans attempted to leverage their fast-track support to bolster other controversial positions. For example, in exchange for their fast-track votes, a group of Republicans wanted the administration to drop certain statistical techniques from the 2000 national census. The Census Bureau planned to estimate part of the population using a method known as sampling, which would account for those missed by other methods. House Republicans believed that statistical sampling could cost them seats when congressional districts were next redrawn.

In addition, a group of between 6 and 10 conservative House Republicans led by James Talent (R-MO) pressed Clinton to reinstate the so-called Mexico City provision, which banned US aid to international health organizations that offered or recommended abortion services. Enacted under President Reagan, it had been repealed by executive order during Clinton's first term. House Democrats on both sides of the debate, including fast-track supporter Robert Matsui, strongly warned the administration not to trade away the Mexico City provision, and President Clinton publicly declared that the issue was not linked to the passage of fast track. Though the census controversy was resolved, conflict over abortion remained. "I think in the end we could have passed the bill if the Mexico City thing had been resolved," the president would say. "But I simply couldn't do that."[81]

## Fast Track Is Withdrawn

A few minutes before midnight, on November 9, 1997, House Speaker Gingrich called the White House to say that fast track was still short of the majority needed for passage. According to one observer, only 154 Republicans and as few as 41 Democrats supported fast track (Shorrock 1997). At 1:15 A.M., President Clinton called Gingrich and asked him to cancel the vote scheduled for the next morning. By pulling the bill, Clinton avoided the potential embarrassment of losing a high-profile House vote. But not all observers agreed with the president's decision; some were convinced that if the vote had been held as planned, the administration would have picked up the needed additional support and fast track would have passed. "Some members will 'do the right thing' if necessary but don't want to commit in advance," said one fast-track proponent.

Some pundits branded the end of the 1997 fast-track effort the first failure of a free trade measure in six decades. With four of five House Democrats against it, the *Wall Street Journal* noted that President Clinton had been dealt "the biggest legislative blow since Republicans killed his health-

---

81. Statement by President Clinton, November 10, 1997.

care plan in 1994."[82] However, not everyone saw the cancellation of the vote in such dramatic terms—the event received only scant coverage on two of the three major broadcast networks, and the third, NBC, failed to mention it at all.[83]

AFL-CIO President John Sweeney welcomed the news, calling the decision to pull the bill "the first bit of blue sky working Americans have seen in US trade policy in many years."[84] The *New York Times* called the defeat of the trade bill "labor's biggest legislative victory in years."[85] Richard Gephardt argued that the collapse of fast track demonstrated that any new attempt must take fuller account of labor and environmental issues. "The real question before us now is whether we connect our values of environmental quality, worker and human rights to our economic policy," he said. Representative Barney Frank (D-MA) had already declared that he and other liberals "will not agree to a continuation of public policies in this country and elsewhere which exalt the mobility of capital and do nothing to provide some offset for the inequality that is exacerbated thereby."[86]

Some had assumed that President Clinton would ultimately prevail. As White House point man Jay Berman puts it, "There were people who thought fast track was one of these issues where at the end of the day the president always wins—so why don't we leave it to the end of the day? And this time it proved to be the exception. Leaving it to the end of the day proved to be one of its fatal flaws."

Ultimately, business interests outspent labor more than 2 to 1 in the fast-track campaign. Editorials were consistently pro–fast track, and the president and the Republican leadership were behind it. "[It] was the political equivalent of the world champion Chicago Bulls playing a pick-up street team," said one fast-track opponent. "[But] the street team won" (Choate 1998, 63).

## The 1998 Vote

Though the White House hoped to wait and deal with fast track in the spring of 1999, Republicans announced that a vote would take place in the

---

82. John Harwood and Jackie Calmes, "Gephardt, Fresh from Victory in Trade Scrap, Flexes His Muscles for More Battles with Clinton," *The Wall Street Journal*, November 12, 1997, A24.

83. John F. Harris and Peter Baker, "Clinton Neglected to Sell 'Fast Track' to US Public," *The Washington Post*, November 12, 1997, A4.

84. Aaron Zitner, "Clinton Is Set Back as Fast-track Vote Is Deferred; Deal-making Fails to Line up a House Majority," *The Boston Globe*, November 11, 1997, A7.

85. Abramson with Greenhouse, "The Trade Bill," A1.

86. Gephardt, quoted in Alison Mitchell, "Clinton Retreats on Trade Power; Prospects Slight," *The New York Times*, November 11, 1997, A1; Frank, quoted in David Broder, "Fast Track: The Fiasco . . . ," *The Washington Post*, November 16, 1997, C7.

fall of 1998—when it would fail again. Many observers say that House Speaker Newt Gingrich brought the issue to the floor six weeks before an election knowing that it would be defeated but also knowing that it would create dissension among the Democrats. The administration withheld its support, and Democrats criticized the vote as intended to drive a wedge in their party ranks and to portray the president as weakened by the scandal involving Monica Lewinsky. Some analysts noted that times had changed since the Clinton administration collaborated with Gingrich to pass NAFTA in 1993.

The September House vote opposing fast track was 243 to 180, with 71 Republicans joining 171 Democrats to defeat the proposal. Only 29 Democrats supported the bill. "Today's exercise on this legislation soils our national trade policy with the mud of partisan politics," said Robert Matsui, one of the staunchest Democratic defenders of free trade. "It is rather an attempt to embarrass members of my party."[87] President Clinton issued a written statement: "Now was clearly the wrong time to vote on [fast track]. At a time when we need to forge a new consensus on trade, Congress has chosen partisanship over progress."[88] Debate over trade would continue, as seen in the collapse of the Seattle WTO ministerial in 1999.

The divisive nature of the fast-track fights and the growing politicization of trade led some trade advocates to wonder if fast track was worth the trouble. Perhaps, some argued, resources would be better used to push for specific trade agreements instead of a seemingly abstract, procedural measure. For example, in 2000 the House voted to grant China permanent normal trade relations (PNTR), 237 to 197 (with the support of 73 Democrats), and business mobilized powerfully behind the legislation. Moreover, one of the brokers of the deal that ensured its passage was a Democrat who opposed fast track in 1997, Representative Sander Levin of Michigan. In 2001, also without fast track in place, Congress passed implementing legislation for the US-Jordan Free Trade Agreement (FTA).[89] Interestingly, that FTA was the first US trade agreement to include a set of labor and environmental provisions directly in its body, making them subject to dispute resolution procedures. Some who questioned the necessity for fast track also pointed out that talks had already begun on the Free Trade Area of the Americas (FTAA) without its renewal. "There is a great deal of mistrust and fear on all sides of the fast-track question," says

---

87. Matsui, quoted in Finlay Lewis, "House Defeats Fast-Track Trade Bill," *The San Diego Union-Tribune*, September 26, 1998, C1.

88. Clinton, quoted in Alan Fram, "House Rejects GOP Effort to Expand President's Trade Powers," Associated Press Newswires, September 25, 1998.

89. The House of Representatives passed the US-Jordan Free Trade Agreement (HR 2063) on July 31, 2001, and the Senate followed on September 24, 2001. President Bush signed the implementing bill on September 24, 2001.

one observer. "In the absence of a specific agreement, people tend to vote their worst fears. They believe that unless they tightly constrain the president, their views will not be represented. That fear is a powerful force."

## A Victory? Trade Promotion Authority

In January 2001, Republican George W. Bush became president of the United States. Soon thereafter, his administration launched an effort to secure fast track, renamed "trade promotion authority" or TPA. In the wake of the September 11, 2001, attacks on New York and the Pentagon, the administration argued that the United States should "counter terror with trade." "Congress needs to enact US trade promotion authority so America can negotiate agreements that advance the causes of openness, development and growth," wrote USTR Robert Zoellick in a *Washington Post* op-ed. "The terrorists deliberately chose the World Trade towers as their target. While their blow toppled the towers, it cannot and will not shake the foundation of world trade and freedom."[90] Observers also noted that the Bush administration methodically sought to win converts to TPA by increasing tariffs on imported steel and Canadian softwood and by approving larger subsidies for US farmers. Though foreign trade partners objected to such policies, nine more steel caucus members would vote for TPA than had voted for fast track in 1998 (Bergsten 2002, 86).

The new chairman of the House Ways and Means Committee, Bill Thomas (R-CA), said he would work to create bipartisan TPA legislation. However, in his search for negotiating partners Thomas bypassed the senior committee Democrats—Charles Rangel and Sander Levin (both of whom had backed China PNTR but opposed fast track in 1997), as well as free trader Robert Matsui. Instead, he turned to more junior protrade Democrats—not all of them committee members—a move that alienated Democratic Party leaders. Rangel, Levin, and Matsui sent out a "Dear Colleague" letter declaring that "Thomas' 'Bipartisan Compromise' Is Neither."[91] However, the committee passed Thomas's bill 26 to 13, with 24 Republicans and 2 Democrats approving it. It included labor and environmental standards in the negotiating goals for the administration, but these goals were not binding—that is, putting such standards in trade agreements was not required. With a Republican now in the White House, business did not believe that labor and the environment would be a priority for trade negotiators and did not hesitate to lobby on TPA's behalf. Labor unions continued to oppose TPA.

---

90. Robert Zoellick, "Countering Terror with Trade" (op-ed), *The Washington Post*, September 20, 2001, A35.

91. Charles Rangel, Sander Levin, and Robert Matsui, "Dear Colleague" letter, September 26, 2001; reprinted in *Inside US Trade*, September 28, 2001.

The House vote on the Bipartisan Trade Promotion Authority Act was scheduled for December 6, 2001. The outcome was uncertain, and many predicted that TPA would not pass. In fact, on the day of the vote, the White House told Republican leaders that the bill should be withdrawn to avoid defeat. But House Republicans pressed on, and TPA went to the floor. As time ran out, there were more votes against the act than for it; the vote was held open while Republican members were pressured to change their positions. As Democrats shouted to end the voting, Representative Jim DeMint (R-SC) switched his vote to "yes" in return for a promise to restrict apparel imports from Caribbean and Andean nations in order to bolster textile manufacturers in his district. That protectionist promise so angered Ways and Means Committee Chairman Thomas that he threateningly waved a red "no vote" card (he ultimately voted "yes," however). The House passed TPA by a one-vote margin (215–214), with only 21 Democrats supporting the bill. The free trade Democrat Robert Matsui voted "no" on TPA, arguing that Congress needed greater input on trade negotiations.[92]

The Senate approved its own version of TPA in May 2002 more decisively, 66 to 30; 41 Republicans were joined by 24 Democrats and an Independent in supporting the bill, while 5 Republicans and 25 Democrats opposed it. The House and Senate versions differed substantially, however, especially over Trade Adjustment Assistance for US workers who lost their jobs as a result of imports. The Senate version included more worker unemployment benefits than the House bill, as well as a new innovation: health care benefits. In a second vote in June 2002, the House voted to take its version to conference with the Senate, also by a one-vote margin (216–215) with support from only 11 Democrats.

In the end, the compromise version of trade promotion authority expanded the Trade Adjustment Assistance program: It increased worker eligibility and financing to partially cover lost wages, lost health insurance, and job retraining for trade-dislocated workers. Thomas agreed to about $1.2 billion a year in benefits (the original Senate version's expansion of TAA had been broader). Thomas had hoped to give laid-off workers a tax credit they could use to buy individual insurance policies, but Democrats secured language allowing workers to access state-run insurance pools or their former employers' plans.[93] Senate Finance Committee Chairman Max Baucus (D-MT), the Democrat who led the Senate negotiations, said the bill "to a large degree protects American workers who may lose their jobs as a consequence of trade," and would therefore "help to restore some

92. Juliet Eilperin, "Trade Bill Passes House by One Vote; Bush Closer to Obtaining More Negotiating Power," *The Washington Post*, December 7, 2001, A1.

93. Michael M. Phillips, "Leading the News: Houses Passes Fast-Track Bill, But Margin of Victory Is Slim," *The Wall Street Journal*, July 29, 2002, A3.

lost American confidence in trade agreements."[94] Some observers believe that the absence of such TAA reform was one reason why earlier fast-track efforts had failed. But even with expanded benefits, AFL-CIO President John Sweeney declared that TPA "will cost millions of family-supporting jobs at a time when America's workers are already struggling."[95]

In addition to enhancing assistance for laid-off workers, the final version of TPA imposed more structure than past fast-track laws on the president's interactions with Congress before entering into trade agreements. It created a new Congressional Oversight Group that would develop guidelines for consultations with the administration and serve as advisers to the negotiators. Baucus and Majority Leader Daschle signaled to USTR Robert Zoellick that they wanted the new Congressional Oversight Group to play an important role in trade negotiations, insisting that it have a good deal of access to negotiating documents and attend negotiating sessions.[96]

Dropped from the final version of the bill, at the administration's insistence, was the Senate version's Dayton-Craig amendment. Both Republicans and Democrats fought to keep Dayton-Craig, which would have allowed Congress to amend any trade deal that altered US antidumping or countervailing-duty laws. The administration had already agreed to discuss antidumping issues in the new round of WTO talks. However, through the fight for the amendment, the Senate sent a strong signal that it wanted antidumping laws to remain unchanged.

In a 3:30 A.M. vote on July 27, 2002, after an intense night of lobbying from the Bush administration, the House narrowly passed the Bipartisan Trade Promotion Authority Act, 215 to 212. Fast track had expired eight years earlier. Although USTR Robert Zoellick and Ways and Means Committee Chairman Bill Thomas continued to present the bill as a bipartisan consensus, the evidence of a near party-line split was hard to miss. Republicans voted for the bill 190 to 27, while Democrats opposed it 183 to 25.

Less than a week after the House vote, the Senate, in a 64 to 34 vote, approved the conference report for a trade package that included extending fast track. President Bush signed the legislation a few days later, saying that the measure would enable his administration to work on trade agreements with Chile, Singapore, and Morocco and to negotiate a Free Trade Area of the Americas, the 34-nation plan to integrate most North and

---

94. Baucus, quoted in Edward Alden, Michael Mann, and Frances Williams, "Bush Poised for Win in Fast-Track Trade Pact Battle," *The Financial Times*, July 27, 2002, 8.

95. AFL-CIO press release, "Statement by AFL-CIO President John J. Sweeney on Passage of Fast Track Trade Legislation in the US House of Representatives," July 27, 2002. Available at www.aflcio.org.

96. See letter from Tom Daschle and Max Baucus, September 9, 2002; reprinted in *Inside US Trade*, September 13, 2002.

South American economies into a single free trade block.[97] Trade promotion authority would be automatically renewed until June 2007, unless either house passed a disapproval resolution before June 2005. A senior European trade official responded to the renewal of fast track/TPA, "It is excellent news. It means the US can engage fully again."[98]

Some celebrated TPA's passage as the beginning of a new era for US trade policy—"a victory for the American economy," as President Bush put it. "Open trade is not just an economic opportunity, it is a moral imperative," Bush said.[99] Others noted that Democratic support for trade in the House had hit an all-time low. While 102 House Democrats had supported NAFTA in 1993, only 25 had supported the so-called bipartisan trade promotion authority act in 2002 (see table 5.1). "This is not the type of authority which facilitates a broadly bipartisan trade policy," said Sander Levin, the ranking Democrat on the House Trade Subcommittee, before the 2002 House vote. "Another narrow vote will not be a victory for US trade policy, but instead will mean trouble for each new trade agreement because all of the same issues and debates will be repeated" (quoted in Shapiro and Brainard 2003).

## Negotiation Analysis of the Case

The success of organized labor in opposing the renewal of fast track in 1997 is, at first glance, surprising. Fast track was supported both by President Clinton and by the Republican leadership in Congress. Powerful business interests, which had a major stake in seeing the drive to liberalize international trade continue, outspent labor 2 to 1 in the lobbying campaign preceding the canceled vote. How then did the unions manage to torpedo fast track? The answer lies in their early, energetic organization to oppose the legislation, as well as their skill in shaping the process.

### Element #1: Organizing to Influence

In deciding how to engage in the debate over fast track, organized labor confronted a classic negotiating dilemma: Was it better to work to shape

---

97. The White House, Office of the Press Secretary, "Remarks by the President at Signing of the Trade Act of 2002," August 6, 2002.

98. Quoted in Edward Alden and Guy de Jonquières, "A Deal, at Last—Trade Promotion Authority Represents an Important Boost for Free Trade," *The Financial Times*, August 1, 2002, 14.

99. President George W. Bush, remarks at the signing of the Trade Act of 2002, Washington, DC, August 6, 2003; Bush, quoted from May 7, 2001, in White House press release, Shannon, Ireland, June 26, 2004.

**Table 5.1    Trade votes in Congress**

### House of Representatives

| Vote | Fast track, 1991[a] | | | | NAFTA, 1993 | | | | GATT Uruguay Round, 1994 | | | | Fast track, 1998 | | | | Trade promotion authority, 2001 | | | | Trade promotion authority, 2002 | | | |
|---|---|---|---|---|---|---|---|---|---|---|---|---|---|---|---|---|---|---|---|---|---|---|---|---|
| | R | D | I | Total | R | D | I | Total | R | D | I | Total | R | D | I | Total | R | D | I | Total | R | D | I | Total |
| Yes | 140 | 91 | — | 231 | 132 | 102 | — | 234 | 121 | 167 | — | 288 | 151 | 29 | — | 180 | 194 | 21 | — | 215 | 190 | 25 | — | 215 |
| No | 21 | 170 | 1 | 192 | 43 | 156 | 1 | 200 | 56 | 89 | 1 | 146 | 71 | 171 | 1 | 243 | 23 | 189 | 2 | 214 | 27 | 183 | 2 | 212 |
| Present | — | — | — | — | — | — | — | — | — | — | — | — | — | 3 | — | 3 | — | — | — | — | — | — | — | — |
| Not voting | 4 | 4 | — | 8 | — | — | — | — | — | — | — | — | 6 | 3 | — | 9 | 4 | 1 | — | 5 | 5 | 2 | — | 7 |

### Senate

| Vote | Fast track, 1991[a] | | | NAFTA, 1993 | | | GATT Uruguay Round, 1994 | | | Trade promotion authority, May 2002 | | | | Trade promotion authority, August 2002 | | | |
|---|---|---|---|---|---|---|---|---|---|---|---|---|---|---|---|---|---|
| | R | D | Total | R | D | Total | R | D | Total | R | D | I | Total | R | D | I | Total |
| Yes | 36 | 23 | 59 | 34 | 27 | 61 | 35 | 41 | 76 | 41 | 24 | 1 | 66 | 43 | 20 | 1 | 64 |
| No | 5 | 31 | 36 | 10 | 28 | 38 | 11 | 13 | 24 | 5 | 25 | — | 30 | 5 | 29 | — | 34 |

— = 0
D = Democrat
I = Independent
R = Republican

a. For the sake of clarity and comparison, the literal "yes" and "no" votes on fast track 1991 have been reversed. House Resolution 101 would have barred extension of fast-track procedures; therefore, a "no" vote was a vote supporting fast track.

*Sources: Congressional Quarterly Almanac* (various issues); Baldwin and Magee (2000, 7).

the legislation into something acceptable, thereby running the risk of allowing momentum to build behind an unacceptable proposal, or to mobilize early in direct opposition? After first trying to shape fast track, labor shifted to outright opposition of the legislation. When business interests delayed their mobilizing efforts until it was too late, labor prevailed.

The AFL-CIO's "Rapid Response" campaign was a key component of labor's strategy to influence Congress. The unions leveraged their traditional strength in grassroots organizing to direct the rank and file to oppose fast track. The results were impressive: numerous letters to Congress (160,000 from steelworkers alone), phone calls, and rallies. Organized labor also made skilled use of advertising. Though business outspent labor, the timing and targeting of labor's advertising—for example, focusing on 13 undecided House members—arguably rendered it more effective.

## Element #2: Selecting the Forum

Despite being motivated to delay or prevent further trade liberalization, labor leaders also recognized the potential benefits of including workers' rights and labor standards on the international trade agenda. The traditional global forum for advancing labor's interests was the International Labor Organization, a single-issue UN agency with little US support for its conventions and essentially no enforcement authority. Should labor issues be successfully moved into the trade arena, improvements in labor standards could be linked to trade liberalization and increased market access. Commitments would also be enforceable under the WTO dispute settlement system. In the words of the AFL-CIO's Thea Lee, labor could then use the "leverage of trade agreements to obtain promises from trading partners to improve their [labor] laws."

Labor's strategy was similar to the approach taken by US knowledge-based industries to put intellectual property onto the Uruguay Round agenda. These industries recognized that the World Intellectual Property Organization (WIPO), a sister agency of the ILO in the UN system, had neither the scope nor the enforcement authority to advance their interests. Business and labor wanted their respective concerns on the trade agenda for the same reason: to increase leverage. At the same time, business vigorously argued that labor (and environmental) issues had no place in trade agreements.

## Element #3: Shaping the Agenda

The parties involved in the fast-track debate were engaged in a monumental battle to shape the agenda of future trade negotiations. The debate hinged, in part, on whether labor and environmental issues belonged in trade talks. As a condition for granting fast-track authority, organized labor and their Democratic allies sought to require the administration to negotiate labor and environmental provisions in future trade agreements. Republican opponents and business groups sought to prevent the expansion of the trade agenda to encompass these issues.

The debate over fast track was an inevitable consequence of the tensions created by this peculiar mechanism and its history. To appreciate these tensions, we need to understand the deal structure implicit in the fast-track process. Fast track was developed in order to give the US administration credibility in international trade negotiations by preventing the ratification problems that had emerged after the Kennedy Round. After making commitments on nontariff barriers in the Kennedy Round trade talks, the administration was embarrassed when Congress refused to pass enabling legislation. In order to avoid future difficulties of this sort, the administration asked Congress to grant it the authority to negotiate agreements that would be ratified by an up-or-down vote held on a strict schedule. In return for giving up its ability to amend or delay the legislation needed to implement trade agreements, Congress received increased overview and consultation privileges during the negotiation process.

But the arrangement created a classical negotiating problem: the principal-agent dilemma. When the principal (here, Congress) sends an agent (the administration) out to negotiate an agreement, how can the principal be sure that the agent will represent his or her best interests? If the principal does not trust the agent, the relationship becomes even more charged.

## Element #4: Building Coalitions

"Organized labor" is, of course, far from monolithic. Therefore, building an internal coalition in favor of defeating fast track was an early priority for those union groups that stood to bear the burden of increased trade liberalization. Representatives of traditional industrial unions such as the Teamsters, Steelworkers, UAW, textile and apparel workers, and Oil, Chemical and Atomic Workers, built a core coalition and then gradually gathered broader support before taking the issue to the AFL-CIO Executive Committee. This strategy enabled them to overcome opposition from some members of the Executive Committee staff and to override concerns on the part of AFL-CIO leaders about directly opposing a Democratic administration.

The unions then focused on building a coalition in Congress to oppose fast track. Here, too, the choice of the battleground was not accidental. While the unions had influence in the Clinton administration, this influence was not sufficient to kill fast-track renewal efforts. President Clinton was pushing a broad liberalization agenda that included negotiating new trade agreements in the Americas, Asia, and Europe. Although some Clinton administration officials opposed moving forward with fast track

**Figure 5.1  The ideological divide on fast track**

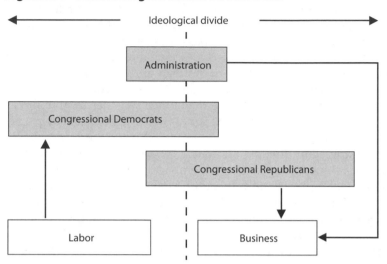

because they feared it would jeopardize other legislative priorities, a critical mass of support for working to win its renewal ultimately formed.

As illustrated in figure 5.1, Congress was a very different story. There, organized labor could expect strong support from its traditional allies, including key members of the Democratic leadership such as Minority Leader Richard Gephardt. They also could fight a public, grassroots campaign to influence undecided members. Furthermore, members of Congress tended to be responsive to labor unions that were well represented in their own districts. At the time, the labor movement provided almost 50 percent of the PAC funding for Democratic members of Congress. This financial support translated into willingness on the part of many Democrats to defer on issues that labor defined as high priority. In short, the history of financial support for Democrats and experience in grassroots organizing enabled labor to hold its own against business lobbying.

In addition, the Democratic leadership in Congress relied on well-established patterns of deference—that is, the tendency of groups to fall in line behind recognized leaders—to solidify opposition to fast-track renewal. For example, Gephardt's "Dear Colleague" letter to his fellow Democrats firmly rejected any fast-track proposal that failed to include labor and environmental protections. Gephardt's motives were complex; he was not only a staunch supporter of organized labor but also harbored presidential ambitions that could not be realized without solid union support. Active and early opposition to fast track by Gephardt and other key Democrats such as House Minority Whip David Bonior translated into broader opposition in Congress, as many members deferred to the Democratic leadership on these issues.

**Figure 5.2    Linkages in fast-track renewal**

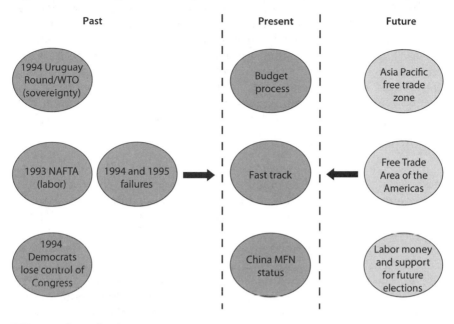

MFN = most favored nation

Finally, organized labor succeeded in mobilizing other interest groups to oppose fast track. Key members of the coalition included environmental groups that wanted to see environmental standards included in trade agreements, antiglobalization groups such as Public Citizen, and more conservative economic nationalists such as Pat Buchanan.

To counter this force, the Clinton administration sought to create a winning coalition to pass fast track, relying heavily on congressional Republicans. This effort failed, in part because of the lack of trust among the parties, but also because the Republicans asked business interests to delay their lobbying efforts in order to try to pressure the Clinton administration on the content of the fast-track bill.

## Element #5: Leveraging Linkages

Negotiations over fast-track renewal in 1997 were tightly linked to an array of other trade negotiations—past, present, and future. As figure 5.2 illustrates, the administration wanted fast track in order to pursue a range of future negotiating initiatives, including a Free Trade Area of the Americas.

The 1997 renewal effort also was linked to previous (failed) efforts to renew fast track in 1994 and 1995. Critically, the 1997 fast-track debate occurred in the shadow of the battles over NAFTA and the implementing legislation for the Uruguay Round. Congress approved NAFTA under fast-track provisions in the face of tremendous opposition by organized labor. The result was residual bitterness in the labor movement, especially because NAFTA was viewed to have resulted in significant union job losses. Efforts by the Clinton administration to negotiate NAFTA side agreements on labor and environmental issues had done little to assuage the unions' sense of defeat. "No more NAFTAs" became a rallying cry for those organizing to oppose fast track. The grim warning of the AFL-CIO pamphlet cited above fell on receptive ears: "Fast Track brought us NAFTA. . . . Now big corporations want to extend the NAFTA deal to other countries."

The 1997 effort to renew fast track also became linked to concurrent negotiations over the 1998 federal budget and the annual renewal of China's most favored nation trading status. Because the Clinton administration needed Democratic support to pass the budget, it decided to delay a vote on fast track. Yet the budget process itself alienated Democrats, who perceived that the administration had worked too closely with Republicans and had curbed funding for traditional Democratic priorities. Moreover, the administration was aware that Democrats in Congress didn't want to side with business and the Republicans on both the China issue and fast track; and because China was the priority, it wanted the vote on China's MFN status to be held first.

## Element #6: Playing the Frame Game

By using anger at NAFTA and the fear of job loss, organized labor framed the debate in ways that were compelling to its constituents and their representatives in Congress. While the administration sought to argue that the choice was between making progress and disengaging from the rest of the world, the unions argued that trade agreements should protect workers as well as investors. The appeal to pocketbook issues proved decisive for the audiences that the AFL-CIO sought to influence.

## Element #7: Creating Momentum

In this case, organized labor was trying to prevent momentum from building toward passage of fast track. That organized labor chose to fight fast track rather than take on specific trade agreements was no accident. The choice reflected labor's sophisticated understanding of fast track as key to the administration's strategy for building momentum toward US acceptance of new international trade agreements. This understanding arose, in part, from labor's failure to oppose NAFTA—whose success, in turn, rested on prior congressional fast-track renewal.

The key insight is that trade agreements negotiated by the administration under fast track are very difficult to defeat in Congress. Because fast track prohibits amendments and imposes a strict time frame for a vote, it blunts the most commonly used tools that single-issue groups use to delay, water down, or defeat legislation in Congress. It thus limits the ability of unions, environmental organizations, and other groups to influence trade agreements. For this reason, labor concluded that it was essential to fight the battle early over fast track and not to wait for "the next NAFTA."

Organized labor also benefited from the administration's miscalculations in attempting to create momentum behind fast track (the decision to wait on submitting proposed fast-track language to Congress, followed by a premature push for a vote). As just mentioned, the administration decided to put fast track on hold until after Congress had voted on the 1998 budget and China's MFN status. The resulting delay from the spring to the fall of 1997 gave fast-track opponents a full summer to organize. At the same time, business was restrained from mobilizing by the Republican leadership, who sought to retain leverage with the administration in negotiating the final language of the bill.

Once the bill was introduced in the fall, business and Republican leaders in Congress began to press hard for a vote. Such pressure, they believed, would force the administration to make deals with undecided members so that the legislation would pass. This strategy backfired when it became evident that there was not enough time to overcome the resistance that had built up against fast track. The resulting decision to cancel the vote and withdraw the legislation illustrates an enduring negotiation lesson: Action-forcing events do force action—but not necessarily the desired action.

## Conclusion

The 1997 failure was, of course, not the end of the story. In August 2002, the Bush administration succeeded in achieving TPA. By renaming fast track "trade promotion authority," the administration reframed what was at stake, focusing not on moving a bill quickly through Congress but on something more positive: promoting trade. In addition, through bipartisan negotiations, Congress succeeded in reforming Trade Adjustment Assistance, providing additional aid to US workers displaced by trade liberalization. Nevertheless, TPA passed in the House by the narrowest of margins, and the close votes underscore the continuing deep partisan divide over fast track. Some believe that such extreme polarization will enable special interest lobbies to exert disproportionate influence over future trade debates. It remains to be seen if a new approach to fast track will emerge that can command bipartisan common ground.

# 6

# The 1999 US-China
# Bilateral Agreement
# and the Battle for PNTR

## Making Trade Policy

On December 11, 2001, China became a member of the World Trade Organization (WTO), a move that would thrust new challenges on the Chinese leadership and people and fundamentally redefine China's relations with the rest of the world—especially the United States. This case describes the prolonged US-China bilateral negotiations over China's WTO accession and the subsequent debate and vote in the US Congress to permanently establish normal trade relations with China. Written from an American perspective, the case presents material that is useful for a discussion of such issues as (1) the problems inherent in conducting trade negotiations under the US system of government; (2) the role of trade policy in advancing America's economic interests; (3) the role trade agreements can and should play in promoting human rights, enhancing domestic reform, encouraging the rule of law, and promoting national security; (4) the costs and benefits of WTO membership; and (5) the nature of the WTO accession process.

In order to join the WTO, China had to negotiate not only a multilateral agreement with all the member countries as a group but also bilateral

*The Eagle and the Dragon: The 1999 US-China Bilateral Agreement and the Battle for PNTR* is an edited and revised version of the case with the same name originally written for the Case Program at the Kennedy School of Government. For copies or permission to reproduce the unabridged case please refer to www.ksgcase.harvard.edu or send a written request to Case Program, John F. Kennedy School of Government, Harvard University, 79 John F. Kennedy Street, Cambridge, MA 02138.

agreements with as many members as requested one. On November 15, 1999, China and the United States signed a bilateral agreement on market access that, many say, paved the way to China's WTO entry. China's commitments included pledges to cut tariffs, to remove trade barriers on US agricultural and industrial products and services, and to eliminate a number of restrictions on foreign investment.

By supporting China's WTO accession, the United States was essentially agreeing that China should receive all the rights of WTO membership. Such a decision was not made lightly, especially given the special challenge that China's application presented to the United States. The central principle of the WTO is nondiscrimination. For example, Article I of the General Agreement on Tariffs and Trade (GATT) requires that imports from all WTO members be subject to the same tariffs without conditions—so-called most favored nation (MFN) treatment. Even though China was not a WTO member, the United States had granted China MFN status since 1979. However, US law required Congress each year to affirm China's MFN status in a vote that entailed scrutiny on China's performance in upholding human rights. In order to support Chinese accession, the United States had to commit to nondiscriminatory treatment by agreeing to make China's MFN status permanent—known as permanent normal trade relations, or PNTR—and thereby giving up the right to annual reviews.

To understand how the United States and China behaved throughout these events, it is useful to reflect on the interests and concerns each side had about China's WTO accession. These considerations also help to explain why the bilateral agreement took the form that it did and why the PNTR vote was considered a landmark event.

## Underlying Interests and Concerns

### US Interests

The United States has major economic and political interests in how China develops. China is an important US supplier and also provides a large market for American goods, services, and investment—a market that is likely to become even larger. China's decisions about how to relate to the rest of the world will also have a significant impact on the global economy. Specifically, because China is a large and important economy, its membership in the WTO could affect the direction in which the WTO evolves.

China is the world's most populous nation and, as a result of sustained economic reform and international engagement, over the past two decades it has grown more rapidly than any other developing country. US trade with China has surged as a result. Domestically, however, China's political evolution has not matched its economic growth. The country remains under the control of the Communist Party, and its administrative system generally reflects the rule of Party bureaucrats rather than the rule of law. Neither human rights nor property rights are firmly protected, making it very difficult for US firms to operate there; US unions in particular have complained about having to compete with workers on unfair terms.

China, as a nuclear power and a potentially dominant nation in the Pacific, is also a key player in global politics and security issues. China's relationship with Taiwan presents one of the most contentious issues in international relations and has led many Americans to view China as a rival. Over time, Chinese power is likely to grow, and the way it wields this power will be largely determined by how its economy and political system continue to change.

## Chinese Interests

China sought WTO membership for several reasons. Participation in the WTO was an important step in China's quest to gain influence on the global scene generally, and China's growing exports would benefit from a system based on rules. The forum that the WTO provides for negotiating international liberalization could help China both to reduce barriers to its exports and to leverage its large domestic market to obtain concessions from its trading partners. As a participant in WTO negotiations, China could work to make the rules of global trade reflect its own interests more closely. Although China's Party-dominated economic system and low wages would expose it to frequent challenges as an unfair trader, its large domestic market would give it bargaining power in bilateral relationships.

China also had specific reasons to seek US approval for its WTO entry. Because the WTO generally functions by consensus, and because members are particularly deferential to the Quad countries (the European Union, the United States, Japan, and Canada), United States could have blocked Chinese accession. Alternatively, the United States could have permitted China to join, but invoked its right under GATT Article XXXV (Non-application of the Agreement Between Particular Contracting Parties) not to extend it benefits. Such a decision would have made WTO membership less useful to China, since the leadership was particularly interested in ending the annual US renewal of MFN status. Though the effectiveness of the MFN review in reducing human rights violations in China is debatable, the votes in Congress and the reviews of China's human rights record in the international press undoubtedly demanded the constant attention of Chinese officials. The votes also created an element of uncertainty regarding access to Chinese markets and discouraged investors who required such access in order to be profitable.

## Domestic Chinese Reform

Entering the WTO has important implications for Chinese domestic reform. China had earlier taken several steps toward introducing a market system to its economy, but the enterprises that played a leading role in these reforms were generally owned by foreign investors and local Chinese governments rather than by private Chinese entrepreneurs. The prospect of WTO membership strengthened the hand of those seeking to hasten China's development toward a market economy, for China could join the organization (and thus gain the benefits of accession) only if it first undertook a number of domestic reforms. WTO entry has enabled China's leadership to make a more credible commitment to creating a system that more fully recognizes private enterprise. In addition, it has mobilized domestic firms to become more competitive through restructuring, acquiring new technologies, and undertaking new alliances and mergers with both domestic and foreign firms.

The requirements of WTO entry forced Chinese policymakers to confront the difficult political issues involved in reforming domestic banking institutions, subjecting state-owned enterprises to hard budget constraints, and allowing private firms to freely engage in international trade. The accession process also served to promote better Chinese governance, because the WTO requires policies to be transparent and enforced by rules rather than at a bureaucrat's discretion. Moreover, the WTO requirement of nondiscrimination (i.e., national treatment) for imported goods and services will have significant internal consequences. China remains a country with considerable domestic barriers and strong provincial governments; if provinces are forced to provide national treatment for imported goods and services, they will find it harder to discriminate against goods from other provinces.

Many of these reforms are changes that China might have chosen to embrace of its own accord, but entry into the WTO will advance their implementation. However, WTO membership also creates political and economic risks both domestically and internationally. At home, nationalists may argue that because the reforms are being imposed from outside, the Chinese people should reject them. Abroad, China exposes itself to scrutiny and challenge in the WTO dispute settlement system as it undertakes binding obligations.

## China's Entry into the WTO and US Economic Interests in China

Historically, US firms operating in the Chinese market have faced many problems. In addition to dealing with formal border barriers, they must surmount the challenges of engaging with an economy in which market forces are not always in play and property rights are not always secure. The hurdles include extensive and discriminatory bureaucratic intervention, restrictions on foreign investment, interventionist industrial policies, the need to compete with state-owned enterprises that are not subject to hard budget constraints, and the need to undertake trade through designated trading agents. While China's entry into the WTO will not eliminate these problems, it promises to ameliorate them, making the Chinese market more penetrable and offering more recourse when US interests are treated unfairly.

## China's Entry and the Broader Political Relationship Between China and the United States

The question of whether to support China's bid to join the international trading system was long debated in the United States. Though no one can be sure how China will develop, President Clinton and many others held that accession to the WTO would reinforce its domestic political and economic reforms. Nonetheless, prominent figures on both the political left and right showed considerable reluctance to support the economic engagement with China that WTO membership would entail. On the left, the central issue related to human rights violations. Unions in particular were concerned about competing against Chinese workers who had low wages, poor working conditions, and limited rights. Political groups objected to the country's human rights violations and believed that the annual scrutiny from the MFN vote was the best way to maintain pressure on the Chinese to improve their record. On the political right, concerns about national security—and specifically to the fate of Taiwan—were at the forefront.

The above considerations suggest why US negotiators found it necessary to be particularly demanding in establishing conditions for Chinese entry into the WTO in the November 1999 bilateral agreement and provide the background for a discussion of its framework.

## Developing Countries

Given its interests in enhancing domestic reform in China, opening the Chinese market to US products and investment, and mitigating any weakening of WTO rules, the United States refused to provide China with the lenient or special and differential treatment that was offered to smaller, less economically significant developing countries. Instead, it insisted that Chinese entry must be "on commercial terms." The US government feared that if China entered the WTO without committing to considerable reform, it might undermine the trading system. WTO members could perhaps turn a blind eye to lax entry terms for a small country but not to China—it was too large a player. In addition, the terms of Chinese accession would surely become the model for other significant potential members that were waiting in the wings, such as Russia and Vietnam.

The United States also had domestic concerns in mind. US firms faced many problems when trying to sell products and services in China—problems that could be resolved only if China began to operate in a significantly different way. In this respect, US demands coincided with the goals of China's domestic reformers, thereby helping them make the case for major policy changes.

## Coverage and Depth

The 1999 US-China bilateral agreement was comprehensive, covering all goods (including agriculture), services, and foreign investment. Its scope and depth were driven both by US objectives and by the objectives of Chinese reformers. China pledged to eliminate or enlarge quotas and reduce tariffs, particularly in sectors that were US priorities, and made additional commitments related to domestic markets. China's concessions in services were considerable: Foreign investment was extensively liberalized for a number of service industries—notably, telecommunications, insurance, banking, and tourism. China would implement the WTO's Agreement on Trade-Related Investment Measures (TRIMs) and would no longer make permission to invest contingent on performance requirements. Restrictions on foreign participation in the distribution sector would be phased out within three years.

## Winners and Losers

WTO membership has the potential to change the distribution of wealth and power in China. Trade liberalization will certainly have an impact on income—typically benefiting those associated with export activities and imposing costs on those competing with imports. Chinese producers in domestic agriculture and financial services are particularly worried about the effects of WTO membership. Workers in state-owned enterprises may also lose jobs when industry subsidies are withdrawn as part of domestic market reforms. WTO membership may also affect the balance of power between the central and provincial governments, reformers and conservatives, private entrepreneurs and state enterprise employees.

The distribution of power within the WTO itself may also change. After all, WTO members participate in the system on the basis of reciprocal concessions, and China's large domestic market gives it a great deal of bargaining power as it seeks to advance its interests in export markets. And since the MFN principle applies in the WTO, any benefits the Chinese are able to obtain in labor-intensive products must automatically be provided to other member countries that export such products. For example, if China is able to obtain lower tariffs on its textile exports to developed countries, all other producers of textiles will benefit. Moreover, China's WTO accession could change the regional balance of power. If WTO membership makes China a more competitive location for production and investment, its gains may come at the expense of other Asian developing countries.

China's accession has affected power relationships among political groups in the United States as well—especially in the wake of the vote to give China PNTR. The annual vote on China's MFN status provided human rights activists with opportunities to advance their cause. The vote also gave those who opposed trade with China, and those who were undecided, an opening to use the threat of a negative vote to obtain concessions from the administration on other issues.

## Governance

The WTO requires members to administer their trade rules transparently: In accordance with GATT Article X, all trade rules must be published and independent judicial tribunals must be available to review administrative actions. The WTO also requires its members to implement legal regimes that enforce intellectual property rights (through the Agreement on Trade-Related Aspects of Intellectual Property Rights, or TRIPS). Accession will therefore force the Chinese government to make significant changes in administration and governance, increasing the use of rules-based systems. WTO members will monitor China's progress. Failure to implement the necessary policies could result in international challenges.

## Enforcement

In the early 1990s, the United States threatened to impose sanctions on China as a way of pressuring Party leaders to enforce intellectual property protection. Now that China has joined the WTO, the United States can no longer make such threats: It is obligated to use the WTO's dispute settlement procedures. Some believe that without the ability to impose sanctions, the United States will have a tougher time enforcing trade agreements with China. On the other hand, if the United States is able to win cases at the WTO, the subsequent multilateral pressure on China to conform may be more effective than bilateral threats. For its part, China will be able to defend itself in a multilateral setting and to pursue its own grievances at the WTO. Indeed, it was China that acted first in a bilateral dispute, bringing a case against US steel tariffs in 2002. As a country with a large market, China will also be able to use the prospect of suspending concessions to increase the compliance of other WTO members.

From an American standpoint, the 1999 US-China agreement was a remarkable success, with Chinese concessions going much further than most observers had hoped or expected. The Chinese agreed to liberalize their market, while the United States was required simply to enforce the status quo, giving up only the right to suspend MFN treatment. Yet despite the advantages of the agreement, passage of PNTR was highly controversial; almost two-thirds of the Democratic party and most American trade unions were strongly opposed to it. One reason the Clinton administration was so firm in its demands in the bilateral negotiations with China was that only a very good agreement was worth the very high political cost that the president knew he would have to pay. In the end, the US success in obtaining such a far-reaching agreement does not necessarily imply that China "lost" in the negotiations. Because the Chinese leadership was able to use the terms of the agreement to strengthen its reform agenda, they may in fact have been the bigger winners.

## CASE STUDY: The Eagle and the Dragon—The 1999 US-China Bilateral Agreement and the Battle for PNTR

President Clinton was in the shower when US National Security Adviser Sandy Berger told him who was on the phone. The president took the call. United States Trade Representative (USTR) Charlene Barshefsky and National Economic Adviser Gene Sperling were standing in a ladies' bathroom at the Chinese Trade Ministry in Beijing. "Mr. President," Barshefsky exclaimed, "it's done."

On November 15, 1999, after six days of high-stakes negotiations, China and the United States signed a bilateral market access agreement. According to many observers, it was this agreement that paved the way to China's entry into the World Trade Organization. In the deal, China agreed to cut tariffs, remove trade barriers on agricultural and industrial products and services, eliminate a number of restrictions on foreign investment, and allow the United States to guard against import surges that could hurt certain domestic industries. Some predicted that the agreement would become a key element in Clinton's presidential legacy.

However, the bilateral agreement was not the final step in the process. While the president had the authority to support China's WTO membership, it was Congress that would decide whether to grant China PNTR with the United States. Previously, China's most favored nation trade status had faced an annual renewal that often became a focal point in

Congress for protests over human rights issues, security concerns, and the growing US trade deficit with China.[1] As a presidential candidate, Bill Clinton had campaigned on making China's trade status conditional on improvements in its human rights record, criticizing George H. W. Bush for "coddling" the Chinese. After opposition from the business community—and seeming indifference from the international community—Clinton backed away from this policy. Ultimately, following a heated fight, the House of Representatives voted to grant China PNTR in May 2000. PNTR was passed by the Senate in September and signed into law in October, during the last months of Clinton's presidency.

The US-China bilateral agreement and the fight for PNTR were not short on drama or strange bedfellows. Negotiations over the November 1999 bilateral deal were often all-night affairs. During the last round of talks in Beijing, USTR Barshefsky sent her luggage to the airport three times to indicate her readiness to walk away. The fight on Capitol Hill for PNTR was of historic proportions—one observer remarked that "The colossal lobbying battle over China's trade status will be studied by political science classes for years to come."[2] Republicans who had led the charge to impeach the president now found themselves working to advance Clinton's goals. Business interests spent record-setting amounts lobbying for the legislation. Labor and consumer groups, invigorated after their forceful and well-publicized protests in November 1999 at the Seattle WTO ministerial, vehemently opposed PNTR. In the end, three out of four Republicans voted for PNTR while two out of three Democrats opposed it. Yet a number of observers say that considerable credit for PNTR's passage belongs to a prolabor Democrat who had voted against the North American Free Trade Agreement (NAFTA)—Representative Sander "Sandy" Levin (D-MI).

## China and the GATT

China was an original signatory of the General Agreement on Tariffs and Trade (1947), the predecessor to the WTO,[3] but its domestic political upheaval led to an unusual withdrawal. When Mao Zedong's Chinese Communist Party defeated Chiang Kai-shek's Nationalist Party in 1949, the People's Republic of China (PRC) was born and the remains of Chiang's Nationalist government fled to Taiwan. In March 1950, UN Secretary-

---

1. The US trade deficit with China rose from $6 billion in 1989 to nearly $84 billion in 2000 (see table 6.1).

2. Paul Magnusson, "The Battle over China—China Trade: Will Clinton Pull It Off?" *Business Week*, May 29, 2000, 74.

3. There were 23 original contracting parties to the GATT.

General Trygve Lie received a cable from Nationalist government officials in Taiwan indicating that "China" was withdrawing from the GATT. The withdrawal took effect a few months later. The mainland Communists refused to recognize the Nationalists' action and contested its validity.[4] The disagreement centered on the charged question of whether there was one China or two. Regardless, mainland China (hereafter called simply "China" or "the PRC") would not play a role in GATT affairs for years to come (see Bhala 2000, Wang 1995).

Economic relations between the PRC and the United States effectively ended when the United States imposed an embargo on trade with China in 1950 at the start of the Korean War. In 1951, under the Trade Agreements Extension Act, President Harry Truman suspended the MFN tariff status not just of China but of all countries in the then Sino-Soviet bloc.

In 1965, the Nationalist government of Taiwan was accorded observer status in the GATT—a status withdrawn in 1971 after the United Nations recognized the Communist government of the PRC as the sole legal Chinese representative in the United Nations in UN General Assembly Resolution 2758 (XXVI). Though the PRC became a full member of the General Assembly, the Chinese government did not seek to reenter the GATT. Observers cite various reasons for this decision, including China's Cultural Revolution of 1966–76, its isolation from the rest of the world, and the Chinese government's insistence (contrary to GATT principles) on controlling foreign trade. Foreign trade was also only a small part of the PRC's economy, for its guiding principle was self-reliance.

In 1980, China joined the International Monetary Fund (IMF) and the World Bank. It also applied for nonvoting observer status at the GATT, a request that was granted in 1982.[5] These moves coincided with Deng Xiaoping's economic reforms (which began in 1978), designed to jump-start China's economy. The reforms profoundly changed China's relationship with the outside world. Merchandise exports grew from $11 billion in 1978 to $24 billion in 1984, reaching $154 billion by 1996 (Kennedy and Marquis 1998, 9).

Trade relations between the PRC and the United States were formally restored in the 1979 US-China Trade Agreement. The 1979 agreement—which entered into force in 1980—provided mutual MFN trading status, significantly lowering tariffs on traded goods.[6] That status was not permanent,

---

4. According to the Communists, the Nationalists could not speak for the Chinese government because they did not control the mainland.

5. In 1983, China participated in negotiations as an observer and became a signatory to the GATT Multi-Fiber Arrangement (MFA).

6. MFN was not the lowest tariff status possible; some developing countries had even lower rates under the Generalized System of Preferences (GSP). The trade agreement with China would be renewed every three years.

however. Instead, as a nonmarket economy, China was subject to an annual review under section 402 of the Trade Act of 1974, the so-called Jackson-Vanik amendment.[7] Each year on July 3, the US president had to waive Jackson-Vanik in order to renew China's MFN status. The president's renewal would go through automatically unless Congress voted to reject it.[8]

## Accession Negotiations Begin . . . and Stall

In 1986, China requested the restoration of its status as a full contracting party to the GATT, arguing that the Beijing government had never agreed to China's withdrawal (Jackson and Rhodes 1999, 498; see also Yang and Cheng 2001, 299–302). Rejoining the GATT would assure China of lower tariffs for its goods when trading with GATT members. Entry would also eliminate other trade barriers China faced, such as quantity restrictions. Overall, the World Bank estimated that by acceding to the GATT, China would increase its exports by 38 percent (Bhala 2000, 1480). With the approval of the US Congress, accession would also mean the end of the US annual review of China's MFN status. In short, GATT membership would garner China all the benefits of belonging to the principal international trade organization.

But the path to that goal was not easy. The GATT accession process had both multilateral and bilateral levels (for more information on the process, see WTO 1995). As an applicant nation, China had to negotiate a *multilateral* Protocol of Accession with all interested members to establish the terms and conditions of GATT entry. To this end, a working party on "China's Status as a Contracting Party" was created in 1987.[9] The first phase of the process required China to submit a memorandum on its trade regime for review by the working party, followed by negotiations on how and when China would revise polices that did not meet minimum GATT standards. Many issues needed to be discussed, including tariffs, market access, transparency of trade laws, and subsidies to state-owned enterprises. In addition, because decisions at the GATT were made by consensus, the opposition of one country could block the working party from concluding its task.

As part of the accession process, each GATT applicant also negotiated *bilateral* market access agreements with members of the working party. Thirty-seven countries requested such negotiations with China, and any

---

7. Jackson-Vanik was designed to deny MFN status to countries with nonmarket economies—notably the Soviet Union, which did not freely allow emigration.

8. Congressional rejection of the extension was subject to presidential veto, which could be overturned only by a two-thirds majority in both the House and the Senate.

9. The working party met at least 20 times: in 1987, 1988 (five times), 1989, 1990, 1992 (three times), 1993 (three times), 1994 (four times), and 1995 (at least three times) (*GATT Activities* [1987–95]).

commitments made by China would apply equally to all GATT members under nondiscrimination rules. In other words, the bilateral talks determined the benefits members could expect when China joined the GATT.

By the end of 1988, the working party had completed the initial phase of exploring China's trade regime and expected to begin considering possible terms of a Protocol of Accession in 1989.[10] But in June 1989, tanks and army soldiers opened fire on unarmed students and other protesters in Tiananmen Square, killing hundreds and leading the United States to withdraw its support for China's accession to the GATT (Ross 1996, 22). Other GATT members were worried about the slowdown of China's economic reform. Citing "political and economic upheaval in China in the early summer," which "led participants to conclude that no useful work could be done at that stage," the GATT Working Party on China canceled its June 1989 meeting. Concerns about China's economy were also voiced at a meeting in December at which members of the working party "were anxious to clarify whether [China's] recent cutbacks in imports and slowdown in the pace of reform were a short-term reaction to an overheated economy or represented a more permanent change of approach."[11] The working party met again in September 1990—and then not until a year and a half later, in February 1992.[12]

Taiwan's 1990 bid to join the GATT heightened the controversy. China, which has never swerved from its policy favoring reunification with Taiwan, demanded that the island not enter the GATT until its own application was accepted. In 1992 the GATT established a working party to consider Taiwan's application as a "separate customs territory" under the name "Chinese Taipei."[13] While China's and Taiwan's accession processes would continue independently, it was decided that China had to be accepted first.

In a final complication, attention sometimes was diverted from China's accession to the multilateral GATT Uruguay Round negotiations (1986–93)—especially when the talks broke down over agriculture at the end of 1990. "A lot of things go on hold while you're trying to complete a new global trade agreement," notes one negotiator. "Accessions tend to be one of them. So that contributed to the slowdown in China's WTO bid."

## US-China Bilateral Trade Tensions

As discussions continued on the multilateral level, the issue of trade with China was becoming more contentious in the United States. From 1980—the year MFN status was restored after having been suspended in 1951—

---

10. *GATT Activities* (1988), 129.

11. *GATT Activities* (1989), 130, 131.

12. *GATT Activities* (1991), 132; *GATT Activities* (1992), 94.

13. *GATT Activities* (1992), 95–96.

until 1989, the annual renewal of China's trade status was relatively uncontroversial in the US Congress. However, Tiananmen Square caused many in Washington to advocate harsh economic sanctions against China. Some in Congress favored withdrawing China's MFN status altogether, or at least using the annual renewal as an opportunity to speak out against China's human rights abuses, use of prison labor, Taiwan policies, and weapons proliferation. Withdrawing MFN status would raise US tariffs on Chinese imports from an average of 8.4 percent to 47.5 percent.

Senate Majority Leader George Mitchell (D-ME) and Representative Nancy Pelosi (D-CA) led the charge on Capitol Hill to restrict China's MFN status during the presidency of George H. W. Bush. In 1990 and 1991, the House voted to set conditions on MFN status for China by overwhelming bipartisan majorities,[14] but the Senate did not give these bills final approval. President Bush argued that retracting MFN status would be a setback for Chinese reformers. "If we withdrew MFN or imposed conditions that would make trade impossible, we would punish South China, in particular Guangdong Province, the very region where free-market reform and the challenge to central authority are the strongest," Bush said when he announced the extension of China's MFN status in 1991.[15] Senate Majority Leader Mitchell criticized the president's comments as lacking "any moral or logical basis."[16]

Many in Congress also worried about the growing trade imbalance with China, which had ballooned from $3.5 billion in 1988 to $10.4 billion by 1990 (see table 6.1). Trade with China was changing—not just in volume, but also in composition. In 1980, the principal Chinese exports to the United States were crude oil and refined petroleum products. By the late 1980s and early 1990s, China's exports were largely composed of labor-intensive manufactures such as electronics, footwear, textiles, apparel, toys, and sporting goods (Sebenius and Hulse 2001a, 7).[17] While the United States had a growing demand for these products, China did not have the same appetite for US goods.

Though President Bush refused to link human rights to MFN treatment, his administration did put pressure on the Chinese to reform their trade regime. Section 301 of the 1974 Trade Act allowed the president to take unilateral action against "unreasonable, unjustifiable, or discriminatory" practices by its trade partners. In 1991, the United States initiated a section 301 case against China over four unfair trading practices affecting US ex-

---

14. In the House, the 1990 bill (HR 4939) to put new human rights conditions on China's MFN status passed 384–30; the 1991 measure (HR 2212) to restrict the president's ability to renew MFN status for China in 1992 passed 313–112.

15. President George H. W. Bush, commencement address at Yale University, May 27, 1991.

16. Mitchell, quoted in *Congressional Quarterly Almanac* (1991), 14-E.

17. By 1997, approximately 87 percent of Chinese exports and 80 percent of Chinese imports consisted of manufactured goods (USITC 1999, 6).

**Table 6.1    US merchandise trade with China, 1980–2003**
(billions of dollars)

| Year | US exports | US imports | US trade balance |
|------|-----------|-----------|------------------|
| 1980 | 3.8 | 1.1 | +2.7 |
| 1981 | 3.6 | 1.9 | +1.7 |
| 1982 | 2.9 | 2.3 | +0.6 |
| 1983 | 2.2 | 2.2 | 0.0 |
| 1984 | 3.0 | 3.1 | –0.1 |
| 1985 | 3.9 | 3.9 | 0.0 |
| 1986 | 3.1 | 4.8 | –1.7 |
| 1987 | 3.5 | 6.3 | –2.8 |
| 1988 | 5.0 | 8.5 | –3.5 |
| 1989 | 5.8 | 12.0 | –6.2 |
| 1990 | 4.8 | 15.2 | –10.4 |
| 1991 | 6.3 | 19.0 | –12.7 |
| 1992 | 7.5 | 25.7 | –18.2 |
| 1993 | 8.8 | 31.5 | –22.8 |
| 1994 | 9.3 | 38.8 | –29.5 |
| 1995 | 11.7 | 45.6 | –33.9 |
| 1996 | 12.0 | 51.5 | –39.5 |
| 1997 | 12.8 | 62.6 | –49.8 |
| 1998 | 14.2 | 71.2 | –57.0 |
| 1999 | 13.1 | 81.8 | –68.7 |
| 2000 | 16.2 | 100.0 | –83.8 |
| 2001 | 19.2 | 102.3 | –83.1 |
| 2002 | 22.1 | 125.2 | –103.1 |
| 2003 | 28.4 | 152.4 | –124.0 |

*Sources:* US Department of Commerce, International Trade Administration, www.ita.doc.gov: US Total Exports to Individual Countries, 1997–2003; US Total Imports from Individual Countries, 1997–2003; US Exports by Country, 1985–2003; and US Imports by Country, 1985–2003.

ports, including tariff and nontariff barriers and a lack of transparency in Chinese trade rules.[18] The case was the most sweeping market access investigation in USTR's history. In August 1992, USTR determined that China had made insufficient progress and threatened to impose $3.9 billion in trade sanctions—which would have been the highest amount ever levied in a section 301 case (Morrison 2001). In October 1992, China and the United States reached an agreement—the Memorandum of Under-

---

18. Specifically, the practices were (1) product- and sector-specific import prohibitions and quantitative restrictions, (2) restrictive import-licensing requirements, (3) technical barriers to trade such as testing and certification requirements, and (4) failure to publish laws, regulations, judicial decisions, and administrative rulings concerning requirements, restrictions, or prohibitions on imports affecting their sale and distribution in China (see USTR, *1992 Annual Report of the President of the United States on the Trade Agreements Program*, 56).

standing Between the Government of the People's Republic of China and the Government of the United States of America Concerning Market Access (hereafter referred to as the 1992 US-China Market Access MOU)—with China pledging to reduce a variety of trade barriers over the next five years. In return, the United States agreed to "staunchly support" the PRC's goal of becoming a GATT/WTO member (1992 US-China Market Access MOU, Article VIII).[19]

The Bush administration also put pressure on the Chinese in the area of intellectual property rights (IPR) violations, especially in the "piracy" of software, compact discs, and videos.[20] In the first visit to China by a US cabinet officer after Tiananmen Square, Secretary of State James Baker told government officials that misuse of American intellectual property stood with the sale of weapons of mass destruction to Iran and human rights abuses as one of three issues impeding better bilateral relations (Alford 1995, 113). In April 1991, China was named a "Priority Foreign Country" under Special 301 for failing to provide adequate protection to patents, trademarks, copyrights, and trade secrets.[21] In May, USTR Carla Hills began an investigation and later warned that $1.5 billion in trade sanctions would be imposed on Chinese products like clothing and electronics if an IPR agreement was not reached by January 1992. When China countered with plans to impose sanctions of its own, the Bush administration threatened to revoke China's MFN status and impede China's accession to the GATT (Sebenius and Hulse 2001a, 8). On January 17, 1992, China and the United States reached a deal: China agreed to significantly improve IPR protections on products such as computer software, agricultural chemicals, CDs, and pharmaceuticals and to join the Berne Convention on copyrights. The agreement reportedly brought about little real change, however.

In 1992, President Bush twice vetoed a conditional MFN bill passed by the House and Senate that linked trade with human rights. "There is no doubt in my mind that if we present China's leaders with an ultimatum on MFN, the result will be weakened ties to the West and further repression," Bush wrote in a veto message.[22] The Senate failed to override the presidential

---

19. 1992 US-China Market Access MOU, Article VIII, 2, "The US Government will staunchly support China's achievement of contracting party status to the GATT and will work constructively with the Chinese Government and other GATT contracting parties to reach agreement on an acceptable 'Protocol' and then China's rapid attainment of contracting party status."

20. In his book *To Steal a Book Is an Elegant Offense,* William Alford (1995, 112) notes: "The Bush administration's professed concerns about interfering in China's internal affairs, which supposedly constrained it from pushing with vigor, either publicly or privately, for a peaceful resolution of the occupation of [Tiananmen] Square, simply did not carry over to intellectual property."

21. On Special 301, see chapter 3.

22. Bush, quoted in his written presidential message to the House of Representatives, March 2, 1992.

vetoes (see table 6.2). In another development on the human rights front, in August 1992 the United States and China signed an MOU that committed China to cease exporting to the United States products made with prison labor (US law prohibits the importation of such goods). But debate continued over the MOU's implementation, focusing especially on visits by US customs officials to production facilities suspected of using forced labor.

As a presidential candidate, Bill Clinton was critical of the Bush policy of engagement with China. During his acceptance speech at the Democratic convention, Clinton declared that the United States needed a government that "does not coddle tyrants from Baghdad to Beijing"—a statement that would be repeated in the press for years to come. Clinton also noted in campaign speeches that "there is no more striking example of Mr. Bush's indifference toward democracy than his policy toward China" and criticized Bush for "signaling that we would do business as usual with those who murdered freedom in Tiananmen Square."[23] The Chinese government expressed "serious concern" at the possibility of Clinton's being elected to the White House.[24] In the lead-up to the election, Clinton continued to denounce Bush's stance on China's MFN status, endorsing legislation that would link China's MFN renewal to improvements in human rights, reductions of overseas arms sales, and fairer trade.

As president, Clinton followed through with his vision, issuing an executive order in May 1993 to make the renewal of China's MFN trade status in 1994 conditional on improvement in six areas, including human rights.[25] He was commended by Senator Mitchell and Representative Pelosi, who said that further congressional action would be unnecessary. Mitchell called Clinton's order "fair, reasonable, responsible."[26]

Clinton's move was unpopular with many in the business community, however. As AT&T Chairman William Warwick told Secretary of State William Christopher, conditional MFN was "well-intentioned" but "in the view of American business interests is ill-conceived."[27] Before signing his

---

23. William J. Clinton, "American Foreign Policy and the Democratic Ideal," campaign speech, Pabst Theater, Milwaukee, WI, October 1, 1992; speech to the Los Angeles World Affairs Council, US Newswires, August 13, 1992.

24. Geoffrey Crothall, "MFN Worry If Clinton Wins," *South China Morning Post*, July 29, 1992, 11.

25. The five other areas were treatment of political prisoners, Tibet's heritage, emigration, international radio and television broadcasts in China, and the use of prison labor. See Executive Order 12850, "Conditions for Renewal of Most Favored Nation Status for the People's Republic of China in 1994," May 28, 1993.

26. Mitchell, quoted in "China's Trade Status Tied to Human Rights Record," *1993 Congressional Quarterly Almanac*, 184.

27. Warwick, quoted in Robert S. Greenberger and Kathy Chen, "China, US Head Toward Trade Collision—Beijing Refuses to be Railroaded by Washington over Human Rights," *The Asian Wall Street Journal*, March 14, 1994, 1. US businesses were not united on this issue; human rights concerns had already led some, such as Levi-Strauss and Timberland, to pull out of China.

## Table 6.2 China MFN votes in Congress

| Year | Vote | Republicans | Democrats | Independents | Total |
|------|------|------------:|----------:|-------------:|------:|
| **House of Representatives** | | | | | |
| 1990 | Conditions on China's MFN (HR 4939) | | | | |
| | Yes | 150 | 234 | — | 384 |
| | No | 19 | 11 | — | 30 |
| 1991 | Conditional MFN for China in 1992 Conference Report (HR 2212) | | | | |
| | Yes | 151 | 257 | 1 | 409 |
| | No | 14 | 7 | — | 21 |
| 1992 | Override veto of HR 2212 | | | | |
| | Yes | 110 | 246 | 1 | 357 |
| | No | 51 | 10 | — | 61 |
| | Conditional MFN for China in 1993 (HR 5318) | | | | |
| | Yes | 112 | 226 | 1 | 339 |
| | No | 47 | 15 | — | 62 |
| | Override veto of HR 5318 | | | | |
| | Yes | 102 | 242 | 1 | 345 |
| | No | 60 | 14 | — | 74 |
| 1993 | Disapprove China MFN (HJ Res. 208; H Rept 103-167) | | | | |
| | Yes | 63 | 41 | 1 | 105 |
| | No | 108 | 210 | — | 318 |
| 1994 | Disapprove China MFN (HJ Res. 373) | | | | |
| | Yes | 36 | 38 | 1 | 75 |
| | No | 141 | 215 | — | 356 |
| | China MFN Executive Order Codification (HR 4590) | | | | |
| | Yes | 129 | 151 | — | 280 |
| | No | 44 | 107 | 1 | 152 |
| 1995 | Disapprove China MFN/ Motion on table (HJ Res. 96) | | | | |
| | Yes | 178 | 143 | — | 321 |
| | No | 52 | 54 | 1 | 107 |
| 1997 | Disapprove China MFN (HJ Res. 79) | | | | |
| | Yes | 79 | 93 | 1 | 173 |
| | No | 147 | 112 | — | 259 |
| 1998 | Disapprove NTR status for China (HJ Res. 121) | | | | |
| | Yes | 78 | 87 | 1 | 166 |
| | No | 149 | 115 | — | 264 |
| 2000 | PNTR for China (HR 4444) | | | | |
| | Yes | 164 | 73 | — | 237 |
| | No | 57 | 138 | 2 | 197 |
| 2000 | Overturn decision to Extend PNTR (HJ Res. 103) | | | | |
| | Yes | 54 | 91 | 2 | 147 |
| | No | 164 | 117 | — | 281 |

*(table continues next page)*

**Table 6.2**   *(continued)*

| Year | Vote | Republicans | Democrats | Total |
|------|------|-------------|-----------|-------|
| **Senate** | | | | |
| 1991 | Conditional MFN for China (HR 2212) | | | |
| | Yes | 6 | 49 | 55 |
| | No | 37 | 7 | 44 |
| 1992 | Conditional MFN for China/ Conference Report (HR 2212) | | | |
| | Yes | 9 | 50 | 59 |
| | No | 34 | 5 | 39 |
| | Override veto of HR 2212 | | | |
| | Yes | 9 | 51 | 60 |
| | No | 34 | 4 | 38 |
| | Override veto of conditional MFN for China (HR 5318) | | | |
| | Yes | 8 | 51 | 59 |
| | No | 35 | 5 | 40 |
| 2000 | PNTR for China (HR 4444) | | | |
| | Yes | 46 | 37 | 83 |
| | No | 8 | 7 | 15 |

— = 0
MFN = most favored nation status
NTR = normal trade relations
PNTR = permanent normal trade relations

Notes:
HR 4939 (1990): Passage of the bill to require the president to certify that the Chinese government is taking action to correct human rights violations before granting China MFN trade status in 1991.

HR 2212 (1991): Adoption of the conference report to allow the president to renew the extension of nondiscriminatory treatment for the products of China (MFN trading status) only if the Chinese government releases nonviolent Tiananmen Square demonstrators, does not sell missiles to Syria or Iran, and makes significant progress in human rights, its nuclear proliferation policy, and certain trade practices. A "nay" was a vote supporting the president's position.

HR 5318 (1992): Conditional MFN for China in 1993: Bill to prohibit the president from waiving the Jackson-Vanik amendment to the 1974 Trade Act for Chinese state-owned enterprises in 1993 unless he certified that China had released and accounted for all prisoners from the Tiananmen Square demonstrations in 1989 and had made significant progress in resolving concerns over human rights violations, trade violations, and weapons nonproliferation. A "nay" was a vote supporting the president's position.

HJ Res. 208—H Rept. 103-167 (1993): Disapprove China MFN: Joint resolution to disapprove President Clinton's waiver of the Jackson-Vanik amendment to the 1974 Trade Act with respect to China for the period beginning July 3, 1993, through July 2, 1994.

HR 4590 (1994): China MFN Executive Order Codification: Substitute amendment to codify President Clinton's May 26 executive order waiving the Jackson-Vanik amendment to the 1974 Trade Act and granting MFN status to China from July 1994 through July 1995, allowing Chinese products to enter the United States at the lowest available tariff rate.

HJ Res. 96 (1995): Disapprove China MFN: Wolf (R-VA), motion to table (kill) the joint resolution to disapprove President Clinton's waiver of the Jackson-Vanik amendment to the 1974 trade act in order to grant MFN status to China for the period July 1995 through July 1996. A "yes" vote was a vote in support of the president's position.

HJ Res. 79 (1997): Disapprove China MFN: Joint resolution disapproving of President Clinton's decision to renew MFN status to China from July 3, 1997, to July 3, 1998. A "no" vote was a vote in support of the president's position.

HJ Res. 121 (1998): Disapprove NTR status for China: Bill to deny president's request to provide "normal trade relations" for items produced in China for the period July 1998 through July 1999.

HJ Res. 103 (2000): Overturn decision to extend PNTR: Disapprove the extension of the waiver authority contained in Section 402(c) of the Trade Act of 1974 with respect to the People's Republic of China.

*Source: Congressional Quarterly Almanac (various years).*

executive order, Clinton had received a letter from 298 companies and 37 trade associations requesting him not to attach conditions to MFN status.[28] The business coalition against conditional MFN, which became known as "the new China lobby," was described by trade experts as "perhaps the most formidable, pro-trade coalition ever sustained by US business on its own initiative" (Destler 1995, 234). Some administration officials, including Treasury Secretary Lloyd Bentsen, National Economic Council Chairman Robert Rubin, and Council of Economic Advisers Chair Laura Tyson also called for moderation with China. Nor did the international community rally to support Clinton's executive order; the European Union and Japan had no plans to link trade with human rights. In the months following the executive order, some say the Chinese made a point of defying US conditions by cracking down on well-known political dissidents.[29] In June 1994, Clinton renewed China's MFN status despite the consensus in the United States that if anything, human rights in China had worsened.

Later that month, USTR once again designated China a Special 301 "Priority Foreign Country" because of its lack of progress in enforcing agreements on intellectual property rights. According to industry estimates, "piracy" of their products in China cost US software publishers $351 million annually.[30] The music industry calculated that China was copying 75 million CDs per year.[31] In negotiations with the Chinese, Deputy USTR Charlene Barshefsky emphasized that improving IPR enforcement would be an important step in their bid for membership in the GATT, demonstrating to the international community that China was serious about making the required changes. But in February 1995, citing a lack of progress in the IPR talks, USTR released a list of more than $1 billion worth of Chinese imports that would be subject to 100 percent tariffs. China retaliated by announcing sanctions of its own on US products, including CDs, cigarettes, Kodak film, and AT&T telecom switches.[32] After a high-risk negotiation, China and the United States reached an agreement on IPR enforcement on February 26, 1995.

---

28. Fifty of these companies had made soft money contributions averaging $30,000 each to the Democratic National Committee (John Kruger and Charles Lewis, "Bill's Long March; When Big Money Talked, Clinton Retreated to George Bush's Policy," *The Washington Post*, November 7, 1993, C3).

29. Greenberger and Chen, "China, US Head Toward Trade Collision," 1.

30. Robert Hurtado, "With Sanctions Set, Companies Rethink Their China Plans," *The New York Times*, February 6, 1995, A1.

31. Kantor said about 70 million of these pirated CDs were exported. See "US Hits China with 301 Case on IPR, Spares Argentina, India," *Inside US Trade*, July 1, 1994.

32. "New Chinese Retaliation List Targets Telecom Switches, Film," *Inside US Trade*, February 10, 1995.

USTR once again put the Chinese on notice for failing to enforce IP rights in May 1996. Some US companies claimed that IPR piracy had actually worsened after the February agreement. For example, while China had conducted thousands of raids and destroyed millions of copied CDs at the retail level, USTR noted that many Chinese factories continued to produce and export pirated products.[33] Some in the administration felt that with Clinton running for a second term as president, a firm stance was important. As negotiations and threats of sanctions continued, Acting USTR Barshefsky turned down a surprise invitation to meet with President Jiang Zemin, explaining to China's trade minister, "I would be honored and delighted to meet with President Jiang, but I am afraid that would be impossible. I cannot meet with President Jiang and then impose sanctions. If all 15 factories are not closed, I will have no choice but to impose sanctions, and I do not want to put President Jiang, or you, in that embarrassing position."[34] Ultimately, in June 1996, China agreed to improve enforcement of the 1995 IPR agreement. "Three years ago, IPR enforcement was an abstract concept," Barshefsky said at a press conference. "Now, the Chinese authorities are taking concrete and tangible actions."[35] Nevertheless, IPRs would remain a potent issue in the years ahead.

## China Sets a Goal

Meanwhile, back at the GATT, China set a goal of January 1, 1995, for reentry—the date the GATT would become the WTO. As Barshefsky remembers, "China viewed entry at the creation of the WTO as a psychologically important target. In large part, this was because China was a founding member of the GATT. Now it wanted to be a founding member of the WTO."[36] The GATT working party met between 1992 and the end of 1994, and China held bilateral market access negotiations with many countries.[37] Numerous issues were discussed, such as tariffs, nontariff bar-

---

33. USTR, *1995 Annual Report of the President of the United States on the Trade Agreements Program*, 88.

34. Barshefsky, interviewed in Sebenius and Hulse (2001b, 10).

35. See Seth Faison, "US and China Agree on Pact to Fight Piracy," *The New York Times*, June 18, 1996, A1.

36. Unless otherwise noted, all quotes from Charlene Barshefsky are from a March 2001 interview with Charan Devereaux. Observers at the GATT agreed with her assessment; e.g., see *GATT Activities* (1993), 105 ("Throughout the year, China expressed its wish that the negotiations on its status as a contracting party be concluded in time for it to become an original member of the World Trade Organization").

37. The countries participating included the United States, Canada, Japan, EC members, Mexico, the Nordic nations, and Switzerland (*GATT Activities* [1993], 104–5; *GATT Activities* [1994–95], 113).

riers, market access for financial services, insurance and telecommunications, labor standards, state-owned enterprises (SOEs), investment, agriculture, and China's lack of transparent trade laws. The United States wanted to see a special safeguard created that would allow restrictions on China to be reimposed if there was a flood of subsidized exports from China's nonmarket sectors. It also insisted that China expand trading rights so that foreign companies could import and export without going through Chinese middlemen.

From the US perspective, China's offers were far below expectations. In 1993, the United States and China held their first bilateral GATT accession meeting since formal talks were cut off in 1989. After two days of negotiations, Assistant USTR for GATT Affairs Douglas Newkirk told reporters that China had stepped back from commitments made before the military crackdown four years earlier—including those on the safeguard issue. "We made progress this week, but we are not as far along as we were in 1989," said Newkirk. "We're a long way from completing the negotiations. . . . I'm going to be retired in seven years, and I'm not sure I can wrap it up at the current pace."[38] For its part, China argued it had made major advances in economic reform and trade liberalization; it hoped to reenter the GATT as early as that year. "The accession process is driven by the acceding country," Newkirk noted. "If they want to agree to very tough obligations, we can do it very quickly. But if they want to draw the process out by talking about the virtues of a socialist market economy, it is going to take a long time."[39]

As working party negotiations went on, US officials continued to express dissatisfaction with China's offers on its trade regime. "There is need for improvement," said one US official. "The offer has got to meet a certain threshold and they are just not there yet."[40] China's offers were "seriously deficient," Barshefsky declared.[41] The European Union and Japan also found China's offers insufficient, though the European Union continued to press for China's entry as a WTO founding member. Some Chinese participants saw the situation differently, saying, "Though China's economic development showed very positive signs, negotiations for China's resumption of

---

38. Newkirk, quoted in David Schlesinger, "US Dashes China Hopes of Early GATT Entry," *Reuters News*, March 2, 1993. Newkirk said that China had to meet five conditions for GATT entry: a "single national trade policy" common to all provinces and regions, full transparency of trade regulations, the elimination of nontariff barriers, a commitment to move to a "full market price economy," and acceptance of safeguards to protect GATT signatories from a possible surge in Chinese exports.

39. Newkirk, quoted in "China's Bid to Join GATT Stalls Following Negotiations with US on Protocol," *Inside US Trade*, March 5, 1993.

40. Quoted in "Officials Say China Services Offer Falls Short, But See IPR Movement," *Inside US Trade*, September 2, 1994.

41. Barshefsky, quoted in "Barshefsky Blasts China for Inadequate Offers in WTO Talks," *Inside US Trade*, December 2, 1994.

membership in the GATT contrarily became more difficult. Western countries demanded more and more. . . ." (Yang and Cheng 2001, 315).

China's wish to become a WTO founding member would not be fulfilled. In December 1994, Working Party Chairman Pierre-Louis Girard said the panel had reached "substantive agreement" in some areas, but other questions of central importance remained unsettled.[42] One particularly difficult question centered on whether China would gain admission to the GATT as a developing or as a developed country. China hoped to secure membership as a less-developed country (LDC), thereby ensuring that it would have "special and different status" under the GATT. For example, less-developed countries were offered certain exemptions, special consideration in dispute settlement, and a longer transition period for meeting international standards.[43] "The obligations to be assumed by China, in principle, should not exceed those that are required of developing countries," said Gu Yongjiang, China's vice minister of foreign trade and economic cooperation.[44] It was "unfair and unrealistic" for Western countries to expect China to achieve quickly what developed countries had accomplished over 100 to 200 years, Trade Minister Wu Yi would later add.[45] But the United States, pointing to China's size and its significance in the world trading system, insisted that it join as a developed country. The European Union indicated that it might support China's membership under less stringent requirements than those advocated by the United States. A European Commission strategy paper noted that the EU's approach reflected "a sympathetic understanding of the fact that China is a country that is rapidly developing, but, in important respects, has not yet become a developed economy" and that some WTO commitments "could be implemented under multilateral surveillance over a specified period of time after entry into the WTO" (European Commission 1995, 11).

## USTR Creates a Road Map

In 1995, China renewed its application under the WTO and requested that the GATT working party continue its activities in the new organization. As the WTO working party's negotiations got under way, differences re-

---

42. *GATT Activities* (1994–95), 113.

43. See Article XVIII of the GATT 1994, which addresses governmental assistance in economic development. In addition, under part IV of the GATT, which was added in 1965, developed countries forgo the receipt of reciprocal benefits for their negotiated commitments to reduce or eliminate tariffs and restrictions on trade with less-developed member countries.

44. Gu, quoted in "Chinese Officials Concede PRC May Not Join WTO As Founding Member," *Inside US Trade*, July 8, 1994.

45. Wu, quoted in James Kynge, "Beijing in Offer on Services," *The Financial Times*, February 18, 1998, 7.

mained. The European Union, Japan, and others seemed willing to settle for China fulfilling some WTO criteria on entry and other requirements later. EU Commissioner Sir Leon Brittan spoke of allowing China to join the WTO "in principle," given its political importance, a position supported by some in the US foreign policy community as well.[46]

USTR disagreed, noting that the WTO was fundamentally not a political club but a contractual agreement—an agreement that contained specific terms enforced through a provision for binding dispute settlement. USTR was also thinking about the US Congress. If China were to enter the WTO (which has unconditional MFN treatment as a fundamental principle), Congress would be asked to end the annual review of China's MFN status. USTR believed that Congress was unlikely to pass legislation making China's MFN status permanent unless the deal that brought China into the WTO was negotiated on a commercial basis.

Therefore, the mantra at USTR was that China must enter the WTO on "commercially meaningful terms," not as a political decision. Meanwhile, President Clinton and his senior policy advisers decided to make a major strategic push to deepen and stabilize relations with China. To communicate the seriousness of the United States, Deputy USTR Barshefsky created a road map for China's WTO accession. In late 1995, her team put together a nine-page document that Barshefsky presented to her counterpart: Trade Minister Wu Yi, the highest-ranking woman in China's government. The road map was designed to indicate the kind of comprehensive and far-reaching internal changes that would be necessary if China was to be admitted to the WTO. The document covered a number of controversial issues, such as reducing nontariff measures on agricultural products and providing market access for the telecom, banking, and insurance industries. As Barshefsky remembers:

> The road map proved to be very helpful in two respects: one, it helped to focus the minds of the Chinese on the substance of what would have to be put together. Second, it was an early warning to the Chinese leadership that this was not a frivolous exercise, and it was not an exercise that could be successfully concluded on a political basis. This was not a political deal. This was a commercial deal. That would mean the leadership would have to come to grips politically at the highest level with the series of changes that would be demanded by the WTO membership.

The United States was taking a tough stance; in response, WTO Director-General Renato Ruggiero publicly called on the United States to offer a "political clarification" of its desire to see China in the WTO. Ruggiero believed that such a step would ensure a political environment conducive to effective negotiations, according to his spokesman.[47]

---

46. Brittan quoted in "Barshefsky Says China's Stall on WTO May Weaken Japan, EU Stance," *Inside US Trade*, November 3, 1995.

47. Ruggiero quoted in "Kantor Rejects EU Proposals for Special Treatment of China in WTO," *Inside US Trade*, October 27, 1995.

US concerns about the multilateral accession process continued, however. Some analysts worried that if a deal was reached first at the multilateral working party level, the European Union might altogether forgo engaging in the bilateral talks that members could also request as part of WTO accession. Some believed that if the European Union did not demand a bilateral agreement, then China would no longer feel inclined to make a meaningful bilateral deal with the United States. Therefore, US officials started to shift their focus. According to one US negotiator,

> There were concerns that the Chinese might push for a political accession—a possibility that might have been supported by the EU—had the working party in Geneva concluded the multilateral part of the accession talks prior to conclusion of the bilateral market access negotiations. Some in Washington thought the EU would say, "They've done enough, just let them in on some special terms," especially since negotiations had dragged on for so long. So the US had that over our shoulder, which is why we switched in mid-1997 to bilateral work.

As bilateral talks between the United States and China continued, interest in the US business community grew. Because the terms of the bilateral agreement would be more specific than those of previous discussions, industry leaders could see the potential benefits for their own companies. As one member of the US negotiating team said:

> Up until that point, no country had engaged in comprehensive bilateral market access talks. In the summer of '97 it was decided that we'd put aside this multilateral process of negotiating working party documents and actually get right down into the nuts and bolts of the bilateral market access talks: the tariffs, the services, the agriculture, the quotas, and so forth. The how-does-it-affect-my-product kind of negotiations. And that also helped focus the wider US business community. It gave them a real sense of the advantages of China joining the WTO.

Also in July 1997, Hong Kong reverted back to Chinese rule after having been administered by the British for more than 150 years. A financial center of Asia, Hong Kong ranked among the world's richest cities and boasted the region's largest port. For the next 50 years, it would be a "Special Administrative Region" of China. President Jiang Zemin announced that Hong Kong would be administered under the "one country, two systems" concept, leaving the city with "a high degree of autonomy."[48]

## Trade Tensions Continue (Domestic Politics)

As the talks moved forward, politicians and others in the United States kept up the debate about the wisdom of engaging China. As she had dur-

---

48. "Remarks by President Jiang Zemin of China at Ceremony Recognizing the Restoration of Hong Kong to the People's Republic of China," Hong Kong, June 30, 1997, transcript by Federal News Service.

ing the Bush administration, Representative Nancy Pelosi led the fight against granting China MFN status, joined by Representative Frank Wolf (R-VA). Despite such protests, the House rejected a 1997 resolution disapproving Clinton's decision to extend China's MFN status.[49]

In October 1997, President Jiang Zemin and President Clinton held a summit in Washington, DC. Both sides hoped that in addition to addressing security issues such as mutual detargeting of nuclear missiles, they could make progress in the bilateral trade negotiations. President Jiang did make promises to reduce tariffs significantly by 2005 and committed to join the March 1997 Information Technology Agreement. However, the US press viewed the summit as showcasing mainly the differences between how the United States and China approach human rights—focusing especially on how the two presidents responded to questions about Tiananmen Square in a joint press conference.

Clinton's announcement in June 1998 that he would renew China's MFN status came against a backdrop of accusations from Republican members of Congress that the Chinese government had illegally contributed to his presidential campaign. The annual debate over MFN also reignited concerns about the US trade deficit with China. US figures indicated that the United States had imported $62.6 billion in goods from China the year before, but exported only $12.8 billion in goods (the differences in how China and the United States calculated imports and exports make such figures controversial).[50] And accusations over Chinese human rights violations continued. House Minority Leader Richard Gephardt (D-MO) declared he would once again oppose MFN status for China. The United States "must not reward the Chinese Communist government for its continuing political repression and tyranny," he said.[51]

---

49. Some MFN supporters believed that withholding MFN status for China would also hurt Hong Kong. Hong Kong was allowed to maintain separate economic and trade offices in the United States under a bill passed by the House and Senate and signed into law on June 27, 1997 (*Congressional Quarterly Almanac 1997*, 8–37).

A group of conservative Republicans and liberal Democrats pushed nine bills through the House that attacked China's human rights record, treatment of religious minorities, relations with Taiwan, support of compulsory abortion, and weapons proliferation (the House leadership delayed the votes on these measures until after President Jiang's state visit in October 1997; all passed by large majorities).

50. China claimed that the trade deficit was only $10.5 billion in 1996. A primary source of disparity was different treatment of goods that passed through Hong Kong. The United States did not count US goods exported to Hong Kong and then reexported to China as exports to China, but it attributed to China the full value of all goods shipped through Hong Kong when calculating the bilateral trade balance. China counted only the value of goods leaving China whose final destination was known when they left the country, and it also claimed that many exports from the PRC were from US-operated companies.

51. Gephardt, quoted in Susan Page, "Clinton: Maintain Trade Ties with China, Annual Review Faces More Difficult Road," *USA Today*, June 4, 1998, 8A.

In addition, worries in Congress about security were growing. One concern was the possibility that the Chinese had used US technology to improve their missile guidance systems. Another centered on China's propensity to share weapons technology with Pakistan and Iran. Moreover, reports surfaced that China's military relied on American-made commercial satellites to transmit coded messages. One of the satellites was sold by a US company whose chairman was also the largest individual contributor to the Democratic Party in 1997.[52] Promoting relations with Beijing, some congressional leaders argued, compromised national security. Nevertheless, the House overwhelmingly rejected a resolution to disapprove of extending China's MFN status in 1998, just as it had in 1997 (see table 6.2).

Concerns about engagement were not limited to the US side. Worries over the pace of domestic reform led many in China to conclude that efforts to join the WTO were premature. Chinese financial institutions were saddled with record levels of bad debts, and state-owned enterprises were experiencing runaway losses. China's state-owned sector included more than 300,000 SOEs, which were responsible for more than one-third of the country's GDP; they also provided livelihood and social welfare for over 200 million employees and pensioners and their families (Blumenthal 1999, 115). In order to comply with WTO principles, China would have to eliminate most subsidies to SOEs. Even in its early stages, SOE reform had increased unemployment and urban poverty in the PRC.

Some in China wondered if the stiff conditions of WTO entry were worth it. After all, the PRC already had trade relationships with 200 countries, many of which included MFN treatment (Bhala 2000, 1491). In addition, the Asian financial crisis of 1997–98—which started with bank defaults in Thailand and spread to Malaysia, Indonesia, the Philippines, and South Korea—revealed weaknesses in the Asian development model. A coalition of central Chinese government ministries, provincial representatives, and major industries petitioned the Beijing leadership to postpone WTO accession efforts, accusing the foreign trade establishment of "excessive impetuosity."[53]

Such internal debates highlighted the larger dynamic on the Chinese side: the struggle between the reformist and conservative elements within the Chinese leadership. This tension would continue to play a key role as negotiations continued. As then deputy USTR Richard Fisher observes, WTO accession "represented part of the struggle between the reformers in China and the conservatives. In the former camp are the Zhu Rongjis and in the latter camp would be the Li Pengs. As one evaluates what hap-

---

52. Bernard Schwartz, chairman of Loral Space and Communications (Jeff Gerth, "Reports Show Chinese Military Used American-Made Satellites," *The New York Times*, June 13, 1998, A1).

53. Willy Wo-Lap Lam, "Open Door May Be Closed," *South China Morning Post*, November 26, 1997, 19.

pened in this story—when the talks pressed forward and when they were lagging—this is the number one point to consider."[54] Some US observers are quick to note that labeling Zhu Rongji and others as "reformers" did not imply they were considered free market enthusiasts. As former Deputy National Economic Adviser Lael Brainard puts it, "We certainly did not see Zhu as somebody who was a pure market-oriented reformer. It was much more complicated than that. He was a Chinese nationalist and would pursue reforms to the extent that he thought it was in China's interest—not because of some ideological desire to be capitalist."[55]

Despite the controversy on both sides, bilateral negotiations on market access went ahead. President Clinton made his historic nine-day state visit to China in June 1998 amid hopes that the deal could be concluded as a part of the summit. "Jiang and Clinton would have liked to conclude," Barshefsky remembers. "We negotiated intensively with the Chinese." Though some progress was made, large problems remained unresolved, especially in the agriculture and service sectors. When no agreement could be reached, President Clinton invited Premier Zhu Rongji to the United States. "Zhu hemmed and hawed," says Barshefsky, "but ultimately he accepted the invitation." The Chinese premier would come to the United States the following year.

In the interim, the US administration was weakened by the yearlong scandal over President Clinton's involvement with former White House intern Monica Lewinsky. Clinton's impeachment by the House on charges of perjury and obstruction of justice in December 1998, and subsequent acquittal by the Senate in February 1999, caused enormous distraction.

## Bilateral Negotiations

At the beginning of 1999, the bilateral talks got a boost when Premier Zhu Rongji indicated a readiness to deal. Zhu told US Federal Reserve Board Chairman Alan Greenspan that despite China's economic slowdown, Beijing was ready to open up its markets as a prelude to joining the WTO.[56] As Lael Brainard recalls,

> We were starting to get signals that Zhu Rongji in his new position as Premier was seriously interested in [the US-China bilateral talks] because it bolstered his reform agenda. We were hearing this, but certainly our negotiators, I think correctly,

---

54. Unless otherwise noted, all quotes from Richard Fisher are from a March 2001 interview with Charan Devereaux.

55. Unless otherwise noted, all quotes from Lael Brainard are from a March 2001 interview with Charan Devereaux.

56. See David E. Sanger, "How US and China Failed to Close Trade Deal," *The New York Times*, April 10, 1999, A2.

were reluctant to put anything on the table or to show any leg until they got more direct evidence—they had gone down this road too many times before. Alan Greenspan was going to China and we knew he had a good relationship with Premier Zhu. We needed somebody that was not directly involved with the administration to probe the degree of seriousness—how to interpret the signals. That conversation came back very positively. *Very* positively. Much more so than anybody had anticipated, I think, even the real boosters. That's when the activity really started to take off.

Zhu sent his chief negotiator Long Yongtu to Washington to meet with USTR Barshefsky. Barshefsky was reportedly heartened by China's "seriousness of purpose,"[57] and sent negotiator Robert Cassidy to China for what became weeks of negotiations.

In February, Deputy Treasury Secretary Lawrence Summers visited Beijing to push forward the talks. "We're looking at a window of opportunity now to get this done that will close for [a lengthy] period," he told reporters.[58] After his trip came a visit by Secretary of State Madeleine Albright. In March 1999, USTR Barshefsky traveled to Beijing to meet with Premier Zhu. She was followed by Commerce Secretary William Daley.

US and Chinese negotiators began working out a number of key substantive issues, including a tariffs package and commitments in particularly sensitive areas such as financial services and telecommunications. "The Chinese conceded more than I thought would be politically possible," said Nicholas Lardy, an expert on the Chinese economy at the Brookings Institution. "You have to remember that unemployment is at a 30-year high in China, corporate profits are falling off a cliff, and here is Zhu arguing that this is a moment to actually allow the foreigners to offer more domestic competition."[59] US officials, led by chief USTR China negotiator Robert Cassidy, were calling from Beijing to report the bold offers from the Chinese.[60] "February and March were great," remembers a USTR negotiator. "We were going great guns. We were putting it together."

At the same time, opposition to the US-China trade agreement was heating up in Congress. On February 25, 1999, the Senate unanimously urged the administration to seek a resolution at the UN Human Rights Commission condemning China's human rights abuses (Senate Resolution 45 passed 99–0). Adding fuel to opponents' rhetoric was a top news story of March:

---

57. Barshefsky, quoted in Ian Johnson, "Talks Between US, China Turn Serious—Sinking Foreign Investment Puts Pressure on Beijing to Join Trade Group," *The Wall Street Journal*, March 5, 1999, A9.

58. Summers, quoted in Matt Forney, "Washington Urges China to Speed Reform—US Says Concessions Vital for WTO Ticket Before New Rules Take Effect," *The Asian Wall Street Journal*, February 24, 1999, 1.

59. Lardy, quoted in Sanger, "How US and China Failed to Close Trade Deal," A2. Lardy is now a senior fellow at the Institute for International Economics.

60. Lee Siew Hua, "The Inside Story of Zhu's WTO Bid," *The Straits Times* (Singapore), April 17, 1999, 64.

the alleged espionage of Wen Ho Lee, a former nuclear weapons scientist at Los Alamos National Laboratory.[61] Senate Majority Leader Trent Lott (R-MS) said on *Fox News Sunday* that China's entry to the WTO "should be out of the question."[62] Concerned about the "exploding US-China trade deficit," Senators Jesse Helms (R-NC) and Ernest Hollings (D-SC) announced that they planned to introduce legislation requiring the administration to win congressional approval before signing any deal allowing China into the WTO. "Continuing problems with Chinese human-rights violations, espionage, and possible technology transfers suggest that this is not the appropriate time for China to enter the WTO," Helms and Hollings added in a March 15 letter to Senate colleagues. "Any trade agreement with China would be premature before these issues are resolved."[63]

In the House, Minority Leader Gephardt likewise proposed legislation making US support for China's WTO accession contingent on congressional approval.[65] Other House Democrats made known their worries about the impact of any China trade deal on domestic labor—especially in import-sensitive areas such as textiles and steel. In short, as a former administration official says, "The US relationship with China was an enormously polarized issue in the US Congress." A US negotiator observes, "There seemed to be a confluence of difficulty in Congress at the same time we were actually getting closer in the substance of the negotiations."

The strong emotions in Congress resonated through the White House. Former administration officials note that every step of negotiating the bilateral deal was deeply informed by political realities. What would be the implications for other items on the administration's legislative agenda? For the Democratic Caucus? Many were wary of what was clearly shaping up to be a difficult fight on Capitol Hill.

In March, Premier Zhu Rongji vented his frustration about the WTO accession process, saying that his black hair had turned white since China started negotiations in 1986. "It's time for a conclusion!" he declared at a televised press conference after the closing session of the National People's Congress.[65] He too was aware of the controversy in Congress. "Originally, the WTO negotiations were proceeding fairly smoothly," Zhu said in an in-

---

61. For example, see James Risen, "US Fires Scientist Suspected of Giving China Bomb Data," *The New York Times*, March 9, 1999, A1; John F. Harris and Vernon Loeb, "Spy Case Tests US Openness with China; Engagement Policy Failing, Critics Say," *The Washington Post*, March 14, 1999, A1.

62. *Fox News Sunday*, March 7, 1999, transcript no. 030700cb.250; cited in "Senators Move to Oppose China's WTO Accession Without Strong Oversight," *Inside US Trade*, March 12, 1999.

63. See Senators Jesse Helms and Fritz Hollings, "Dear Colleague" letter, March 15, 1999.

64. Gephardt's bill (HR 884), introduced March 1, 1999, required the United States to withdraw from the WTO within six months if China joined the WTO without congressional approval.

65. Zhu, quoted in Irene Ngoo, "Finishing Line in Sight, China's WTO Marathon," *The Straits Times* (Singapore), April 4, 1999, 28.

terview. "But recently—we believe, due to pressure from the US Congress—the US government has shown a change in attitude during this round of negotiations."[66]

In the lead-up to Zhu's visit to the United States, some Democrats signaled that any move to close an agreement would be premature. Sandy Levin, the ranking Democrat on the House Ways and Means Trade Subcommittee, was troubled by the failure to include a provision against dumping that would require that China continue to be treated as a nonmarket economy for an extended period of time. Levin also saw the need for a special product-specific safeguard provision to address import surges from China. As a result, one observer recalls, "Levin and others urged the president to go back to the negotiating table and not seal the deal during Premier Zhu's visit." Perhaps a source of congressional resistance greater than the trade concerns of Democrats was the growing security concerns of Republicans. The administration knew that within the next few months, a congressional panel headed by Representative Christopher Cox (R-CA) would release a report accusing China of nuclear espionage. As a former senior White House official remembers, "There was a conjuncture of anti-China sentiment that was largely driven on the Republican side by the Cox Report. The problems that we had on China were not confined to your traditional trade problems. They were much more driven by the Republican majority on security, espionage, and Communist fears."

Administration officials debated the bilateral China deal. "There was true intense division within the administration," says one observer. USTR Barshefsky, National Security Adviser Sandy Berger, and Secretary of State Madeleine Albright argued that China's concessions were sufficient and that Zhu's visit offered a historic opportunity for coming to an agreement. Signing a deal was also important as a means of supporting Premier Zhu, some argued, a reformer who was betting his political capital on WTO accession. The key goal was to conclude the bilateral negotiations, the strongest supporters said; it was not critical to secure Congressional approval immediately.

Other officials—including White House Chief of Staff John Podesta and National Economic Council Chairman Gene Sperling—remained unconvinced that Zhu's visit was the best time to finalize an agreement. The agreement on the table lacked key elements, they said, and rushing it forward would make it impossible to achieve congressional approval of PNTR during the president's term—an element they believed was absolutely critical to success. In particular, sticking points remained, especially in the areas of textiles, brokerage firms, and auto financing. Officials

---

66. Zhu, quoted in Peter Krann, Karen Elliot House, Ian Johnson, and Matt Forney, "The Wall Street Journal interview with Chinese Premier Zhu Rongji," *The Asian Wall Street Journal*, April 6, 1999, A23.

said that given the strength of Republican anti-China sentiment in Congress and the size of the US trade deficit with China (in 2000, China would surpass Japan to become the largest deficit trading partner of the United States), the deal had to be airtight. They also worried about political opposition from Democrats and labor unions—especially in the steel industry. Finally, some officials were concerned that there was not enough active support from the business community, support they deemed crucial if the deal was to succeed.

As these discussions continued, the meetings became smaller and smaller in a vain effort to maintain secrecy. Almost daily, news stories appeared detailing the debates within the administration over the China deal. The week before Zhu's arrival, Ambassador Barshefsky again went to Beijing to hammer out the terms of a bilateral agreement. According to reports, she returned to the United States with the makings of one of the strongest trade deals the United States had ever negotiated.[67]

## An Opportunity Lost?

Premier Zhu came to Washington on April 7, 1999, and on the following day met with President Clinton for two and a half hours in the private residence of the White House. Clinton concluded that this was not the time to sign an agreement. "We have made significant progress toward bringing China into the World Trade Organization on fair commercial terms, although we are not quite there yet," President Clinton said after the meeting.[68] A US-China joint statement noted that "certain matters remain to be resolved" in banking, securities, and audiovisual services as well as in rules governing textiles trade. The joint statement also affirmed that China's admission to the WTO was in the interest of the United States, China, and the global trading system.[69]

Observers say that beyond any specifics, the deal was brought down by political concerns and some confusion about the best time to move forward. As Richard Fisher notes,

> I think case studies always try to make things neat. But this wasn't a neat process. Some of us were very unsettled by the confusion surrounding the deal. At USTR, you build a logic chain and you figure out the pieces that need to be filled in. But when that process intersects with the politics of reality—I quote Henry James: "Courtship is poetry and marriage is hard prose." In this case, the poetry, as hard

---

67. Helene Cooper and Bob Davis, "Barshefsky Drove Hard Bargain, But Lost to Politics," *The Wall Street Journal*, April 12, 1999, A24.

68. White House Briefing, Press Conference with President Bill Clinton and Chinese Premier Zhu Rongji Following Their Meetings, Washington, DC, April 8, 1999.

69. Joint US-China Statement on China's WTO Accession, April 8, 1999.

as it was to structure and negotiate, was a deal. The hard prose was making sure the politics all lined up. And at that point, they didn't seem to line up.

With groups of both Democrats and Republicans in opposition, "the critical middle that you need to support a deal like this is shrinking," said Commerce Secretary William Daley.[70] In a press conference following the meeting with President Clinton, Zhu noted (through an interpreter) that the differences between the two sides on the agreement "were not very significant. . . . If you want to hear some honest words," he told reporters, "then I should say that now the problem does not lie with this big difference, or big gap, but lies with the political atmosphere."[71]

Apparently some in the administration hoped that the tenor of the press coverage of Zhu's visit would be positive, focusing on the broad progress that had been made. Instead, the decision not to go ahead with the agreement was widely criticized as a mistake. It was reported that Clinton had rebuffed Zhu and the Chinese delegation was furious. A new word was created in the White House vocabulary to describe someone who had been undercut politically: "Zhu'd."[72]

The Chinese premier immediately embarked on a six-city tour of the United States to drum up support for the bilateral agreement. Zhu worked rooms like a seasoned American politician, observers said, encouraging farmers and business representatives to call President Clinton and push for completion of the deal. Thousands of people heard his speeches, which often brought standing ovations. In Chicago, 1,500 businesspeople, including the chief executives of Motorola, United Airlines, and Bank One, gathered at a banquet for Zhu.[73] They, as well as many others, were impressed by his relaxed style and sense of humor. While visiting Denver, the premier flattered his hosts, declaring that if the Chinese ever came to play American-style football, he was sure that they could never beat the Denver Broncos.

Zhu's visit was not played up in the Chinese media, however, reportedly taking second billing to more mundane stories. Such treatment demonstrates the care that China's media took to keep the spotlight on President Jiang Zemin. "If Zhu's trip is given much merit, it could take away from the glory" of Mr. Jiang, said a former editor for the *People's Daily*, the

---

70. Daley, quoted in David E. Sanger, "The World: Clinton Foreign Policy; China: A Hot Issue That Takes the Back Burner," *The New York Times*, April 18, 1999, sec. 4, 5.

71. White House Briefing, Press Conference with Clinton and Zhu.

72. Helene Cooper, Bob Davis, and Ian Johnson, "To Brink and Back: In Historic Pact, US Opens Way for China to Finally Join WTO—with Deal, Bigger Market Beckons, But Washington Falls Short on Telecom—New Words for Old Songs," *The Wall Street Journal*, November 16, 1999, A1.

73. Joseph Kahn, "Why the Chinese Are Fretting: Is Clinton Fickle?" *The New York Times*, April 13, 1999, A14.

official paper of the Chinese Communist Party.[74] The lack of coverage apparently also reflected divisions in the Chinese leadership over Zhu's quest. The premier, who had once lost power in an internal fight, joked that if he were to openly describe the concessions he offered the United States, "I'm afraid I would be kicked out of office again."[75]

Chinese officials did in fact learn the specifics of Zhu's offer, after the Clinton administration released a 17-page summary of China's concessions. The hope was that the summary would generate enthusiasm for the deal among business interests and in Congress. But the summary was also published on the Internet—though some say that the posting was never explicitly authorized—and the Chinese delegation was angry. Back in Beijing, ministry officials read the summary on the Web and immediately claimed that Zhu had made his concessions without sufficient consultation with them and without receiving approval. As a result, observers say, the Chinese premier's political stature suffered. "That was probably the single most bizarre episode in US policymaking," remembers a senior White House official.

> Nobody gave approval for [the summary] to go on the Internet. I think the Press Office just put it on the Internet because they put everything on the Internet. In our society, when you have an agreement that's public, you put it on the Internet right away. But how it happened was really quite remarkable because everything about this negotiation had been quadruple checked at the highest levels of government. Cabinet secretaries sat in meetings for hours and hours arguing things backwards and forwards and upside down—everything had been thought through. And then there was this Internet release, to which nobody had given previous consideration.

Some US business interests were furious that an agreement had not been signed. In one meeting, executives applauded USTR Barshefsky for her efforts but chastised Gene Sperling for his opposition to the deal. (Sperling pointed out Trent Lott's opposition after a business representative argued that there was sufficient congressional support.)[76] The Business Coalition for US-China Trade ran a full-page ad in the *Washington Post* on April 13 calling for the administration to "finalize the trade agreement." Business representatives declared that they would intensely lobby members of Congress to push for a quick conclusion to the deal.

With business now voicing such enthusiasm, some believed that the decision not to close the agreement during Zhu's visit would ultimately help

---

74. Quoted in Matt Forney, "China's Press Plays Down Zhu's Visit to US Lest It Upstage Jiang at Home," *The Wall Street Journal*, April 14, 1999, A23.

75. Zhu, quoted in Gerald F. Seib, "Kosovo, China May Spur Some Isolated Thoughts," *The Wall Street Journal*, April 14, 1999, A28.

76. "Democrats Offer Conflicting Views on China WTO Accession, MFN," *Inside US Trade*, April 16, 1999.

the cause. President Clinton "wants and still intends to get a trade agreement with China over the next half-year or so," wrote Jim Mann in the *Los Angeles Times*. "But the president also knows that such a deal will have to be approved by Congress, which must pass new legislation giving China permanent trading rights. . . . By saying 'no,' Clinton temporarily angered the business community. Yet he also galvanized corporate America to begin campaigning hard for congressional support for a WTO deal later on." He quoted Scott Parven, vice president of Aetna: "Before Zhu's visit, [the White House] wanted the business community to come out publicly, big time, for such a deal. But it's a chicken-and-egg kind of thing. Business people were saying, 'Until we see what the deal is, we can't push for it.' Now that we have the makings of a good deal, we're ready to roll."[77]

On April 13, President Clinton called Premier Zhu, who was then visiting New York's financial district, and asked if negotiations could reconvene by the end of the month. In addition, after an all-night negotiating session, China and the United States concluded an agriculture cooperation agreement that resolved disputes over Chinese imports of US wheat, meat, and citrus. For example, China had previously banned all US citrus products, arguing that an infestation of Mediterranean fruit flies in Los Angeles County might pose a threat to its own crops. Now, imports of US citrus would be permitted—a key issue for the Florida congressional delegation, Fisher notes.

Negotiators met again at the end of April for more work on the bilateral agreement, but spirits were low. Everyone was tired.

## Setback and Regrouping

On May 7, the unimaginable happened. American B-2 bombers flying over Belgrade mistakenly targeted China's embassy, killing three Chinese journalists. Robert Cassidy, the chief USTR China negotiator, almost drove off the road when he heard the news over his car radio.[78] Initially, Chinese officials said they believed the embassy was intentionally hit, despite US insistence that its destruction was an accident.[79] Anti-US protests erupted in China, with thousands attacking the US Embassy in Beijing. Some labeled Zhu a traitor for his WTO concessions. Understandably, the tragedy transformed the dynamic of the US-China bilateral negotiations; China halted the talks.

---

77. Jim Mann, "National Perspective: China Summit May Yet Pay Off," *Los Angeles Times*, April 14, 1999, A5.

78. Cooper, Davis, and Johnson, "To Brink and Back," A1.

79. Charles Hutzler, "Chinese Expresses Optimism, Calls for Pragmatism in WTO Talks with US," Associated Press Newswires, November 9, 1999.

As if this weren't enough, on May 26, a congressional panel created by House Speaker Newt Gingrich (R-GA) officially released the so-called Cox Report, which accused China of systematically stealing secret American nuclear designs. Top Republicans expressed outrage.

In July, US-China relations warmed a little when the United States signaled that Taiwan should back away from toughening its stance toward the mainland. Taiwan's President Lee Teng-hui had announced that contacts between Taiwan and China should be on a "nation to nation" basis, pulling back from the 50-year-old "one China" policy. Beijing regarded Taiwan as a rebel province. "The US is showing some sincerity over Taiwan. This is positive. It should create a better atmosphere," said one Chinese official.[80]

In August, an exchange of letters commenced between the US and Chinese presidents, with Clinton urging Jiang to restart the talks. In a reversal of roles, Clinton was the one actively seeking a deal. One of Clinton's letters was hand-delivered to the Chinese president by Senator Dianne Feinstein (D-CA). The ice thawed further on September 11 at an economic summit in Auckland, New Zealand. There, Clinton met with President Jiang—the weakened Chinese premier no longer seemed to be taking the lead. Again, Clinton encouraged a new start to the negotiations. One of the challenges faced by the US officials was that President Jiang's position on WTO accession, unlike Premier Zhu's, was something of a mystery.

US-China trade negotiations began again, but talks were tense. The Chinese proposals lacked the breadth of those Zhu had offered months before, and Chinese negotiators often lectured the US team on a variety of economic matters. There were long statements, but little progress. "This was payback," says Barshefsky. "We went through months of payback: September, October, and November."

In October, President Clinton and President Jiang began a series of telephone conversations. On November 6, Jiang hinted that he was ready to conclude a deal. What followed were long conference calls involving the president, Sandy Berger, John Podesta, Gene Sperling, Madeleine Albright, Robert Rubin, and Charlene Barshefsky. The question was, Should Barshefsky go to China? Certainly, there was the possibility that, as the ultimate payback, Barshefsky could be sent home empty-handed—just as had happened to Zhu. Administration officials worried that such a move by the Chinese would rekindle stories in the press about the mishandling of Zhu's visit. Clinton made a decision. As Barshefsky remembers, "The president had the right instinct. He said, 'Perhaps a really vindictive trade minister might say to another minister, "Yes, come," and then not do a deal. But the president of a country would not do that to another president.' Therefore,

---

80. Quoted in James Kynge, "Beijing Applauds Washington Stance on Taipei," *The Financial Times*, July 23, 1999, 4.

President Clinton's view was that the Chinese would negotiate in good faith and that one could reasonably envision the talks concluding."

USTR Barshefsky insisted that Gene Sperling accompany her to China. The economic adviser had been one of the key officials who counseled the president against concluding a deal during Zhu's April visit. As Barshefsky remembers,

> At the time, the question was: What can we do that will tangibly demonstrate to the Chinese that Bill Clinton is ready to do the deal? One answer was, let's send one of the White House people who the Chinese knew was against it before. I was very concerned that if the Chinese thought that President Clinton was in any way ambivalent about concluding, they would not negotiate in good faith towards conclusion. I suggested to John Podesta and our small group that Gene Sperling should come. Some in the group were very against this, but there was no question it was absolutely the right thing to do. When the Chinese learned that Gene was going to accompany me, they understood Bill Clinton would not be advised to delay a second time.

## Closing the Deal

On November 8, Barshefsky and Sperling headed to Beijing. Other key participants included lead negotiator Robert Cassidy and USTR General Counsel Bob Novick. Six days and six sleepless nights of negotiations ensued. For the first several days, Barshefsky met in long sessions with Chinese trade negotiator Shi Guangsheng, but the US team felt as if they were treading water. Barshefsky eventually told her Chinese counterpart that she had had just about enough and was sending her baggage to the airport.[81] This declaration prompted Premier Zhu to enter the negotiations directly, and he and Barshefsky proceeded to work out a number of remaining issues. When Shi returned to the table, however, he reopened a new set of concerns.

Frustrated, Barshefsky told her team to pack up—they would all head to the airport in the morning. As she climbed into her taxi the next day, Barshefsky directed the car to stop one last time at the trade ministry. When she arrived, she found that Premier Zhu was awaiting her arrival—a highly unusual event, since premiers rarely visited the ministries.[82] It was then that the deal started to come together; later that morning Zhu and Barshefsky shook hands. In the moments before the signing ceremony, Shi Guangsheng attempted to reopen the deal, but it was too late—the negotiations were over.

Richard Fisher notes that an awareness of US politics played a role in China's willingness to reach a final agreement. "I'm convinced that the

---

81. John F. Harris, Michael Laris, " 'Roller-Coaster Ride' to an Off-Again, On-Again Trade Pact," *The Washington Post*, November 16, 1999, A26.

82. Cooper, Davis, and Johnson, "To Brink and Back," A1.

Chinese regime was motivated to close the deal with us because they were concerned that a Republican administration might be a little bit tougher," he says. "I think we were very tough and it's a very good deal. But once they closed with us, China would take their time in terms of completing their accession to the WTO."

Barshefsky and the USTR team returned home triumphant, with the 250-page agreement in hand. Short on diplomatic language, said one journalist, the deal was "less a treaty than a spreadsheet."[83] In some respects, this market access deal was viewed as stronger than the agreement that would have been signed during Zhu's April visit. For example, the November deal contained provisions that labor unions and some Democrats had advocated, including a nonmarket economy methodology for antidumping that could be used for 15 years and special safeguards for such US domestic industries as textiles and apparel. However, one important April concession did not make it into the November deal: In the spring Zhu had offered foreign firms 51 percent ownership of telecommunications ventures, but the agreement that was signed allowed only 49 percent ownership.

When presenting the deal to the press, Barshefsky noted that the significance of the US-China bilateral deal went beyond any commercial achievements. "Consider the broader picture," she said.

> That is, moving China in the direction of a rule of law . . . basic obligations such as transparency, judicial review, the publication of all regulations, the notion that China will be held accountable to the contracts that it makes. These are extraordinarily important principles, which go well beyond the commercial side and indeed will have, I think, positive spillover effects in other areas of Chinese practice and Chinese law.[84]

## The Battle on the Hill

Congress would not vote on China's accession to the WTO. Under existing authority, the president had already made the decision to support China's membership. The issue Congress would decide was whether to grant China permanent normal trade relations upon its entry into the WTO. (In 1998, the term *most favored nation* was replaced with the "less misleading" *normal trade relations*.)[85] More precisely, Congress had to vote to exempt China from the review process conducted annually under the Jackson-Vanik Amendment to the Trade Act of 1974.

---

83. Joseph Kahn, "From Minks to Mules, US Issues China Trade Details," *The New York Times,* March 15, 2000, A10.

84. Charlene Barshefsky, interview by Jim Lehrer, *The NewsHour with Jim Lehrer,* PBS, November 18, 1999.

85. The change occurred as part of a measure overhauling the Internal Revenue Service (PL 105-206), signed into law by President Clinton on July 22, 1998.

On January 10, 2000, President Clinton announced that Commerce Secretary Bill Daley would lead the administration's PNTR war room. Daley, who had also run the administration war room on NAFTA, would coordinate the PNTR efforts on Capitol Hill along with White House deputy chief of staff Steve Ricchetti. "There's no one better at politics in the administration than Bill," Barshefsky says. "No one. I mean, this guy's DNA is political." Observers add that the choice of Daley gave confidence to business and Republicans. Other administration officials right away declared their resolve to secure PNTR. "I do not plan on spending five minutes on anything other than an all-out effort to pass this [permanent NTR] through both Houses of Congress," said Gene Sperling in a November 19 press briefing. "We are one hundred percent committed."[86] Many House Republicans came out early in support of permanent NTR for China. A smaller group of protrade Democrats, led by Representative Robert Matsui (D-CA), would also fight for the legislation.

Business sources confirmed that the PNTR vote would be their priority for the upcoming session of Congress. When lobbying for the legislation, companies and trade associations focused on the boost the agreement would give to US exports to China.[87] Many CEOs and company chairmen were involved in the lobbying effort, which participants on all sides of the PNTR debate admit was tremendously effective; leaders included Maurice Greenberg (AIG), Joseph Gorman (TRW), and Christopher Galvin (Motorola). "For business, [supporting PNTR] was a very practical decision," says one former administration official. "That is why they were so well organized." Some observers noted that the business lobby was much more effective in using the Internet to organize than it had been in past trade battles.

Business also emphasized that the China agreement was good for labor. It "will expand opportunities for the US chemical industry and the more than 1 million American men and women who work in it," said Fred Webber, president of the Chemical Manufacturers Association.[88] Hewlett-Packard president and CEO Carly Fiorina summed up the position of business: "In reality, a vote against trade with China is a vote against US business, employees, American citizens and the people of China."[89]

---

86. Sperling, quoted in "Sperling Says Administration Determined to Fight for Permanent MFN," *Inside US Trade*, November 26, 1999, 9.

87. Among the groups active in the campaign were the Business Roundtable, the US Chamber of Commerce, the Business Coalition for US-China Trade, the Information Technology Industry Council, and the Electronics Industries Alliance. Agribusiness interests included Archer Daniels Midland and the American Farm Bureau.

88. The Business Coalition for US-China Trade, "A Terrific Deal for America: Part Five: Manufacturers," February 15, 2000, www.uschina.org.

89. Carly Fiorina, "Commentary—The Proper Way to Promote Change in China Is from Within; World Trade: Increasing US Presence There Will Encourage Greater Positive Reform Faster and More Effectively," *Los Angeles Times*, May 18, 2000, B11.

Business interests were not as eager to emphasize the investment benefits that would come with China's WTO accession, though they would be significant. In fact, declared Joseph Quinlan, an economist with Morgan Stanley Dean Witter, "The deal is about investment, not exports. US foreign investment is about to overtake US exports as the primary means by which US companies deliver goods to China." But many feared that this argument would be used by labor unions to show that the deal would prompt US companies to move to China—taking American jobs with them. "US exports will increase, over time," said Greg Mastel, director of global economic policy at the New America Foundation. "But not at the rate of investment, and the corporate community has been quiet about that. They've been able to avoid telling that story."[90] Already, the United States was the third-largest investor in China. US corporations with major interests included Motorola, Kodak, Atlantic Richfield, Coca-Cola, Amoco, Ford Motor, Lucent Technologies, General Electric, and General Motors (Morrison 2001). For example, three days before the November 1999 bilateral agreement was signed, Kodak announced that the first phase of building a new plant in Xiamen was complete, part of its $1.2 billion investment in manufacturing plants in China.[91]

## Opposition to PNTR

The American public showed little support for PNTR. A February 2000 poll by the Pew Research Center for the People and the Press found 2-to-1 opposition to granting China PNTR (56 percent to 28 percent), and 62 percent said they had never heard of the November US-China bilateral agreement.[92] A *Business Week*/Harris poll found that 79 percent of Americans believed China should be given permanent access to the US markets only when it agreed to meet human rights and labor standards.[93]

---

90. Quinlan and Mastel, quoted in Helene Cooper and Ian Johnson, "Opening Doors: Congress's Vote Primes US Firms to Boost Investments in China—Debate Focused on Exports, But for Many Companies, Going Local Is the Goal—'Looking for Predictability,' " *The Wall Street Journal*, May 25, 2000, A1.

91. Kodak press release, "Breakthrough Milestones in Chinese Imaging Industry, Kodak Grows with China into New Millennium," Shanghai, November 11, 1999, www.kodak.com.

92. The nationwide poll of 1,330 adults took place between February 9 and 14, 2000, under the supervision of Princeton Survey Research Associates with a 3.5 percent margin of error (Pew Research Center 2000).

93. *Business Week*/Harris Poll, "Globalization: What Americans Are Worried About," *Business Week*, April 24, 2000, 44. The poll, a total of 1,024 interviews, was conducted by Harris Interactive between April 7 and 10, 2000. Interviewees were asked "Which of the following statements comes closest to your views on trade with China"; the answers were "15 percent—The best way to improve human and worker rights in China is not to restrict trade but to engage China and include it in the World Trade Organization and give it permanent access to US markets; 79 percent—Congress should only give China permanent access to the US markets when it agrees to meet human rights and labor standards; Five percent—Don't know; One percent—Refused."

Organized labor led the opposition to PNTR. Two days after the conclusion of the US-China bilateral agreement, the AFL-CIO and 12 industrial unions sent a letter urging all members of the House and Senate to oppose permanent normal trade relations with China. In a speech at the National Press Club on November 19, AFL-CIO president John Sweeney told an applauding audience, "It is disgustingly hypocritical for the White House to posture for workers' rights in the global economy at the same time it prostrates itself for a deal with China that treats human rights as a disposable nuisance." Sweeney vowed to wage a "full and vigorous campaign" against PNTR.[94] Labor leaders said that unions would fight this issue as hard as they had fought the extension of fast-track trade negotiating authority—a battle they had won.

The China deal put the AFL-CIO president in a difficult position. Some observers believe that Sweeney had carefully picked his path, supporting globalization while insisting on the inclusion of labor standards in trade deals. But the US-China bilateral agreement alienated the industrial unions of the AFL-CIO, including the UAW, Teamsters, and Steelworkers. China's workforce was estimated at 700 million, and these workers were denied the right to join collectively to bargain for wages and benefits; their average manufacturing wage was about $0.25 an hour (for a summary of labor's position, see Bolle 2000). "The Teamsters Union has fought long and hard for workers' rights in the US," said a union official. "We should not be made to compete with a workforce that has no rights."[95] Unions claimed that 872,000 American jobs would be lost over 10 years as the result of the China deal (figures disputed by some economists).[96] In public statements, union leaders also frequently compared PNTR to NAFTA. Working families "know that dirty trade agreements

---

94. John J. Sweeney, "Making the Global Economy Work for Working Families: Beyond the WTO," National Press Club, Washington, DC, November 19, 1999. Outbursts of applause continued throughout Sweeney's speech and the audience was asked to refrain at least twice by the National Press Club's president, Larry Lipman (National Press Club, "Excessive Applause at NPC Lunches Misleads Radio/TV Audience," *The National Press Club Record* 49, no. 44 [November 25, 1999]).

95. Michael E. Mathis, Teamsters Union director of government affairs, "China Trade Debate," *Online NewsHour Report*, May 2000, www.pbs.org.

96. According to the Economic Policy Institute, "The China-WTO deal under consideration will eliminate at least 872,091 jobs between 1999 and 2010, even with the US [International Trade Commission's] highly optimistic assumptions. If China devalues its currency or fails to live up to the terms of the agreement, job losses will be even larger" (Scott 2000, 2). The Cato Institute criticized these conclusions as based on "flawed economic reasoning," arguing that passage of PNTR with China "will create not more or fewer jobs in the US economy, but better jobs" (Daniel T. Griswold, "Economic Policy Institute Publishes Flawed China Job-Loss Estimates," Cato Institute, May 19, 2000).

like PNTR and NAFTA cost jobs in this country," declared Teamsters general president James Hoffa.[97]

In addition to labor unions, some human rights groups, family farmers, consumer groups, and environmental organizations opposed PNTR. Many of these interests were further energized by the well-publicized protests at the November 1999 WTO ministerial meeting in Seattle, Washington, that led to mass chaos (on some accounts, the focus on completing the China deal had left the US administration underprepared for the ministerial). When the ministerial meeting collapsed, many protesters claimed victory and turned with enthusiasm to the next fight. "The coalition that opposed China PNTR was very similar to the coalition that was active in Seattle," said one House Democratic aide. "Seattle gave them a lot of momentum." Opposition to PNTR also included a number of religious and veterans groups, including the US Conference of Catholic Bishops and the American Legion. Reform Party presidential candidate Pat Buchanan and Green Party candidate Ralph Nader opposed the bill as well.

Large numbers of traditional Democrats came out strongly against PNTR. House Minority Whip David Bonior (D-MI) organized the fight against the legislation. Many Democrats supported labor's position that the China deal would result in domestic unemployment. Some also pointed to China's weak record in implementing trade agreements such as the 1992 US-China Market Access MOU. Many Democrats were concerned as well about the human rights implications of eliminating the annual review of China's trade status. Representative Nancy Pelosi spoke for them: "We have been told over the last decade that human rights in China would improve if we had unconditional trade benefits for China. Not so. More people are imprisoned for their beliefs in China today than at any time since the Cultural Revolution."[98] Many cited the US State Department's 1999 annual human rights report, which noted that "the [Chinese] government's poor human rights record deteriorated markedly throughout the year."[99] Some Democrats also believed that PNTR for China would hurt their party. In an election year, members were not eager to alienate traditional constituencies such as labor and consumer groups.

And though most Republicans supported permanent NTR for China, a sizable minority of the caucus opposed it on grounds of US national security as well as China's policies restricting religious freedom. Citing the recent controversy over Chinese military use of US satellite technology

---

97. Hoffa, quoted in "A Free Pass for Tyrants," *The Teamster Leader*, June 2000.

98. Nancy Pelosi, in "Four Voices from the Debate in the House on the Trade Bill," *The New York Times*, May 24, 2000, A14.

99. US Department of State, Bureau of Democracy, Human Rights, and Labor, *Country Reports on Human Rights Practices 1999* (February 2000), see www.state.gov.

and allegations of Chinese espionage, some Republicans claimed that the security risk posed by China was vastly underrated.

## When to Vote in the House?

When to hold the House vote was a key question for PNTR supporters, made more complicated by the upcoming presidential and general elections. As one analyst put it, "Usually, Congress would sooner cut its own pay than pass controversial legislation during an election year."[100] Among the relatively few Democrats who came out strongly in support of PNTR, the hope was to distance the vote from the Democratic Party's national convention. More time between the tough fight and the election campaign would enable protrade Democrats, Vice President Al Gore, and the labor unions to get over their anger and make up.

Republicans may have had a different plan. On February 15, 2000, the House Republican leadership—House Speaker Dennis Hastert (IL), Majority Leader Richard Armey (TX), and House Whip Tom DeLay (TX)—promised support for the White House PNTR effort. But observers say that Republicans hoped to draw out the process, delaying a vote until just before the August convention—a move intended to maximize the damage to Gore.

However, on April 5, Boeing CEO Phil Condit and FMC chairman Robert Burt led a delegation of business interests to Tom DeLay's office and insisted that the GOP leadership set a date for the vote. Partisanship, they said, would kill PNTR, just as it had killed fast-track trade legislation in 1998 when Republicans scheduled a controversial vote six weeks before election day. "The Republicans had to stop playing games," said Lisa Berry, a lobbyist for American Online. "We just told DeLay, 'You can't do this.' "[101] A former White House administration official quipped, "DeLay was told not to delay." Soon after, Speaker Hastert announced that the House would vote on PNTR during the week of May 22, 2000.

Other factors also came into play in determining the vote's timing. Some Republicans wanted to wait until the European Union had negotiated its bilateral market access agreement with China. In late February, however, after negotiators failed to resolve a number of outstanding technical issues, EU trade commissioner Pascal Lamy canceled a trip to Beijing that had been intended to close the deal with Chinese trade minister Shi Guangsheng. EU officials said the US-China agreement covered about 80 percent of what the European Union wanted, and the remaining issues

---

100. Paul Magnusson, "China Trade: Will Clinton Pull It Off?" *Business Week*, May 29, 2000, 74.

101. Quotation and general information on the Republicans and business in Magnusson, "China Trade," 74.

needed to be covered in the EU-China bilateral.[102] Areas of concern included automotive tariffs and the level of EU participation in the telecommunications and life insurance markets. The European Union also hoped to eliminate tariff differentials for products similar to those made in the United States. For example, EU cognac faced different import duties than US whiskey.

## Levin Builds a Bridge

Surprisingly, one person working to bridge concerns about PNTR was Representative Sandy Levin, a Democratic with a 94 percent career record of voting with organized labor.[103] Like lead PNTR opponent David Bonior, Levin was from Michigan and his suburban Detroit district bordered the United Auto Workers' Union headquarters. Levin had voted against NAFTA and opposed the renewal of fast-track trade authority. Over the years, he had voted both for and against MFN status for China. In other words, Levin was not a classic free trader. He was, however, the ranking Democrat on the House Ways and Means Trade Subcommittee.

As noted above, Levin pressed Clinton not to sign a deal during Premier Zhu's April 1999 visit, pointing to the lack of safeguards needed by US producers. In anticipation of the November 1999 agreement, Levin joined an ad hoc group of Democrats discussing how to address concerns that would be raised by the bilateral deal. One Democratic staffer describes it as

> a broad spectrum of the caucus trying to come up with ideas, at both the member and the staff level. What can we do to address the legitimate concern that by granting permanent NTR, we're giving up a mechanism for exerting leverage when it comes to human rights? What can we put in its place? What can we do to enhance our oversight of China's compliance with its WTO obligations once it accedes? What about our own self-interest—the ability of US producers of goods and services to compete with Chinese producers of goods and services?

In January 2000, Levin made a 10-day visit to China, where he spoke with artists, students, and activists about how free trade would change Chinese society. "I came back feeling that changes in China are irreversible, but that the direction is not inevitable," he said. Levin did not believe that social progress would automatically accompany economic changes; "You have to shape globalization," he noted.[104] Levin set to work on drafting a

---

102. For example, see "EU, China to Meet on WTO Accession; EU Does Not Expect Deal," *Inside US Trade*, January 14, 2000.

103. Eric Schmitt, "Public Lives; An Unlikely Champion of a New Trade Pact with China," *The New York Times*, April 17, 2000, A12.

104. Levin, quoted in Schmitt, "Public Lives," A12.

plan to do just that. One of the most widely discussed aspects of his proposal was the creation of a congressional-executive commission to monitor human rights in China. Modeled on the Helsinki Commission that investigated human rights conditions in Eastern Europe during the Cold War, the China Commission would issue policy recommendations but would not have power of enforcement; it was intended to keep pressure on the PRC after the end of the annual MFN renewal process.

Levin's proposal included language codifying product-specific safeguards to protect American workers from job-threatening surges of Chinese imports. In addition, it established new procedures to ensure that China complied with its trade commitments. "Mr. Levin felt it was important to have regular reviews of China's level of compliance," says a source, "a more detailed level of scrutiny than you might have for other new members of the WTO." Programs would also be established to develop China's commercial and labor laws and monitor China's compliance with existing US statutes barring the use of prison labor.[105] Moreover, Levin's proposal stated a sense of Congress that Taiwan should be allowed to enter the WTO on the same schedule as China.

Initially, some say, Levin's ideas drew little interest. "The administration expressed concerns about different elements of the package," says one observer. "And I think there were some doubts as to whether [Levin's proposal] was needed at all." But former White House insiders say Levin's proposals were taken seriously. "Congressman Sandy Levin was key to obtaining broad House Democratic support," says Lael Brainard, "which is one of the reasons Chief of Staff John Podesta and Steve Richetti asked the National Economic Council to put together a senior group to work with him on his substantive proposals." By April 2000, Levin's ideas were attracting more notice. The vote count in the House was uncertain—the administration, business supporters, and the Republican leadership were not sure they had the votes to pass PNTR. Levin's language might be able to pull some undecided members to the "yes" side.

Representative David Dreier (R-CA), the powerful chairman of the House Rules Committee, appointed Representative Doug Bereuter (R-NE) to work with Levin. In a bipartisan move, Levin and Bereuter cosponsored the proposal, with support from Dreier. "I think getting Mr. Bereuter on board was what helped us get this moving," says a Democratic supporter of the proposal, "to get some momentum developing around it to the point where there was a critical mass." Levin also received support from business

---

105. As mentioned above, in August 1992 the United States and China signed an MOU to ensure that goods produced by prison labor were not exported to the United States. Disputes over its implementation led to the signing of a Statement of Cooperation (SOC) on March 14, 1994, whose provisions clarified procedures by which US officials could gain access to Chinese production facilities suspected of exporting such products.

interests. Levin "has been very, very helpful," noted the legislative director from the Business Roundtable, a coalition of chief executives from large corporations.[106] As former USTR Barshefsky remembers,

> Sandy Levin was terrific in the sense that, contrary to many of his Democratic colleagues, he recognized the fundamental importance of doing this. He then set about to find a way to try and make it happen. I can't overstate how helpful this was in terms of his basic attitude and his constancy in this mission to come up with companion legislation that would help ease the way for protrade Democrats to make the right vote.

Not all were supportive, however. China blasted the human rights provisions, calling the proposed commission an interference in its internal affairs. US labor unions also faulted the proposal. "It's a well-meaning effort," said the AFL-CIO's Thea Lee. "But it's redundant with what's already done and may even be counterproductive."[107] Some were even more critical. "Levin-Bereuter is meaningless," said a spokesman for the UAW. "It's pure political cover."[108] Other PNTR opponents used terms such as "fig leaf" or "toothless" in characterizing its language.

As the PNTR bill (HR 4444) came closer to markup in the Ways and Means Committee, one source of debate was which (if any) of the Levin-Bereuter proposals would be included in the bill. The Republican leadership reportedly gave Ways and Means Chairman Bill Archer (R-TX, and one of the original authors of the Jackson-Vanik amendment) the go-ahead to attach the safeguard issue. Negotiations ensued, particularly between Levin and Trade Subcommittee Chairman Phil Crane (R-IL), over the specifics. For example, under ordinary safeguard law, the president had fairly broad discretion in choosing a response after the International Trade Commission (ITC) recommended action. What degree of presidential discretion would the PNTR bill grant?

Once the bill was reported out of committee, the handling of the rest of the Levin-Bereuter proposals remained at issue. Levin wanted to ensure that his provisions were part of the PNTR package, but the Republican leadership considered moving Levin-Bereuter as a separate bill—after the PNTR vote. "That idea caused us a lot of heartburn," recalls a Levin-Bereuter supporter. "Once PNTR was passed, that commitment would have been meaningless. Even if a vote [on Levin-Bereuter] was allowed in the House, it was not clear that the Senate would have taken it up."

---

106. Carolyn Brehm, quoted in Owen Ullmann, "A Labor Liberal's Efforts Make the Difference," *USA Today*, May 25, 2000, 5A.

107. Lee, quoted in Joseph Kahn, "Former Critics of Trade Bill Are Swaying Vote in House," *The New York Times*, May 21, 2000, A16.

108. Quoted in Matt Kelley, "Bereuter in the Thick of China Trade Vote," *Omaha World-Herald*, May 21, 2000, 17A.

## The Lead-Up to the Vote

In the weeks leading up to the vote, Federal Reserve Chairman Alan Greenspan publicly endorsed PNTR, and former presidents Gerald Ford, Jimmy Carter, and George Bush issued a letter supporting the measure. The administration also mobilized 149 economists—10 former Council of Economic Advisers chairs and 13 Nobel laureates among them—to sign an open letter, released in late April, in support of China's entry into the WTO. (Because federal law prohibits the administration from using federal funds to urge others to lobby Congress, PNTR was not explicitly mentioned.) The presumptive Republican presidential nominee, George W. Bush, also backed the bill, as did Taiwan's new president, Chen Shui-bian.

President Clinton made his most comprehensive case for establishing PNTR with China in a speech at Johns Hopkins University on March 8, 2000. He argued that supporting China's participation in the WTO

> represents the most significant opportunity that we have had to create positive change in China since the 1970s. . . . I believe the choice between economic rights and human rights, between economic security and national security, is a false one. Membership in the WTO, of course, will not create a free society in China overnight, or guarantee that China will play by global rules. But over time, I believe it will move China faster and further in the right direction—and certainly will do that more than rejection would.

PNTR was also required if the United States was to receive the economic benefits of China's WTO accession, Clinton said.

However, some PNTR opponents put forward the argument that extending permanent MFN treatment to China was unmerited and even unnecessary. They called the idea that without PNTR the United States would lose out on the benefits of China's WTO entry "the Big Lie" (Public Citizen's Global Trade Watch 2000, ii). Citing a memo by Columbia Law School's Mark Barenberg (Barenberg 2000), groups like Public Citizen's Global Trade Watch held that MFN provisions in the 1979 US-China agreement would give the United States all the benefits of China's WTO accession. Public Citizen therefore maintained that members of Congress should not feel pressured to vote for PNTR by the administration, the Chinese, or US corporations.[109] Georgetown University's John Jackson and others countered that the Jackson-Vanik amendment was indeed a legal obstacle to a full WTO relationship between the PRC and the United States. The 1979 bilateral agreement applied mainly to tariffs and would not cover market access or other WTO commitments, Jackson argued (Jackson and Rhodes 1999, 504). "A vote against PNTR, or no vote at all,

---

109. See testimony of Lori Wallach, Public Citizen's Global Trade Watch, "Permanent NTR for China: Neither Merited nor Necessary," Hearing of the Senate Commerce, Science and Transportation Committee, 106th Congress, 2nd Session, April 11, 2000.

means that . . . the United States would miss out on the most valuable elements of China's concessions: the nontariff liberalization," researchers at the Institute for International Economics claimed (Hufbauer and Rosen 2000, 1). The argument that PNTR was unnecessary did not appear strong enough to persuade lawmakers to oppose the bill.

As debate over PNTR continued, a surprising alliance formed between President Clinton and Republican House Majority Whip Tom DeLay, who was perhaps Clinton's harshest critic on Capitol Hill and had led the charge to impeach the president. However, in the PNTR fight, DeLay found himself in the position of Clinton's point man for rounding up Republican votes. "I have a fundamental disagreement with this president about how he's done his job," said DeLay. "But when he's doing something I think is important, I'm going to support him because he doesn't do it very often." DeLay's support of PNTR was also striking because he was a fierce anti-Communist as well as coauthor of the proposed Taiwan Security Act, a bill strongly opposed by Beijing that would strengthen the relationship between Taiwan and the Pentagon. "Exporting American values undermines the Communist regime in China," DeLay explained.[110]

The rhetoric of leaders in the House grew more sweeping. Ways and Means Chair Bill Archer "sternly told his colleagues that this was the most important vote they could cast in their entire congressional career."[111] Business interests also heightened their lobbying efforts in the lead-up to the vote. Ultimately, corporate America mounted its largest-ever trade campaign in favor of PNTR.[112] The United States Chamber of Commerce and the Business Roundtable alone spent almost $10 million on ads, against about $2 million spent by labor opposing PNTR.[113] Executives walked the halls of the Capitol, targeting representatives whose districts would benefit from the China deal. "This is the most contested trade battle I've ever seen," said the international vice president of the National Association of Manufacturers.[114] PNTR opponents attacked the business effort as "the most forceful and aggressive corporate legislative campaign in history" (Public Citizen's Global Trade Watch 2000, 1).

President Clinton met with more than 100 lawmakers to rally support for PNTR. In a last-minute effort to secure votes, Clinton and Speaker Hastert announced a set of tax breaks and public investments aimed at

---

110. DeLay, quoted in Eric Schmitt, "Unlikely Alliance Is Formed to Pass Bill on China Trade," *The New York Times*, May 9, 2000, A1.

111. "A Much-Needed Victory," *The Economist,* May 27, 2000, 27.

112. Jonathan Peterson, "Trade Debate Shows Force of Social Issues," *The Los Angeles Times*, May 25, 2000, A1.

113. Joseph Kahn and Eric Schmitt, "House, by Wide Margin, Grants Normal Trade Rights to China," *The New York Times*, May 25, 2000, A1; "A Much-Needed Victory," 27.

114. Franklin J. Vargo, quoted in Peterson, "Trade Debate Shows Force of Social Issues," A1.

helping distressed rural and urban areas—the New Markets and Community Renewal initiative. Observers say the move was meant to sway undecided members of the Black Caucus. Representative Martin Frost (D-TX) announced he would vote "yes" after the Navy told the Northrop Grumman defense plant in his district that it would receive enough business to stay open. Among other district matters receiving attention were the construction of a gas pipeline in western Texas and the fate of a National Weather Service monitoring station in Alabama.

In the week before the House vote, on May 19, Trade Commissioner Pascal Lamy completed Europe's bilateral market access talks with China. The EU-China agreement in certain regards also helped US business interests. For example, the deal included a commitment to end discriminatory policies for pharmaceuticals. Some Republicans would later credit the EU-China bilateral deal with being a key factor in their decision to support PNTR. The European Union knew that "having US congressional approval would be very good for the world trading system," says Lael Brainard. "So in the end they were helpful and it worked out."

On May 21, the White House canceled a planned televised address by President Clinton on the importance of granting PNTR to China. White House spokesman Joe Lockhart said the action was taken after discussions with congressional Democrats. "In talking to Democrats on the Hill, we realized that in the context of this debate, that speech might be counterproductive, [and] certainly wasn't likely to produce the retail-oriented votes that we needed to get," he said.[115] The administration was also concerned about who would provide the response to Clinton's comments. One possibility was House Minority Leader Dick Gephardt, creating the problematic scenario of a leader of the Democratic Party speaking out against a Democratic president.

The day before the vote, union workers, environmental activists, and human rights activists rallied against PNTR on the steps of the Capitol. Harry Wu, a prominent human rights advocate, drew cheers when he called out to the crowd, "Vote your conscience, not just for profit."[116] In the final hours of lobbying, AFL-CIO president John Sweeney focused his efforts on undecided Republicans. By some accounts, however, labor did not fight the battle against PNTR with the same intensity that it had marshaled against fast track in 1997.

The night before the vote, Levin won support from House leaders to amend the PNTR bill with his proposal. Vote counters reported that Levin-Bereuter helped to recruit about two dozen undecided representatives. One of the most influential legislators who pointed to Levin-

115. Lockhart, quoted in "White House Cancels China Speech for Fear of Backlash," *Inside US Trade Special Report*, May 23, 2000, 12.

116. Wu, quoted in Eric Schmitt and Joseph Kahn, "The China Trade Wrangle: The Overview; The House Opens a Spirited Debate over China Trade," *The New York Times*, May 24, 2000, A1.

Bereuter as making the difference in his decision to support PNTR was Representative Charles Rangel (D-NY), the ranking minority member of the Ways and Means Committee.

When the House vote on PNTR was finally taken, the tally was not as close as some had expected; indeed, the bill passed quite comfortably, 237 to 197. Some observers, including Charlene Barshefsky, believe that House members recognized the historic implications of China joining the WTO and deferred to the specialized knowledge of those who were more closely involved. She thinks that "what really became the ace was that members of Congress are reluctant to let their own judgment on the security implications of a given piece of legislation override that of the president of the United States, the secretary of defense, and the secretary of state."

But it is important to note that only 73 out of 211 Democrats voted for PNTR—a lower percentage than had voted for NAFTA (35 percent of Democrats voted for China PNTR, while 102 out of 258 Democrats, or 40 percent, voted for NAFTA). One hundred and sixty four Republicans out of 221 supported the legislation. Some Democrats think that timing was an important factor in PNTR's passage. According to one congressional staffer, "If this had dragged out much longer, I think a lot of the Democrats who were sitting on the fence wouldn't have voted for it. As you got closer to the convention and the election, PNTR would have become more and more viewed as a political liability. It would have been very hard for a lot of Democrats to support it."

After the vote in the House, President Jiang Zemin took the step— "unusual," according to White House officials—of telephoning President Clinton to express his thanks. The usual protocol would be a formal exchange of letters, not a 40-minute conversation. One senior official involved in China policy remarked, "I don't recall Jiang ever [before] initiating a call."[117]

## The Senate

The next step was to get PNTR through the Senate. Though the bill's passage was expected, suspense remained. Any amendments would result in HR 4444 being sent back to the House, where supporters feared that further deliberations would doom it. Leading supporters of PNTR in the Senate included most Republicans and many Democrats, Max Baucus (D-MT) among them.

Many PNTR proponents were frustrated with Senate Majority Leader Trent Lott, who delayed in getting the measure to the floor. The bill was

---

117. Quoted in Marc Kaufman and John F. Harris, "Chinese Leader Telephones Thanks for Trade Bill Vote; White House Officials Describe Call to Clinton as Unusual," *The Washington Post*, May 29, 2000, A2.

not taken up by the Senate until the week of September 4. Representative Robert Matsui criticized the move as "a major tactical error. A bill like that should never be brought up in the last month of Congress."[118] While the bill awaited debate in the Senate, President Clinton announced on June 2 that he would extend China's NTR status for the next year. On July 18 the House defeated a resolution to overturn the president's decision (HJ Res. 103), 147 to 281.

Many Senate proponents of the China trade bill joined in a pact to block any attempts to amend it. PNTR supporters thought a proposed amendment by Senators Fred Thompson (R-TN) and Robert Torricelli (D-NJ) was the biggest threat to passing a "clean" version of PNTR, and business groups lobbied hard for its defeat. Some tried to convince Thompson not to offer his amendment, which would have imposed sanctions on Chinese companies caught exporting nuclear, chemical, or biological weapons, but Thompson held firm.[119] In the end, the amendment was killed on September 13 (despite Lott's support).[120]

Before HR 4444 was brought to a vote, the Senate rejected a total of 18 amendments. One, proposed by Paul Wellstone (D-MN), required the president to certify that China was not exporting goods made with prison labor before granting PNTR; another, from Senator Jesse Helms (R-NC), would have delayed granting PNTR until the president certified that China had made substantial strides toward permitting greater religious freedom. Senator Robert Byrd (D-WV) proposed an amendment requiring the United States to support the transfer of clean energy technology as part of programs aimed at assisting China's energy sector. Before Byrd's amendment was defeated, the Senator expressed his anger on the floor saying, "Why have any debate? Why call up amendments? Why go through this charade? I have called up an amendment. We all know it is going to be rejected because some senators are going to vote against any amendments, no matter what the amendment provides. . . . What kind of legislative process is that?"[121]

---

118. Matsui, quoted in Chuck McCutcheon with Lori Nitschke, "China Trade Bill Remains Intact as Senate Rejects Arms Sanctions," *Congressional Quarterly*, September 16, 2000, 2152.

119. "Senate Poised to Approve China PNTR After Thompson Failure," *Inside US Trade*, September 15, 2000.

120. Senator Thompson, a former Watergate prosecutor, wanted the Senate to add an amendment to the intelligence authorization bill for fiscal 2001 that would require the president to punish the Chinese government or individual Chinese companies if they were found to be supplying weapons of mass destruction or components of such weapons to other nations. However, the White House, many business interests, Senate Democrats, and some Senate Republicans opposed the effort. Thompson also directed a yearlong probe of alleged Democratic Party fund-raising improprieties centered on Chinese donations (*Congressional Quarterly Weekly*, July 29, 2000, 1901).

121. Comments by Robert C. Byrd (D-WV) on the Senate floor, September 7, 2000.

Observers agreed that the debate on PNTR had a "going-through-the-motions feel."[122] The anterooms of the Senate, unlike those of the House, were not filled with business and union lobbyists in the lead-up to the vote. After 10 days of deliberations, the Senate voted on HR 4444 on September 19. PNTR passed, 83 to 15, without additional amendments and was signed by President Clinton on October 10 (for a timeline, see appendix 6A). The law would not enter into force until China's accession to the WTO.

## Conclusion

Analysts viewed the passage of PNTR as a historic bookend to the Clinton presidency, which also began with landmark measures expanding trade—the passage of the North American Free Trade Agreement and the implementation of the Uruguay Round Agreements that created the WTO. Some noted the irony that Clinton began his presidency determined to link China's trade status to human rights, and ended it with the most important US-China trade deal in history. In the aftermath of the congressional battle over PNTR, many contrasted the success of the China bill with the failed efforts to pass fast track in 1997 and 1998. "The China debate became a debate on the overall course of the China relationship," said Myron A. Brilliant, a lobbyist for the US Chamber of Commerce. "On trade agreements and on fast track, it centers much more on the role of labor and environmental issues."[123] The loss on fast track also added to the importance of the PNTR victory, "because," noted *The Economist*, "it shows that trade bills can actually be passed in Congress, something that even the most ardent free-traders were beginning to question."[124]

China would become the 143rd member of the WTO on December 11, 2001, after a 15-year accession effort. The signing ceremony was postponed by one day so that it would follow the WTO's endorsement of Taiwan's membership as a "separate customs territory" under the name "Chinese Taipei." On December 27, 2001, President George W. Bush issued a proclamation extending PNTR status to China, effective January 1, 2002. Though the journey to WTO entry was over, China and the rest of the world would now embark on a new journey. WTO membership would "inevitably exert widespread and far-reaching impact on China's economy and on the world economy," said Chinese trade minister Shi Guangsheng.[125] The full nature of that impact remains to be seen.

---

122. Andrew Taylor, "China Trade Bill Nears Its Finale as Senators Spurn Amendments," *CQ Weekly*, September 23, 2000, 2224.

123. Lori Nitschke, "After the China Bill: Fresh Start for the Trade Expansion Debate," *CQ Weekly*, September 23, 2000, 2224.

124. "A Much-Needed Victory," 27.

125. Shi, quoted in Frances Williams, "China and Taiwan Join World Trade Body," *The Financial Times*, November 12, 2001, 10.

# Negotiation Analysis of the Case

When viewed in isolation, the US-China negotiations that paved the way for China's accession to the WTO are unremarkable. Certainly, there were difficult issues that needed to be resolved. Certainly, the parties vigorously engaged in bluff and brinkmanship. But little distinguished this process from myriad other tough bilateral negotiations.

When placed in their larger context, however, the US-China market access talks prove a rich subject for analysis. These bilateral negotiations were just one link in a complex negotiating game over China's WTO accession, which also included other bilateral negotiations over market access (especially between China and Europe) and multilateral negotiations over accession within the WTO, as well as linkages to the Uruguay Round negotiations, human rights issues, national security concerns, and perceptions of performance in implementation of earlier agreements.

The US-China negotiations also have to be situated in the larger context of US trade politics. The bilateral market access agreement was *not* negotiated under the auspices of fast track. In part, the negotiations succeeded because the United States was dealing with a single large partner rather than engaging in a broader multilateral process. In addition, the president already had the authority to approve China's accession to the WTO. Crucially, business mobilized an unprecedented campaign in support of PNTR, taking action much earlier than it had done to aid NAFTA or the fast-track efforts of the 1990s.

## Element #1: Organizing to Influence

China's accession to the WTO was propelled forward by a powerful combination of economic and political forces. Economically, the vast expansion of trade between China and the rest of the world de facto made the Chinese players in the international trading system. Politically, the end of the Cold War and liberalization in China made WTO membership acceptable to the West.

As is true of all the case studies in this volume, however, outcomes do not result solely from evolving macro forces. China's WTO accession was catalyzed by vigorous organizing efforts on the part of dedicated groups of business players and government officials in the United States, Europe, and China. These groups created momentum in the external negotiations and mediated the significant internal differences within their respective sides.

Chinese trade and foreign policy officials engaged in a long-term effort to gain accession to the GATT/WTO. Beginning as early as 1986, China had requested the restoration of its status as a party to the GATT. When stymied by the desire of US and European officials to first complete the

Uruguay Round, the Chinese persevered by pressing to become founding members of the WTO in 1995. Failing to meet that goal, the Chinese worked to lay the diplomatic groundwork for entry. They also successfully dealt with significant internal conflicts between reformers and conservatives over the pace of liberalization and the timing of accession.

On the US side, USTR was the focal point for pushing forward China's accession process, as well as for advancing US interests in bilateral and multilateral negotiations. Under the leadership of Charlene Barshefsky, USTR took control of the process by creating a road map for Chinese entry. Like their Chinese counterparts, Barshefsky and her colleagues in the administration had to deal with serious internal differences. For example, many in Congress were reluctant to relinquish the opportunity that the annual MFN renewal process offered them for criticizing various Chinese policies. Concerned about issues ranging from China's human rights record to competition in low-wage manufacturing industries to national security, some legislators opposed granting China PNTR. Only through energetic and focused organization, such as creating a PNTR war room under the command of Commerce Secretary Bill Daley, was the administration able to win the battle in Congress.

Finally, critical support for brokering a creative compromise in Congress came from the work of Representative Sandy Levin—a somewhat surprising torchbearer for PNTR, given his prolabor background. By energetically advocating the codification of product-specific safeguards and the creation of a congressional-executive commission on China's human rights record, Levin helped to pave the way for the bill's passage.

Outside Congress, the so-called new China lobby of export-oriented US business interests mobilized very strongly in support of passing PNTR. Mounting their largest-ever campaign, businesses coordinated efforts and created alliances among leading organizations ranging from the Business Roundtable to the American Farm Bureau.

## Element #2: Selecting the Forum

In 1997, the US administration decided to focus on bilateral market access negotiations with China rather than the multilateral entry negotiations. Concerned that the European Union might forgo a bilateral agreement altogether, thereby reducing the pressure on China to make hard economic concessions, the administration decided to change its focus to gain more bargaining leverage. In addition, US policymakers knew that agreements reached in the bilateral forum would set the standard for subsequent negotiations over accession. The Europeans were happy to garner the benefits of allowing the United States to play "bad cop."

The trajectory of the negotiations among European, US, and Chinese forums is also worthy of attention. Much of the early negotiating took place in the multilateral forum in Geneva. But as the focus shifted to bilateral negotiations, the venue also changed. Proponents of a US-China agreement sought to use a visit to the United States by Premier Zhu Rongji to increase pressure on holdouts in the Clinton administration. When this failed and no agreement was reached, Zhu was humiliated. The Chinese responded to this incident by essentially forcing the US negotiators to come to them if they wanted to renew negotiations. To signal US seriousness, and avoid another division in the administration, Barshefsky brought National Economic Council Chairman Gene Sperling with her to China.

## Element #3: Shaping the Agenda

Once the US-China bilateral negotiating forum became the focus of attention, the economic relationship between the two countries largely established the agenda for the talks. China sought permanent MFN treatment, while the United States sought concessions in the areas of trade in services and agriculture. Complementary goals created the potential for joint gains.

More interesting were the efforts to shape the agenda for the congressional debate over granting China PNTR. Opponents attempted to link passage of PNTR to issues ranging from human rights violations (as exemplified by the violent crackdown on protesters in Tiananmen Square) and labor conditions to trade safeguards and national security. Many in Congress were reluctant to give up the stick provided by the annual requirement that the administration waive Jackson-Vanik in order to renew China's MFN status.

In addition, a comparison of the fast-track and China PNTR agendas helps to illustrate why business mobilized much more strongly in the latter case. The fast-track agenda concentrated on the rules that would determine how trade agreements would be negotiated in the future. This complexity rendered the potential benefits ambiguous and uncertain. By contrast, the issues on the agenda of granting PNTR status to China were often direct, bottom-line concerns affecting many companies. As a result, key business sectors mobilized early and very effectively.

## Element #4: Building Coalitions

The fight to win passage of PNTR in the US Congress was a classic exercise in legislative coalition building, albeit one with a few twists. Though a Democrat, President Clinton created a successful alliance with protrade Republicans in the House, led by his archenemy Tom DeLay. House Democrats opposed PNTR by a margin of nearly 3 to 1, more than had op-

**Figure 6.1    Potential coalitions on PNTR for China**

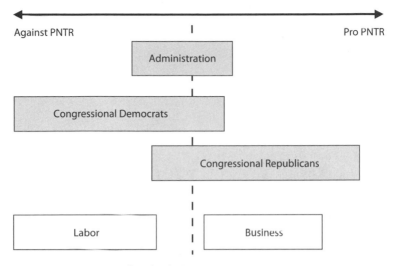

PNTR = permanent normal trade relations

posed NAFTA. At the same time, a sizable minority of House Republicans opposed PNTR because of their concerns about China's record on human rights and religious freedom, as well as worries about US national security interests in the aftermath of the Wen Ho Lee affair and revelations about the transfer of sensitive satellite technology. The coalitional possibilities are summarized in figure 6.1.

Opposition to PNTR emanated primarily from organized labor in import-competing industries. As they faced increased trade with China, the Steelworkers, UAW, Teamsters, and other major industrial unions in the United States were concerned about potential job losses. Environmental organizations, human rights groups, family farmers, and consumer groups also joined the anti-PNTR coalition. Opposition was further energized when antiglobalization protesters effectively disrupted the Seattle WTO ministerial. Collectively, these groups exerted pressure on Democrats who were beholden to them for financial and political support.

Because positions had already hardened during the NAFTA and fast-track battles, the PNTR fight was ultimately waged for the hearts and minds of moderate Republicans and protrade Democrats. In concert with business lobbyists, the president and his key advisers—notably Commerce Secretary Bill Daley—waged a tireless and ultimately successful battle to secure the middle ground.

Well-timed endorsements also played a role in tipping the balance. In the weeks before the final vote, the administration secured the public support of Alan Greenspan; former presidents Gerald R. Ford, Jimmy Carter, and George Bush; and 149 economists, including 10 former Council of Economic Advisers chairs and 13 Nobel laureates. Moreover, incorporating the Levin-Bereuter provisions directly into the PNTR bill (rather than presenting them as separate legislation) gave some members of Congress political cover to vote for passage.

## Element #5: Leveraging Linkages

Linkages can propel negotiations forward and create opportunities for joint gains. But they can also act as barriers to progress. When linkages act as barriers, negotiators must find ways to neutralize them. The process through which China acceded to the WTO is notable for the broad array of such blocking linkages that had to be overcome.

In the United States, trade with China had long been linked to a range of other issues, notably human rights and labor conditions, but also increasingly to national security. The annual renewal of China's MFN status had enabled critics to focus a spotlight on Chinese conduct each year, as well as to implicitly threaten to hold MFN renewal hostage until there were changes in behavior. The Chinese, of course, resented these linkages, seeing them as unacceptable meddling in their domestic affairs. The Levin-Bereuter proposal was a way of breaking the tie between trade and human rights, while still providing critics with a mechanism for focusing attention on Chinese behavior.

The passage of PNTR was also strongly linked to previous battles between business and labor over NAFTA and fast track as well as to the protests at the Seattle ministerial. After losing the fight on NAFTA, organized labor had hardened its opposition to further expansion of international trade. By failing to mobilize effectively to press for passage of fast track in 1997, business had lost that fight. Both sides were therefore determined to win in the next round of the game.

Other linkages helped to propel the process forward while at the same time providing certain players with strategic advantage. There was an important linkage, for example, between the GATT negotiations over accession and bilateral US-China negotiations over market access. The working party for China, formed in 1987, was the largest such body ever in the history of the GATT. Thus as early as 1987, China knew that it would have to conclude a record number of bilateral agreements before it became a member. And in the accession of any individual country, the final agreement has to incorporate *all* of the concessions made in *each* of the bilateral agreements.

But precedents set in earlier accession negotiations can influence subsequent ones. Japan, which had finished its bilateral first, was willing to settle for less stringent terms than the United States would press for. The

Clinton administration was concerned that the Europeans would give away too much in the accession negotiations, in effect helping to build momentum for a more lenient overall accession agreement. Therefore, the United States decided to take control of the process by initiating bilateral negotiations before the EU and through its agreement shaping subsequent bilateral negotiations between the European Union and China (and ultimately the multilateral accession process). Of course, this approach allowed the European Union to pocket what the United States had already negotiated and focus entirely on winning concessions for its own special interests.

Conversely, bilateral negotiations between the European Union and China likewise helped to create momentum for passage of PNTR. Just prior to the vote in Congress, the European Union completed its bilateral negotiations with China. These negotiations incorporated about 80 percent of the provisions of the US-China bilateral agreement, validating the US decision to press ahead on this front. But they also provided some important additional benefits for US business interests that strengthened Republican support for passage of PNTR.

## Element #6: Playing the Frame Game

The case of China's PNTR provides some notable examples of effective framing. USTR sought to frame China's entry to the WTO in terms of economics, not politics. To support their argument that the WTO was not a political club but a contractual agreement, USTR established "commercially meaningful terms" as the standard by which WTO entry should be judged.

The domestic debate in the United States over passage of PNTR likewise evoked creative framing efforts on both sides, as demonstrated by quotations already cited above. Favoring PNTR, Hewlett-Packard CEO Carly Fiorina stated that "a vote against trade with China is a vote against US business, employees, American citizens and the people of China." Framing the opposing point of view, Representative Nancy Pelosi denied the claim "that human rights in China would improve if we had unconditional trade benefits for China," pointing out that "more people are imprisoned for their beliefs in China today than at any time since the Cultural Revolution."

At the same time, business intentionally downplayed some potential arguments in favor of PNTR to avoid strengthening the opposition. They sought, for example, to avoid talking about the significant investment benefits of the WTO agreement, fearing that this argument would be used by organized labor to bolster the argument that passage of the legislation would lead to job loss.

## Element #7: Creating Momentum

The case of PNTR for China provides a wealth of examples of how multi-stage processes, sequencing, creative compromises, and action-forcing events can be used to create (and to impede) momentum toward agreement. For example, by creating a road map for China's accession in 1995, Charlene Barshefsky shaped a multistage process that could progressively overcome key barriers and build momentum toward agreement. In another example of momentum building, the Chinese linked their accession negotiations to the WTO ministerial meeting in Seattle. Knowing that the administration was anxious to close the US-China deal before the Seattle ministerial, the Chinese effectively backed the United States up against the deadline.

The scheduling of the vote in the House exemplifies the use of an action-forcing event to create momentum. The Republican leadership sought to delay a vote on PNTR in order to hurt Vice President Gore in the lead-up to the presidential elections. But business interests perceived this postponement as a threat to passage of PNTR and pressed the Republicans to move swiftly toward a vote.

Not all efforts at momentum building worked out so well. The visit to the United States by Chinese premier Zhu Rongji, for example, was an unsuccessful effort by supporters of agreement in the Clinton administration to force the negotiations to closure. By inviting Zhu to the United States and then not just failing to finalize the agreement but also publishing the Chinese concessions, the administration unquestionably set the process back and also undermined a key Chinese reformer. It took many months of hard work to get the process back on track.

## Conclusion

The case of China's PNTR offers rich material for exploring how players employ the key elements of strategic negotiation to advance partisan interests, particularly in the area of linkages. The ability to create and neutralize linkages in time (e.g., between NAFTA and PNTR), among issues (e.g., trade and human rights), and between international negotiations and domestic ratification processes is critically important for trade negotiators. Linkages are indispensable tools for improving one's own best alternative to a negotiated agreement and also can function effectively as action-forcing events. The right linkages can spur people to make choices they would rather avoid.

# Appendix 6A
## Timeline: The 1999 US-China Bilateral Agreement and the Battle for PNTR

| Date | Event |
|------|-------|
| 1947 | China is one of the 23 original GATT contracting parties. |
| 1949 | The Chinese Communist Party defeats the Nationalist Party. |
| 1950 | Nationalist China pulls out of the GATT. |
| 1951 | President Truman suspends China's most favored nation (MFN) trading status. |
| 1971 | The United Nations recognizes the Communist government of the People's Republic of China as the sole legal Chinese representative in the United Nations. |
| 1978 | Deng Xiaoping launches economic reform in China. |
| 1980 | The United States conditionally restores MFN trading status to China to be reviewed annually under the Jackson-Vanik amendment of the Trade Act of 1974. |
| 1982 | The GATT grants China's request for nonvoting observer status. |
| 1986 | China requests the restoration of its status as a full contracting party to the GATT. |
| 1989 | Unarmed protesters are killed at Tiananmen Square. |
| 1993 | President Clinton issues an executive order to make China's MFN trade status conditional on improvement in six areas, including human rights. |
| 1994 | Clinton renews China's MFN status. |
| | Beijing accelerates efforts to join the GATT, hoping to become a founding member of the WTO. |

*(timeline continues next page)*

## Timeline: The 1999 US-China Bilateral Agreement and the Battle for PNTR   *(continued)*

| Date | Event |
| --- | --- |
| 1995 | The WTO replaces the GATT. |
| October 1997 | President Jiang Zemin and President Clinton hold a summit in Washington, DC. |
| 1999 | Chinese Premier Zhu Rongji tells US Federal Reserve Board Chairman Alan Greenspan that he is ready to make a deal. |
| March 1999 | USTR Charlene Barshefsky visits China. |
| April 1999 | Premier Zhu Rongji comes to the United States. In a controversial move, President Clinton chooses not to close the US-China bilateral. |
| May 7, 1999 | The United States mistakenly bombs the Chinese Embassy in Belgrade. |
| September 11, 1999 | President Clinton and President Jiang Zemin discuss restarting trade talks during New Zealand Economic Summit. |
| November 8, 1999 | Clinton sends USTR Charlene Barshefsky and his economic adviser Gene Sperling to China. |
| November 15, 1999 | The US-China bilateral deal is reached. |
| May 24, 2000 | The US House of Representatives votes to grant China permanent normal trade relations (PNTR) status upon its accession to the WTO. |
| September 19, 2000 | The US Senate passes PNTR. |
| October 10, 2000 | President Bill Clinton signs PNTR. |
| December 11, 2001 | China becomes the 143rd member of the WTO. |

# 7

# The US-EU Mutual Recognition Agreements

## Making Trade Policy

The mutual recognition agreements (MRAs) negotiated by the United States and the European Union highlight the role that standards and certification procedures can play in creating obstacles to trade. The case points to the possibilities of overcoming these obstacles without complete international harmonization. It raises questions about the pressures created by MRAs on domestic regulators, and it demonstrates how private-sector actors can form international coalitions to influence national trade policies. The case also underscores the institutional differences between the United States and the European Union and how these affect the transatlantic relationship.

## Coverage

Should trade agreements include rules for regulatory standards? The introduction to the General Agreement on Tariffs and Trade (GATT) speaks of achieving both "the substantial reduction of tariffs and other barriers to trade" and the elimination of "discriminatory treatment in international commerce." Even when tariffs and other border barriers are eliminated,

*International Trade Meets Domestic Regulation: Negotiating the US-EU Mutual Recognition Agreements* is an edited and revised version of the case with the same name originally written for the Case Program at the Kennedy School of Government. For copies or permission to reproduce the unabridged case please refer to www.ksgcase.harvard.edu or send a written request to Case Program, John F. Kennedy School of Government, Harvard University, 79 John F. Kennedy Street, Cambridge, MA 02138.

however, international markets are not as integrated as national markets. One reason is that national regulations and standards often differ. Firms have higher market entry costs if they are required to adapt their products to meet different standards to sell products in another country. The testing and certification of compliance with these different national standards imposes additional costs. A particular concern in international trade is that such standards can be a cover for protectionism. In other words, a country may enact a regulation solely for the purpose of keeping outside firms from entering the domestic market. Thus, standards and product certification pose legitimate concerns to those seeking an open trading regime.

## Depth

Under the original GATT rules, countries were expected to provide foreign goods with national treatment and to treat goods from all contracting parties equally (i.e., with most favored nation status).[1] As long as goods from all sources were treated equally, countries could set any standards they desired. During the Tokyo Round, concluded in 1979, negotiators developed codes for sanitary and phytosanitary standards and technical barriers to trade. These codes were extended in the Uruguay Round. Today, World Trade Organization (WTO) members are expected to follow certain basic principles when setting standards, avoiding any measure that restricts trade more than is necessary to achieve its objective. Countries are also encouraged, but not required, to use international standards. Members are allowed to adopt standards more stringent than the international norm, but their regulations must be based on sound science and risk analysis. Thus, while the WTO rules set certain constraints on regulation, countries are not required to adopt the same standards—a process known as harmonization.

### Harmonization

The case for harmonizing standards internationally involves complex trade-offs and judgments. In principle, uniform international standards could make international markets more efficient and more easily contestable by reducing transactions costs and improving transparency. But the devil lies in the details. These positive outcomes are not guaranteed if the common standard is too stringent or is poorly designed. Such a stan-

---

1. National treatment applies only after a product, service, or item of intellectual property has entered the market. Therefore, charging customs duty on an import is not a violation of national treatment even if locally produced products are not charged an equivalent tax.

dard might reduce efficiency or, if it favors firms from a particular nation, actually hinder international competition. In addition, international standards restrict the choices of domestic governments. In national standards, countries can reflect their domestic institutions, values, and conditions more precisely. At the same time, however, domestic standards can enhance domestic monopolies and hinder international trade.

Choosing to harmonize standards leaves open the question of how these standards would be determined. One approach is to rely on negotiation, as was done in Europe until the early 1980s. Europeans originally sought to establish common standards through a process that required consensus among all members of the European Community—but because member countries had different interests, progress was extremely slow. Following complaints by European firms that these differences had dramatically increased their costs by preventing the creation of a single market, in the early 1980s a different approach was taken: mutual recognition.

## Mutual Recognition

Mutual recognition served as a pillar in the EU92 initiative that sought to complete the internal European market. Under the European system, if a product met the standards of any one EC member country, then it could be sold throughout the Community. This approach avoided the problems inherent in negotiating universal standards, and it also introduced a new dynamic. If a firm could obtain access to the entire European market by meeting the standard of any EC member, it would choose the most attractive national standard. Therefore, competition existed between standards and between standards setters.

Despite these advantages of mutual recognition, the coexistence of several standards could also lead to confusion and impose information costs on consumers trying to understand them. Some also argue that competition in standards setting will lead to "a race to the bottom"—that is, it will encourage the continued weakening of standards. Because of such concerns, one country will not grant mutual recognition before it trusts the standards set by the other. Indeed, even within Europe, mutual recognition is sometimes accompanied by an agreement on minimum standards.

Mutual recognition does not automatically result in a race to the bottom, however. For example, suppose Germany has a more rigorous standard than France for sink faucets. Faucet manufacturers seeking to convince consumers that their products are superior might actually prefer to be certified in compliance with the German standard. On the other hand, if the regulation does not add value (or if it functions like a tax), the least costly would be the most attractive.

The US-EU MRAs did not seek full mutual recognition of standards but mutual recognition of inspection, testing, and certification requirements for a range of traded products. While the United States and Europe would continue to set their own domestic standards, they would agree that producers could test in the United States to Europe's standards, and test in Europe to US standards. Therefore, the US-EU MRAs introduced competition between assessors. Such competition was familiar in Europe, where private firms had long provided certification, but was quite new for Americans, particularly the government agencies that had enjoyed a monopoly in providing certification in the United States. While some US officials believed that competition would lead to cheaper and more rapid certification, others worried about its implications for product safety.

## Enforcement

Introducing competition into setting standards and assessing conformity also introduces pressure, which, some fear, might result in less meticulous enforcement. For example, a certifier could be deliberately lax as a way of attracting more firms. The need for mutual trust suggests that countries will be unwilling to sign MRAs without first extensively examining the procedures and integrity of the mechanisms that ensure continued compliance. In the United States, some products are assessed by private institutions; but many argue that health and safety concerns should preclude those products under the purview of the Food and Drug Administration (FDA) from being certified in a competitive environment.

## Developing Countries

In general, mutual recognition is easier when countries are at similar levels of development, with similar standards. Understandably, such arrangements are particularly difficult to create between developed and developing countries. Developing countries with small markets would likely be forced to conform to the standards of countries with larger markets, because firms in the latter would be reluctant to cover the costs of certifying their standards. Indeed, developing countries may not have the capacity to establish standards at all, whether their own or others'. Developing countries are therefore unlikely candidates for MRAs, although certified laboratories in developing countries may be able to attest to conformity with European or US standards.

## Participation

Should international trade agreements be negotiated multilaterally, bilaterally, plurilaterally, or at all levels simultaneously? The United States emphasized multilateralism through the early 1980s but then turned to a multitrack approach. Europe has followed both regional and multilateral strategies. During the late 1980s, however, both major trading economies strengthened their regional focus, Europe with EU92 and the United States with the North American Free Trade Agreement (NAFTA). In 1994, agreements were made at the Asia Pacific Economic Cooperation group (APEC) summit in Bogor to achieve free trade and investment among members by 2010 for developed and 2020 for developing countries, and at the meeting of 34 nations from the Western hemisphere in Miami to conclude an agreement for free trade in the Americas.

These events naturally raised the question of whether the world's two largest economies should enhance their trading relationship bilaterally. They might negotiate a formal free trade agreement—but this approach had two problems. First, a US-EU bilateral agreement would inevitably be seen as a challenge to the multilateral system. Second, WTO rules required coverage of essentially all trade—including agriculture, which was extremely problematic for Europe. Accordingly, transatlantic dialogues took the place of a full-scale bilateral agreement. These dialogues led quite naturally to efforts to implement regional measures that could not be easily achieved multilaterally.

## Winners and Losers

Europe's success in implementing MRAs internally suggested that they might be a potential area of agreement between the United States and the European Union. But full mutual recognition was a radical step that would have dramatically altered the role of regulators in the United States. In the area of pharmaceuticals, for example, firms wishing to sell products in the United States would have had only to meet European standards rather than undergoing the more taxing process of obtaining FDA approval. Instead, therefore, the parties took a smaller step: the mutual recognition of conformity assessment procedures. Thus, while continuing to set their own standards for domestic sales of goods and services, they agreed to allow European and American certifiers to verify compliance with both US and European standards—allowing firms to choose where they certified their products. The agreement reduced costs and improved efficiency, but it also reduced the traditional power of regulators and added to the options, and consequently the power, of the firms that needed such assessments. Moreover, the dialogues provided firms in the United States and Europe with new opportunities to form international coalitions and thus advance their agendas at home and abroad.

## Governance

The MRA case points to the growing importance of nongovernmental actors in international economic relations and dramatizes the functional pressures that are leading to deeper integration. The US and the EU governments helped to construct transatlantic dialogues between business, labor, consumer, and environmental groups. The MRA emerged from the business dialogue, clearly driven by the interests of firms on both sides of the Atlantic in greater efficiency in compliance certification. The virtue of this approach is that it allows private groups to consensually find mutually advantageous policy solutions to common problems. But although such alliances may yield better policies, they also affect the balance of power between the regulators and the regulated. Moreover, the agreements they reach may move policy in a direction considered unacceptable by parties who are not included in the dialogue. Participation by government officials is therefore crucial to ensure that a broad array of interests are considered and that trade-offs are made when consensus does not exist (a difficult task).

In short, mutual recognition has significant implications both for regulators and for those who are regulated. The competition created by MRAs may be useful in limiting the danger of one particular regulatory system being captured by special interests. At the same time, mutual recognition will curtail the ability of domestic governments to construct protectionist regulations. MRAs may also be viewed as undermining local (or national) control; alternatively, they may be viewed as expanding local or national jurisdiction, because decisions taken at that level will extend to other countries.

## CASE STUDY: International Trade Meets Domestic Regulation—Negotiating the US-EU Mutual Recognition Agreements

In 1998, the United States and the European Union (EU) recognized each other's inspection, testing, and certification requirements for a wide range of traded products in a set of agreements known as mutual recognition agreements. The MRAs applied to nearly $50 billion in transatlantic trade in six sectors: medical devices, pharmaceuticals, recreational craft, telecommunications, electromagnetic compatibility (EMC) testing services, and electrical equipment.[2] The Commerce Department estimated that the agreement would save US industries more than $1 billion annually in testing and certification costs.[3] According to Stuart Eizenstat, then

2. USTR, *1999 Trade Policy Agenda and 1998 Annual Report of the President of the United States on the Trade Agreements Program*, 1999, 217.

3. Charles Ludolph, deputy assistant secretary for Europe, US Department of Commerce, hearing before the House Subcommittee on Oversight and Investigations of the Committee on Commerce, "Imported Drugs: US-EU Mutual Recognition Agreement on Drug Inspections," 105th Congress, 2nd session, October 2, 1998, 24.

undersecretary for economics, business, and international affairs at the State Department, the MRAs proved that the United States could simultaneously protect its citizens, promote public health, and encourage trade. The MRAs "are a groundbreaking step in President Clinton's policy to break down trade barriers, because they address the proliferation of requirements brought on by the growth in foreign trade," said Eizenstat. "They cut red tape and save money for industry, consumers, and regulators and make the USA more competitive."[4]

Champions of the MRA negotiations argued that the proliferation of differing standards, licenses, and certificates had created a formidable system of barriers to transatlantic trade. The MRAs were intended to eliminate duplicative testing, streamline procedures, lower costs, and decrease the time required to bring new products to market. Companies doing business internationally complained that they were often forced to retest their products at the border to standards that were very similar to those of the country of origin. For example, US companies exporting consumer electronics to Europe reported that the administrative burden alone of complying with double testing and certification cost them $70 million each year.[5] MRA proponents argued that performing all needed testing at one time would increase efficiency and reduce costs to consumers. "The basic concept behind the MRAs was the simple proposition that products could be tested once and considered to have been tested in both markets," Eizenstat said.[6]

In addition to seeking changes that would streamline international trade, some industries hoped the MRA process would encourage domestic regulatory reform. The US medical device industry, for example, was frustrated that navigating the FDA approval process to bring a product to market took four years, on average. Industry observers hoped the MRA negotiations would help stimulate regulatory changes at the FDA modeled on the European approval system—a system viewed by industry as much more efficient. Champions of the MRAs also believed that the agreement would set a powerful precedent for increased international regulatory cooperation and future efforts to harmonize standards for traded goods. "The longer-term benefit that industry saw was a continued acceleration towards harmonization and standardization," said one pharmaceutical executive. "Moving towards more harmonized standards is good for us. MRAs were a building block to that."

---

4. Eizenstat, quoted in "US Industry Urged to Back MRAs with EU," *Pharma Marketletter*, October 13, 1997.

5. Editorial, "The Strength of Dialogue," *Journal of Commerce*, June 5, 1997, 6A.

6. Eizenstat, hearing before the Senate Foreign Relations Committee, "US-EU Cooperation on Regulatory Affairs," October 16, 2003.

Industry played a key role in the MRA negotiations. Especially important was a new government-initiated organization of CEOs from Europe and the United States called the Transatlantic Business Dialogue (TABD). "This government-business dialogue is unique in the world, and has contributed immensely to the reduction of trade barriers across the Atlantic," declared David Aaron, undersecretary of commerce for international trade. "No other forum has risen so rapidly to become as effective as the TABD."[7] But some observers, including consumer groups like Public Citizen, were suspicious of the TABD's part in the MRAs. Was it appropriate for industry to be involved in negotiations over testing requirements for their own products? Why was there no comparable role for consumer and safety groups? Industry representatives noted that their participation was necessary since it was business that faced the inefficiencies and duplication in testing. Policymakers needed to have an understanding of the practical implications of any agreement, they said.

Though business played an important role, US and EU governments led the MRA negotiations. The talks presented a number of unprecedented institutional challenges to US and European officials. In Europe, the negotiation tested the relationship between the European Commission and the member governments of the European Union. In the United States, government agencies ordinarily uninvolved in trade discussions, such as the FDA and the Occupational Health and Safety Administration (OSHA), became central players—yet the idea of considering domestic regulatory and certification issues within the framework of a trade agreement made some participants uneasy. The primary mission of a regulatory agency, after all, is not to facilitate trade but to safeguard consumers. As Representative Henry Waxman (D-CA) put it, "There is no question that international agreements of this kind can enhance the efficiency of commerce, but it is equally clear that they can potentially depress American health and safety standards."[8] Such concerns made some regulators reluctant to participate in the MRA process.

Bilaterally, Europe and the United States had dissimilar ideas about how to structure the agreement; each was understandably eager to promote its own industries, cultural values, and institutions. In addition, differences in the way US and European businesses relate to government (and vice versa) affected the negotiations. Because of such challenges, completing the MRAs took four years of tough on-again, off-again talks, and implementation efforts continue.

---

7. Aaron, hearing before the House Ways and Means Committee, "Trade Relations with Europe and the New Transatlantic Economic Partnership," 105th Congress, 2nd session, July 28, 1998.

8. Waxman, Hearing before the House Subcommittee on Oversight and Investigations, 4.

# Background

## What Is a Mutual Recognition Agreement?

The US-EU mutual recognition agreements aim to reduce what are technically known as *conformity assessment procedures:* the testing, certification, and inspection processes used to determine if a product meets specified standards and regulations. Ralph Ives of the office of the US Trade Representative (USTR), who served as lead US MRA negotiator, explains: "An MRA basically allows you to test [your products] in the US to Europe's standards, and in Europe to US standards."[9] MRAs were negotiated on a sectoral basis; that is, separate talks were held for each industry sector.

The impetus to negotiate a US-EU agreement on conformity assessment procedures grew out of the mutual recognition of standards in Europe. Under full mutual recognition, if a product meets the standards of any one EC member country, then it can be sold throughout the European Community. Europe came to this practice of mutually recognizing standards after a failed attempt to pursue regulatory *harmonization,* which would have required all EC member countries to adopt the same standards.

## Harmonization Efforts Within Europe

The free movement of goods within Europe was guaranteed in Articles 30–36 of the 1957 Treaty of Rome, which established the European Economic Community. Article 30 prohibited "qualitative restrictions on imports . . . between the Member States." Article 36 allowed exemptions to this rule for reasons such as public security, protection of health and life, and the protection of national treasures. However, such permissible restrictions could not "constitute a means of arbitrary discrimination or a disguised restriction on trade between the Member States."

The 1970s saw efforts in the Community to pursue regulatory harmonization, a move that would have made national barriers irrelevant by creating pan-European standards for products. But the process of creating such standards required consensus among all EC members, and directives for the harmonization became so detailed and technical that developing a standard could take 15 years. As a result, this effort, later dubbed the "Old Approach," proved largely ineffective.

---

9. Unless otherwise noted, all quotes from Ralph Ives come from a November 1999 interview with Charan Devereaux.

The New Approach toward standards emerged from a series of cases at the European Court of Justice interpreting Articles 30–36. In an often-cited 1979 case (120/78), the court ruled that West Germany had violated EC free trade laws by banning a French liqueur on the grounds that it didn't have enough alcohol to be classified as a liqueur by German standards. The decision confirmed that goods should be allowed free circulation within the European market as long as they were safe and did not threaten public health or the environment.

Using such cases as a precedent, the European Commission adopted the principle of mutual recognition of standards based on essential safety requirements and ceased to pursue complete harmonization. It thereby avoided the complications inherent in negotiating universal standards. In 1985, the EC Council adopted a resolution titled "A New Approach to Technical Harmonization and Standardization." Mutual recognition of standards became a major element of Europe's Single Market Program, also approved in 1985. The governments of the 12 Community member countries, as well as the governments of 6 of the 7 members of the European Free Trade Association (EFTA), committed themselves to achieving mutual recognition by the end of 1992 in the Single European Act (SEA).

The New Approach directives were limited to essential safety and performance requirements for most manufactured products traded on the EC market.[10] Under mutual recognition in Europe, if a product met the standards of any member country, then it could be sold throughout the Community. After products were issued a "CE" (Conformité Européenne) mark, they could be sold anywhere in Europe without undergoing further testing by individual countries.[11] Many New Approach directives required third-party certification before a manufacturer could affix the CE mark. As a part of this system, "notified bodies," or private third-party institutions to certify compliance, were developed. The Community also forbade the recognition or acceptance of most non-EC inspections and product certifications.

This decision not to recognize outside inspections required many non-EC manufacturers to retest their products at the borders of European member states. "Seen from the outside, the Community was perceived to be setting up a major obstacle to trade against third countries because our own products would be favored," says Karl Falkenberg, the European Commission's lead negotiator on the US-EU MRAs. "It was the origin of the debate about 'fortress Europe.'" The intent, Falkenberg argues, was

---

10. For some products, including food, automobiles, and airplanes, the Community continued to rely on the Old Approach.

11. The CE mark was an international symbol of quality management and product safety, earned after a manufacturer was inspected and audited by a "notified body" authorized under EU regulations. Once the mark was granted, the manufacturer could market its products throughout the European Union unregulated by individual countries.

not to create new barriers: "We were trying to liberalize as much as we could within Europe, but we were quite prepared to recognize any other country that would reciprocally recognize our standards or certification bodies."[12]

## The United States Organizes to Meet the Challenge

As the pursuit of a single market gained momentum in Europe, the US government became concerned about its implications for trade. The Europe-US trade and investment relationship was the largest in the world. Some experts predicted that a fortress Europe was indeed imminent and that EC-wide trade barriers would drive out US exports. The US Commerce Department was charged with the unenviable task of reviewing the proposed changes to European regulations.

In 1987, Charles Ludolph, director of the Commerce Department's Office of European Community, became chair of the new US Interagency Working Group on European Standards and Regulatory Issues. In addition to drawing on such traditional players in trade as the Commerce Department, the State Department, and USTR, the working group also included officials from a wide spectrum of regulatory agencies such as the Federal Communications Commission (FCC), the FDA, the Environmental Protection Agency (EPA), the Federal Aviation Agency (FAA), the Department of Labor, OSHA, and the Department of Agriculture (USDA). Between 1987 and 1991, the group typically met at least once every six weeks.

Many regulators found that taking part in discussions led by the trade-related agencies was a relatively new experience. "We are not a trade agency," explains Walter Batts, the FDA's director of international relations. "Until very recently, there hasn't been anything in our legislation that indicates we should be involved in these kind of things. . . . But at the same time, because we regulate such a wide range of products, we obviously have impact on trade."[13] Nor had regulators traditionally played much of a role in international trade talks. Trade negotiations had concerned themselves with "border barriers," such as tariffs and quotas, as opposed to "beyond-the-border barriers" such as domestic regulation. Ludolph's interagency group was therefore somewhat unusual.

Of particular concern to Ludolph were the implications of the new CE marks, which would be legally required for most manufactured goods distributed or sold within Europe's single market. Between 1987 and 1992,

---

12. Unless otherwise noted, all quotes from Karl Falkenberg are from a November 1999 interview with Charan Devereaux.

13. Unless otherwise noted, all quotes from Walter Batts are from a 1999 interview with Charan Devereaux. The FDA regulates over $1 trillion worth of products, which accounts for 25 cents of every consumer dollar spent in the United States each year (US Department of Health and Human Services, Food and Drug Administration, *Fiscal Year 2000 CFO's Annual Report*, 2001, I-1).

"we stared at these 25 CE marking directives," Ludolph recalls. "It was clear that no US manufacturers were prepared to send their products all the way to Europe to be tested and certified—the cost was too high—and that was what CE marking required."[14]

The United States needed to find a different approach. Negotiating complete mutual recognition of standards between Europe and the United States was not feasible. For example, under full mutual recognition companies could sell pharmaceuticals in the United States after meeting European standards without first obtaining FDA approval. An agreement on testing and certification procedures was a smaller step, but appeared to be a more realistic goal. Through an MRA on conformity assessment procedures, the United States and Europe could continue to set their own domestic standards, but agree that producers could test in the United States to Europe's standards, and test in Europe to US standards.

Ludolph was also interested in the efforts of telecommunications companies to address the same concerns. Some analysts believe that the MRAs were inspired by an agreement between the US and German telecom industries to facilitate trade in the face of the changes in how Europe treated standards. Subsequently, Lucent Technologies' Chuck Berestecky and Nortel's Vic Boersma encouraged the US government to address the issue with Europe more broadly.

In early 1992, drawing on the interagency working group discussions and the telecom industry efforts, Ludolph sent 400 letters to a range of US companies outlining his recommendations regarding the new European approach to standards. An alternative to having US products tested in Europe, Ludolph wrote, was an MRA—an alternative codified in the GATT Technical Barriers to Trade Agreement (TBT).[15] "Under the TBT, there are fairly tough conformity assessment requirements," Ludolph explains. "You either give national treatment to testing and certification services—which means you treat foreign producers the same as domestic producers—or if you deny national treatment you must offer MRAs. . . . I decided that MRAs were something we should recommend as an option to the business community." Of the 25 business sectors Ludolph contacted, 11 expressed interest in MRAs.

That same year, the European Council empowered the European Commission to engage in MRA negotiations with a certain number of coun-

---

14. Unless otherwise noted, all quotes from Charles Ludolph come from one of several interviews conducted by Charan Devereaux in 1999 and 2000.

15. After years of negotiations at the end of the Tokyo Round in 1979, 32 GATT Contracting Parties signed the TBT. It laid down the rules for preparing, adopting, and applying technical regulations, standards, and conformity assessment procedures. The new WTO Agreement on Technical Barriers to Trade, negotiated during the Uruguay Round, strengthened and clarified the provisions of the Tokyo Round code (see www.wto.org).

tries. According to Giacomo Mattinò, an MRA negotiator from the Commission's Directorate-General for Enterprise, "The mandate identified MRAs as an instrument to achieve the objective of trade facilitation. The immediate cause was not the New Approach directives themselves. It was the overall perspective of broadening trade facilitation."[16] In selecting the countries with which it would negotiate, the Commission weighed the volume of trade, the sectors in question, the types of legislation that were applicable, and the level of existing technical regulations. "It is easy to understand why the US was at the top of the list," adds Mattinò.

Later in 1992, Ludolph entered into "prediscussions" with European Commission officials to explore what an MRA would look like. "Those talks were totally useless," he says. Formal talks did not begin until October 1994. What caused the holdup? US observers say the European Commission had no incentive to enter into talks immediately. The New Approach directives were being phased in at different times for different sectors, and no real effects would be felt until January 1995. At that time, the Electromagnetic Compatibility Directive would be implemented, affecting all electronic products and at least $13 billion worth of US computer exports.[17] Ludolph wanted to have the MRAs in place and signed by 1995 to prevent any break in testing services. The main concern of the European Commission, in contrast, was simply to open negotiations early enough to avoid being brought before the WTO. If talks did not begin in a timely fashion, the United States could bring a case against Europe at the new trade dispute settlement body and penalties might result.

## Getting to the Table

In 1994, an agreement was reached to begin MRA negotiations in earnest. In preparation, the Commerce Department took steps to directly involve the US business community. Ludolph approached a variety of trade associations and companies, asking them to "come together and advise us about how to proceed with the negotiations." The department formed advisory committees of businesspeople for each sector (except for recreational craft). The most active participants were those from the telecom industry, followed by representatives of the pharmaceutical and the medical devices industries.

---

16. Unless otherwise noted, all quotes from Giacomo Mattinò come from a December 1999 interview with Charan Devereaux. Since May 1998, Mattinò has been responsible for the overall coordination within DG Enterprise of the MRA dossier. Since January 2001, he has served as principal administrator at DG Enterprise. The views expressed are those of Giacomo Mattinò and do not represent any official view of the European Commission.

17. Interview with Ludolph.

**Table 7.1  Bilateral trade in seven sectors under MRA negotiation, two-year average, 1994–95** (billions of dollars)

| Sector | US exports to EU-15 | US imports from EU-15 |
|---|---|---|
| **Sectors already deemed essential in agreement** | | |
| IT equipment and terminal telecommunications (telecom sector annex) | 7.8 | 2.8 |
| Aircraft, machinery, and appliances subject to FCC and/or OSHA requirements (electrical and electronic sector annex) | 21.3 | 18.0 |
| *Subtotal* | 29.1 | 20.8 |
| **Sectors in which US-EU agreement is being sought** | | |
| Class I and II medical devices | 2.3 | 1.0 |
| Pharmaceutical GMPs | 2.7 | 3.4 |
| *Total* | 34.1 | 25.2 |

FCC = Federal Communications Commission
GMPs = good manufacturing practices
OSHA = Occupational Safety and Health Administration

*Source:* Hearing before the House Subcommittee on Oversight and Investigations of the Committee on Commerce, 105th Congress, 2nd session, October 2, 1998, 75 (Commerce Department Analysis of Trade, 1996).

## Telecommunications

"It was primarily the [US] telecommunications sector that thought the agreement would be useful," says lead USTR MRA negotiator Ralph Ives—unsurprisingly, given its earlier enthusiasm. In 1994, the United States exported about $7.8 billion in telecommunications equipment to the European Union while Europe sent only about $2.8 billion to the United States (see table 7.1). As noted above, the industry's attempts to streamline testing and certification processes preceded any formal government-led initiative.

Several US industry groups, including the Telecommunications Industry Association (TIA) and the American Council of Independent Laboratories (ACIL), approached the FCC (which regulated the industry) to express interest in the talks. "The Telecom Industry Association was a major part of what actually motivated the MRAs," says the FCC's MRA negotiator, Art Wall. "We [the FCC] got involved mainly because industry came to us, and because we saw the handwriting on the wall that change was going to come. We also saw the handwriting on the wall that the FCC's resources were dwindling. If change was going to come about, it was better to be part of the process so that we could continue to monitor the things we cared about."[18]

The stakes were high for the telecom industry because the duration of any testing process directly affects the manufacturer's bottom line. "The objective of an MRA is to reduce the time and cost of bringing equipment to market," says Joanne Wilson, Lucent Technologies' director of global public affairs.

> In order to get a product approved for sale, you often have to send the product to that country to be tested and have a conformity assessment body in that country do the testing. So this means that for every new market, you have another round of testing and you have another delay of getting the product into market. Product life cycles are getting shorter and shorter, and your profitability associated with the product depends on its life cycle. The more you delay getting to market, the shorter the lifetime of that product, which reduces its profitability. Particularly now in our computer-based products, the life cycle is getting very short. And so the only way to be profitable is to be able to get product into market very quickly.[19]

The FCC's Wall echoes her assessment: "The bottom line is that manufacturers need to get products to the market quicker. They can't wait three months for each country to do its product approvals, because the life cycle of some products is less than three months." Some also suspected that some delays had more to do with protectionism than with product approval. "That was definitely a real concern to the industry," said one industry representative.

European officials were less enthusiastic about pursuing an agreement in the telecom sector. "Europeans were initially somewhat cool to the idea," recalls Ives, USTR's lead MRA negotiator. "They saw trade being heavily in our favor. So the EC came back with a number of sectors they wanted to include, particularly pharmaceuticals, medical devices, and electrical safety. The package started to develop around those basic sectors." Falkenberg of the European Commission points out, "The package for us included, necessarily, pharmaceuticals and medical devices because we are large exporters of those products." For European negotiators, including these sectors in the talks was essential to balance the package.[20]

---

18. Unless otherwise noted, all quotes from Art Wall come from a 1999 interview with Charan Devereaux.

19. Unless otherwise noted, all quotes from Joanne Wilson come from a December 1999 interview with Charan Devereaux.

20. The European Union was the world's largest producer and exporter of pharmaceutical products, with production totaling $99.3 billion in 1993 ("Europe's Pharmaceutical Industry in 1993," *Pharma Marketletter*, October 24, 1994).

## Pharmaceuticals

The US pharmaceutical industry as well as the European Commission was interested in pursuing an MRA. As matters stood, drug manufacturing facilities were inspected by each country that imported their products, resulting in much duplication of effort. The immediate goal of the industry was to streamline these testing procedures. Laura Peralta-Schulte, director of government affairs and public policy worldwide of Warner-Lambert (a company since merged with Pfizer), explains:

> Industry was never saying we wanted to modify the Food, Drug, and Cosmetic Act. Nor did we want shoddy standards. We just wanted to modify the process so we could have one rather than multiple inspections with varying requirements and procedures because it is costly, time-consuming and slows the ability to get a product to market. That was short term. The longer-term benefit that industry saw was a continued acceleration towards harmonization and standardization. Moving towards more harmonized standards is good for us. MRAs were a building block to that. If we could get more of these issues under our belt, the thought was that at some point we could look towards a more harmonized transatlantic marketplace for other issues as well.[21]

This was not the first time that the United States and Europe had entered into regulatory discussions on pharmaceuticals. A conference of regulatory officials from Japan, Europe, and the United States, together with industry representatives, had laid the groundwork for the International Conference on Harmonization (ICH) in 1989.[22] The ICH had two major goals. First, the participating countries and companies sought to harmonize the scientific requirements of pharmaceutical regulations in the United States, the European Community, and Japan. They hoped that if the various regulatory agencies required the same data, the differences in their approval processes would become less significant. Second, they wished to shorten the time from development to marketing of new drugs (Kidd 1996).[23]

In addition, since the 1970s, the FDA had entered into memoranda of understanding, or MOUs, with Switzerland, Sweden, Canada, and Japan. In this MOU, foreign governments made a commitment that their regulated exports to the United States would meet FDA standards. The FDA

---

21. Unless otherwise noted, all quotes from Laura Peralta-Schulte are from a 1999 interview with Charan Devereaux.

22. The full title was the International Conference on Harmonization of Technical Requirements of Pharmaceuticals for Human Use.

23. The first ICH, held in Belgium in 1991, drew more than 1,000 government and industry representatives. The second ICH, in Florida in 1992, had 1,600 attendees. In 1995, some 2,400 delegates representing pharmaceutical companies and 40 governments took part in the third ICH in Japan (Kidd 1996).

also sent inspectors to certify that plants producing medications in those countries complied with FDA "good manufacturing practices," or GMPs.[24] Since 1989, the FDA had been participating in discussions with the European Commission's Directorate-General (DG) for Enterprise about entering into an agreement to exchange inspection information.[25]

However, the mandate of the Commission's trade directorate (DG Trade) to negotiate MRAs superseded DG Enterprise's authority to pursue MOUs with the FDA. Any future discussions would therefore take place under the umbrella of the MRA. "FDA would have preferred to continue the bilateral MOU approach rather than getting sucked into the MRA," admits Ives. Trade agencies were not involved in the MOU process.

FDA's experience in trade-related negotiations was fairly limited. The agency first became involved in GATT negotiations during the Uruguay Round of trade talks (1986–94). "When the Uruguay Round negotiations began, it wasn't something on our radar screen," says the FDA's Walter Batts. "The trade agencies didn't actively seek out FDA in the early stages of the negotiations to be involved in establishing the US government position." However, Batts explains, new items on the Uruguay Round agenda drew FDA into the process: "There was a totally new agreement being negotiated, the Sanitary and Phytosanitary [SPS] Agreement.[26] [As a result], a USDA representative contacted us and said, 'Hey, we think you folks need to be aware and involved in this.' We agreed and realized that we needed to be actively involved in the Technical Barriers to Trade negotiations as well." In the latter part of the Uruguay Round, FDA therefore participated in negotiations for the SPS and TBT agreements. "We actually had people including myself and other FDA members as part of the negotiation teams," Batts points out. "This was unprecedented for FDA."

---

24. GMPs are practices and procedures for manufacturing, processing, and packing products to ensure their quality and purity. FDA investigators conduct both periodic and "for cause" inspections of manufacturers for compliance with GMPs (Horton 1998, 697).

25. During the MRA negotiations, DG Enterprise was known as DG III. The mission of DG III was to "promote the competitiveness of industry in the EU," ensure the free movement of products as a "central role in the Internal Market Program," promote innovation and R&D—particularly in information technology, and "ensure that other EU policies and activities contribute to improving industrial competitiveness." ("Industry: European Commission Directorate-General Goes Public on Aims," *European Report*, April 16, 1997.) In 1999, Europe ended the practice of numbering the DGs, and combined DG III, DG XXIII (Enterprise policy, tourism and SMEs), as well as parts of the DG XIII (telecommunications and information technology) to form DG Enterprise.

26. The Agreement on the Application of Sanitary and Phytosanitary Measures concerned the application of food safety and animal and plant health regulations. According to the WTO, the problem addressed in the agreement was "How do you ensure that your country's consumers are being supplied with food that is safe to eat—'safe' by the standards you consider appropriate? And at the same time, how can you ensure that strict health and safety regulations are not being used as an excuse for protecting domestic producers?" (see www.wto.org).

## Medical Devices

Even as the European Commission was pressing for the inclusion of the medical device sector in the MRA talks, the US medical device industry was gaining interest in the negotiations. As a part of the EC92 Single Market Program, the European Community had created a pan-European system intended to harmonize and streamline the regulation of medical devices, replacing the different standards of each different member country. The new system allowed manufacturers (a) to self-certify that low- and medium-risk devices met European requirements and (b) to employ third-party bodies to review and approve higher-risk devices. In short, the European regulatory system represented a public-private partnership in which the government established medical device requirements and private notified bodies actually approved the products. In the United States, Congress and the FDA established requirements and the FDA was responsible for approving the products. "The net result of the new European system," according to a US Health Industry Manufacturers Association (HIMA) report, "is that European governments are able to approve advanced medical devices more than three times faster than FDA with only a small fraction of the staff that FDA has devoted to regulating devices" (HIMA 1997, 59). (In June 2000, HIMA changed its name to AdvaMed, the Advanced Medical Technology Association.)

The US industry considered the new European system to be much more modern, efficient, and highly developed than that of the FDA. The new system also freed US medical device manufacturers from having to meet a different standard for each individual country in the European Community. As a result, some US medical device companies moved their research facilities to Europe. A HIMA survey of 500 US medical device firms found that more than 45 percent of manufacturers and 55 percent of start-up companies were increasing their R&D activities in Europe. Many US companies were also introducing products into the European market earlier than the US market. When asked why, more than 90 percent cited the US process of product review, saying that they had to generate cash flow from European markets to fund the more costly and time-consuming US approval and commercial requirements (Wilkerson Group 1995). Guidant's chief compliance officer, Michael Gropp, explains the implications:

> If you look at companies such as Guidant, at any point in time, 50 to 60 percent of our revenue comes from products introduced in the preceding 12 months. So, for us, speed to approval of safe products is really important. At the time we started talking about the MRA, the gap between EU and US approval was much worse. So the idea was to find a way that you could go through a single approval process in one country and have it be accepted by authorities in another.[27]

27. Unless otherwise noted, all quotes from Michael Gropp come from a 1999 interview with Charan Devereaux.

As in the pharmaceutical sector, efforts had been undertaken to pursue international harmonization in medical device regulation. The Global Harmonization Task Force (GHTF), founded in 1992, was an informal group that included regulatory and industry officials from the European Community, United States, Japan, Canada, and Australia. It defined its purpose as "encourag[ing] convergence in regulatory practices related to ensuring the safety, effectiveness/performance and quality of medical devices, promoting technological innovation and facilitating international trade."[28] "The GHTF is FDA's highest priority for international [medical] device activities," declared the FDA's Linda Horton in 1998 (Horton 1998, 720).

While an MRA would not harmonize standards, it would allow a body in the European Union to inspect a medical device to verify that it met US requirements, and vice versa. What analysts found particularly intriguing about this idea was that it introduced the notion of international competition between bodies tasked with conformity assessment. While the United States and Europe remained sovereign over their own standards, industry could choose to work with the most efficient body to certify that standard—be it the FDA or a private European notified body.

In addition, many in the medical device industry saw the MRA process as part of a broader effort to encourage the FDA to adopt what was considered a "more modern approach" to regulation through greater exposure to the European system. In the words of one industry representative:

> First, the MRA would take steps towards eliminating duplicative regulatory requirements between Europe and the US. For example, instead of having two GMP inspections—one by FDA and one by a European notified body—you could have one inspection and it would suffice in both countries. Second, the Europeans had developed a new regulatory system that turned out to be very reasonable, providing for timely reviews and using very little in terms of government resources because it relied on third-party notified bodies. US industry saw that and said, "This is a good model for pushing the FDA reform process." So ultimately, that is what the MRA negotiations turned into. A way to help us in our broader efforts to encourage FDA reform.

Domestic efforts were already being undertaken to encourage such changes, but the MRA talks were another venue for introducing that kind of thinking.

## The MRA Negotiations

### The First Two Years

Official MRA negotiations kicked off in 1994. The lead US negotiators were the Commerce Department's Charles Ludolph and USTR's Richard

---

28. Global Harmonization Task Force, "General Information," November 17, 2004, www.ghtf.org.

Meier.[29] The rest of the US delegation was essentially the interagency working group on standards and certification that Ludolph had been meeting with for some time. He describes them as "the same group where people from FDA got to learn trade and people in USTR and Commerce got to know regulation." Each sector had a regulator in charge of the technical negotiations who reported to Ludolph and Meier. For telecommunications, the negotiator was Art Wall of the FCC; for pharmaceuticals, Walter Batts of the FDA; and for medical devices, FDA's Joe Levitt and Linda Horton. The MRAs progressed slowly, but Ludolph was relieved that at least negotiations had begun.

For the European Commission, DG Trade took the lead on the MRA negotiations; Karl Falkenberg was head of the unit, which was in charge of external relations and commercial policy with North America, the Far East, Australia, and New Zealand.[30] Officials from DG Enterprise also participated in the talks. Their unit's key objective was to promote the competitiveness of European industry, and its responsibilities included coordinating regulatory and legislative activity in the European Union. "The Commission works very differently from a national government," explains Falkenberg.

> It particularly works very differently from the relationship between government and independent agencies in the United States. Within the Commission, we have different directors-general who have different prime responsibilities. But the Commission is working as a collective entity. We don't have the sort of independence that you see in the States between, say, USTR on one hand and FDA on the other. Decisions here are made collectively at the level of the Commission with all the commissioners represented on all decisions.

Other fundamental differences between US and EU governmental structure were highlighted by the MRA initiative. DG Enterprise's Mattinò points out, "In most cases, the US approach to regulation is that the conformity assessment organization intervenes directly—which means the public authority itself, such as FDA or OSHA, has to approve the products directly. Our approach, at least in sectors covered by the MRAs, is different. The public authority is not itself directly certifying products but entrusts this responsibility to third parties, independent certification organizations."

The Commission also had an obligation to coordinate with the national governments of its member states. The coordinating body in trade negotiations was the 133 Committee. When the MRA negotiations were launched, the 133 Committee established an ad hoc MRA Committee to advise the

---

29. Ludolph was with the negotiations for their entire duration, from 1992 to 1998. Richard Meier was the lead negotiator for USTR until he retired. Ralph Ives became the lead USTR MRA negotiator after the TABD's Chicago meeting in November 1996.

30. During the MRA negotiations, DG Trade was known as DG I.

Commission. "But 133 is a consultative committee," Falkenberg emphasizes. "It can give views but it has no decision-making force." According to Mattinò, the process of coordination and consultation with business and the member states was especially challenging because MRAs were a new idea:

> The concept itself of an MRA in the format under negotiation between the EU and the US was so recently developed that this process of interrogating and receiving feedback from a number of economic operators was going hand in hand with a learning process where all the operators were trying to better understand what an MRA was. So on one hand we were asking for feedback from industry and on the other hand we were trying to explain exactly what an MRA could be. That's sort of a strange situation, but that's how it developed.

During the first two years, US and European negotiators met every six months, alternating between Brussels and Washington. "I think, in the beginning, it was a reasonable pace because we each had a lot of reading to do," says lead European negotiator Karl Falkenberg.[31] "We had to familiarize ourselves with certification procedures in the other market. We had to look into standards and understand which were mandatory standards and which were voluntary." Many participants describe the initial phase of negotiations as a process of mutual education. Regulators from each side of the Atlantic presented the requirements of their respective markets, and business representatives were included in the discussion. As Commerce's Ludolph explains: "We invited laboratories and manufacturers to accompany us on our negotiations and so every time we negotiated with the Europeans we brought a delegation of US companies and trade associations. Sometimes they were in the room and sometimes they were not in the room for the talks themselves."

## The Transatlantic Business Dialogue

As the MRA talks were getting under way, so too were efforts to organize a high-level dialogue between EU and US businesses. In December 1994, seeking ways to further facilitate trade between Europe and the United States, Commerce Secretary Ron Brown went to Brussels. While there, Brown outlined his vision of a business-to-business dialogue in a speech to the EU Committee of the US Chamber of Commerce. "He said that Europe and the US didn't need a free trade agreement and there were plenty of government-to-government dialogues," Ludolph remembers. "What was missing was a private-sector, high-level business dialogue."

Initially, neither the European Commission nor European business representatives showed much enthusiasm for such discussions. In January 1995,

---

31. Falkenberg also was the Commission's lead negotiator for MRAs with Canada, Japan, Australia, New Zealand, Switzerland, and countries in Eastern Europe.

Commerce Department officials proposed initiating a business-to-business dialogue in meetings with European Commissioner Sir Leon Brittan and other EC officials. Skeptical EC officials said they would wait to see if the European business community supported the idea.

Such support was by no means guaranteed. For one thing, as Ludolph explains, "the nature of the European business community is that they are much less connected to these kind of government initiatives." For example, European business was not known for lobbying government. Instead, as one American business representative puts it, "they just took their lumps." Over the years, according to some observers, European business had come to see its relationship with government as top-down. "The idea of the business community telling government to do something that they otherwise wouldn't do was a novel concept," Ludolph says. "There was not the kind of aggressive, pointed contact to influence the outcome of either the executive or the legislative branches anywhere in Europe" that there was in the United States. Falkenberg concurs: "In the US, aggressive lobbying is normal, so when US lobbying groups or large companies arrive in Brussels, the first thing they have to learn is to forget about their Washington ways, because they don't work in Brussels. That's part of the cultural difference."

Another unusual feature of the Commerce Department's proposal was that the point of contact for business would be the European Commission. Normally, the government officials with whom European businesses dealt were ministers from the 15 member states, who would then convey their thoughts and concerns to the Commission in Brussels. The idea of business working directly with the Commission was untested. Falkenberg also notes the differences between the advisory processes of the Commission and those of US agencies.

> In the US, you have institutionalized advisory committees, where industry is used to working very directly with the administration. In Europe, our institutionalized counterpart is the member states—the 133 Committee, the Council of Ministers. Traditionally, the CEOs of industries were one step further away. That link existed between the CEOs and their national administration; the Commission was not used to involving us directly with individual enterprises and individual CEOs.

In light of these concerns, the Department of Commerce and the European Commission sent 1,400 US and European businesses and trade associations a survey accompanied by what one business recipient called "the three-B letter." Signed by European Commission Vice President Sir Leon Brittan, Commissioner for Industry Martin Bangemann, and US Commerce Secretary Ron Brown, the letter asked how the Commission and the US administration could improve and deepen the transatlantic business relationship. The survey also asked whether there should be a US-EU business dialogue. According to the Commerce Department, approximately 80 percent of the respondents answered yes.

Observers suggest that promoting a business-to-business dialogue made sense for the Commerce Department from an institutional standpoint. In 1995, there were proposals from Republicans on Capitol Hill to eliminate the department as part of a plan to balance the budget. Commerce Secretary Brown denounced the idea, saying that it amounted to "suggesting unilateral disarmament in the battle for global competitiveness."[32] Initiating a transatlantic dialogue was one way to demonstrate the Commerce Department's relevance and value, some said.

In addition to showing support for a US-EU dialogue, the responses to the three-B letter also indicated that businesses put a high priority on standards and regulatory issues. "When we got the survey back and tallied the results," Ludolph recalls, "40 percent of all the respondents in Europe and the US said standards were the most important thing to the US-EU commercial relationship. The next-nearest thing was intellectual property at 8 percent. Standards just stood out as a huge issue." Stephen Johnston, who later became the lead European staff person for the TABD, agrees: "Because of the success of the GATT, access to other nation's markets was easy enough. The problems came once you were in the market."[33]

### The Seville Meeting

The initial meeting of the TABD was scheduled to take place in Seville, Spain. Its goal was to make recommendations to participants in the December 1995 US-EU Summit about the US-EU economic relationship. The Commerce Department and the European Commission approached several key business executives to lead the TABD meeting. The two US cochairs were two CEOs, Paul Allaire of Xerox and Alex Trotman of Ford. On the European side, the cochairs were BASF CEO Dr. Jürgen Strube and Chairman Peter Sutherland of Goldman Sachs International. Working groups on regulatory policy, multilateral issues, third-country issues, and investment were chaired by other CEOs. According to Selina Jackson, the US director for the TABD:

> The notion behind the TABD was that the Cold War had ended, and the US government and the European Commission looked at their relationship and identified the key issues on which they should be focusing. And rightly, they identified business and economics as one of the key priorities for the transatlantic relationship. They thought to seek input from the business community, which is why they sent out this questionnaire and convened the Seville conference.[34]

---

32. Martha M. Hamilton, Stephen Barr, "Brown Blasts Plan for Commerce Dept.; Elimination Would Hurt US Firms in Global Trade, Secretary Suggests," *The Washington Post*, May 10, 1995, A5.

33. Unless otherwise noted, all quotes from Stephen Johnston come from a 1999 interview with Charan Devereaux.

34. Unless otherwise noted, all quotes from Selina Jackson are from a 1999 interview with Charan Devereaux. Jackson went on to work for United Parcel Service (UPS).

In September, a US steering committee began meeting daily at 8 A.M., hosted by the head of Xerox's Washington, DC, office. Jackson, a representative from Ford, and representatives of each of the TABD working groups attended these sessions. For example, because the CEO of Tenneco chaired Working Group 1 on standards and regulatory policy, a Washington staff person from Tenneco participated.

The Washington meetings focused on the logistics of the Seville conference and on drafting position papers. There were also some efforts to work with the group's European counterparts but Jackson notes, "there just weren't the relationships, because we had not met face-to-face." Though bilateral relationships began to develop at an October US-European full steering committee meeting at the staff level in Brussels, the preparations for the Seville conference were largely pursued separately.

In November 1995, the TABD held its conference. Commerce Secretary Brown addressed the group of European and US CEOs, encouraging their involvement in the trade negotiation process and declaring, "We should put the business 'horse' before the government 'cart.'"[35] The Seville meeting could not be called an overwhelming success, however. Attendance was modest, and a European observer frankly admits, "There weren't many high-quality European CEOs." Commission officials also note the lack of coordination between industry and the Commission.

But the conference did create some momentum for the MRAs. In the report published by the TABD, participating executives declared that they had come to Seville "not to negotiate between US and EU industry but to present joint recommendations" to government—in other words, to see what they could agree on. They stressed to political leaders that the transatlantic business relationship was one of the great successes of the postwar period, and business on both sides urged their governments to "eliminate, as soon as possible, the remaining obstacles to trade and investment" (TABD 1995, 1). Many of the US companies that sent representatives to Seville had also participated in Ludolph's advisory process for negotiating the MRAs. The final report for Working Group 1 on standards, certification, and regulatory policy recommended that the MRA talks be completed by January 1997.

### The Dialogue Continues

Originally, the TABD was intended to last only three months; there were no plans to continue after the Seville meeting. Toward the close of the conference, however, Ford's Alex Trotman suggested that follow-up might be in order since some good first steps had been made. Ron Brown stepped forward to say that the United States would host the next TABD confer-

---

35. Brown quoted in Jeff Gerth, "Where Business Rules; Forging Global Regulations that Put Industry First," *The New York Times*, January 9, 1998, D1.

ence. The Americans knew that the US government was not prepared to underwrite such a meeting. "It was sort of funny," recalls Jackson. "When Ron Brown said 'We will host the conference,' he was not committing the Commerce Department. He was committing the US business community." It was agreed that the TABD would meet again the following year, but many executives were wary of creating yet another business organization. "A lot of the businesspeople didn't want to set up another institution— there were quite a few already," says European TABD director Stephen Johnston. The consensus was that the process should remain flexible.

An ongoing dialogue appealed to some members of the European Commission. There was a sense that continuing discussions could be an important element in reducing transatlantic trade tensions. According to Guidant's Michael Gropp:

> I think that there was an interest on the European side in trying to create some kind of forum that wouldn't replace the GATT process, but where there could be a less argumentative approach in trying to resolve issues and build some consensus in ways that didn't always lead to threats. The Europeans and the Japanese resented US trade policy and Super 301 threats. The European approach to these issues tends to be much less legalistic and much more one of consensus building. Partly that's a cultural issue; partly it is the way that progress is made in the European Union. In many cases, disputes are not settled through legal channels as they are in the US, but through diplomatic initiatives, through consensus-building mechanisms. This of course frustrates some in the US industry and government, because it's seen as slow and inefficient. But Europeans wonder if there isn't a way to create a forum where you can achieve consensus in a more collegial manner without resort to threat and law.

Returning to the United States, Trotman tasked his Washington staff with figuring out what needed to be done to follow up on the Seville recommendations. Jackson calls the moment "really wide open—it was a tremendous opportunity." On the European business side, there was a similar response. BASF's Strube asked his vice president of international trade, Ilsa Stübinger, to take charge of the day-to-day running of the TABD. As a result, a small TABD office was opened on each side of the Atlantic. Selina Jackson was hired as director in Washington and Stephen Johnston was named her counterpart in Brussels.[36] And so the Transatlantic Business Dialogue was born.

## The MRA Talks Gain Momentum . . . and Lose It

One month after the Seville conference, the MRA talks gathered new steam at the December 1995 US-EU Summit in Madrid, where US and EU presidents Clinton and Santer sought to expand transatlantic cooperation

---

36. Jackson had recently finished a graduate degree at Tufts University's Fletcher School of Law and Diplomacy; Johnston had worked at the European Commission.

through an initiative called the New Transatlantic Agenda (NTA). The inauguration of the NTA marked the first time that the United States recognized the European Union as a major political institution. The centerpiece of the NTA's economic component was a commitment to create a New Transatlantic Marketplace (which later evolved into the Transatlantic Economic Partnership, or TEP), to be achieved by "progressively reducing or eliminating barriers that hinder the flow of goods, services, and capital" across the Atlantic.[37] Among those barriers were technical standards.

A few months later, in March 1996, US officials announced that a breakthrough in the MRAs was imminent, touting it as the first substantial fruit of the TABD's launch in Seville.[38] But the announcement was premature: The MRA talks broke down when European negotiators rejected a US proposal to drop two sectors where progress was lagging—pharmaceuticals and medical devices—refusing to delink them from the other areas still under negotiation. "There had been a lot of discussion about this concept of unbundling, of separating out the sectors," Falkenberg explains:

> The Community had always said that these negotiations had to be a package, and that we would only conclude an MRA if there was an economic balance. That package for us included medical devices and pharmaceuticals because we are large exporters of those products, and because the obstacles we had identified in the US market because of the FDA were extremely burdensome, costly, and time-consuming. We needed those to be addressed.

### The Debate over Pharmaceuticals

The pharmaceutical MRA would apply not to certification—any new drug still had to meet FDA standards—but to *production* of the drug once it had been approved. The US Food, Drug, and Cosmetic Act of 1938 (amended in 1993) aims to ensure that pharmaceuticals are safe and efficacious—that they actually do what their labels claim. The Act also seeks to guarantee that they are made safely, through regulations that govern so-called good manufacturing practices. GMPs are based on the premise that finished-product testing does not suffice, and that safety and quality must be built into products during their manufacture (Horton 1998, 697). Foreign firms were expected to comply with the same product requirements and the same GMP regulations as US domestic firms.

Typically, a company that wanted to export pharmaceutical products would invite the importing country to inspect its plant; once the manu-

---

37. *The New Transatlantic Agenda,* adopted December 3, 1995 at the EU-US Summit in Madrid, Spain.

38. Eurowatch, "Transatlantic Dialogue Spurs Progress on Mutual Recognition," April 15, 1996.

facturing process was deemed appropriate, the drug's importation would be allowed. For example, Europeans might visit Puerto Rico to inspect a US manufacturer's plant, which would also be inspected by the FDA to ensure that it met US GMPs. "The problem," Peralta-Schulte explains, "is that the ways different countries perform these inspections are different. Industry gets caught in between." Charles Ludolph's assessment is similar: "It is not standards, but the practice of the inspections that are different. If Europe does one process and the US does another, a company often got caught in between as to what standards they ought to be applying on a practical basis."

European MRA negotiators argued that EU and US testing bodies had comparable competence. It seemed reasonable to hope that facilities in the United States could test a product to European standards, and vice versa. But the FDA saw the situation differently. "Generally speaking, the EU took the position that US regulatory systems were good and acceptable to them," says the FDA's Walter Batts.

> They were willing to accept our decisions on the marketability of products in return for us accepting their decisions. But from FDA's standpoint, we just couldn't accept that at all. We have a statutory requirement to review and approve certain products before they are marketed—including certain medical devices and pharmaceuticals. We can't delegate that authority to anyone else, to another government. We could not pursue an MRA on that basis.

FDA officials felt the need to educate US and European trade officials on the parameters of the Food, Drug, and Cosmetic Act, the central piece of legislation governing FDA operations. The agency wanted everyone to understand that any negotiations related to pharmaceuticals were constrained by the act's directives.

The FDA appeared to be in a tough position. As expanding international trade made growing demands on the agency, its resources had not increased comparably. Moreover, the problems of the FDA were symptomatic of a larger issue: conflicts caused by the distinct mission (and therefore the different priorities) of each federal agency. USTR and the Department of Commerce were pushing for MRAs as a trade issue. Meanwhile, the FDA insisted that inspections were regulatory matters that fell under its purview. The FCC and OSHA felt similarly about their sectors. And the State Department wanted a final say on any international pact.

As a result, European negotiators viewed the US government as unwilling to make any changes to its own procedures. This recalcitrance was especially frustrating in light of the US role in initiating the MRAs. As one European negotiator put it,

> The US was saying that mutual recognition within Europe was creating trade barriers against the US and therefore, please do something about it. When we said we would be prepared to do something about it, but it implied some change in US legislation, the answer was, "No, no, no, that was not the deal." The deal was that

Europe should just recognize US certification procedures, but without any reciprocity, without any change to US legislation. That has been a major problem. We have developed recognition within the European territory. We have said that we are prepared to modify legislation and to extend this recognition to third countries, but on a reciprocal basis. Therefore, we can only accept recognizing third-country testing if those countries are prepared to recognize Community testing. And that has been the major problem, most vociferously argued by FDA. But we had similar concerns voiced by FCC and OSHA, really by all the agencies we talked to.

Some negotiators felt that European regulators had a head start in the MRA process because of the European Commission's New Approach directives. In Falkenberg's judgment,

The underlying issue is that every regulatory authority believes that it's the only entity that can do a job properly. These bodies believe that the only safe products are those tested by the agency itself—every foreign body is unfit. That attitude existed in Europe as it exists in the US, or anywhere else. In Europe, the New Approach to recognition within the EU basically broke this monopoly. Member states were forced to recognize what their Portuguese, Spanish, British, Swedish, French, or other colleagues were doing. In the US, we were still up against a complete monopoly. There was only the FDA. There was only the FCC. Our regulators had been forced inside the Community to recognize that someone else could do as good a job as they could themselves. For the US, this negotiation was the first exposure to that kind of thinking.

After some negotiation, the European Commission asserted that a series of FDA proposals for a system of equivalency in pharmaceutical plant inspections failed to constitute true mutual recognition in practice or in spirit (Gopal 1997, 38). According to several US observers, DG Trade was in effect saying to the departments of Commerce and State and to USTR, "You folks need to tell the FDA that this is not the kind of agreement we are going to have." The disagreement over pharmaceuticals held up the talks in all the other sectors. "It was such a divisive issue and nobody was thinking very creatively," admits Peralta-Schulte. "Both governments were basically at a standstill."

In early January 1996, the State Department's Stuart Eizenstat wrote FDA Commissioner David Kessler that "the [European] Commission has made it clear in its negotiations and to me personally that without the US-EU agreement on pharmaceutical GMPs, the Commission is not prepared to commit to agreements in another 4 to 5 sectors. Therefore I would like to ask you to personally look at these negotiations to help move the whole MRA process forward."[39]

---

39. Quoted by Representative Ron Klink, Hearing before the House Subcommittee on Oversight and Investigations, *US-EU (European Union) Mutual Recognition Agreement on Drug Inspections*, 81.

## Narrowing the Agenda

By August 1996, Charles Ludolph had concluded that, in his words, "the MRA talks were severely wounded." He decided that he needed help to get them going again: "The European Commission wasn't getting what they wanted in pharmaceuticals and I think they were very confused about what their business community *wanted* them to get. So in August of 1996, I went to the TABD and said, 'These MRAs are going to die if I don't get direct help, participation, and support from the pharmaceutical industry. And TABD has got to orchestrate that.' "

The US pharmaceutical company Warner-Lambert was "very responsive," Ludolph says, and enlisted SmithKline Beecham to be the interlocutor on the European side. Both companies were members of the TABD. From August to November, the parties spent hours "in rooms arguing with each other" over the minimum that would benefit the pharmaceutical industry and the maximum that the FDA could give. "This was done at the expert level," Ludolph emphasizes. "The CEOs provided the strategic umbrella and overall focus." SmithKline Beecham and Warner-Lambert worked with other members of the pharmaceutical industry and with the trade association PhRMA (the Pharmaceutical Research and Manufacturers of America) to "help the European Commission and the FDA understand what the pharmaceutical industry needed at a minimum—what they couldn't walk away from the MRAs without." Ludolph adds, "It also gave an opportunity for the FDA and the European Commission to make their case directly to industry about what they were trying to get."

Industry representatives worked to focus the scope of the talks. "I think where we were effective was in helping to narrow the focus to two issues," says Warner-Lambert's Laura Peralta-Schulte. "Once they were resolved, the other issues fell in line." The two major issues were Good Manufacturing Practices and the public disclosure of inspection reports.

Manufacturing processes were actually subject to scrutiny at two points. The first was during the preapproval stage, when a pharmaceutical company was about to launch a new drug. As Peralta-Schulte notes, "A slowdown or miscommunication there can keep your product off the market until the issue has been resolved." The second point was post-approval: Once a product was on the market, the manufacturer might change the production process in some way.

The US government position was that negotiations should focus on postapproval and not preapproval inspections. The Europeans believed that both stages should be within the scope of the agreement, and were supported by the pharmaceutical industry. "From a company standpoint, most problems are in the preapproval period," explains Peralta-Schulte, "so to only focus on the postapproval stage and not on preapprovals, you are not solving the problem." Industry suggested that the negotiations be staggered to address postapproval first, and then preapproval.

The second sticking point in the pharmaceutical negotiations concerned not the timing of inspections but their publication. While the US Food, Drug, and Cosmetic Act required disclosure of inspection reports to the public, the European negotiators believed that it was inappropriate for certain documents to be made public. US pharmaceutical companies recognized that the FDA could not ignore its legislated mandate, and therefore the TABD pharmaceutical representatives saw their role as explaining the US government position to European business and the Commission. As one US pharmaceutical representative says,

> Europeans were coming at this from a place where there was not a thorough understanding of how important it was [in the United States] to maintain the Food, Drug, and Cosmetic Act. And quite frankly, that was the litmus test. We were not as an industry, or as the FDA, going forward to seek modifications to that act because any changes would take a lot of time. It was our theory that you could resolve these issues without going to that degree of activity.

Walter Batts sees the role of US industry in communicating the FDA's position to the European negotiators as important: "I think they were extremely helpful in that regard. They assisted the European Commission in understanding the US Constitution, FDA statutory authority, and the Food, Drug, and Cosmetic Act. [They also assisted the Commission in understanding] political reality in the US government. The US government cannot change its laws or policies on a whim."

In their efforts to move the talks forward, US pharmaceutical interests worked with several US agencies, but their major point of contact was the FDA. "Because the TABD process brought together various US departments and agencies, industry worked with the Commerce Department, USTR, the State Department, and numerous regulatory agencies," says Peralta-Schulte. "But no participant was more important than the FDA, because they were the ultimate decision maker on these issues."

## The Search for Consensus

Before August 1996 the TABD was keeping an eye on the MRA talks, but the negotiations weren't a priority. "It wasn't really until that four-month exercise—from August to November—that things really got pointed up," says Charles Ludolph. In October, Ludolph, the FDA's Batts, and a State Department official visited "virtually everyone in Europe involved in pharmaceutical MRAs," including the health ministries of many of the EU member states, numerous European trade associations, and a number of companies active in the TABD. Ludolph continues, "By November 3, everybody in the business knew what the stakes were in the MRA and we brought the issues to their attention. At the same time, Warner-Lambert and SmithKline Beecham were getting companies to realize how important this was to their overall commercial agenda with US regulators."

Some MRA participants say it was this broader agenda with regulators that convinced pharmaceutical companies to exert effort on the MRA negotiations. One explains,

> Mainly, they felt no matter how small the actual MRA was—because it only covered GMPs, which are a very small part of the total drug approval process—just getting the two regulatory communities to be exposed to each other's procedures, and to be formally reporting to each other and exchanging information, was a huge accomplishment. Their goal was to get this improved dialogue between the two regulatory communities. And MRAs helped that. And so that's why they were so willing to put so much into it.

As noted above, the medical device industry also had broader goals for participating in the MRAs: encouraging reform at the FDA. As one industry representative remembers:

> FDA's position was "We are the gold standard." We could sit there and talk all day to them, saying, "How come you have 600 employees in the Office of Device Evaluation and it takes you five years to approve a device that's been on the market for three years in Europe and there's no evidence of safety problems?" But FDA really didn't move until the trade agencies and other senior US officials, as well as the Europeans, began to put concerted pressure on them.

But industry's hopes to keep pharmaceuticals and medical devices in the talks did not mean that its goals coincided with those of the European Commission. "The US industry had a slightly different interest," notes DG Trade's Falkenberg:

> They were trying to effectively modernize FDA procedures through these MRAs, which was not necessarily what we wanted. We were not opposed to that, and we still favor that the FDA would review some of their burdensome procedures. But there was a bit of a danger for the negotiations because obviously it is much more difficult to modify existing domestic legislation than to seek recognition that a body in Europe could carry out existing procedures. Therefore, we were not necessarily supportive of these tactics.

Challenges persisted in other sectors as well. European negotiators were particularly dissatisfied with the negotiations on electrical safety. That issue was often bundled with the telecom and EMC sectors "because most of the products that are subject to legislation in one area are also subject to legislation in the other areas," according to DG Enterprise's Mattinò. But European negotiators felt they had no leverage in electrical safety. As Mattinò puts it,

> US manufacturers already had full market access in Europe because they didn't have to submit their products for certification to an independent organization. They could certify themselves, which meant they had direct responsibility and minor costs. What we wanted was to break what is regarded in Europe as the US monopoly by Underwriters Laboratories [UL]. We said to the US, "If you don't accept terms we can live with in electrical safety, we will never accept the conclusion

of EMC or telecom." But the EU and US telecom industries were so successful in lobbying they put pressure to conclude EMC and telecom. So from the perspective of a negotiation, we didn't have anything to offer. We didn't have any leverage.

At the same time, the negotiations over telecom were progressing more smoothly. The US Telecom Industry Association's MRA task force met regularly with the two European telecom industry associations, ECTEL and EUROBIT.[40] "We held those joint meetings so that US and European industry were on the same page," recalls Lucent's Global Public Affairs Director Joanne Wilson. The TIA also worked with the US government on the substance of the agreement.

Of particular concern to industry were restrictive rules of origin. As Wilson notes, "We wanted the agreement to be strictly about conformity assessment, and not include issues related to where the product was sourced from, because we're all global companies. So we were adamant about that. We wanted all parts of a piece of equipment to be covered under the scope of the agreement." The Commission took the opposite position, initially seeking an agreement that would specify where a product could be manufactured. US negotiators attribute this stance to a hope of encouraging more manufacturing in Europe. In any case, the European telecom industry agreed with the US position that there should be no restrictions based on rules of origin. "The fact that the US [government] held a hard line on that issue and succeeded in keeping it out of the agreement is because the US and European industry made it very clear that it was a problem," said one representative of the US telecom industry.

US industry representatives note that they and their European counterparts had different relationships with government. As one telecom industry executive observes,

> We worked very closely with Commerce and USTR. They'd let us know how things were going in terms of their negotiations, the sticking points and so forth. We would give them feedback on our views, and the important points that we wanted them to dig their heels in on. We also shared with them areas where we could find some flexibility. It would have been easier had there been a closer working relationship between the Commission and companies in Europe. . . . The problem in general on the European side is that the Commission is not as easily influenced by industry. Because the Commission is appointed, they have much more autonomy [than the US government]. It is easier for the Commission to take positions that industry opposes than it is for the US government to do the same thing. I also think Europeans have a much more programmatic approach that expects more management by government of industry.

---

40. ECTEL is the Association of the European Telecommunications and Professional Electronics Industry. EUROBIT is the European Association of Manufacturers of Business Machines and Information Technology Industry.

## The Chicago Breakthrough

While discussions continued in the various MRA sectors, the TABD was looking for a site—and, more specifically, a local organization that would help with expenses—for its next conference. The task fell to Alex Trotman and Ford's Washington office, and the Chicago Executive Club agreed to host the November 1996 meeting. As the conference approached, some believed that movement on the MRA talks had become the true test of the TABD's utility. "Breaking the long-standing MRA impasse has emerged as the clearest test of the TABD's potential to be a true catalyst for free and unregulated trade and investment, rather than simply a forum to discuss issues," declared one observer.[41] As a result, according to USTR's Ralph Ives, "the TABD really dramatized the importance of the MRA. Basically, what the TABD was saying was, 'Look, we're a new organization. You, the government, encouraged us to do this. We haven't seen a lot of results for our efforts and we're putting in high-priced help here, CEOs of large companies. The MRA is a symbol for whether there is any utility to going to these meetings.'"

Nearly 70 CEOs from a cross section of American and European companies attended the Chicago conference, led by cochairs Alex Trotman and Simon DeBree, CEO of the Dutch petrochemicals firm DSM. Participants included Chrysler, Warner-Lambert, Xerox, and Sara Lee, as well as small and medium-sized businesses. Among the European participants were Ericsson, Daimler-Benz, Pirelli, and Pechiney (Breitfelder 1996, 22). Although the Chicago TABD meeting attracted more business representatives than did the first meeting in Seville, some European business leaders remained unconvinced of the forum's efficacy. "The people in Seville by and large came back," says European TABD director Stephen Johnston. "But a number of other European CEOs were still cautious. There was still a feeling that this was new and untested. And we weren't quite sure whether it was legitimate. Nobody wants to be caught out." The CEOs that did attend were particularly interested in the opportunity to speak face-to-face with government representatives.

Indeed, many participants remarked on the presence of high-level officials from the US government and the Commission. Mickey Kantor, who became commerce secretary after Ron Brown's death in an airplane crash, led the US delegation. On the European side, two commissioners, Sir Leon Brittan and Dr. Martin Bangemann, were in attendance. As Ives notes, "If you expect CEOs to be someplace, you have to expect cabinet-level officers to be at those meetings." Government, according to a TABD

---

41. "With No MRAs in Sight, TABD Participants Prepare for Second Annual Meeting," *Eurowatch* 8, November 1, 1996.

participant, had "a slight feeling of responsibility [for the TABD] because they had started it."

Some analysts have observed that TABD involvement both raised the profile of the European Commission and provided the institution with information it could not otherwise have attained. The European member states did not play an active role in the TABD, and the Commission preferred it that way. One observer comments,

> On the European side, there was always the issue that the Commission was not government, that they were not elected but the administrative arm of the common European institutions. The TABD raised the profile of Commission trade negotiations by giving them first-class information about what European business was asking for. It was useful to the Commission to be able to say to the member states, "We have a rather powerful, influential group of business people who want this agreement."

Falkenberg echoes these sentiments: "The Commission welcomed the opportunity to speak with CEOs very much. It's the member States who reacted jealously because it's clear that direct contact between the Commission and individual national industrial interests weakened the position of the member states in the 133 and council advisory procedures. [Contact with industry] gave the Commission direct information that was otherwise filtered through the national administrations."

A breakthrough on the MRAs came about on the second day of the conference, during the "Chairmen's Breakfast." The breakfast included the CEOs chairing the conference, the CEOs who would chair the following year, and key cabinet-level government officials. After some discussion, the group moved from the breakfast into the pharmaceutical breakout session. There Kantor, Brittan, and Bangemann joined several pharmaceutical industry CEOs—Warner-Lambert's Lodewijk de Vink, Smith-Kline Beecham's Jan Leschly, and Glaxo Wellcome's Robert Ingram. Also present were the chief negotiators of the MRAs from Commerce, USTR, and DG Trade and regulators from the FDA and DG Enterprise. When Commerce Secretary Kantor walked into the room he reportedly said, "We're going to make this happen. Let's get this thing finished."

The pharmaceutical industry understood that other sectors—especially telecom—were willing to throw pharmaceuticals overboard in order to reach an agreement. This understanding brought industry representatives to the table eager to work things out. On the subject of the pre- and post-approval of good manufacturing processes, one observer characterized US industry as "very supportive of the European position" that the agreement cover both. But the FDA continued to resist an agreement that addressed preapproval processes. In the end, negotiators decided to focus only on postapproval. Peralta-Schulte explains why industry conceded on this point: "The industry had to take a pragmatic standpoint. There is a cultural difference between government and industry. Industry lives by deliverables, what can be accomplished in the near term. In working with government, however, we are often forced to accept incremental victories."

On the second major stumbling block, the Commission declared that it could not support public disclosure of plant inspection reports because the European business community wouldn't endorse it. But reportedly, the European CEOs of SmithKline Beecham and Glaxo Wellcome both contradicted this claim; in one observer's paraphrase, they responded, "No, it's OK. This is something we can live with." In fact, they insisted, the European pharmaceutical industry was not as sensitive on this issue as the European Commission imagined. "It was quite compelling," says one industry representative. "It is the difference between having someone unfamiliar with actual business practices articulate a point of view as opposed to someone who does this every day for a living."

This discussion led directly to an agreement in principle between the United States and the European Commission. Europe conceded on the disclosure of inspection reports. In return, the FDA agreed to carry out second inspections of EU pharmaceutical imports only in special circumstances (Gopal 1997, 38). "Once these issues were discussed, not in a broad manner, but coming down to the central issues of concern," says one observer, "you had reasonable people sitting together who could come to an agreement on how to move forward."

Commerce Secretary Kantor declared that the MRA talks would be completed by January 1997—only two months away. "Mickey loved to establish deadlines," says one observer. Though few saw this goal as reasonable, one participant asserts its importance: "For the first time, you had very high-level attention on the MRA negotiations." Ralph Ives, the USTR lead negotiator, agrees:

> For three or four years, the MRAs had been kind of floundering around, largely because nobody at high levels was paying attention to it. There were a lot of domestic political problems on both sides that people at my level just can't overcome. So once you had leaders from both the US and EC saying, "We want this done within the particular period of time," that gives a pretty good push. You know you're going to have to report to these leaders every six months at the summit. It put a lot of pressure on both sides, both the US and the EC side, to try to reach an agreement.

The agreement in principle was considered a major breakthrough— "really the highlight of the conference," says Johnston. One executive praised the effectiveness of the business-government session that advanced the MRAs, commenting that more real communication had taken place in two hours of dialogue than had occurred in the entire preceding year (Breitfelder 1996, 22). Another participant recalls Sir Leon Brittan telling the conference, "If business agrees on something on both sides of the Atlantic, it is up to the governments to say, 'Why can't it be implemented?' " But little is ever so simple. Charles Ludolph notes that the

TABD still was engaged in "making sure the consensus reached in Chicago was truly lived up to. And that was quite a job in itself. We still had several more months of negotiations where everyone was trying to slip out of that consensus."

## A Done Deal?

On December 16, 1996, at a press conference with Ireland's Prime Minister Bruton and EC President Santer, President Clinton announced that the transatlantic commitment to reduce trade barriers was paying off:

> Next month our negotiators will finish work on a set of mutual recognition agreements, which will abolish requirements that a broad range of products, including telecommunications and medical equipment, be reinspected and recertified for each other's markets. This will remove barriers on $40 billion worth of trade between the United States and the European Union, cutting red tape for our businesses and prices for our consumers. One standard, one test, one time.[42]

Of course, the MRAs did not establish "one standard, one test, one time," and some US negotiators were dismayed to hear these words. "Unfortunately he said it right after the US-EU Summit and it was not cleared with anybody," says one negotiator. "My European counterparts would play it back to me, but what could we say?" President Clinton also thanked the Transatlantic Business Dialogue for its leadership in the MRA process, and asked the European and American co-chairs—Jan Timmer, former chairman of the Philips Electronics Corporation, and Dana Mead, chairman of Tenneco—to stand and be recognized.

### To Create a Framework or Not to Create a Framework

Despite the president's announcement, EU and US negotiators missed their January 1997 deadline for agreeing on the MRA package. One emerging problem centered on the concept of an overarching framework or umbrella agreement for the MRAs. While some Commission negotiators strongly favored it, "The US said, 'We don't need a framework agreement, for God's sake,' " said one US negotiator. "We don't need this big structure.' But it became increasingly apparent to us that one reason the Europeans wanted this was largely for internal reasons—that is, to ensure that DG-1 [Trade] was in charge of all other DGs in the MRAs."

In the United States, a specific regulatory agency (the FDA, FCC, etc.) had jurisdiction over each sectoral annex. Similarly, various Directorates-General in the Commission had responsibility for their respective sectors.

---

42. Press conference by President Clinton, Prime Minister of Ireland John Bruton, and President of the European Commission Jacques Santer, December 16, 1996, Washington, DC.

A framework agreement would put DG Trade in charge of the overall MRA. "In fairness to the Commission," said one US participant, "there was probably a need for some type of a committee or structure to oversee all of this, particularly as you bundled more sectors into the package." But if DG Trade was in charge on the European side, then USTR would be in charge on the US side. And that idea, according to Ives, created a dilemma:

> The FDA has a much-deserved reputation as an independent regulatory authority, and this is something that the Europeans envy. It is an authority that has relatively little influence from outside trade or political influence. The downside of that for us, in negotiating something like the framework agreement, is FDA says, "Wait a minute. We have authority over regulating pharmaceutical products and medical devices, and you, USTR, can't speak for us." If you have a framework agreement where it's clear that USTR is in charge, of course USTR could say in a meeting with the EC, "FDA will change that regulation." But that carries absolutely no weight with FDA. I said to FDA, "It makes no sense that I would go into a meeting with the Europeans and say something that FDA won't support." But then it became largely a perception issue with the FDA and constituents, both on the Hill and public interest: does it look like USTR is speaking for FDA?

In addition, broader concerns were raised on the US side about the overall MRA effort. EPA officials organized a public hearing on the MRA to air worries about the agreement, though none of the sectors being negotiated were directly under its purview. Commerce's Charles Ludolph characterizes the EPA's efforts this way:

> It took four years to do this thing [the MRA] and nobody really believes that something that takes four years is actually going to happen. But toward the end, when everybody saw it was really going to happen, agencies came out of the woodwork trying to stop it or influence it. The EPA essentially undertook a campaign to disengage completely from the MRA. There is solidarity among regulators in the US government. They seem to have an unspoken agreement to try and keep about the same policy positions, in a general way. The effect was that, when EPA had a problem, all of a sudden people who had been on board for four years suddenly had a problem. It was a hard thing for me to absorb.

Ives says the hearing failed to meet the EPA's hopes because the public had little interest in the MRA negotiations and press coverage of the talks was sparse. As he describes it,

> EPA saw the MRA as being this evil monster that was subjecting environmental concerns to trade concerns. Something that for the life of me—and we went through numerous interagency meetings—I just could not understand. I really couldn't, because we assured FDA that there is nothing in this that was going to undermine their authority and we kept putting that in almost every other sentence of the MRA. But anyway, EPA had this public hearing, expecting that there would be a lot of public outcry. In fact, there was very little. There was just very little attendance. And very few call-in questions. So my point is, there has been throughout the process a number of attempts to elicit public comments, and there hasn't been a lot of public interest in it. Nevertheless, FDA has a legitimate concern that it does not want the perception that its regulatory authority is being subjected to trade concerns.

Another factor that prolonged the process, according to industry executives, was European "culture shock" at the initiative taken by the private sector. "The Europeans had enormous problems with industry sitting at the table," says telecom executive Vic Boersma of Nortel (quoted in Schick 1997, 18). European negotiators also balked at what they perceived to be the FDA's intransigence. "The EU understands what's at stake," said the Commission's Brittan. "Europe is prepared to go the last mile . . . but it is not prepared to become a sub-agency of the [US] Food and Drug Administration" (quoted in Journal of Commerce Staff 1997, 2A).

Finally, language surfaced as a problem. European negotiators insisted that the MRA be signed in all 11 official languages of the European Union. US negotiators countered that the agreement itself specified that the only authentic text was the English version. The Europeans agreed that the authentic MRA was in English, but remained adamant that all 11 versions had to be signed. US treaty lawyers refused to sign the 10 new versions until all were translated back into English and verified.

### The Final Push

Senior US administration officials decided to push forward on the MRAs before they stalled under the weight of bureaucratic resistance. In May 1997, Secretary of State Madeleine Albright called EU President Santer to say that the time had come to resolve the remaining issues. Later that month, at a ministerial meeting of the Organization for Economic Cooperation and Development in Paris, USTR Charlene Barshefsky met with European Commissioner Sir Leon Brittan, but they failed to resolve all the outstanding issues. The next day, Barshefsky and Brittan met again with Jeff Lang, Stuart Eizenstat, Charles Ludolph, and Ralph Ives. Brittan put a new proposal on the table, and the leaders finally agreed on a deal. As Ives tells it,

> This is where having high-level attention really helped. A combination of Jeff Lang and Stu Eizenstat calling various people—for example, the acting FDA commissioner at the time, Mike Friedman—and getting his staff involved in going through some of the new EC proposals. Then Charles Ludolph and I worked with FDA and came back with a counterproposal. The bottom line was: by the time we left Paris, over that three-day period, we had a text that both the US and EC negotiators could accept, and this was basically at the ministerial level. That meeting was a huge breakthrough.

The MRAs were initialed by all parties but not officially signed, because the translation-and-verification process still had to be completed. "This is a new way of doing business," said Barshefsky. "The MRA package is an important breakthrough in the US-EU trade agenda. We could not have achieved this package without the Transatlantic Business Dialogue." Sir

Leon Brittan of the European Commission added that the "massive red-tape-cutting" deal "will oil the wheels of transatlantic trade by cutting costs, shortening delays and reducing red tape in some of the most important sectors for the next century. With vital input from the TABD, it has assured that the US-EU relationship will bring real benefits to business and consumers."[43] But because the agreement wasn't signed, the game wasn't quite over yet.

In November, Congress overwhelmingly passed the Food and Drug Administration Modernization Act of 1997 (FDAMA) with the goal of "improv[ing] the regulation of food, drugs, devices, and biological products" (Public Law 105-115). The legislation, meant to speed the FDA's approval process for new drugs and medical devices, was the result of a three-year campaign by Republicans to reform the FDA. An attempt in 1996 to institute more sweeping changes had been blocked by Democrats. Health and Human Services Secretary Donna Shalala had threatened to recommend a presidential veto over provisions in the 1997 act on medical device approvals, but compromise language paved the way for President Clinton's approval. Senator Edward Kennedy (D-MA) praised the legislation as a victory for public health saying, "the health of the American people will be enhanced through faster availability of pharmaceutical drugs and medical devices."[44]

Among the FDAMA's provisions was a section on "mutual recognition agreements and global harmonization" (see appendix 7A) directing the FDA to support the efforts of Commerce and USTR to implement MRAs. The act also required that a plan be established within 180 days to achieve mutual recognition of pharmaceutical GMPs. Observers say that the inclusion of MRA language in the FDAMA was an important step toward finishing the agreement.

The FDAMA also made changes to the 1976 medical device amendments that also affected the MRAs—inadvertently. "Just as we were tying things up, of course, Murphy's law kicked in," jokes Charles Ludolph. As an unintended consequence of the law, four of the medical device products listed in the MRA could no longer be included (Horton 1998, 726). Negotiators were incredulous. "We had to amend the damned agreement," says Ludolph, even though the agreement had already gone through the language-verification process. "Because we had already translated it, bureaucratically no one could figure out how to amend it." But somehow the necessary changes were made.

---

43. Barshefsky and Brittan, quoted in "Transatlantic Business Dialogue Praises Conclusion of MRA," US Newswire, June 13, 1997.

44. Mark Suzman, "Compromises Pave Way for FDA Reform: New Law Is Widely Hailed as a Victory for US Public Health," *The Financial Times*, November 21, 1997, 7.

## The Agreement

The MRAs were signed on May 18, 1998, by USTR Charlene Barshefsky, Commerce Secretary William Daley, European Commission Vice President Sir Leon Brittan, and European Commissioner for Industry Martin Bangemann (see appendix 7B).[45] The six sectors covered in the agreements were telecommunications, medical devices, pharmaceuticals, electromagnetic compatibility services, electrical equipment, and recreational craft.

For pharmaceuticals, the MRA governed good manufacturing practices and the exchange of inspection reports. Though the FDA ultimately agreed to include preapproval as well as postapproval GMP inspections, the agency prevailed in its demand for a three-year transition period—rather than the 18 months requested by the Europeans—to determine which EU inspection processes would be deemed equivalent to its own. Once the MRA was implemented, the FDA and its EU counterparts would each inspect domestic production facilities and make sure they were in compliance with the regulations of the country to which they were exporting.

The agreement also provided for the exchange of product evaluation reports by third parties in the United States and the European Union under the existing FDA pilot program for selected medical devices. These reports would be accepted and used by the receiving regulatory authority.

On electrical safety, European negotiators were dissatisfied. Giacomo Mattinò remarks that political pressure forced a bad outcome and was "detrimental to reaching fair and unambiguous conclusions."

> At the negotiating level, we were having a number of serious difficulties in the electrical safety sector. An important point about the TABD is that—at the time of negotiation—the most successful industry in lobbying on the issue was the big telecommunication industry on both sides, EU and US. They created such pressure to conclude the telecom and EMC sectors that basically we had to conclude electrical safety even though the terms were not what we were expecting. I personally would not have signed an agreement according to those terms. Even if that implied delaying an agreement in EMC and telecom.

Other observers heralded the innovative and precedent-setting role of the TABD. Ellen Frost, a senior fellow at the Institute for International Economics, told the House Ways and Means Committee's Subcommittee on Trade: "This is the first time in the history of trade negotiations that a transnational business coalition has taken quite such a prominent and high-level initiative in defining an agenda of this kind. This makes sense

---

45. In 1998, the European Union comprised 15 countries: Austria, Belgium, Denmark, Finland, France, Germany, Greece, Ireland, Italy, Luxembourg, the Netherlands, Portugal, Spain, Sweden, and the United Kingdom.

because these companies are most familiar with real-life transatlantic trade and investment and can identify the barriers most readily."[46]

Some saw the TABD as part of an emerging trend, pointing out that with increased frequency, international trade initiatives are being spearheaded by business. Guidant's Michael Gropp comments:

> I think [the TABD] is a reflection of a phenomenon. More and more, it is business that drives these multilateral initiatives because it's business that is forced to confront the inefficiencies and the duplication, more than governments. If you think about FDA, they deal with issues that come to them in the US, but they don't deal day-to-day with the problems of moving medical devices into markets or introducing pharmaceuticals around the world. These initiatives become even more important in view of pressures in most societies to reduce the growth of health care costs for aging populations.

But some saw this trend—and the TABD—as worrying. Public Citizen's Global Trade Watch, a US nonprofit consumer organization, was alarmed by the role of business in the MRA talks. If business groups were involved in determining how their own products were certified, wouldn't compromises in health and safety inevitably follow? In response to such concerns, the Clinton administration assured the public that the MRA would not jeopardize the safety of American consumers. One administration official declared that the MRA "in no way undermines the capacity of US regulatory agencies to inspect or test where they feel the health or safety of the American people is concerned."[47]

TABD officials perceive these worries to be unfounded. "The dumbing-down of standards is not what we are about at all," says Selina Jackson, former director of the TABD. "The business community does not mind if there are high standards, they just want one standard. It is very difficult to conform to one standard in the United States and another in Europe. They would rather take the highest of standards, just as long as there is one. I am not sure consumer groups understand that." Some industry representatives also consider the suspicion of industry efforts a knee-jerk response, emphasizing that industry involvement was in fact necessary to reaching a final agreement. As Lucent's Joanne Wilson explains, "People think of lobbying as industry or interest groups just trying to have their way. But the reality is that those who are creating policy need to have an understanding of the implications of that policy in practice. It is a very valid and valuable process that industry plays to ensure that the policies are ones that are useful."

---

46. Frost, testimony before the House Subcommittee on Trade of the Ways and Means Committee, "New Transatlantic Agenda," 105th Congress, 1st session, July 23, 1997.

47. Dan Tarullo, assistant to the President for International Economic Affairs at the National Economic Council, White House press briefing, May 28, 1997.

The Commerce Department's Charles Ludolph sees no need to defend the idea of business and government working together, for such interactions are inevitable: "The US Commerce Department works with the business community. I would expect consumer groups to hope that the business community wouldn't be working with government, or vice versa. But in a democracy, in an open government, that is impossible to achieve. Every citizen, every interest group, has the right to work with the US government. If they don't want the government to talk to business anymore, that's clearly illegal."

But Public Citizen argued that while government was becoming more responsive to the concerns of business, it was becoming less responsive to the needs of consumers. For example, the White House had recently closed its Office of Consumer Affairs. In addition, even as government-initiated organizations like the TABD were being developed to improve dialogue with business, little effort had been made to include other constituencies, such as consumer and environmental groups, in discussions of international trade, Public Citizen noted. In response to such concerns, the Transatlantic Consumer Dialogue (TACD), an association of US and European consumer associations, was founded in September 1998.

Some business representatives claim that consumer groups could have been more active in the MRA process than they chose to be. "I don't remember any participation from consumer groups," says one pharmaceutical executive. "The FDA solicited public comment in the *Federal Register* and held hearings to seek input. The only thing I have seen from consumer groups has been post-MRA."

## Concerns in Congress

As the MRAs were being completed, further concerns were raised in the US Congress, particularly over the pharmaceutical annex. For three years, the House Commerce Committee's Subcommittee on Oversight and Investigations had been studying the FDA's program of inspecting foreign drugs. "The amount of pharmaceutical products being imported into the US was exploding," explains the senior oversight counsel of the subcommittee, Alan Slobodin, "and there were concerns about the safety of these products."[48]

In the summer of 1998, subcommittee staff traveled to Europe to meet with regulators and pharmaceutical industry representatives about the MRA. Staff members were trying to learn more about pharmaceutical GMP inspections in Europe. "We had very little information and we were trying to find some answers," says Slobodin. "No one seemed to know

---

48. Unless otherwise noted, all quotes from Alan Slobodin come from a 2000 interview with Charan Devereaux.

much about how these inspections took place. With 80 percent of the bulk pharmaceuticals used by US manufacturers being imported, this was a cause of great concern."

Soon after the trip, several ranking members of the subcommittee and the full committee—including Subcommittee Chair Joe Barton (R-TX), John Dingell (D-MI), Henry Waxman (D-CA), and Ron Klink (D-PA)—wrote to the FDA requesting more information about the MRAs. One observer called this letter, signed by John Dingell, "the Dingell-gram from Hell," since the FDA was not eager to be the subject of congressional investigation. In October 1998, the subcommittee convened a hearing titled "Imported Drugs: US-EU MRA on Drug Inspections." Opening the session, Chairman Joe Barton declared: "The Congress is open-minded about this MRA and we are very supportive of the FDA cooperating with foreign health authorities. However, this agreement raises serious questions that Congress must address. As my mentor Ronald Reagan has stated so elegantly regarding international relations, 'Trust, but verify.' "[49]

Committee members voiced their questions and concerns to Charles Ludolph, Ralph Ives, Walter Batts, and FDA Deputy Commissioner for External Affairs Sharon Smith Holston. "We are already experiencing a severe negative trade balance in drug products with the EU," asserted Commerce Committee Chairman Tom Bliley. "In the last six years, this trade balance has become over 24 times larger, amounting to a negative trade balance of $4 billion."

Waxman, coauthor of the 1984 Waxman-Hatch Act on pharmaceuticals, also expressed reservations. "There is no question that international agreements of this kind can enhance the efficiency of commerce. But it is equally clear that they can potentially depress American health and safety standards." Klink ruminated,

> It only makes sense to reduce the number of duplicative inspections and processes that manufacturers have to go through to get their products on the market. But . . . during the negotiations, I fear that the FDA—the agency most responsible for protecting the health and safety of our citizens—may have been reduced to a large poker chip in a game of high stakes trade worth tens of billions of dollars.

Along those lines, one committee member read an internal FDA e-mail in which a former member of the FDA's MRA negotiation team suggested that the agency should consider withdrawing from the talks.

Some observers and participants saw the congressional hearing as proof that the US political process was working—that federal agencies were held accountable and asked to explain their reasoning and decisions.

---

49. All quotations from House members in this passage are drawn from the Hearing before the House Subcommittee on Oversight and Investigations of the Committee on Commerce, "US-EU (European Union) Mutual Recognition Agreement on Drug Inspections" October 2, 1998.

In the end, the MRA remained intact, though the subcommittee asked the General Accounting Office (GAO)—now the Government Accountability Office—to keep it informed on the FDA's progress in devising a means to assess the EU GMPs. According to the GAO's John Hansen,

> The biggest concerns were what criteria FDA was going to use to measure equivalency, and how those criteria were going to be applied to the respective inspection programs of each of the EU member states. What the FDA was telling Congress was very general. In order to learn more about FDA's plans, members of Congress asked us to look into how FDA intended to implement the MRA in more detail.[50]

Though an agreement had been signed, the story clearly was not over.

## Implementation

Negotiation of the MRAs was just the beginning of the process—next came implementation. Many issues required further discussions to determine their terms. "The tough issues in negotiation became the tough issues in implementation," says Lucent's Joanne Wilson. Some called the negotiation of the MRA elementary compared to the challenge of implementing the agreement. According to DG Enterprise's Giacomo Mattinò, "The MRA often implies regulatory changes that the responsible parties on the internal front are not always ready to put in place, have not conceded to, or did not expect would come so quickly. I think some have been taken by surprise." Another negotiator says, only half-joking, "It's never over. As far as I'm concerned, we will have to be vigilant the rest of our lives."

Events in Europe during the MRA negotiations had underscored the importance of protecting public safety, heightening public awareness of controversies over trade and public health. A Commission official explains:

> In Europe there's been a series of problems—for example the mad cow experience, the problem in Belgium with Coke—that attracted the attention of the wide public, pointing out how particular attention should be given to protecting public safety. GMOs [genetically modified organisms] and the beef hormone case can also be seen in the same perspective. On one hand there is trade liberalization, and on the other hand the fact that public safety must be safeguarded appropriately. We are trying to promote an appropriate approach to those issues with the ultimate objective of overall deregulation. But again, not deregulation just for the sake of deregulation.

Though some concerns about health and safety were legitimate, regulators were keenly aware of the frequent use of standards and certification

---

50. Unless otherwise noted, all quotes from John Hansen come from a 2000 interview with Charan Devereaux.

as trade barriers. As a European Commission staff member notes, "conformity assessment has traditionally been used everywhere as an instrument for each state to be somewhat protectionist."

The ultimate long-term relevance of the MRAs was also debated. Some, including Michael Gropp, saw the MRAs as a step along the way toward further harmonization of standards:

> My view is that the work of the Global Harmonization Task Force will eventually eclipse MRAs, but that's a long time down the road. In my mind, the bigger game and the better outcome would be harmonization, not a growing web of bilateral MRAs, because they become difficult to manage. I think that five to ten years out, we could have harmonization in the leading markets in the world, and maybe even some of the smaller markets. If that's the case, then I expect that the MRAs would essentially drop by the wayside as being superfluous.

The suggestion that MRAs were a temporary fix raised concerns that too great a proportion of scarce regulatory agency resources were being devoted to a project that might have limited use. Others worried that perceived lack of success in negotiating and implementing MRAs might jeopardize future international agreements on regulatory issues. One negotiator gave voice to that view: "They say, 'after all, MRAs are a little part of a bigger idea. If this little part is not successful then why should we try for a more ambitious one?'" Finally, some suggested that success in implementing the MRAs could make future regulatory reform more difficult. Charles Ludolph explains, "One of the criticisms which has been said of the MRAs is that they tend to freeze the regulatory situation of each party instead of pushing them to change. If you accept my legislation as such and I accept yours, then probably we don't have an interest in changing anything in the future."

Though disagreement over these broad questions remained, implementation was under way. The telecommunications section of the MRAs took effect in December 2000, as planned, and the US-EU MRA became the pattern for future telecom agreements. The US industry later entered into MRAs with the 17 nations of APEC and then with the Inter-American Commission of Telecommunications. "The real benefit was not so much the agreement itself, it was the process," says one industry official. "It became a model. What's happening in various countries—not just in Europe, but around the world—is that the regulatory agencies are changing their product approval programs to accommodate the MRAs."

Other sectors did not enjoy such obvious success. The three-year confidence-building period for the medical device sector of the MRAs began in December 1998. Industry continued to hope that the United States and Europe would agree to a joint implementation plan with action steps and benchmarks. "You may have an agreement signed," says Bernie Liebler, HIMA's director of technology and regulatory affairs, "but until you actually have a plan, it's difficult to move forward."[51] For example, when it began conducting routine European inspections in 1999, the FDA asked medical device companies if they wanted to include a European Conformity Assessment Body (CAB) as part of the MRA process. When Europeans wondered how the FDA could move forward with joint audits in the absence of a joint implementation plan, the FDA countered that it was just trying to move forward. "There's been some miscommunication," admits Liebler. "As a result, the process has been slow to get under way." The United States and the European Union therefore agreed to defer implementation in the medical device sector until November 2003.

The biggest problems in implementing the MRAs arose in the electrical safety and pharmaceutical sectors. In a letter to USTR Charlene Barshefsky written in October 2000, EU Trade Commissioner Pascal Lamy accused the United States of "being hardly within the letter and even less in accordance with the cooperative spirit of the MRA." Efforts to implement the agreement were "drifting dangerously," he wrote.[52] The European Union believed that US regulatory agencies—particularly OSHA and the FDA—were undermining the deal by refusing to recognize European product safety testing as equivalent to tests in the United States. Some business leaders were especially frustrated by the holdup because they had made the MRAs a top priority. In a document presented to both EU and US governments, the TABD noted that failure to implement the MRAs by the December 2000 deadline "will have far-reaching negative consequences for both the governments and industry. . . . Full implementation of the agreement is essential to maintain the credibility of these processes and future EU-US trade negotiations" (TABD 2000, 23). The TABD called on the governments to apply the group's objective of "Approved Once, Accepted Everywhere" (TABD 2001, 4).

OSHA maintained that it had sole authority to determine whether EU electrical safety inspection labs met US standards. The European Union disagreed, arguing that authorities in the 15 member states should certify these European labs. Three European testing laboratories went ahead and applied directly to OSHA for approval to certify products for the US market; two of these applications received no consideration because they were made in French and Spanish, not English. "We are a domestic health and safety agency," said Steven Witt, the director of technical support at

---

51. Unless otherwise noted, all quotes from Bernie Liebler are from a 2000 interview with the author.

52. Pascal Lamy, letter to US Trade Representative Charlene Barshefsky, October 20, 2000; reprinted in *Inside US Trade*, November 10, 2000.

OSHA. "We don't do translations."[53] In the pharmaceutical sector, the European Union proposed extending the implementation period for the pharmaceutical GMPs annex to 2003, but the FDA was hesitant to set any firm deadline. EU officials also considered increasing the pressure on the US government by suspending or terminating portions of the MRAs (such as the telecom agreement) that were of key interest to US industry.

Ultimately, the European Union withdrew entirely from participation in the MRA electrical safety agreement when the European Council suspended the annex in January 2003. The impasse over implementing the MRA's pharmaceutical annex continued as well. As a result, some characterized the MRAs as a failure. "The efforts that we've made to date—the MRA process for example—are, I think, failures or seen as failures by authorities and the business community," said Jean-François Boittin, minister for economic and commercial affairs at the French embassy in Washington. According to Boittin, the lack of progress showed that the United States and European Union had failed to find "the right framework" for discussing and resolving regulatory issues in a way that facilitates trade.[54]

Not all officials shared his assessment. Assistant USTR for Europe and the Mediterranean Cathy Novelli observed that although the United States and European Union "have not figured out all the pieces" of solving regulatory problems, "to me, that doesn't mean we simply cease and desist and say this is a failure. . . . I take a less dim view of the efforts we've had to date, because we are trying to work our way through this difficult period." She suggested that progress on regulatory issues tends to be slow: "For now at least, we are doomed to incrementalism in terms of thinking about this."[55] Perhaps the most important aspect of the MRA process, some said, was learning more about the other side. As Mattinò notes,

> I would say a good half of the negotiating process was spent exchanging information. This is one of the good things that came out of the MRA. It made an incredible contribution, surprisingly, to a better understanding between the regulatory communities. I say it's surprising because I'm surprised myself that people didn't have the chance to get more familiar with procedures in different countries before. But in fact it is the truth that the MRAs have greatly contributed to the experts at the same level from each side of the Atlantic talking to each other. In the end this will hopefully lead us to greater confidence in each other.

---

53. Witt, quoted in Edward Alden, "Mismatch on Product Safety Puts Accord on Danger List: The European Union Is Accusing the US of Undermining Their Deal on Mutual Recognition of Tests and Standards," *The Financial Times*, November 9, 2000, 23.

54. Boittin, quoted in "US, EU Seek Way Ahead on Stalled Regulatory Cooperation Agenda," *Inside US Trade*, March 21, 2003.

55. Novelli, quoted in "US, EU Seek Way Ahead."

Despite their setbacks in dealing with pharmaceutical good manufacturing practices, medical devices, and electrical safety, at a June 2003 summit meeting the United States and European Union agreed to regulatory cooperation in five more areas: cosmetics, automotive safety, nutritional labeling, food additives, and metrology. European officials characterized the agreement as involving no detailed commitment on any particular regulation, serving instead as a promise to cooperate on new regulatory issues and to look for ways to coordinate rule making between US and EU agencies.[56] In February 2004, the United States and the European Union signed an MRA on marine safety equipment covering $150 million to $200 million annually in two-way trade. "Regulatory cooperation between us is the way forward to foster trade and investment," said the Commission's Pascal Lamy.[57]

## Negotiation Analysis of the Case

When the MRA talks are viewed through the lens of negotiation analysis, it is clear why they proved to be so challenging. The rationale for pursuing MRAs is easy to understand: Companies were often forced to retest their products in different countries to similar standards, a costly and time-consuming requirement. But when the process of international trade met the process of domestic regulation and certification, challenges inevitably arose. In the MRA talks, US and European officials confronted unprecedented institutional issues. Government regulatory agencies, ordinarily uninvolved in trade discussions, became central players. Their involvement complicated the negotiations, for their primary mission was to protect public safety, not to facilitate trade. The reluctance of some FDA officials to participate in the process was an obvious sign of this tension. One lesson that can be drawn from the MRA story is that new issues in trade necessarily draw new players into trade negotiations, leading to new complexities in the negotiating dynamic.

In the face of such challenges, participants in the MRA talks sought to advance the negotiations by engaging in a number of classic game-changing moves. One such move was the creation of the Transatlantic Business Dialogue (TABD). By leveraging this unofficial negotiating forum, business and government representatives were able to move the official MRA negotiations forward. The MRA talks can also be seen as part of a longer-term strategy of certain export industries to achieve greater harmonization in international standards and to increase pressure on domestic US regulatory agencies (notably the FDA, the FCC, and OSHA) to change how they regulate their sectors.

---

56. "Lamy Spells Out Areas for US-EU Regulatory Cooperation," *Inside US Trade*, June 20, 2003.

57. Lamy quoted in European Commission press release no. 33/04, "EU-US Sign Mutual Recognition Agreement on Marine Equipment," February 27, 2004.

## Element #1: Organizing to Influence

The evolution of the MRA negotiations was strongly shaped by two initiatives originating in the US Commerce Department. The first effort, spearheaded by Charles Ludolph in 1987, supported and launched MRA negotiations between the United States and Europe. Anticipating the impact of the introduction of CE marks by the European Union, Ludolph and his interagency working group surveyed US industries to gauge interest in negotiating MRAs. When a critical mass of industry sectors expressed support, Ludolph initiated a dialogue with the European Commission that eventually led to the MRA negotiations. He also created supporting business advisory groups for each industry sector.

The second MRA organizing effort, begun in 1994, resulted in the creation of the TABD. The brainchild of Commerce Secretary Ron Brown, the concept of the TABD initially met with a cool response from EC officials, who wanted evidence of interest on the part of European business. Secretary Brown and his staff involved the European Commission by convincing the EC to undertake a joint survey of European and US business interest in the idea. Positive results and subsequent success in engaging business leaders on both sides of the Atlantic led to the first TABD event in Seville.

## Element #2: Selecting the Forum

Arguably the most interesting aspect of the MRA case, like the Multilateral Agreement on Investment (MAI) case, is the effort to create a new negotiating forum. A key difference, of course, is that the MRA negotiations ended in an agreement (though tenuous in some sectors), in part because the TABD forum played a constructive role in helping the negotiators to overcome significant barriers to reaching a deal.

The TABD is an example of a particular type of game-changing move: the use of "track two" diplomacy. The creation of a parallel forum allowed informal discussions to take place that helped advance the formal negotiations. Because the TABD's status as an MRA negotiating forum was unofficial, the key parties could talk without the pressure of committing themselves to specific positions. The TABD forum also provided government negotiators with an important channel for learning about business perspectives on standards issues. This learning function was especially helpful in Europe, where businesses had traditionally worked with national governments, not the Commission. Through the TABD, European business and EC officials could communicate directly.

The case also illustrates the implications for regulatory agencies of negotiating standards and certification issues in a multisector trade forum. Before the MRA negotiations began, the FDA was engaged in focused bilateral talks with Europe's DG Enterprise to complete a memorandum of understanding that would have committed EU countries exporting drugs to the United States to meet FDA standards. But because the MRAs superseded the MOU process, the FDA was pulled into a new negotiating forum, where multiple sectors were being dealt with in the context of a broader trade relationship. The parallel negotiations made cross-sector trades feasible—a possibility that understandably made the issue-focused US regulatory authorities quite nervous.

Moreover, the involvement of the FDA in the MRA negotiating forum advanced the interests of the medical device industry. The US industry preferred the European regulatory process, which it found less costly and time-consuming than the FDA's. By broadening awareness of the differences in the two systems, the MRAs helped to create pressure within the US government to reform the regulation of medical devices.

### Element #3: Shaping the Agenda

Rather than seek a broad agreement to completely harmonize regulatory standards, a goal that they realized was probably unreachable, the organizers of the MRA negotiations decided to focus narrowly on mutual recognition. By concentrating on the modest objective of recognizing each other's testing and certification processes, the negotiators had a fighting chance of finding a zone of agreement. The deal structure also established precedents that would help to create momentum toward future regulatory agreements.

European and US officials engaged in "prenegotiations" over which industry sectors would be included in the talks. Negotiators sought to identify a package of sectors that both represented a reasonable aggregate balance of trade between the United States and European Union and provided sufficient potential for creating value through cross-sectoral trades. The US telecommunications industry was very interested in negotiating an MRA with Europe, for example, but European Commission officials refused to include telecom unless pharmaceuticals, medical devices, and electrical safety (strong export industries for Europe) were added to the package. The United States agreed to include these sectors, in part because the US pharmaceutical and medical devices industries believed that they could advance their own agendas through negotiating an MRA. In this way, mutually beneficial trades shaped the agenda.

Negotiators also made the important decision to narrow the agenda when disagreement in the pharmaceutical sector threatened to derail the whole process in 1996. When the FDA objected to preapproval inspections of pharmaceutical manufacturing processes, the MRA negotiators— believing that an agreement, however modest, that advanced the harmonization agenda was key—avoided breakdown by agreeing to focus only on postapproval inspections. In fact, the FDA eventually accepted preapproval inspections.

Finally, the parties needed to decide whether the MRAs should be placed into a broader, longer-term negotiation framework. After initially opposing such a framework, which might seem to confirm the perception that the trade agencies were "in charge" of the regulatory agencies, US negotiators realized that the real issue was intra-European bureaucratic politics. DG Trade was trying to solidify its control over the other EC directorates-general in the administration of the MRAs. Its maneuvers, as well as the FDA's discomfort with domestic regulatory issues being moved onto the trade agenda, illustrate how government bureaucracies incorporate agenda setting into their efforts to win internal competitions for policymaking influence.

## Element #4: Building Coalitions

The organizers of the TABD sought to support the MRA process by fostering coalition building between US and European businesses. Traditionally, the US and EU business communities had influenced trade negotiations by cooperating on an ad hoc, issue-specific basis (as seen, for example, in the case of the Agreement on Trade-Related Aspects of Intellectual Property Rights). The TABD provided a new institutional structure that broadened and formalized transatlantic business cooperation (see figure 7.1).

The TABD also provided a forum for direct dialogue between European business and the European Commission. Through the TABD, business interests could explore common interests and better educate negotiators on their positions. For example, European negotiators initially believed they were acting in the interests of their pharmaceutical companies by demanding that plant inspection reports remain confidential; but when direct dialogue between US and EU CEOs and government officials revealed it to be a nonissue, the roadblock in the pharmaceutical negotiations was removed.

## Element #5: Leveraging Linkages

As illustrated in figure 7.2, the MRA negotiations were linked to a number of prior sets of talks. These included the negotiations in Europe that created the CE marking process in 1985 and an agreement between US and German telecommunications companies. The efforts of companies to negotiate common positions in forums such as the International Conference on Harmonization (for the pharmaceutical industry) and the Global Harmonization Task Force (for the medical device industry) also helped to shape the MRA negotiations.

**Figure 7.1   The TABD and coalitions in transatlantic trade
            negotiation**

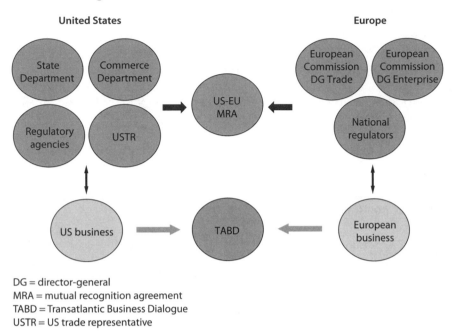

DG = director-general
MRA = mutual recognition agreement
TABD = Transatlantic Business Dialogue
USTR = US trade representative

The negotiators also were bargaining in the shadow of future talks. They knew that an MRA would establish important precedents for reaching future bilateral agreements on standards. In fact, the US-EU MRA in the telecommunications sector became the template for later agreements both between the United States and APEC and between the United States and the Inter-American Commission of Telecommunications.

In addition, the MRA negotiations set the stage for subsequent (and problematic) linked negotiations over the agreement's implementation. Difficulties were especially acute in electrical safety and pharmaceuticals. When negotiations over the rules are problematic, it should come as no surprise if negotiations over implementation are equally fraught with difficulty.

## Element #6: Playing the Frame Game

While framing played a limited role in the MRA negotiations, there are some notable examples of the use of this tactic. One is found in the argument that the talks were an important step in creating momentum in the direction of harmonization of standards, which helped to increase the support of pharmaceutical companies for the MRA negotiations. Another

### Figure 7.2 Linkages in MRA negotiations

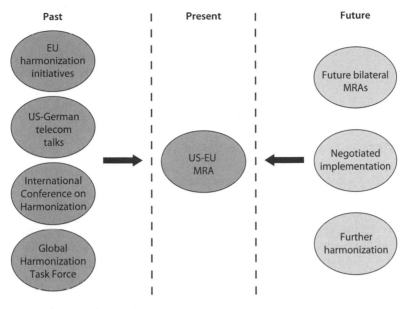

MRA = mutual recognition agreement

is Ron Brown's statement, "We should put the business 'horse' before the government 'cart,' " which framed business as playing a central role in the process.

The EPA tried to play the frame game at the end of the process by holding a public hearing intended to undermine the MRA process. But it didn't work. Some in Congress, with similar lack of success, tried to frame the agreement as threatening the integrity of domestic regulation. Perhaps the technical nature of the negotiations provided opponents with limited raw material to create a compelling frame, or perhaps those opponents were somewhat lacking in focus or creativity.

## Element #7: Creating Momentum

In both Europe and the United States, action-forcing events created momentum in the MRA negotiating process. The European Union's move to create new pan-European standards and testing procedures, the CE marks, together with its prohibition on non-European testing organizations, spurred US interest in negotiating MRAs. The negotiations showed limited movement until 1994, however. The Europeans felt little urgency, because the first standard on electromagnetic compatibility would not come into force until 1995. The deadline for implementing that standard, another action-forcing event, eventually goaded the European side into action; they had to initiate talks with the United States in a timely manner or face the likelihood of a US challenge at the WTO.

The Commerce Department skillfully used surveys as action-forcing events that progressively pushed MRAs onto the trade negotiation agenda—an example of step-by-step involvement. Charles Ludolph's early survey of US businesses regarding the US-EU trade relationship clearly identified regulation as their biggest concern. The survey also demonstrated that many sectors had substantial interest in pursuing an MRA. The joint survey of US and EU businesses undertaken by the Commerce Department and the European Commission likewise proved a potent tool for establishing a critical mass of support to create the TABD.

As the negotiations progressed, key meetings of TABD and high-level government officials helped to maintain momentum. After the negotiations in the pharmaceutical sector bogged down in 1996, for example, the TABD meeting in November was instrumental in achieving a breakthrough. Similarly, the final high-level meetings between USTR Charlene Barshefsky and European Commissioner Sir Leon Brittan facilitated high-level agreement on some remaining difficult issues, while at the same time spurring the bureaucracies on both sides to bring the process to closure.

The FDA unsuccessfully tried to slow momentum by arguing that the Food, Drug, and Cosmetic Act constrained what it could agree to. This argument was undercut when Congress included provisions in the FDA Modernization Act of 1997 that directed the FDA to support the MRAs. The act also gave the FDA a 180-day deadline for presenting a plan to achieve mutual recognition of good manufacturing practices inspections.

Though enough momentum was created to successfully reach agreement, some was lost in the MRA implementation phase, as seen in the European Union's decision to cancel altogether its participation in the electrical safety sector. Struggles over implementation might indicate that more guidelines, deadlines, and high-level government participation in the negotiations are needed to ensure follow-through.

## Conclusion

Reaching an agreement is by no means the end of the story: Further talks are necessary to bring an agreement into force. As noted above, while the US administration was successful in garnering support for the MRAs, significant problems emerged in implementing their terms. Challenges in implementing the MRAs were principally due to continuing (and understandable) reluctance in the US regulatory agencies to recognize European safety standards and testing as equivalent to those of the United States. Some believed that the MRAs required too much too soon. To repeat the words of one European negotiator, "The MRA often implies regulatory changes that the responsible parties on the internal front are not always ready to put in place, have not conceded to, or did not expect would come so quickly." Though the prospects for full implementation remain unclear, the MRAs are one link in a larger ongoing process of dealing with the significant challenges of domestic regulation in a globalizing economy.

# Appendix 7A
## Excerpt from the FDA Modernization Act of 1997
## Section 410: Provisions for Mutual Recognition Agreements and Global Harmonization

(c)(1)  The Secretary shall support the Office of the United States Trade Representative, in consultation with the Secretary of Commerce, in meetings with representatives of other countries to discuss methods and approaches to reduce the burden of regulation and harmonization regulatory requirements if the Secretary determines that such harmonization continues consumer protections consistent with the purposes of this Act.

(2)  The Secretary shall support the Office of the United States Trade Representative, in consultation with the Secretary of Commerce, in efforts to move toward the acceptance of mutual recognition agreements relating to the regulation of drugs, biological products, devices, foods, food additives, and color additives, and the regulation of good manufacturing practices between the European Union and the United States.

(3)  The Secretary shall regularly participate in meetings with representatives of other foreign governments to discuss and reach agreement on methods and approaches to harmonize regulatory requirements.

(4)  The Secretary shall, not later than 180 days after the date of enactment of the Food and Drug Administration Modernization Act of 1997, make public a plan that establishes a framework for achieving mutual recognition of good manufacturing practices inspections.

(5)  Paragraphs (1) through (4) shall not apply with respect to products defined in Section 201(ff).

# Appendix 7B
## Agreement on Mutual Recognition Between the European Community and the United States of America (1998)

### Framework

The EUROPEAN COMMUNITY, and the GOVERNMENT OF THE UNITED STATES OF AMERICA, hereinafter referred to as "the Parties,"

CONSIDERING the traditional links of friendship that exist between the United States of America (US) and the European Community (EC);

DESIRING to facilitate bilateral trade between them;

RECOGNIZING that mutual recognition of conformity assessment activities is an important means of enhancing market access between the Parties;

RECOGNIZING that an agreement providing for mutual recognition of conformity assessment activities is of particular interest to small and medium-sized businesses in the US and the EC;

RECOGNIZING that any such mutual recognition also requires confidence in the continued reliability of the other Party's conformity assessments;

RECOGNIZING the importance of maintaining each Party's high levels of health, safety, environmental and consumer protection;

RECOGNIZING that mutual recognition agreements can positively contribute in encouraging greater international harmonization of standards;

NOTING that this Agreement is not intended to displace private sector bilateral and multilateral arrangements among conformity assessment bodies or to affect regulatory regimes allowing for manufacturers' self-assessments and declarations of conformity;

BEARING IN MIND that the Agreement on Technical Barriers to Trade, an agreement annexed to the Agreement establishing the World Trade Organization (WTO), imposes obligations on the Parties as Contracting Parties to the WTO, and encourages such Contracting Parties to enter into negotiations for the conclusion of agreements for the mutual recognition of results of each other's conformity assessment;

RECOGNIZING that any such mutual recognition needs to offer an assurance of conformity with applicable technical regulations or standards equivalent to the assurance offered by the Party's own procedures;

RECOGNIZING the need to conclude an Agreement on Mutual Recognition (MRA) in the field of conformity assessment with sectoral annexes; and

BEARING in mind the respective commitments of the Parties under bilateral, regional and multilateral environment, health, safety and consumer protection agreements.

HAVE AGREED AS FOLLOWS: . . .

ARTICLE 2
PURPOSE OF THE AGREEMENT

This Agreement specifies the conditions by which each Party will accept or recognize results of conformity assessment procedures, produced by the other Party's conformity assessment bodies or authorities, in assessing conformity to the importing Party's requirements, as specified on a sector-specific basis in the Sectoral Annexes, and to provide for other related cooperative activities. The objective of such mutual recognition is to provide effective market access throughout the territories of the Parties with regard to conformity assessment for all products covered under this Agreement. If any obstacles to such access arise, consultations will promptly be held. In the absence of a satisfactory outcome of such consultations, the Party alleging its market access has been denied may, within 90 days of such consultation, invoke its right to terminate the Agreement in accordance with Article 21.

# References

AFL-CIO. 1997. *Stop Fast Track: America Can't Afford Any More NAFTAs.* Washington.

Alford, William. 1995. *To Steal a Book Is an Elegant Offense: Intellectual Property Law in Chinese Civilization.* Stanford: Stanford University Press.

Allison, Graham T. 1971. *Essence of Decision: Explaining the Cuban Missile Crisis.* Boston, MA: Little Brown.

Attaran, Amir, and Lee Gillespie-White. 2001. Do Patents for Antiretroviral Drugs Constrain Access to AIDS Treatment in Africa? *JAMA: The Journal of the American Medical Association* 286 (October 17): 1886–92.

Baldwin, Robert E., and Christopher S. Magee. 2000. *Congressional Trade Votes: From NAFTA Approval to Fast-Track Defeat.* POLICY ANALYSES IN INTERNATIONAL ECONOMICS 59. Washington: Institute for International Economics.

Barenberg, Mark. 2000. Legal Issues in the Congressional Debate over Permanent MFN for China. Columbia Law School, New York. Written statement (March 1).

Bergsten, C. Fred. 2002. A Renaissance for US Trade Policy? *Foreign Affairs* 81, no. 6 (November-December): 86–98.

Bhala, Raj. 2000. Enter the Dragon: An Essay on China's WTO Accession Saga. *American University International Law Review* 15, no. 6 (October): 1469–538.

Blumenthal, David M. 1999. Applying GATT to Marketizing Economies: The Dilemma of WTO Accession and Reform of China's State-Owned Enterprises (SOEs). *Journal of International Economic Law* 2, no. 4 (January).

Bolle, Mary Jane. 2000. *China and the WTO: Labor Issues.* Congressional Research Service Report for Congress, RS20582. Washington: Congressional Research Service. www.ncseonline. org (accessed on July 21, 2005).

Braga, Carlos A. Primo. 1995. Trade-Related Intellectual Property Issues: The Uruguay Round and Its Economic Implications. In *The Uruguay Round and the Developing Economies,* ed. Will Martin and L. Alan Winters. Washington: World Bank, 381–411.

Breitfelder, Matt. 1996. The Transatlantic Business Dialogue: Chicago Conference Exceeds Expectations and Confirms the TABD as a Major Force for a More Open Transatlantic Market. *Business America* (November): 22.

Canner, Stephen J. 1998. The Multilateral Agreement on Investment. *Cornell International Law Journal* 31, no. 3: 657–81.

Chaudhry, Peggy, and Michael Walsh. 1995. Intellectual Property Rights: Changing Levels of Protection Under GATT, NAFTA, and the EU. *The Columbia Journal of World Business* 30, no. 2 (Summer): 80–92.

Choate, Pat. 1998. Redressing the "Democratic Deficit" in US Trade Policy. In *Future Visions for US Trade Policy*, ed. Bruce Stokes. Washington: Council on Foreign Relations.

Cialdini, Robert B. 1993. *Influence: The Psychology of Persuasion*. New York: William Morrow.

Cohen, Richard E. 1997. Democrats Feel the Squeeze on Fast Track. *National Journal* 29 (October 19): 2084.

Correa, Carlos. 2000. Integrating Public Health Concerns into Patent Legislation in Developing Countries. University of Buenos Aires, Argentina.

Deal, Timothy. 1998. Investment E-paranoia. *The Journal of Commerce* (January 7): 7A.

Destler, I. M. 1997. *Renewing Fast-Track Legislation*. POLICY ANALYSES IN INTERNATIONAL ECONOMICS 50. Washington: Institute for International Economics.

Destler, I. M. 1995. *American Trade Politic*, 3rd ed. Washington: Institute for International Economics and the Twentieth Century Fund.

Drahos, Peter. 1995. Global Property Rights in Information: The Story of TRIPS at the GATT. *Prometheus* 13, no. 1 (June): 6–19.

Drahos, Peter, with Braithwaite, John. 2002. *Information Feudalism: Who Owns the Knowledge Economy?* New York: New Press.

Dobson, John M. 1976. *Two Centuries of Tariffs: The Background and Emergence of the US International Trade Commission*. Washington: US International Trade Commission, GPO.

Dymond, William. 1999. The MAI: A Sad and Melancholy Tale. In *Canada Among Nations, 1999: A Big League Player?*, ed. Fen Osler Hampson, Martin Rudner, and Michael Hart. New York: Oxford University Press.

Encarnation, Dennis, and Boris Velic. 1998. *Competing for Foreign Direct Investment: Government Policy and Corporate Strategy in Asia*. New York: Oxford University Press.

European Commission. 1995. Communication of the Commission: A Long-Term Policy for China-Europe Relations. COM (1995): 279.

Fisher, Roger, and William Ury. 1981. *Getting to Yes: Negotiating Agreement Without Giving In*. New York: Houghton Mifflin.

GAO (General Accounting Office). 1998. *Food and Drug Administration: Improvements Needed in the Foreign Drug Inspection Program*. Report to the Chairman, House Subcommittee on Oversight and Investigations, Committee on Commerce. 105th Congress, 2nd session (March).

Geiger, Rainer. 1998. Towards a Multilateral Agreement on Investment. *Cornell International Law Journal* 31, no. 3: 467–75.

Gephardt, Richard A. 1997. Letter to Democratic Colleagues on Fast Track from House Leader Richard A. Gephardt. Attachment to press release: News From the House Democratic Leader: Gephardt Lays Down Markers on Fast Track Trade Negotiating Authority, February 26.

Gibbs, Murray, and Mina Mashayekhi. 1998. *The Uruguay Round Negotiations on Investment: Lessons for the Future*. Geneva: United Nations Conference on Trade and Development.

Gillespie-White, Lee, and Paul Salmon. 2000. *Patent Protection and Access to HIV/AIDS Pharmaceuticals in Sub-Saharan Africa*. Washington: International Intellectual Property Institute. www.iipi.org (accessed on December 1, 2005).

Goffman, Erving. 1974. *Frame Analysis: An Essay on the Organization of Experience*. Cambridge, MA: Harvard University Press.

Good, Mary Lowe. 1996. Technology and Trade; Symposium: Free Trade Areas the Challenge and Promise of Fair vs. Free Trade. *Law and Policy in International Business* 27, no. 4 (June 22): 853–64.

Gopal, Kevin. 1997. Discordant Voices. *Pharmaceutical Executive* (May 17): 38.

Gorlin, Jacques J. 1999. *An Analysis of the Pharmaceutical-Related Provisions of the WTO TRIPS (Intellectual Property) Agreement*. London: Intellectual Property Institute.

Graham, Edward M. 1999. Regulatory Takings, Supernational Treatment, and the Multilateral Agreement on Investment: Issues Raised by Nongovernmental Organizations. *Cornell International Law Journal* 31, no. 3: 599–614.

Graham, Edward M. 2000. *Fighting the Wrong Enemy: Antiglobal Activists and Multinational Enterprises*. Washington: Institute for International Economics.

Graham, Edward M., and Paul R. Krugman. 1999. Trade-Related Investment Measures. In *Completing the Uruguay Round: A Results-Oriented Approach to the GATT Trade Negotiations*, ed. Jeffrey J. Schott. Washington: Institute for International Economics.

Hammond, John S., Ralph L. Keeney, and Howard Raiffa. 1999. *Smart Choices*. Boston, MA: Harvard Business School Press.

Harbinson, Stuart. 2002. Lessons from the Launching of the Doha Round Negotiations. Cordell Hull Institute, Trade Policy Roundtable, Washington, April 18. Published in *Trade Policy Analyses* 4 (May).

Harries, Owen. 1984. A Primer for Polemicists. *Commentary* 78, no. 3: 57–60.

Henderson, David. 1999. *The Multilateral Agreement on Investment: A Story and Its Lessons*. Wellington, NZ: New Zealand Business Roundtable.

Hill, Eileen. 1985. Commerce Department Program Seeks Greater Protection for US IPR. *Business America* 8 (March 18): 3.

HIMA (Health Industry Manufacturers Association). 1997. *1997 Global Medical Technology Update: The Challenges Facing US Industry and Policy*. Washington: Health Industry Manufacturers Association.

Horton, Linda. 1998. Sixth Annual Health Law Symposium: Pharmaceuticals and Medical Devices: International Harmonization and Mutual Recognition Agreements. *Seton Hall Law Review* 29: 692–735.

Hufbauer, Gary Clyde, and Daniel H. Rosen. 2000. *American Access to China's Market: The Congressional Vote on PNTR*. Policy Brief 00-3. Washington: Institute for International Economics. www.iie.com (accessed in April 2005).

Human Rights Clinical Program, Harvard Law School. 1999. *The Multilateral Agreement on Investment: Advocacy History and Prospects for the Future*. Cambridge, MA: Harvard Law School.

IIPA (International Intellectual Property Alliance). 1985. *Piracy of US Copyrighted Works in Ten Selected Countries*. Washington: IIPA.

Iklé, Fred C. 1964. *How Nations Negotiate*. Millwood, NY: Kraus Reprint Co.

International Chamber of Commerce (ICC) Commission on International Trade and Investment. 1998. Business States Its Views on OECD Investment Agreement. www.iccwbo.org (accessed on January 16, 2005).

Jackson, John H., and Sylvia A. Rhodes. 1999. United States Law and China's WTO Accession Process. *Journal of International Economic Law* 2, no. 3 (September): 497–510.

Johnson-Laird, P. N. 1983. *Mental Models: Towards a Cognitive Science of Language, Inference and Consciousness*. Cambridge, UK: Cambridge University Press.

Journal of Commerce Staff. 1997. US, EU Race to Meet Looming Deadline for Products Standards. *The Journal of Commerce* (May 8): 2A.

Juillard, Patrick. 1998. MAI: A European View. *Cornell International Law Journal* 31, no. 3: 477–84.

Kennedy, Robert E., and Katherine Marquis. 1998. *China: Facing the 21st Century*. Harvard Business School Case Study 9-798-066. Boston, MA: Harvard Business School.

Kidd, Dan. 1996. The International Conference on Harmonization of Pharmaceutical Regulations, the European Medicines Evaluation Agency, and the FDA: Who's Zooming Who? *Indiana Journal of Global Legal Studies* 4, no. 1 (Fall): 183–206.

Kingdon, John W. 1995. *Agendas, Alternatives, and Public Policies*. 2d ed. New York: Longman.

Kobrin, Stephen J. 1998. The MAI and the Clash of Globalizations. *Foreign Policy*, no. 111 (Fall): 97–109.

Kosterlitz, Julie. 1997. The Wages of Trade. *National Journal* 29 (October 18): 2076–79.

Krackhardt, David, and Jeffrey R. Hanson. 1993. Informal Networks: The Company Behind the Chart. *Harvard Business Review* (July–August). Reprint 93406.

Lalumière, Catherine, and Jean-Pierre Landau. 1998. *Rapport sur l'Accord mulilatéral sur l'Investissement* (Report on the multilateral agreement on investment). Paris: Ministère de l'Économie, des Finances et de l'Industrie. www.finances.gouv.fr (accessed in September 2005).

Lang, Jeffrey. 1998. Keynote Address. *Cornell International Law Journal* 31, no. 3: 455–66.

Lax, David A., and James K. Sebenius. 1986. *The Manager as Negotiator: Bargaining for Cooperation and Competitive Gain.* New York: Free Press.

Lax, David A., and James K. Sebenius. 1991. Thinking Coalitionally: Party Arithmetic, Process Opportunism and Strategic Sequencing. In *Negotiation Analysis,* ed. H. Peyton Young. Ann Arbor, MI: University of Michigan Press.

Love, James. 2002. Some Personal Notes on the Access to Medicines Campaign. Draft Version 2.0. March 26.

Love, James. 2003. The Access to Medicines Campaign, a Personal Note. Photocopy (modified March 16).

Maggs, John. 1998. OECD Advisory Panel Slams Proposed Investment Treaty. *The Journal of Commerce* (January 16): 3A.

Maskus, Keith. 1990. Intellectual Property. In *Completing the Uruguay Round: A Results-Oriented Approach to the GATT Trade Negotiations,* ed. Jeffrey J. Schott. Washington: Institute for International Economics.

Maskus, Keith. 1993. Intellectual Property Rights and the Uruguay Round. *Economic Review* 78, no. 1: 11–25.

Mayer, Frederick. 1998. *Interpreting NAFTA: The Science and Art of Political Analysis.* New York: Columbia University Press.

Mitchell, Mitchell G. 1970. *Propaganda, Polls, and Public Opinion: Are the People Manipulated?* Englewood Cliffs, NJ: Prentice-Hall.

Moran, Theodore H. 1998. *Foreign Direct Investment and Development: The New Policy Agenda for Developing Countries and Economies in Transition.* Washington: Institute for International Economics.

Moran, Theodore. 2002. *Parental Supervision: The New Paradigm for Foreign Direct Investment and Development.* POLICY ANALYSES IN INTERNATIONAL ECONOMICS 64. Washington: Institute for International Economics.

Morrison, Wayne M. 2001. *China-US Trade Issues.* Congressional Research Service Issue Brief for Congress, IB91121. Washington: Congressional Research Service. Available at www.ncseonline.org.

Myerson, Roger B. 1997 (1991). *Game Theory: Analysis of Conflict.* Cambridge, MA: Harvard University Press.

OECD (Organization for Economic Cooperation and Development). 1995. *A Multilateral Agreement on Investment: Report by the Committee on International Investment and Multinational Enterprises (CIME) and the Committee on Capital Movements and Invisible Transactions (CMIT).* Paris. www.oecd.org.

OECD (Organization for Economic Cooperation and Development). 1996a. *Multilateral Agreement on Investment, Progress Report by the MAI Negotiating Group.* OECD/GD(96)78, April. Paris. www.oecd.org.

OECD (Organization for Economic Cooperation and Development). 1996b. *Report to the Negotiating Group by Expert Group No. 2 on Treatment of Tax Issues in the MAI.* DAFFE/MAI/EG2(96)9, December 17. Paris. www.oecd.org.

OECD (Organization for Economic Cooperation and Development). 1997. *Multilateral Agreement on Investment, Report by the Negotiating Group.* OECD/GD(97)82, May. Paris. www.oecd.org.

OECD (Organization for Economic Cooperation and Development). Negotiating Group on the Multilateral Agreement on Investment (MAI). 1998a. *Summary Record, Meeting on 19 February 1998.* DAFFE/MAI/M(98)2, March 16. Paris. www.oecd.org.

OECD (Organization for Economic Cooperation and Development). Negotiating Group on the Multilateral Agreement on Investment (MAI). 1998b. *Summary Record, Meeting on 14–16 April 1998.* DAFFE/MAI/M(98)4, May 22. Paris. www.oecd.org.

Oxfam. 2001. *Patent Injustice: How World Trade Rules Threaten the Health of Poor People.* Oxford. www.oxfam.org.uk (accessed in February 2005).

Patel, Tara. 1995. Developing Nations Could Provide Input in OECD Investment Talks, Officials Say. *The Journal of Commerce* (May 24): 2A.

Pew Research Center for the People and the Press. 2000. Post-Seattle Support for WTO. http://people-press.org (accessed on March 2, 2005).

Pfizer. 2002–04. *Global HIV/AIDS Partnerships: Diflucan® Partnership Program.* Caring for Community: Global Health. www.pfizer.com.

PhRMA (Pharmaceutical Research and Manufacturers of America). 2002. *Delivering on the Promise of Pharmaceutical Innovation: The Need to Maintain Strong and Predictable Intellectual Property Rights.* Submitted to the US Federal Trade Division and the Department of Justice, Antitrust Division, April 22.

Public Citizen's Global Trade Watch. 2000. *Purchasing Power: The Corporate–White House Alliance to Pass the China Trade Bill over the Will of the American People.* Washington: Public Citizen's Global Trade Watch. www.citizen.org (accessed in October 2005).

Putnam, Robert. 1988. Diplomacy and Domestic Politics: The Logic of Two Level Games. *International Organizations* 42, no. 3: 427–60.

Raiffa, Howard. 1982. *The Art and Science of Negotiation.* Cambridge, MA: Belknap Press of Harvard University Press.

Ratner, Steven R. 1998. International Law: The Trials of Global Norms. *Foreign Policy,* no. 110 (Spring): 65–80.

Riker, William H. 1986. *The Art of Political Manipulation.* New Haven: Yale University Press.

Ross, Robert S. 1996. Enter the Dragon. *Foreign Policy,* no. 104 (Fall): 18–35.

Ryan, Michael P. 1998. *Knowledge Diplomacy: Global Competition and the Politics of Intellectual Property.* Washington: Brookings Institution.

Santoro, Michael A. 1992. *Pfizer: Protecting Intellectual Property in a Global Marketplace.* Harvard Business School Case Study N9-392-071. Boston, MA: Harvard Business School.

Scherer, F. M. 1998. The Patent System and Innovation in Pharmaceuticals. Paper presented at the AIDE Conference on Pharmaceutical Patents, Innovation and Public Health, Toulouse, France (December).

Schick, Shane. 1997. Canada, Europe in Mutual Recognition Agreement Deadlock. *Computer Dealer News* 13 (November 3): 18.

Scott, Robert E. 2000. *China and the States.* EPI Briefing Paper. Washington: Economic Policy Institute. www.epinet.org (accessed in May 2005).

Sebenius, James K. 1984. *Negotiating the Law of the Sea.* Cambridge, MA: Harvard University Press.

Sebenius, James K. 1992. Negotiation Analysis: A Characterization and Review. *Management Science* 38, no. 1: 18–38.

Sebenius, James. 1996. Introduction to Negotiation Analysis: Structure, People, and Context. Harvard Business School Note 896-034. Boston, MA: Harvard Business School.

Sebenius, James K., and Rebecca Hulse. 2001a. *Charlene Barshefsky (A).* Harvard Business School Case Study 9-801-421. Boston, MA: Harvard Business School.

Sebenius, James K., and Rebecca Hulse. 2001b. *Charlene Barshefsky (B).* Harvard Business School Case Study 9-801-422. Boston, MA: Harvard Business School.

Sell, Susan K. 2003. *Private Power, Public Law: The Globalization of Intellectual Property Rights.* Cambridge: Cambridge University Press.

Shapiro, Hal, and Lael Brainard. 2003. Trade Promotion Authority Formerly Known as Fast Track: Building Common Ground on Trade Demands More Than a Name Change. *George Washington International Law Review* 35, no. 1 (January 1): 1–53.

Sherwood, R. M. 1990. *Intellectual Property and Economic Development.* Boulder, CO: Westview Press.

Shorrock, Tim. 1997. Fast Track Is Dead: Now for the Fallout; President, GOP Allies Scramble for Ways to Open Overseas Markets. *Journal of Commerce* (November 12): 1A.

Siebeck, Wolfgang E., Robert E. Evenson, William Lesser, and Carlos A. Primo Braga. 1990. *Strengthening Protection of Intellectual Property in Developing Countries.* World Bank Discussion Paper 112. Washington: World Bank.

Simendinger, Alexis. 1997. Slowpoke on Fast Track. *National Journal* 29 (June 28): 1338.

Soloway, Julie A. 1999. Environmental Trade Barriers Under NAFTA: The MMT Fuel Additives Controversy. *The Minnesota Journal of Global Trade* 8, no. 1 (Winter): 55–95.

Stokes, Bruce, ed. 1998. *Future Visions for US Trade Policy.* Washington: Council on Foreign Relations.

Stone, Peter H. 1997. Business Pushes for Fast Track. *National Journal* 29 (September 27): 1903.

Stumberg, Robert, Thomas Singer, and Paul Orbuch. 1997. *Multilateral Agreement on Investment: Potential Effects on State & Local Government.* Denver, CO: Western Governors' Association. www.westgov.org.

TABD (Transatlantic Business Dialogue). 1995. *1995 Seville Transatlantic Business Dialogue.* www.tabd.com (accessed in January 2006).

TABD (Transatlantic Business Dialogue). 2000. *2000 Mid Year Report.* www.tabd.com (accessed in January 2006).

TABD (Transatlantic Business Dialogue). 2001. *Transatlantic Business Dialogue (TABD) 2001 CEO Report.* www.tabd.com (accessed in January 2006).

Trebilcock, Michael, and Robert Howse. 1999. *The Regulation of International Trade.* London: Routledge.

UNAIDS (Joint United Nations Programme on HIV/AIDS) and WHO (World Health Organization). 1998. *Report on the Global HIV/AIDS Epidemic.* www.who.int (accessed in June 2005).

UNCTAD (United Nations Conference on Trade and Development). 1996. *The TRIPS Agreement and Developing Countries.* UNCTAD/ITE/1. New York: United Nations.

UNCTAD (United Nations Conference on Trade and Development). 2000. Bilateral Investment Treaties, 1959–1999. UNCTAD/ITE/IIA/2. New York: United Nations. www.unctad. org.

UNCHR (UN Economic and Social Council/United Nations High Commissioner for Human Rights). 2001. *The Impact of the Agreement on Trade-Related Aspects of Intellectual Property Rights on Human Rights: Report of the High Commissioner.* E/CN.4/Sub.2/2001/13. Geneva: United Nations. www.eldis.org (accessed on June 27, 2005).

US Commerce Department. 1998. Bilateral Trade in Seven Sectors under MRA Negotiations. Published in hearing before the House Subcommittee on Oversight and Investigations of the Committee on Commerce, "Imported Drugs: US-EU (European Union) Mutual Recognition Agreement on Drug Inspections." 105th Congress, 2nd session, October 2, 75.

USITC (US International Trade Commission). 1993. *Potential Impact on the US Economy and Selected Industries of the NAFTA.* USITC Publication 2596. Washington: US International Trade Commission.

USITC (US International Trade Commission). 1999. *Assessment of the Economic Effects on the United States of China's Accession to the WTO.* Executive Summary, Investigation 332–403. Washington: US International Trade Commission. www.fas.org (accessed in August 2005).

Valley, Kathleen L., and Angela T. Keros. 2000. It Takes Two: Improvisations in Negotiation. Draft HBS Working Paper. Harvard Business School, Boston, MA.

Vallianatos, Mark. 1998. *License to Loot: The MAI and How to Stop It.* Washington: Friends of the Earth. www.foe.org.

van Thiel, Servaas. 2003. Public Health Versus Intellectual Property: or How Members of the World Trade Organization (WTO) Without Pharmaceutical Production Capacity Could Have Access to Affordable Medicines in Public Health Emergencies by Using Compulsory Licenses. www.cid.harvard.edu (accessed in July 2005).

Velásquez, German, and Pascale Boulet. 1999. *Globalization and Access to Drugs: Perspectives on the WTO TRIPS Agreement.* Health Economics and Drugs DAP Series 7 Revised 1998 (WHO/AAP/98.9 Revised). Geneva: World Health Organization. www.who.int.

Walton, Richard E., Joel Cutcher-Gershenfeld, and Robert B. McKersie. 1994. *Strategic Negotiations: A Theory of Change in Labor-Management Relations.* Boston, MA: Harvard Business School Press.

Walton, Richard E., and Robert B. McKersie. 1965. *A Behavioral Theory of Labor Negotiations: An Analysis of a Social Interaction System.* Ithaca, NY: ILR Press.

Wang, Guiguo. 1995. China's Return to the GATT—Legal and Economic Implications. *Journal of World Trade* 28, no. 3 (June): 51–65.

Watal, Jayashree. 2001. *Intellectual Property Rights in the WTO and Developing Countries.* The Hague: Kluwer Law International.

Watkins, Michael. 1998. Building Momentum in Negotiations: Time-Related Costs and Action-Forcing Events. *Negotiation Journal* 14, no. 3: 241–56.

Watkins, Michael. 2000. Negotiation Analysis: A Synthesis. Harvard Business School Note 9-800-316. Boston, MA: Harvard Business School.

Watkins, Michael, and Samuel Passow. 1996. Analyzing Linked Systems of Negotiations. *Negotiation Journal* 12, no. 3: 325–39.

Wilkerson Group. 1995. *Forces Reshaping the Performance and Contribution of the US Medical Device Industry.* Washington: Health Industry Manufacturers Association.

WHO (World Health Organization), Department of HIV/AIDS. 2002. *Leading the Health Sector Response to HIV/AIDS.* WHO/HIV/2002.16. www.who.int (accessed in September 2005).

WIPO (World Intellectual Property Organization), International Bureau of. 1988. *Existence, Scope and Form of Generally Internationally Accepted and Applied Standards/Norms for the Protection of Intellectual Property.* GATT Document MTN.GNG/NG11/W/24/Rev.1.

WTO (World Trade Organization). 1995. *Accession to the World Trade Organization—Procedures for Negotiations under Article XII—Note by the Secretariat.* WT/ACC/1 (95-0651). www.wto.org (accessed in March 2005).

WTO (World Trade Organization). 2001. *GATS—Fact and Fiction.* Geneva: World Trade Organization.

Yang, Guohua, and Cheng Jin. 2001. The Process of China's Accession to the WTO. *The Journal of International Economic Law* 4, no. 2 (June): 275–96.

# Additional Readings

## General

Burtless, Gary, Robert Z. Lawrence, Robert E. Litan, and Robert J. Shapiro. 1988. *Globaphobia: Confronting Fears about Open Trade.* Washington: Brookings Institution.

Hoekman, Bernard M., and Michel M. Kostecki. 2001. *The Political Economy of the World Trading System: The WTO and Beyond.* Oxford: Oxford University Press.

International Forum on Globalization. 2002. *Alternatives to Economic Globalization: A Better World Is Possible.* San Francisco: Berrett-Koehler.

Jackson, John H. 1997. *The World Trading System: Law and Policy of International Economic Relations.* Cambridge, MA: MIT Press.

Nader, Ralph, ed. 1993. *The Case Against "Free Trade": GATT, NAFTA, and the Globalization of Corporate Power.* San Francisco: Earth Island Press; Berkeley, CA: North Atlantic Books.

## Scope

Bhagwati, Jagdish, and Robert E. Hudec, eds. 1996. *Fair Trade and Harmonization: Prerequisites for Free Trade?* Cambridge, MA: MIT Press.

Elliott, Kimberly Ann, and Richard B. Freeman. 2003. *Can Labor Standards Improve under Globalization?* Washington: Institute for International Economics.

Esty, Daniel C. 1994. *Greening the GATT: Trade, Environment and the Future.* Washington: Institute for International Economics.

Graham, Edward M., and J. David Richardson. 1997. *Competition Policies for the Global Economy.* POLICY ANALYSES IN INTERNATIONAL ECONOMICS 51. Washington: Institute for International Economics.

Krugman, Paul R. 1997. What Should Trade Negotiators Negotiate About? *Journal of Economic Literature* 35 (March): 113–20.

Nivola, Pietro, ed. 1987. *Comparative Disadvantages? Social Regulations in the Global Economy.* Washington: Brookings Institution.

Scherer, F. M. 1994. *Competition Policies for an Integrated World Economy.* Washington: Brookings Institution.

Vogel, David. 1995. *Trading Up: Consumer and Environmental Regulation in a Global Economy.* Cambridge, MA: Harvard University Press.

Wilson, John Sullivan. 1996. *Standards and APEC: An Action Agenda.* POLICY ANALYSES IN INTERNATIONAL ECONOMICS 42. Washington: Institute for International Economics.

## Depth

Lawrence, Robert Z., Albert Bressand, and Takatoshi Ito. 1996. *A Vision for the World Economy: Openness, Diversity, and Cohesion.* Washington: Brookings Institution.

Oates, Wallace E. 1999. An Essay on Fiscal Federalism. *Journal of Economic Literature* 37, no. 3 (September): 1120–49.

Rodrik, Dani. 1997. *Has Globalization Gone Too Far?* Washington: Institute for International Economics.

Rodrik, Dani. 2000. Governance of Economic Globalization. In *Governance in a Globalizing World,* ed. Joseph S. Nye and John D. Donahue. Washington: Brookings Institution.

Wilson, John D. 1996. Capital Mobility and Environmental Standards: Is There a Theoretical Basis for a Race to the Bottom? In *Fair Trade and Harmonization: Prerequisites for Free Trade?,* ed. Jagdish N. Bhagwati and Robert E. Hudec. Cambridge, MA: MIT Press.

## Enforcement

Bayard, Thomas O., and Kimberly Ann Elliott. 1994. *Reciprocity and Retaliation in US Trade Policy.* Washington: Institute for International Economics.

Bhagwati, Jagdish, and Hugh T. Patrick, eds. 1990. *Aggressive Unilateralism: America's 301 Trade Policy and the World Trading System.* Ann Arbor: University of Michigan Press.

Lawrence, Robert Z. 2003. *Crimes and Punishments? An Analysis of Retaliation Under the WTO.* Washington: Institute for International Economics.

Pauwelyn, Joost. 2000. Enforcement and Countermeasures in the WTO: Rules and Rules—Toward a More Collective Approach. *American Journal of International Law* 94 (April): 335–47.

## Regionalism

Frankel, Jeffrey A. 1997. *Regional Trading Blocs in the World Economic System.* Washington: Institute for International Economics.

Lawrence, Robert Z. 1995. *Regionalism, Multilateralism, and Deeper Integration.* Washington: Brookings Institution.

Schott, Jeffrey J., ed. 2003. *Free Trade Agreements: US Strategies and Priorities.* Washington: Institute for International Economics.

## Developing Countries

Amsden, Alice. 1999. Industrialization Under New WTO Law. Paper prepared for UNCTAD X (December).

Bergsten, C. Fred. 1999. *The Global Trading System and the Developing Countries in 2000.* Working Paper, Institute for International Economics, Washington, DC. www.iie.com/publications/wp/1999/99-6.htm.

Birdsall, Nancy, and Robert Z. Lawrence. 1999. Deep Integration and Trade Agreements: Good for Developing Countries? In *Global Public Goods: International Cooperation in the 21st Century*, ed. Inge Kaul, Isabelle Grunberg, and Marc A. Stern. New York: Oxford University Press for the United Nations Development Program.

Finger, J. Michael, and L. Alan Winters. 1998. What Can the WTO Do for Developing Countries? In *The WTO as an International Organization*, ed. Anne O. Krueger with the assistance of Chonira Aturupane. Chicago: University of Chicago Press.

Hoekman, Bernard, Aaditya Mattoo, and Philip English, eds. *Development, Trade, and the WTO: A Handbook*. Washington: World Bank.

Trebilcock, Michael J., and Robert Howse. 1999. Trade and Developing Countries. Chapter 14 in *The Regulation of International Trade*. London: Routledge.

# Winners and Losers

Lawrence, Robert Z. 1996. *Single World, Divided Nations? International Trade and OECD Labor Markets*. Washington: Brookings Institution; Paris: OECD Development Centre.

Scheve, Kenneth F., and Matthew J. Slaughter. 2001. *Globalization and the Perceptions of American Workers*. Washington: Institute for International Economics.

Wood, Adrian. 1994. *North-South Trade, Employment, and Inequality*. Oxford: Clarendon Press.

# Governance and Politics

Barfield, Claude E. 2001. *Free Trade, Sovereignty, Democracy: The Future of the World Trade Organization*. Washington: AEI Press.

Bolton, John R. 2000. Should We Take Global Governance Seriously? *Chicago Journal of International Law* 1, no. 2 (Fall): 205–21.

Esty, Daniel. 1998. Non-Governmental Organizations at the World Trade Organization: Cooperation, Competition, or Exclusion. *Journal of International Economic Law* 1, no. 1 (March): 123–47.

Goldstein, Judith. 1998. International Institutions and Domestic Politics. In *The WTO as an International Organization*, ed. Anne O. Krueger with the assistance of Chonira Aturupane. Chicago, IL: University of Chicago Press.

Goldstein, Judith, and Lisa L. Martin. 2000. Legalization, Trade Liberalization and Domestic Politics. *International Organization* 54, no. 3: 603–32.

Jackson, John H. 1997. The Great 1994 Sovereignty Debate: United States Acceptance and Implementation of Uruguay Round Results. *Columbia Journal of Transnational Law* 36: 157–88.

Martin, Lisa L. 2000. *Democratic Commitments: Legislatures and International Cooperation*. Princeton: Princeton University Press.

Nivola, Pietro. 1993. *Regulating Unfair Trade*. Washington: Brookings Institution.

Nye, Joseph N., and John D. Donahue, eds. 2000. *Governance in a Globalizing World*. Cambridge, MA: Visions of Governance for the 21st Century; Washington: Brookings Institution.

Porter, Roger, Pierre Sauvé, Arvind Subramanian, and Americo Zampetti, eds. 2001. *Efficiency, Equity and Legitimacy: The Multilateral Trading System at the Millennium*. Washington: Brookings Institution.

Rogowski, Ronald. 1989. *Commerce and Coalitions: How Trade Affects Domestic Political Alignments*. Princeton: Princeton University Press.

Sampson, Gary P., ed. 2001. *The Role of the World Trade Organization in Global Governance*. New York: United Nations University Press.

Wallach, Lori, and Michelle Sforza. 1999. *The WTO: Five Years of Reasons to Resist Corporate Globalization*. New York: Seven Stories Press.

# Negotiation Theory

Bazerman, Max H., and Margaret A. Neale. 1992. *Negotiating Rationally.* New York: Free Press.

Cialdini, Robert B. 1993. *Influence: The Psychology of Persuasion.* New York: William Morrow.

Susskind, Lawrence, and Patrick Field. 1996. *Dealing with an Angry Public: The Mutual Gains Approach to Resolving Disputes.* New York: Free Press.

Ury, William. 1993. *Getting Past No: Negotiating Your Way from Confrontation to Cooperation.* Rev. ed. New York: Bantam.

Watkins, Michael, and Susan Rosegrant. 2001. *Breakthrough International Negotiation: How Great Negotiators Transformed the World's Toughest Post-Cold War Conflicts.* San Francisco: Jossey-Bass.

# TRIPS

Bradley, A. Jane. 1987. Intellectual Property Rights, Investment and Trade in Services in the Uruguay Round: Laying the Foundations. *Stanford Journal of International Law* 23 (Spring): 57–98.

Maskus, Keith E. 2000. *Intellectual Property Rights in the Global Economy.* Washington: Institute for International Economics.

Watal, Jayashree. 2000. *Intellectual Property Rights in the World Trade Organization: The Way Forward for Developing Countries.* New Delhi: Oxford University Press.

# The Multilateral Agreement on Investment

Encarnation, Dennis, and Boris Velic. 1998. *Competing for Foreign Direct Investment: Government Policy and Corporate Strategy in Asia.* New York: Oxford University Press.

Graham, Edward M. 2000. *Fighting the Wrong Enemy: Antiglobal Activists and Multinational Enterprises.* Washington: Institute for International Economics.

Graham, Edward M. 1999. Regulatory Takings, Supernational Treatment, and the Multilateral Agreement on Investment: Issues Raised by Nongovernmental Organizations. *Cornell International Law Journal* 31, no. 3: 599–614.

Moran, Theodore H. 1998. *Foreign Direct Investment and Development: The New Policy Agenda for Developing Countries and Economies in Transition.* Washington: Institute for International Economics.

Moran, Theodore H. 2002. *Parental Supervision: The New Paradigm for Foreign Direct Investment and Development.* POLICY ANALYSES IN INTERNATIONAL ECONOMICS 64. Washington: Institute for International Economics.

# Fast Track/Trade Promotion Authority

Baldwin, Robert E., and Christopher S. Magee. 2001. *Congressional Trade Votes: From NAFTA Approval to Fast-Track Defeat.* POLICY ANALYSES IN INTERNATIONAL ECONOMICS 59. Washington: Institute for International Economics.

Elliott, Kimberly Ann. 2001. *Dealing with Labor and Environment Issues in Trade.* Policy Brief 01-8. Washington: Institute for International Economics.

Schott, Jeffrey J., ed. 1998. *Restarting Fast Track.* Special Report 11. Washington: Institute for International Economics.

# The 1999 US-China Bilateral Agreement and PNTR

Lardy, Nicolas R. 2002. *Integrating China into the Global Economy.* Washington: Brookings Institution.

Rosen, Daniel H. 1999. *China and the World Trade Organization: An Economic Balance Sheet.* Policy Brief 99-6. Washington: Institute for International Economics. www.iie.com/publications/pb/pb99-6.htm (June).

Zhang Shuguang, Zhang Zansheng, and Wan Zhongxin. 1998. *Measuring the Costs of Protection in China.* Washington: Institute for International Economics.

# US-EU Mutual Recognition Agreements

Frost, Ellen L. 1997. *Transatlantic Trade: A Strategic Agenda.* POLICY ANALYSES IN INTERNATIONAL ECONOMICS 49. Washington: Institute for International Economics.

Nicolaïdis, Kalypso Aude. 2001. Harmonisation and Recognition: What Have We Learned? In *Trade and Regulatory Reform: Insights from Country Experience.* Paris: OECD.

Nicolaïdis, Kalypso Aude. 2001. Regulatory Cooperation and Managed Mutual Recognition: Developing a Strategic Model. In *Transatlantic Regulatory Cooperation: Legal Problems and Political Prospects,* ed. George A. Bermann, Matthias Herdegen, and Peter L. Lindseth. Oxford: Oxford University Press.

# Index

Accelerating Access Initiative, 90–92, 90*n*–91*n*, 117–18
Access to Essential Medicines Campaign, 85–88
ACT UP. *See* AIDS Coalition to Unleash Power (ACT UP)
action-forcing events, 34
  and multilateral agreement on investment, 182
  and TRIPS agreement, 113, 117
  and US-EU mutual recognition agreements, 353–54
activists. *See also* coalitions; nongovernmental organizations (NGOs)
  AIDS, 86–87, 101, 114
  and developing nations, 104
  environmental (*See* environmental groups)
  organizing by, 84–89
    using Internet, 82, 141–42, 162–63, 166, 177–78
  and US free trade agreement TRIPS-plus provisions, 109
advertising, 80, 162, 181, 210, 220, 234, 273, 287
AFL-CIO, and fast-track renewal
  1991 campaign, 195, 197
  1994 campaign, 201, 209–10, 217, 220, 232, 234–35, 238
Africa, 78, 80, 87, 92. *See also* South Africa

agenda shaping, 22–23, 27, 29–31. *See also* goals; *specific agreement*
  and preliminary negotiations, 350–51
Agreement on Mutual Recognition Between the European Community and the United States, 357–58
Agreement on Trade-Related Aspects of Intellectual Property Rights (TRIPS), 2–3, 37–133
  Article 6, 82, 95, 122
  Article 8, 122
  Article 8.1, 95
  Article 27, 97, 122
  Article 28, 79*n*, 83, 122–23
  Article 31, 83, 123
  and China WTO accession, 247
  coverage of, 38–39
  and definition of intellectual property, 43–46
  depth of, 10, 38
  and developing countries, 13, 56–57, 96
  Doha Declaration
    paragraph 6 implementation, 108, 128–33
    on public health, 103–104, 126–27
  enforcement of, 12, 190
  experts, 122–23
  governance, 41–42
  intellectual property protection prior to, 46–52
  minimum standards under, 38

**373**

Baucus, Max, 230–31
Berne Convention for Protection of
    Literary and Artistic Works, 46, 54, 75
bilateral agreements. *See also specific*
    *agreement*
    on investments, 140, 140*n*, 142–43, 142*n*,
        143*t*, 180
bilateral dispute resolution
    consultation and, 97, 97*n*
    US-Brazil, 97, 97*n*
    US-Korea, 52, 115
    US–South Africa, 82–84, 87–88
bilateral investment
    and MAI, 140, 140*n*, 180
    treaties, 137, 142–43, 142*n*, 143*t*
    and TRIMs, 147
bilateral negotiations
    EU-China, 282–83, 287
    as forum in China WTO accession,
        293–94
    on GATT accession market access,
        260–61, 260*n*–61*n*
    on TRIPS agreement, 51, 115
    US-China, 248–49, 265, 267–77
    without fast-track legislation, 191
Bipartisan Trade Promotion Authority Act
    (TPA), 109, 230–31
black market, 90*n*–91*n*, 91, 111
blocking. *See also* opposition; protest(s)
    of Chinese WTO membership, 243
    of Doha compulsory licensing
        negotiations, 106
    and globalization, 207
    of TRIPS, 60, 62–63
blocking coalitions, 24, 29
    avoidance of, 31
    against China MFN status, 259
    and China PNTR and WTO accession,
        281
    and fast-track legislation, 210–11
    against MAI, 169
    against NAFTA, 199
    and TRIPS negotiations, 113, 117
Brazil
    drug patent dispute consultation with
        US, 97, 97*n*
    generic drug industry development
        and, 98–99
    HIV/AIDS drugs program, 91–92,
        96–97
    opposition to TRIPS, 63
    and Special 301, 62
Brittan, Leon, 72, 153–54, 263, 338–39
Brundtland, Gro Harlem, 81

Buchanan, Pat, 211
bureaucratic politics, 178, 243, 350–51
Bush, George H. W., 196, 255
    and audiovisual services intellectual
        property rights exemption, 71
    on China most favored nation (MFN)
        status, 253, 255–56, 257*t*–58*t*
    and labor and environmental
        standards, 191
    and NAFTA negotiations, 195
Bush, George W., 229, 231, 239
    on AIDS drugs availability, 107
    and fast-track authority, 4
    on open trade, 232
    and trade promotion authority, 191
business, 61. *See also* industry
    and CE marks, 312
    and China WTO accession, 278–79,
        278*n*, 287, 292–94, 297
    and Chinese human rights issues, 256,
        256*n*, 259
    on consumer groups, 341
    and fast-track renewal, 196, 214, 218–19,
        225, 227, 234
    government relationship with, 308
    intellectual property revenue losses,
        44–45
    losses of, and intellectual property,
        44–45, 44*n*, 48, 52–52*n*
    and Multilateral Agreement on
        Investment, 153, 163, 171, 181
    and mutual recognition agreements,
        306–307
    and NAFTA, 199
    and Paris Convention revision, 47
    and standards issues, 232
    and trade promotion authority, 229
    and Uruguay Round, 70, 73, 76
    and US-China trade agreements, 264,
        273–74
    and US-EU mutual recognition
        agreement, 306, 308, 313, 341, 348
business and government. *See also*
    Transatlantic Business Dialogue
    (TABD)
    in Europe, 322, 331, 338
    in international negotiations, 61
    in MAI negotiation, 171
    partnership in TRIPS talks, 43
    and South Africa Medicines Act, 80
    in trade negotiations, 308
    views of consumer group, 342
Business and Industry Advisory
    Committee, 171–72

and TRIPS negotiations, 115–16
Uruguay Round implementation, 73–74
and US-China trade agreement, 243, 253, 263, 268–71, 277
and US-EU mutual recognition agreements (MRA), 343, 353
and US trade policy, 188, 192
Congressional Oversight Group, 231
consensus, 53, 67, 170, 189, 225, 243, 325, 330–36
and negotiation momentum, 34
Constitution (US), 43, 43*n*, 187–88
consultation
and bilateral dispute resolution, 97, 97*n*
with Congress, 194, 200–201
on MAI, 167–70, 219
consumer electronic products, 307
consumer groups, 45, 249, 308, 341–42
Consumer Project on Technology, 77*n*
copying products, 45–46, 71, 116
copyright, 44, 53–54
corporations, 40, 164
costs, 45, 47
Council of Canadians, 161–62, 161*n*
counterfeiting, 49–50, 59
countervailing-duty laws, 231
Cox, Christopher, 270
creative compromise, 293, 298
cross-issue negotiations, 21, 27
and TRIPS negotiation forum selection, 112
cross-sanctions, dispute settlement machinery for, and developing countries, 64
cross-sectoral agenda, in US-EU mutual recognition agreement negotiations, 350–51
cross-sectoral retaliation, 12, 41, 137–38
cross-sectoral trades
for market access and TRIPS framework, 63–64, 64*n*
and TRIPS negotiation forum selection, 112
in US-EU mutual recognition agreement negotiations, 350–51
and US regulatory authorities, 349–50
Cuba, 158–59
Cuban Liberty and Democratic Solidarity Act, 158
cultural industries, 148, 159–60, 179. *See also specific industry*
culture, 170, 322
Cunningham, Bill, 197
cyberspace. *See* Internet

Declaration of International Investment and Multinational Enterprises, 149
Declaration on the TRIPS Agreement and Public Health, 3, 103–104, 126–27
paragraph 6 implementation, 105–109, 128–33
DeLay, Tom, 225, 287, 294
democracy, 163–65, 209, 256
Democratic Party
and fast-track renewal, 196
1995 request, 203
1997 request, 205, 212–13, 215–17, 219–22, 225, 238
1998 vote, 228
agenda shaping, 234–35
and labor and environmental issues, 191
and labor coalition building, 236
and US-Mexico free trade agreement, 197
funding by labor, 213
and NAFTA passage, 200
and trade liberalization, 187, 191
and trade promotion authority, 229–32
and Uruguay Round legislation, 73
and US-China bilateral agreement, 248–49, 269, 281–82, 289
coalition building in Congress, 294–96
and safeguard proposal, 284
Deng Ziaoping, 250
developed countries, 45. *See also specific country*
and intellectual property protection, 56–57
and multilateral agreement on investment, 137, 179–80, 182
and mutual recognition with developing countries, 304
NAFTA investment talks between, 144
developing countries. *See also specific country*
and activists, 104
agricultural tariff reductions, 64*n*
and bilateral investment treaties, 142–43, 143*t*
and Cancún WTO ministerial meeting, 108–109
and China WTO membership, 245–47, 262
and counterfeit goods, 59
and Doha Declaration, 103–109, 129, 131–32
and Doha WTO ministerial meeting, 99, 101–102

drug(s), 47, 79–80, 85–86. *See also*
pharmaceutical industry
access to, 78, 84–89
AIDS, 78–82, 86–87, 89–94, 90*n*–92*n*,
96–99, 107, 110
and developing countries, 77–78, 77*n*
definition of, 128
and developing countries, 41–42, 69–70
generic, 78–79, 90*n*–91*n*, 93, 96, 98–99,
104, 110
prices of, 78–80, 80*n*, 87, 90–92,
90*n*–91*n*, 96, 98
reexportation of, 131
and TRIPS negotiations, 66, 108, 108*n*
and US-EU mutual recognition
agreements, 312, 315, 315*n*, 326–28,
340, 346–47
drug patents, 76–111
Accelerating Access Initiative and, 91
anthrax emergency, 98
and compulsory licensing, 66, 79,
95–96, 106, 130–31
defense of, by US government, 82*n*
and Doha WTO ministerial meeting,
100
and drug prices, 82*n*
on manufacturing process and
products, 52*n*
and South Africa AIDS drug program,
79–80
and TRIPS public health negotiations,
112–13
Dunkel, Arthur, 69–70

e-mail, 162
EC92 initiative, 9
economic integration
in Europe, 144–45, 302, 310–11
as governance issue, 305–306
and international markets, 302
and multilateral agreement on
investment, 140
economic regulation, international,
305–306
elections, 228, 282
electrical safety mutual recognition
agreement, 331, 340, 346–47
Electromagnetic Compatibility Directive,
313
electromagnetic compatibility standards,
353–54
employment. *See* labor
Enabling Clause (GATT), 13

enforcement mechanisms, 11–12
and Chinese trade agreements, 247
and competition in standards, 304
GATT, 11–12
and intellectual property rights, 46–47
and investment agreements, 137–38
MAI, 12
and multiround negotiations, 26–27
as OECD code limitation, 150
and product standards conformity, 304
TRIPS agreement, 12
WTO, 12, 190
engagement policy, 264–65
entertainment industry, 70–73
environmental groups, 195–96
and fast track, 189, 195–96, 211, 237
and MAI, 164–65
and NAFTA, 198–99, 198*n*
environmental issues
as economic policy, 222
as fast-track objectives, 200–201,
203–204, 214
and Gephardt fast-track protection
requirement, 212
and TRIPS agreement, 190
and US-EU MRAs, 337
and US-Mexico free trade agreement,
197
environmental policy, 139
environmental protection
Canada and Mexico side agreement
negotiations on, 198
and Ethyl Corp. expropriation
complaint against Canada, 164–65
and global economy, 207
and US-Jordan Free Trade Agreement,
228
Environmental Protection Agency (EPA),
337–38, 353
environmental standards, 189, 208
cost-benefit analysis of, 15
of developing countries, 190–91
and governance issues, 15
and intellectual property rights, 40
and MAI, 170–71, 171*n*
and NAFTA, 139, 198, 200–201
epidemics, 105–107, 107*n*
espionage, 269–70
essential medicines coalition, 85–86, 113
Ethyl Corp., 164–65
EU92 initiative, 303
European-American Business Council,
158

European Association of Manufactures of
Business Machines and Information
Technology Industry (EUROBIT),
332
European Commission, 320–21
and business interests, 322
and mutual recognition of standards
principle, 310
and Transatlantic Business Dialogue,
334, 351
and US-Europe MRAs, 308, 312–13,
331–32
European Free Trade Association (EFTA),
310
European Union, 151, 262. *See also specific
country*
agricultural policies in, and TRIPS
agreement, 65, 65n
bilateral and regional talks in, 109
and bilateral investment treaties, 142
business interests in, 322, 329
government relationship with, 308,
338
and China WTO accession, 262–63,
282–83, 287, 293–94
EC92 initiative, 9
electrical safety mutual recognition
agreements, 346–47
free movement of goods in, 309–10
good manufacturing practices, 342–43
governmental structure of, and MRA
negotiations, 320–21
and Helms-Burton Act, 159
integration of, 144–45, 302, 310–11
and intellectual property rights, 62–63
investment barriers in, liberalization of,
157
and Madrid Summit, 325–26
and national treatment of cultural
industries, 148
negotiators from, 61, 67, 327–28, 331–32
officials from, 308, 315, 348–49
and pharmaceutical industry, 315n, 327
and product standards, 309–11
product standards harmonization in,
309–10
as single market, 303
standards, 303, 309–12
trade sovereignty in, 11
and TRIPS agreement, 66–68, 113
and TRIPS negotiations, 100–101
US bilateral trade with, 314t
and US-China agreements, 259, 297
and US product assessors, 304

European Union of Industrial and
Employers' Confederations (UNICE),
55, 55n, 60–61
EU-US mutual recognition agreements
(MRAs), 4–5, 301–58
and conformity assessment, 309, 312
cost-benefit analysis of, 15
coverage of, 301–302
depth of, 10–11, 302–304
and developing countries, 304
and drug inspections, 343–44
and electrical safety negotiations, 331–32
enforcement of, 304
EPA hearing on, 337–38
as export industry strategy, 348
and globalization, 355
governance issues, 16, 305–306
harmonization of, 301–303
implementation of, 345–47
and industry cost savings, 306–307
inspection, testing, and certification
coverage, 303–304, 306
long term relevance of, 345
and marine safety equipment, 348
and medical devices, 326
negotiation of, 306–48
agenda shaping, 329–30, 350–51
agreement in, 340–42
analysis of, 348–55
background on, 309–13
beginning of, 319–21
coalition building, 351, 352f
completion of, 336–44
congressional concerns about,
342–44
consensus in, 330–36
delegations in, 319–20
forum selection for, 349–50
frame game, 337–38, 352–53, 357–58
implementation of, 342–48
linkage leveraging, 351–52, 353f
momentum building, 324–30, 353–54
organizing to influence, 349
preliminary, 313–19
results of, 336
and Transatlantic Business
Dialogue, 321–25, 333–36
US organizing for, 311–13
winners and losers in, 305
as organizing for CE mark
introduction, 349
and pharmaceutical issues, 326–28,
334–35
and policymaking, 301–306

scope of, 9
and sovereignty over standards, 319
and telecommunications, 331–32, 352
and US-EU trade relations, 305, 314
export(s)
and China, 250, 253, 278, 278n
computer, 313
Europe to US, 315n
and fast-track authority, 193
of US electronic products, 307, 313
US to Europe, 311–12
export-related employment, 193, 208
exporting companies, testing
requirements, streamlining, 307
expropriation
and bilateral investment treaties, 143
Ethyl Corp. complaint against Canada,
164–65
and property trafficking suits by US
nationals, 158
and regulatory taking under NAFTA,
139
externally imposed events, and
negotiation momentum, 34

fall-back options, 20
fast-track authority, 3–4, 187–239. *See also*
trade promotion authority (TPA)
agenda shaping, 31, 234–35
and bilateral and multilateral trade
negotiations, 191
and business lobbying, 218–19
and China PNTR, 291, 294
coalition building, 235–37, 236f
congressional implementation
legislation voting, 189
coverage of, 189–90
depth of, 189–90
derailed, 192
and developing countries, 190–91
enforcement of, 190
and environmental standards, 189
explanation of, 193
and federal budget, 205, 216, 222, 238
forum selection, 234
frame game, 200–201, 238–39
free trade talks without, 202, 228
governance, 188–89
and governance issues, 15
ideological divide over, 236, 236f
linkage leveraging, 226, 237–38, 237f
momentum creation, 238–39
and NAFTA, 189, 195–201, 209, 212,
217, 237–38

necessity for, 191
organizing to influence, 232–34, 233t,
234, 239
and policy making, 187–91
renewal of, 201–204
administration proposal for, 219–20
and business interests, 218–19
and Clinton agenda, 204–205
final push for, 224–25
history of, 194
and labor, 189, 206–10
Mexico City provision, 226
and NAFTA, 195–201
opponents of, 210–11
and political climate, 192, 213–15
pressure for, 222–24
response to, 220–21
summer delay, 215–18
vote on, 222–27
and scope of trade agreements, 9
and social issues, 15
as trade promotion authority, 229
and Uruguay Round, 72, 197–98, 202
value in making trade agreements,
228–29
vote on (1998), 227–29
winners and losers in, 191
film and television business, 44, 173
financial flows, and bilateral investment
treaties, 143, 143t
Food, Drug, and Cosmetics Act, 326
Food and Drug Administration (FDA)
and Global Harmonization Task Force,
319
and medical device mutual recognition
agreement, 307, 345–46
and multiple sector parallel
negotiations, 349–50
and pharmaceutical US-EU MRA,
326–28
and pharmaceuticals inspections, 343
on pharmaceuticals inspections,
326–27
reform, 307, 319, 331, 339
regulatory and trade-related
discussions, 316–17
Food and Drug Administration
Modernization Act of 1997, 354, 356
Ford, Gerald, 194
foreign investment, 136, 139, 165. *See also*
investment
agreements on [*See also* Multilateral
Agreement on Investment (MAI)]
cultural industries exception, 159–60

goods
  counterfeit, developing countries and, 59
  free movement of, in European Union,
    309–10
  national treatment of, 302
  trade in, focus on, 8–9
Gore, Al, 83–84, 86–87, 200
governance, 15–16. *See also specific agreement*
  and China WTO accession, 247
  and functional pressures for
    integration, 305–306
  of intellectual property rights, 41–42
  and investment agreements, 139
  and trade policy making, 188–89
government
  and business (*See* business and
    government)
  and foreign direct investing, 139, 142
  and organizing to influence, 178
government agencies, 304. *See also specific
  agency*
government officials. *See also* regulators
  at Chicago Transatlantic Business
    Dialogue, 333–34
  and MAI negotiations, 172–73, 181
  and transatlantic dialogue, 306
grassroots organizing, 199, 209–210, 234
Green Room process, 68
GSP. *See* Generalized System of
  Preferences
Guidelines on Treatment of Foreign Direct
  Investing, 145

Havana Charter, 145
health. *See* public health
Health Action International (HAI), 78,
  78*n*, 81, 85, 112, 114
Helms, Jesse, 269, 290
Helms-Burton Act, 158, 158*n*, 159
Hills, Carla, 62, 255
HIV. *See* AIDS
Hong Kong, 264, 265*n*
host countries. *See also* forum selection;
  *specific country*
  investment benefits for, 136, 138
  and national treatment terms, 143
House of Representatives. *See also*
  Democratic Party; Republican Party
  and China PNTR status, 253, 265–66,
    282–83, 298, 2253*n*
  and fast-track renewal, 192, 223–27
  Subcommittee on Criminal Justice,
    Human Resources, and Drug Policy,
    87

  Subcommittee on International
    Relationships, 169–70
  Subcommittee on Oversight and
    Investigations, 342
  and trade policy, 188
  and trade promotion authority, 230
  Ways and Means Committee, 203–204,
    223, 229
  Trade Subcommittee, 213–15
human rights
  in China (*See* Chinese human rights
    issues)
  and governance issues, 16
  trade as enforcement mechanism for, 9
Hungary, 48

ideology, 236*f*
ILO. *See* International Labor Organization
  (ILO)
IMF. *See* International Monetary Fund
  (IMF)
incentives, 47
income inequality, 208
India
  at Doha WTO ministerial meeting, 24,
    100–102
  and generic drug industry, 78, 98–99,
    104
  and national treatment, 146
  and Singapore issue, 102
  and TRIPS agreement, 63, 63*n*
Indian National Working Group on
  Patents, 78
industry. *See also* business
  coalition building in, 31, 61
  indigenous, 57
  and intellectual property protection,
    48–49
  and mutual recognition agreements, 308
industry representatives, 67–68
information sharing, in multi-issue
  negotiations, 23
innovation
  and intellectual property, 39, 39*n*, 43, 43*n*
  and pharmaceutical development, 80
  as public good, 56–57
inspections
  pharmaceutical
    FDA, 326–27, 342–44
    and US-EU mutual recognition
      agreements, 343–44
    under pharmaceutical MRA, 316–17,
      326–27, 334–35
      report disclosure, 330, 335, 340

investors
protection and sovereignty of, 136, 164, 166
rights under NAFTA, 165
IPC. *See* Intellectual Property Committee (IPC)
IPR. *See* intellectual property rights (IPR)
issue sequencing in negotiations. *See* sequencing strategy

Jackson-Vanik Amendment, 251, 251*n*, 277, 286–87
Japan
and cultural industries investment exception, 160
and MFN for China, 259
negotiators from, 61
Structural Impediments Initiative with US, 9
and TRIPS, 66–68, 113
Jiang Zemin, 260, 265, 272–73, 275–76, 289
jobs. *See* labor
Jospin, Lionel, 173, 175

Kantor, Mickey, 72, 201–203, 334–35
Keidanren, 55, 60–61
Kennedy Round, 188–89, 194, 235
knowledge, 43, 43*n*. *See also* intellectual property
as public good, 38–39
knowledge-based industries, 43, 43*n*, 234
Korea, South, 33, 52, 115

labor
and China, 280, 280*n*
and fast-track renewal opposition, 192
and foreign investment, 138
and globalization, 207
and workers' rights, 195, 209
labor standards, 208, 256, 256*n*, 259, 284, 284*n*, 290
and China PNTR status, 246–47, 249, 278, 278*n*, 279–81, 280*n*, 296–97
cost-benefit analysis of, 15
and developing countries, 190–91
and environmental standards inclusions, 189
and fast-track authority, 189, 200–201, 203–204, 206, 209–10, 212, 214, 217–18, 220–22, 225, 227, 229, 232–39
as framing issue, 238
and global trade, 207–209
and governance issues, 15
and intellectual property rights, 40

and linkage leveraging, 209
and MAI, 140, 170–71, 171*n*
and NAFTA, 195, 198–201, 206
prison labor, 256, 256*n*, 259, 284, 284*n*, 290
and Seattle WTO ministerial conference, 89
and TRIPS agreement, 190
and US-Jordan Free Trade Agreement, 228
and US-Mexico free trade agreement, 197
labor unions
and China, 243, 248
and fast-track renewal, 207–209
and NAFTA, 198
Lalumière Report, 174, 182
Lamy, Pascal, 106, 282, 348
language
ambiguous, 25, 102, 106, 220
and framing tactics, 34
Latin America, 202
liberal investment regimes, 137
liberalization. *See* trade liberalization
licensing
and Brazil drug price negotiations, 96
and Doha Declaration paragraph 6, 105–106, 130–31
of drug patents, 66, 79, 91, 95–96, 106, 129–31
and national emergencies, 98
and public health, 95
linkage(s). *See also specific agreement or issue*
leveraging of, 29, 32–33
types of, 32
lobbying
and Access to Essential Medicines Campaign, 85–86
by business in Europe and US, 322
and China PNTR status, 249, 278, 278*n*
and fast-track negotiations, 218–19, 224–25, 227, 231
for FDA Modernization Act, 354
by industry of trade negotiating teams, 67–68
for multilateral agreement on investment, 172
for NAFTA, 200
for OECD investment talks, 151
and US-EU MRAs, 341
local content, 136, 143
Lott, Trent, 269, 289–90

Maastricht Treaty on the European Union, 145

macroeconomic forces
  and negotiation momentum, 34
  role in policymaking, 17
MAI. *See* Multilateral Agreement on
    Investment (MAI)
Mandela, Nelson, 79
marine safety equipment mutual
    recognition agreement (MRA), 348
market access
  and EU-China bilateral agreement,
    282–83, 287
  as foreign investment inducement, 138
  investment as important means of,
    152–53
  and multinational corporation
    competitiveness, 141–42
  and TRIPS framework, 63–64, 64*n*
  and US-China bilateral agreement,
    243–45, 255–55*n*, 260–61, 260*n*–61*n*,
    267, 277, 292–98
market delay costs, 315
Mbeki, Thabo, 92
Médecins Sans Frontières (MSF), 85–86, 109
media. *See* press coverage
medical devices industry, 307, 331
medical devices mutual recognition
    agreement
  and FDA Modernization Act, 339
  implementation issues, 345–46
  negotiation of, 318–19
medicines. *See* drug(s)
Medicines and Related Substances Act of
    1965 (South Africa), 82, 82*n*
Medicines and Related Substances
    Control Amendment Act of 1997
    (South Africa), 121
mental models, in framing tactics, 33
Merck and Co., 45
Mexico, 189, 197–98
Mexico City provision, 226
MFA. *See* Multi-Fiber Arrangement (MFA)
MFN. *See* most favored nation (MFN) status
mobilization. *See also* organizing;
    organizing to influence
  on access to medicines, 81–82
  on China WTO and PNTR status, 286,
    292–93
  on fast-track renewal, 209–13, 219
  on intellectual property rules, 42
  as negotiating dilemma, 234
momentum creation, 29, 34–35, 348. *See*
    *also specific agreement*
  and frame game, 352–53
  as negotiating dilemma, 234

monopolies
  and innovation, 39*n*
  on intellectual property, and
    developing countries, 57
  and knowledge creation, 43, 43*n*
  and mutual recognition agreements,
    328
  by US government agencies, 304
Monsanto, Inc., 48, 51
Montreal (Canada), 62–65
moral issues. *See also* human rights;
    *specific issue*
  with open trade, 232
  and Tiananmen Square, 252–53, 256,
    265
  and TRIPS agreement, 38, 51–52, 66, 115
most favored nation (MFN) status, 10
  and bilateral investment agreements, 143
  for China [*See* China most favored
    nation (MFN) status]
  as core MAI principle, 156–57
  for Hungary, 49
  as nondiscrimination principle, 242
Motion Picture Association of America
    (MPAA), 44
MRAs. *See* mutual recognition
    agreements (MRAs); *specific agreement*
Multi-Fiber Arrangement (MFA), 33, 64,
    64*n*, 112
Multilateral Agreement on Investment
    (MAI), 135–86
  analysis of, 177–82
  benefits of, 171–72
  cost-benefit analysis of, 15
  coverage, 135–36
  depth of, 10, 136–37
  and developing countries, 14, 138
  enforcement of, 12, 137–38
  and environmental standards, 170–71
  failure of, 9, 22, 30
    factors in, 141
    and MAI negotiations, 139–77
  and fast-track authority, 168
  and France, 172–75, 180
  and global civil society, 167, 170, 174
  as global model, 140
  governance, 16, 139
  and international investment, 141–49
  and labor standards, 170–71
  and NAFTA, 139, 144–45, 161, 164–66,
    171, 181
  Negotiating Group, 156, 160
  negotiation of, 3, 156–61
    agenda shaping, 179

coalition building, 180
draft text leak during, 161–62
forum selection, 149, 176, 178–79
frame game, 153–54, 181–82
goals, 153–54
linkage leveraging, 179–81
momentum creation, 176, 182
organizing to influence, 177–78
participation in, 137, 156–57
parties involved in, 156, 167–68,
172–73
process of, 157
structure of, 156–57
and OECD, 149–53, 167, 171–73
opposition to, 138, 140–41, 161–68,
176–78
secrecy in, 161–64, 167–68
and taxation, 157–58
and trade liberalization, 142
and WTO, 160
multilateral trade
and fast-track legislation, 191
and foreign direct investment, 145
intellectual property protection and,
76
and TRIPS negotiation, 115
multinational corporations, 138–39,
141–42, 141n
mutual recognition agreements (MRAs).
*See also specific agreement*
bilateral template, 352
conformity assessment in, 305, 309, 312,
314–15, 314t, 345
and developing countries, 304
as market approach in Europe, 310–11
as national treatment alternative, 312
negotiation of, advisory committee for,
313
as precedent for bilateral agreements,
352
and US and European regulatory
approaches, 312

Nader, Ralph, 91
NAFTA. *See* North American Free Trade
Agreement (NAFTA)
National Agricultural Chemicals
Association, 48
national emergencies, 95, 98–99, 129
national security
breaches of, 269–70
and China, 243, 245, 265–66, 281–82
and Congress, 289
and MAI negotiations, 179

national sovereignty
and depth of trade agreements, 10
and enforcement issues, 11–12
and foreign investment, 136
and medical device mutual recognition
agreements, 319
and multilateral agreement on
investment, 164, 166, 175
and TRIMs agreement, 145–46
national treatment, 10
of bilateral investment treaties, 143
and China WTO accession, 244
on conformity assessment provisions,
312
and developing countries, 146
of European investors, 144–45
and French entertainment copying
taxation, 71
and GATS, 148
and India, 146
as MAI principle, 156–57
OECD provisions on, 150
for patent protection, 46–47
and tariffs, 302n
and Technical Barriers to Trade
Agreement, 312
and US policy, 54
National Treatment Instrument, 180
National Wildlife Federation, 211
negotiation(s), 17–35. *See also specific
agreement or issue*
across issues, 21, 27
agenda shaping in, 22–23, 27, 29–31,
350–51 (*See also* goals)
analysis of, foundations of, 18–19
balance of power in, 104
on "beyond-the-border" barriers, 311
coalition building during, 29, 31–32
complex
strategies in, 28, 28f
structure of, 20–27
complexity of, levels in, 24–26
and democracy, 163–65, 209, 256
distributive, 20
division of, 22–24, 27
effect of prior relationships on, 26
forum selection for (*See* forum
selection)
frame game in, 29, 33–34, 308
implementation of, difficulty with, 252
information sharing in, 23
integrative, 21–22
internal, synchronization with external,
25

negotiation(s)—*continued*
  issues in
    number of, 21–23, 27
    sequencing of (*See* sequencing
      strategy)
  like-mindedness in, 109, 155, 157, 167
  linkage leveraging in, 29, 32–33
  mixed-motive bargaining in, 20*n*, 23*n*
  momentum creation during (*See*
    momentum creation)
  objectives of (*See* goals)
  organizing to influence in, 29–30
  paradigm, 67
  parties in, number of, 23–24, 27
  positions in, 21, 21*n*
  preliminary, 31, 350–51
  process dynamics in, analyzing, 27–35
  rounds in, number of, 26–27
  shifting focus of, 1
  simple, structure of, 19–20
  structure of, 19, 19*f*, 19*n*
  influence on strategy, 27–28, 28*f*
  time factors, 26–27
  venue for (*See* forum selection)
negotiation games, 17–19, 18*n*, 24*n*
  in complex negotiations, 28, 28*f*
  designing, 29–35
  effect on structure, 28, 28*f*
  guiding questions for, 35
  tactical elements of, 29
negotiation strategy, 23, 23*n*
  of big labor, 210
  of Clinton administration, 200
  of developing countries and Punte del
    Este, 57
  and forum selection, 234
  in government and industry health
    issues, 80
  of India at Doha WTO ministerial
    meeting, 102
  and Internet use, 82, 141–42, 162–63,
    166, 177–78
  of packaging trade on intellectual
    property, 42
  of pharmaceutical industry on AIDS
    drugs, 94
  and principle-agent dilemma, 188, 235
  of TRIPS negotiators, 67
negotiators. *See also specific country, party,*
  *or agreement*
  and agenda narrowing, 350–51
  aims of, 139–40
  and business interests, 61
"negotiator's dilemma," 23, 23*n*, 27

network games, 26
New Approach to standards, 310, 328
"new China lobby," 259
New Transatlantic Agenda (NTA),
  325–26
noncompliance, and policy enforcement,
  11
nondiscrimination, 97, 145, 242, 244
nongovernmental organizations (NGOs).
  *See also specific organization*
  and MAI
    consultations with OECD
      representatives, 167–68
    consultations with US
      representatives, 168–69
    frame game, 181
    governmental response, 170
    opposition organizing, 138, 140–41,
      161–68, 176–78
      using Internet, 140–41, 141*n*,
        162, 166
    process capture, 174
  and TRIPS
    coalition building, 114
    and Doha WTO ministerial
      meeting, 98
    frame game, 116
    mobilization, 81–82
    and pharmaceuticals, 77–78, 84–89,
      94, 105, 108
normal trade relations. *See* China
  permanent normal trade relations
  (PNTR) status; most favored nation
  (MFN) status
North American Free Trade Agreement
  (NAFTA), 2*n*, 9
  and China PNTR status, 280–81, 295,
    295*f*
  and Clinton presidency, 291
  and environmental standards, 189, 198
  Ethyl Corp. expropriation complaint,
    164–65
  expropriation protections and
    regulatory takings, 139
  and fast-track renewal, 195–201, 206,
    211–12, 217, 237–38
  and labor standards, 189, 198,
    200–201
  and multilateral agreement on
    investment, 161, 181
  and regional investment, 144
North-South issues, 56–57, 147
nuclear design theft, 275
nuclear power, 243

Occupational Safety and Health
Administration, 346–47
OECD. *See* Organization for Economic
Cooperation and Development
(OECD)
Omnibus Trade and Competitiveness Act,
115
Special 301 provision (*See* Special 301
provision)
opposition. *See also* blocking; protest(s)
advertising, 162, 210, 220, 234, 273, 287
to agricultural subsidies phase out, 99
to China PNTR, 272, 279–82, 286–87,
294
to fast-track renewal, 206–13, 217,
220–21
to globalization, 138, 191–92
to MAI, 138, 140–41, 161–69, 180
to NAFTA, 73, 206, 209, 211, 217
as negotiating dilemma, 234
to TRIPS, 45–46, 56–57, 62–63, 63*n*,
68–69, 71, 85, 101, 117
to Uruguay Round implementation, 73
to WTO talks, 102
Organization for Economic Cooperation
and Development (OECD), 11, 149*n*,
160–61
bilateral investment treaties, 142
Codes of Liberalization, 149, 149*n*, 150
Committee on Capital Movements and
Invisible Transactions (CMIT), 149
Committee on International Investment
and Multinational Enterprises
(CIME), 150–51
as host of investment agreement
negotiations, 149–53
and investment negotiations, 137,
151–52
and MAI, 22, 135, 138–39, 167–74,
178–81
members, 157, 176
ministerial meetings, 160, 173–74, 338
negotiators, 167
organized labor. *See* labor unions; *specific
organization*
organizing to influence, 29–30. *See also*
coalitions; mobilization; *specific
agreement*
by activists, 84–89
using Internet, 82, 141–42, 162–63,
166, 177–78
on AIDS drugs, 82, 86–87
by business on China, 259, 273–74, 278,
278*n*

by Clinton administration, 200, 216–17
grassroots, 199, 209–10, 234
for intellectual property protection, 54–56
by labor, 209–10, 212–13, 232, 234
of MAI opposition, 161–66, 177–78
by NGOs, 82, 84–89, 161–66, 161*n*
by Transatlantic Business Dialogue,
321–25
by US government, 54, 56, 311–13

parallel forums, 349
parallel importing, 79, 82*n*, 83, 95
Paris Convention for the Protection of
Industrial Property, 46–47
partisanship, 228, 239, 282
patents
compulsory licensing in national
emergencies, 95, 98, 129
as development policy obstacle, 57
drug (*See* drug patents)
as intellectual property protection
policy, 43–44, 43*n*
law on, 78
link to development priorities, 65*n*
medical discoveries and, 56–57
and national treatment, 46–47
piracy costs, 45
and TRIPS negotiations, 66, 115
patterns of deference, 24, 32
Pelosi, Nancy, 256, 265, 281, 297
performance requirements
and bilateral investment treaties, 143
in Europe, 310
permanent normal trade relations (PNTR)
status of China. *See* China permanent
normal trade relations (PNTR) status
Perot, Ross, 199–200
Pfizer, Inc., 45, 47, 92–93
pharmaceutical industry. *See also* drug(s)
Accelerating Access Initiative, 90– 92
and Africa health care infrastructure,
87, 92, 99, 117–18
and anthrax public health emergency,
98
and developing countries, 133
and Doha Declaration on public health,
103–104, 106, 133
and drug prices, 78–80, 80*n*, 87, 90–92,
90*n*–91*n*, 96, 96*n*, 98
and FDA Modernization Act, 354
and intellectual property rights, 80
on intellectual property rights, 90
manufacturing practices, 329 (*See also*
Good Manufacturing Practices)

pharmaceutical industry—*continued*
  and parallel importing, 83
  and South Africa, 79–80, 88, 93–94
  and TRIPS negotiations, 70, 74–75, 114,
    116–18
  and US-EU mutual recognition
    agreements, 316–17, 329–31, 334–35
  and US patent piracy costs, 45
Pharmaceutical Manufacturers of
  America, 79–80
pharmaceutical patents. *See* drug patents
Pharmaceutical Research and
  Manufacturers Association, 329
PhRMA. *See* Pharmaceutical Research and
  Manufacturers Association
piracy of intellectual property, 34, 44–45,
  50–51
  by China, 259
  as frame game, 116
  by Hungary, 49
  losses to, 52–52*n*
  as product copying, 45–46
PMA. *See* South Africa Pharmaceutical
  Manufacturers Association (PMA)
PNTR. *See* China permanent normal trade
  relations (PNTR) status
policy commitments, credibility of, 136
politics
  of China WTO accession, 244, 262–64
  effect on negotiation momentum,
    34–35
  and governance issues, 15–16
  and liberal investment regime
    concessions, 137
  and negotiations, 25, 27, 33–35
  of protest, 109
  and trade policymaking, 7
poor countries. *See* developing countries;
  *specific country*
poverty, 93, 225
power
  of AIDS activists, 86–87
  balance of, 104, 247, 306
  and China WTO membership, 246–47
  negotiating
    congressional, 3, 15, 26
    in multilateral agreement on
      investment, 169, 172–73
    in multiround negotiations, 27
    of president, 3, 15, 26
    of United States, 3, 25–26, 193
  nuclear, 243
  regulatory, 165–66

power relationships, in domestic
  government, effect of trade
  agreements on, 15–16
president (US)
  consultation with Congress on trade
    negotiations, 194, 200–201, 219, 231
  negotiating power of, 3, 15, 26 (*See also*
    fast-track authority)
  and trade agreements, 188–89, 191, 193
presidential campaigns, 117, 213, 256, 265
President's Advisory Committee on Trade
  Negotiations (ACTN), 52–53
press coverage
  of Clinton-Zhu meeting, 272
  of fast-track renewal, 203, 213, 224–25
  of Jiang-Clinton summit, 265
  of MAI negotiations, 162–63, 162*n*, 181
  of pharmaceutical industry and AIDS
    drugs, 94
  Ruggiero misquotation, 163–64, 164*n*
  of TRIPS negotiations, 124–25
principle-agent dilemma, 188, 235
prison labor, 256, 256*n*, 259, 284, 284*n*, 290
private assessment institutions, 304
private sector. *See also* business
  and European culture, 338
  and fast-track authority, 196
  interest in MAI, 153
products. *See also specific product*
  inspection of
    and certification mutual
      recognition, 303–304
    and US-EU mutual recognition
      agreements, 340
  standards for (*See* standards)
profits, 93–94
property rights. *See* intellectual property
  rights (IPR)
protectionism
  and conformity assessment, 345
  in Congress, 221
  and French copyright compensation, 71
  of indigenous industry by developing
    countries, 57
  of labor unions, 207
  and mutual recognition agreements,
    306
  and regulatory standards, 189, 302
  and US antidumping provisions, 100
protest(s). *See also* blocking; opposition
  on AIDS and Gore, 86–87
  against MAI, 140–41, 167, 174
  against Pfizer, 92

"Old Approach" to, 309
and product superiority, 303
public health, 165, 304
regulatory
safety, 165, 304, 310, 344–45
as trade barriers, 301–302
rigorous, 303
as transatlantic trade barrier, 323, 326
State Department, 82n, 169, 172, 179
strategy
negotiating (See negotiation strategy)
sequencing (See sequencing strategy)
Structural Impediments Initiative, 9
structure-strategy-process-outcomes
model, 19, 19f, 19n
subnational government, 150, 179
subnegotiations, 22–24, 27
summit meetings, 265, 325–26
Supachai Panitchpakdi, 108
Super 301, 115
surveys, 279, 279n, 322–23, 354
Sweeney, John, 227, 231, 280, 287–88
synergistic linkages, 32

TABD. See Transatlantic Business
Dialogue
tactics. See negotiation strategy
Taiwan, 250, 252, 275, 291
Talloires text (TRIPS), 68
tariffs, 64n, 188, 194, 229, 302n
taxation, 71, 157–58
Teamsters Union, 210
Technical Barriers to Trade Agreement
(TBT), 312, 312n, 317
technology, 50–51, 57, 132, 136, 266
Telecom Industry Association (TIA), 314
telecommunications
life cycle of, 315
and US-EU mutual recognition
agreements, 314–15, 314t, 331–32
US-German industry standards, 312,
351–52
terrorism, 98, 229
testing
and cost of telecommunication
products, 315
requirements for exporting companies,
307
and US-EU mutual recognition
agreements, 303–304
textiles, 64, 247
theft of intellectual property, 48
third-party certification, 310
Tiananmen Square, 252–53, 256, 265

time factors, in negotiations, 26–27
Tokyo Round, 49–50, 189, 194, 302, 312n
Enabling Clause, 13
scope of, 8–9
TPA. See trade promotion authority (TPA)
Trade Act of 1974, 194, 251, 251n
Trade Act of 1984, 115. See also Section 301
trade adjustment assistance (TAA),
207–208, 207n, 217, 230–31, 239
trade agreements. See also specific
agreement
binding, 11
Chinese negotiation of, 241–42
cost-benefit analysis of, 14–15
depth of, 10–11
as domestic regulatory issue
framework, 308
enforcement of, 11–12 (See also
enforcement mechanisms)
and foreign direct investment, 136
governance of, 15–16
negotiating [See negotiation(s)]
nonbinding, 11
and presidential authority, 188
scope of, 8–10
expansion of, 9–10
trends in, 16
and WHO, 84
Trade Agreements Extension Act, 250
trade barriers. See also market access;
protectionism
and China, 144–45, 253–54, 254n, 255
as domestic regulations, 189
and foreign investment, 138, 157
liberalization of (See trade
liberalization)
and regulations and standards, 189,
301–302, 326
and US-EU mutual recognition
agreements, 307, 311–12, 312n, 317,
326
and US trade negotiations, 194
trade deficit (US), 52, 193
and China, 253, 265, 265n, 271
trade in goods, focus on, 8–9
trade liberalization
and African AIDS drug access, 89
and China, 246, 248
Democrat opposition, 191
and domestic policies, 137
and forum selection by labor leaders,
234
and India on national treatment, 146
and intellectual property rights, 40

USCIB. *See* United States Council of
International Business (USCIB)
USTR. *See* United States Trade
Representative

value claiming, 20–21, 23, 29
agenda shaping and, 22–23
and linkages, 33
and momentum building, 35
tension between value creating and,
23*n*
value creating, 21, 23, 29, 179, 350–51
and linkages, 33
and momentum building, 35
in multi-issue negotiations, 22
tension between value claiming and,
23*n*
venue for negotiations. *See* forum
selection
vetoes, 255–56, 257*t*–58*t*

weapons of mass destruction, 255, 290,
290*n*
winning coalitions, 24, 29, 31
workers' rights, 195, 209. *See also* labor
standards
Working Party for China, 262, 296–97
World Bank, 145, 250
World Health Assembly, 81
World Health Organization (WHO)
and access to medicine under TRIPS,
80–81, 95–96, 114
developing country forum
selection, 112–13
Revised Drug Strategy, 81, 84
World Intellectual Property Organization
(WIPO), 11, 46–47, 53, 55, 111
World Trade Organization (WTO)
and China-US bilateral trade
negotiations, 262–64
China's accession to (*See* China WTO
accession)

as contractual agreement, 263
cross-sectoral retaliation enforcement,
137–38
and developing countries, 13–14, 104
dispute resolution mechanism, 12
and China trade, 247
and intellectual property rights, 38
organization for, 12
as replacement of GATT, 73
and TRIPS negotiation forum
selection, 112
and US-EU mutual recognition
agreements, 313
and US Section 301, 64
and drug access, 95–97
enforcement mechanisms, 12, 190
and intellectual property rights, 38–41,
83, 97
as investment agreement negotiating
forum, 148
and MAI negotiations, 160, 178
and market barrier reduction, 244–45
membership in, economic impact of,
14
ministerial meetings (*See specific
meeting*)
negotiation of, 19
nondiscrimination principle, 242
politics of protest and US role, 109
reorganization and Seattle ministerial,
100
scope of, 8
standard setting principles, 302
and US-EU mutual recognition
agreements, 313
Working Group on Trade and
Investment establishment, 176

Yeutter, Clayton, 45*n*, 53–54, 58

Zhu Rongji, 35, 266–74, 294, 298
Zoellick, Robert, 97, 102, 106, 109, 229

# Other Publications from the Institute for International Economics

POLICY ANALYSES IN
INTERNATIONAL ECONOMICS Series

## DISTRIBUTORS OUTSIDE THE UNITED STATES

**Australia, New Zealand,
and Papua New Guinea**
D. A. Information Services
648 Whitehorse Road
Mitcham, Victoria 3132, Australia
Tel: 61-3-9210-7777
Fax: 61-3-9210-7788
Email: service@dadirect.com.au
www.dadirect.com.au

**India, Bangladesh, Nepal, and Sri Lanka**
Viva Books Private Limited
Mr. Vinod Vasishtha
4737/23 Ansari Road
Daryaganj, New Delhi 110002
India
Tel: 91-11-4224-2200
Fax: 91-11-4224-2240
Email: viva@vivagroupindia.net
www.vivagroupindia.com

**Mexico, Central America, South America,
and Puerto Rico**
US PubRep, Inc.
311 Dean Drive
Rockville, MD 20851
Tel: 301-838-9276
Fax: 301-838-9278
Email: c.falk@ieee.org
www.uspubrep.com

**Southeast Asia** (*Brunei, Burma, Cambodia,
Indonesia, Malaysia, the Philippines,
Singapore, Taiwan, Thailand, and Vietnam*)
APAC Publishers Services PTE Ltd.
70 Bendemeer Road #05-03
Hiap Huat House
Singapore 333940
Tel: 65-6844-7333
Fax: 65-6747-8916
Email: service@apacmedia.com.sg

**Canada**
Renouf Bookstore
5369 Canotek Road, Unit 1
Ottawa, Ontario KlJ 9J3, Canada
Tel: 613-745-2665
Fax: 613-745-7660
www.renoufbooks.com

**Japan**
United Publishers Services Ltd.
1-32-5, Higashi-shinagawa
Shinagawa-ku, Tokyo 140-0002
Japan
Tel: 81-3-5479-7251
Fax: 81-3-5479-7307
Email: purchasing@ups.co.jp
*For trade accounts only. Individuals will find
IIE books in leading Tokyo bookstores.*

**Middle East**
MERIC
2 Bahgat Ali Street, El Masry Towers
Tower D, Apt. 24
Zamalek, Cairo
Egypt
Tel. 20-2-7633824
Fax: 20-2-7369355
Email: mahmoud_fouda@mericonline.com
www.mericonline.com

**United Kingdom, Europe**
(*including Russia and Turkey*), **Africa,
and Israel**
The Eurospan Group
c/o Turpin Distribution
Pegasus Drive
Stratton Business Park
Biggleswade, Bedfordshire
SG18 8TQ
United Kingdom
Tel: 44 (0) 1767-604972
Fax: 44 (0) 1767-601640
Email: eurospan@turpin-distribution.com
www.eurospangroup.com/bookstore

**Visit our Web site at:
www.iie.com
E-mail orders to:
IIE mail@PressWarehouse.com**